Library of
Davidson College

RE-ELECTING THE GOVERNOR

The 1982 Elections

Edited by

Thad L. Beyle

UNIVERSITY
PRESS OF
AMERICA

RE-ELECTING THE GOVERNOR

The 1982 Elections

Edited by

Thad L. Beyle

UNIVERSITY
PRESS OF
AMERICA

LANHAM • NEW YORK • LONDON

324.973
R327

Copyright © 1986 by

University Press of America,® Inc.

4720 Boston Way
Lanham, MD 20706

3 Henrietta Street
London WC2E 8LU England

All rights reserved

Printed in the United States of America

Co-published by arrangement with the
Center for the Study of Federalism

Library of Congress Cataloging in Publication Data
Main entry under title: 87-5443

Re-electing the governor.
  Bibliography: p.
  1. Governors—United States—Election—Case studies
I. Beyle, Thad L., 1934-   .
JK2447.R44   1986   324.973'0927   85-31582
ISBN 0-8191-5252-8 (alk. paper)
ISBN 0-8191-5253-6 (pbk. : alk. paper)

All University Press of America books are produced on acid-free
paper which exceeds the minimum standards set by the National
Historical Publications and Records Commission.

ACKNOWLEDGMENTS

Many people were part of this project and contributed in various ways. Obviously, the analysts in the states in which governors were re-elected were the most important contributors and we thank them for their time, insight, and analyses. Dan Garry of the National Governors' Association also provided valuable support throughout the project as did Jim Tait, Director of The Governors Center at Duke University. Tina Carter, Belinda Hedgpeth, and Joan Shipman were most helpful with their assistance at the word processor, as was Dawn Lewis of the Department of Political Science at the University of North Carolina at Chapel Hill. Finally, the considerable editorial skills of Marsha Vick of the President's Office at Duke University made all of the parts of this project more readable, and just better.

I thank all of them for staying the course on this project, and hope this book is worth their effort. If it is not, that is my problem and I accept it.

> Thad L. Beyle
> Chapel Hill, North Carolina
> October 1984

CONTENTS

Re-electing the Governor: The 1982 Elections
Thad L. Beyle, Editor

ACKNOWLEDGMENTS

    - Thad L. Beyle.................................iii

PREFACE

    - Terry Sanford, Duke University.................ix

INTRODUCTION

    "Gubernatorial Re-elections: The 1982 Experience"

    - Thad L. Beyle..............................xiii

FINANCING THE 1982 GUBERNATORIAL RACES

1. "Political Money and Gubernatorial Primaries"
   - Malcolm Jewel, University of Kentucky.......1

2. "The Costs of Becoming Governor"
   - Thad L. Beyle, University of North Carolina at Chapel Hill..........................11

THE STATE ANALYSES

3. "Arizona Gubernatorial Politics: 1982"
   - Ruth Jones, Arizona State University.......33

4. "The Lamm Landslide in Colorado: Incumbent Popularity and a Divided Opposition"
   - Rodney Hero, University of Colorado........51

5. "Connecticut: The Governor Fills His Own Shoes"
   - Sarah McCally Morehouse, University of Connecticut, Stamford....................67

6. "The Incumbent Wins: The Politics of Gubernatorial Re-election in Florida"
   - Richard K. Scher, University of Florida....89

7. "Hawaii: Placid Reaffirmation"
   - Daniel W. Tuttle, Jr., University of Hawaii 113

8. "The Idaho Re-election: Politics as Usual"
   - H. Sydney Duncombe and Robert H. Blank, University of Idaho......129

9. "The 1982 Illinois Gubernatorial Election: Historic on Many 'Counts'"
   - Boyd Keenan, University of Illinois at Chicago......141

10. "The Re-election of a Governor and the Aftermath: The Case of Kansas, 1982-1983"
    - Marvin A. Harder, University of Kansas....169

11. "Preparing for the Second Term: The Gubernatorial Experience in Maine"
    - Kenneth T. Palmer and Alex N. Pattakos, University of Maine......181

12. "The Gubernatorial Re-election of Harry R. Hughes: A Non-Event?"
    - Patricia G. Florestano, University of Maryland......201

13. "Oklahoma: A Historic Gubernatorial Succession"
    - Jean McDonald and David R. Morgan, University of Oklahoma......217

14. "The 1982 Oregon Gubernatorial Election: The Politics of Continuity"
    - Sheldon M. Edner, Charles R. White, and Cathy Clark, Portland State University....237

15. "Have the Terms Changed?: South Carolina Re-elects a Governor"
    - Mark Tompkins, University of South Carolina 257

16. "The 1982 Gubernatorial Election in South Dakota"
    - Don Dahlin, University of South Dakota 281

17. "The 1982 Gubernatorial Election in Tennessee"
    - Michael Fitzgerald, Floydette C. Cory, Stephen J. Rechichar, and Abigail S. Hughes, University of Tennessee......299

18. "Wyoming Re-election: From Affluence to Recession with Stability"
    - Janet Clarke, University of Wyoming......323

Contributors

Janet Clark, Department of Political Science, University of Wyoming, Laramie.

Donald C. Dahlin, Department of Political Science, University of South Dakota, Vermillion.

H. Sydney Duncombe, Bureau of Public Affairs Research and Robert H. Blank, Department of Political Science, University of Idaho, Moscow.

Sheldon M. Edner, Charles R. White, and Cathy Clark, School of Urban and Public Affairs, Portland State University, Portland.

Michael R. Fitzgerald, Floydette C. Cory, Stephen J. Rechichar, and Abigail S. Hudgens, Department of Political Science and Bureau of Public Administration, University of Tennessee, Knoxville.

Patricia C. Florestano, Institute for Governmental Service, University of Maryland, College Park.

Marvin A. Harder, Center for Public Affairs, University of Kansas, Lawrence.

Rodney Hero, Graduate School of Public Affairs, University of Colorado, Colorado Springs.

Ruth Jones, Department of Political Science, Arizona State University, Tempe.

Boyd Keenan, Department of Political Science, University of Illinois at Chicago.

Jean G. McDonald and David R. Morgan, Department of Political Science, University of Oklahoma, Norman.

Sarah McCally Morehouse, Department of Political Science, University of Connecticut at Stamford.

Kenneth T. Palmer, Department of Political Science and Alex N. Pattakos, Bureau of Public Administration, University of Maine at Orono.

Richard K. Scher, Department of Political Science, University of Florida, Gainesville.

Mark E. Tompkins, Department of Government and International Studies, University of South Carolina, Columbia.

Daniel W. Tuttle, Jr., Department of Educational Administration, University of Hawaii, Honolulu.

PREFACE

Being able to succeed oneself in the governor's chair is an increasing luxury that our states' chief executives enjoy. As I argued in 1967, however, "Succession is not a right given to a governor; it is a right retained by the people--the right to choose whomever they want as their governor."[1]

In 1967, twelve states denied their four-year term governors such an opportunity; now only four states do so. At that time, two other states with two-year term governors allowed only one successive term, or four total years as governor. Over the last decade or so, states have changed the electoral rules lodged in their constitutions to permit incumbent governors and other elected officials to seek successive terms and, thereby, to have the opportunity to be more effective leaders in their states.

This change has an important influence on and broad implications for the government, policies, and politics of our states. A highly successful governor can be allowed to continue directing the state toward worthy goals. Continuity in leadership rather than constant change can be the byword. Programs and innovations can be suggested, passed into being, implemented, and evaluated without being discontinued or disrupted by changes in the governorship. If an incumbent and his or her administration fail to fulfill the contract made with the citizens, the result will be in the ballot box when he or she seeks re-election.

I served as governor of North Carolina between 1961 and 1965, when there was a one-term limit on this state's governor. I would like to have served another four years to make sure that the ideas, innovations, and programs that we started could and would grow. I think I might have been able to convince the citizens of North Carolina to let me do so. At a minimum, I and those in my administration would have been able to discuss with the citizens of North Carolina what we saw as the future and the ways in which we were at work to provide a better future for them. They would have been able to weigh our record against those proposed by others.

The one-term limit was not all bad, however, because it forced me as it did others to get on with what I had planned to do as governor. We needed more money for our schools, and taxes had to be raised, which we did early in my administration. Other steps were taken quickly rather than being placed "on hold" for later. I was not tempted to wait for the second term.

Re-elections are significant political statements at all levels of government. The people of a particular constituency confirm that they approve of what an office holder is doing when they give him or her a mandate to continue.

The evidence in recent years shows that our governors are doing a good job, if measured by the support they receive when seeking re-election. Most likely they receive support for this reason; at any rate, there is much evidence that people are more aware of what states are and should be doing, so such mandates are even more significant than they may have been in the past. The other side of the coin is equally important--it may mean that the governor has been spending much of his time running for re-election and has been taking advantage of the powerful political tools that an incumbent governor has at his command. Defeat may mean that the governor's record was not what the people hoped it would be. The citizens of a state speak through the ballot box, but, admittedly, it is not always clear why the voters speak as they do.

In this book there are excellent analyses of the gubernatorial re-election campaigns in 1982 and of the subsequent administrations of incumbent governors who sought and received a continuation of their tenure. While the focus in these chapters is on the campaign for re-election and the early steps of the new administration, the reader is able to glean a sense of how a close interaction with the voters after the first election affects a gubernatorial administration and the governor. If our system of democracy is working as it should work, this political interaction is of considerable significance.

                                        Terry Sanford
                                        Durham, North Carolina
                                        October 1984

NOTES

[1] Terry Sanford, *Storm Over the States* (New York: McGraw Hill, 1967), p. 191.

GUBERNATORIAL RE-ELECTIONS: THE 1982 EXPERIENCE

THAD L. BEYLE

Our electoral system operates on a fixed schedule at all levels. This ensures that we know when the leaders of our executive branches will be selected. Unless there is a death, incapacity, or malfeasance while in office, our state governors will be selected every four years in 46 states and every other year in 4 states (Arkansas, New Hampshire, Rhode Island, and Vermont).

These regularities create a certain rhythm to politics in our states. For those states with four-year terms, the first year is one of "learning the ropes," getting acquainted with personnel, processes, agencies, problems, and ways of working with those relevant others so important to a gubernatorial administration--the legislature and the media. It is also the period of time in which the governor usually has his greatest amount of power flowing from the mandate received at the polls. The second and third years are those in which the governor's administration can and often is fine-tuned to fit the style of the governor and the needs of the state. The final year gives way to politics, since the incumbent or his successor looks toward the election. Electoral politics pervade the first and fourth years by calendar, while receding in significance in the middle two years. For those states with two-year terms, states there are no middle years, only the first year, in which the electoral mandate pervades, and the last year, in which the next election does so; thus, any mistakes made are difficult to overcome.

Many states have moved to separate the rhythm of their own political system from that of national politics. To do so, gubernatorial elections, and other state elections, are held in off-presidential election years. Thus, there were two gubernatorial elections held in 1981, thirty-six in 1983, and there will be two in 1985. Only thirteen states held a gubernatorial election in 1984 coinciding with the presidential contest, and four of these were the two-year term states.

Succession, the ability to succeed oneself in the governorship, has gradually become the rule in the states and their constitutions. Only four states now deny their governors the ability to seek a second term: Kentucky, Mississippi, New Mexico, and Virginia. In those states, the governor's initial political strength undergirded by the victory at the polls is immediately eroded, as the threat to run and win again is not available. In fact, it may be that in those states the greatest power the governor has is on the day of the election.

Twenty-four other states limit their governors to two consecutive terms, and three of these, Delaware, Missouri, and North Carolina, have an absolute two-term limit for any one person to serve as governor. The remaining twenty-two states set no limitation on how many terms a governor can serve, so only politics and personal desires set the limits.

Governors who can and do seek re-election run as incumbents with not only higher name recognition but also a record of accomplishment and non-accomplishment. The campaign can and most often does revolve around the governor and his or her administration and policies. Such knowledge is beneficial to everyone concerned in the electoral process because a good part of the fear of the unknown is removed by one candidate's record. Voters can make their choices based on the record they know versus the promises they hear. Interest groups can pledge their allegiance in the same manner, as can the monied political action committees (PACs), and others who work in or close to government, such as those in the bureaucracy, other officials, and those in the media. Incumbency is a powerful political tool because with it goes power, access to media, degrees of control over a vast state bureaucracy, and a sizeable personal staff. The defeat of an incumbent governor means not only the rejection of the current governor and his or her administration but also indicates that the challenger had significant wherewithal to overcome the built-in strengths of an incumbent governor. So, in most cases, an incumbent will win re-election unless there is a serious problem concerning his or her governorship. The 1982 gubernatorial elections uphold this point: Twenty-five governors sought re-election and nineteen of them were successful, for a 76-percent winning rate.

The focus of this volume is on the re-election of the nineteen governors in the 1982 general elections. We established a state analysts' network throughout the thirty-six states undergoing a gubernatorial election in 1982 in order to look at two phenomena. For the seventeen states in which a transition occurred following the election, the questions concerned how the transfer of gubernatorial power, authority, and responsibility was handled.[1] For the nineteen states in which an incumbent was successful in the bid for re-election, the questions concerned how that success occurred and, importantly, what changes, if any, followed the re-election in the new administration. State analysts provided studies in all but three of the states involved: Pennsylvania, Rhode Island, and Vermont.

The Study of Incumbency's Effect on Gubernatorial Re-election

Clearly, incumbency has been viewed as an important part of understanding and analyzing elections. While most attention has been focused on the national-level incumbents such as congressmen, senators, and presidents, there is a growing literature and understanding of the effect of incumbency for governors seeking re-election.[2] Several of the findings are relevant to this study of the 1982 gubernatorial elections.

First, during the twentieth century there has been an increasing number of incumbent governors who are constitutionally able to seek re-election, and who do seek re-election. Between 1900-1909, forty-six percent of the gubernatorial elections involved incumbents seeking to hold their seats; by the 1940s the number had risen to 68 percent of the elections,[3] and between 1980 and 1982, to 77 percent.

Second, incumbency is an important factor in seeking and holding the governor's chair. Between 1900 and 1969, Turett found that approximately two-thirds of the gubernatorial incumbents seeking re-election were winners in the selected states he studied.[4] Morehouse found that nearly three out of every four were successful across all the states between 1970 and 1979,[5] while in the early 1980s, the success rate was seven out of every ten (26 of 37). These data support Piereson's argument that incumbency is "a growing advantage" for governors, and Patterson's finding that incumbency made a positive contribution to vote shares in the 1978 gubernatorial elections.[6]

Third, hidden within these overall averages are variations based on the impact of national politics on state politics. Morehouse notes that Republican governors seeking re-election in the 1970s were considerably less likely to win (23 of 39, or 59 percent) than were Democrats seeking to hold their seats (35 of 39, or 90 percent).[7] The difference is attributed to the problems of the national Republican party and President Nixon concerning Watergate and related issues. In the 1980 Reagan presidential sweep, five of twelve incumbent Democratic governors seeking re-election lost. They represented one-half of the Democratic governors seeking re-election. But, Morehouse cautions, the pulling effect of presidential coattails can vary considerably as witnessed by the "too slippery coattails" of Nixon in 1972 when the Republicans lost a net of two governorships to the Democrats.[8]

Therefore, when the national political party is suffering a major setback, incumbent governors seeking to serve another term can find considerable difficulty in doing so. However, the converse can also be true: In off-presidential-year gubernatorial races, incumbent governors of the non-presidential party can have a better chance to win, partly in reaction to the presidential administration. Since 1950, in the even-year midterm elections, the average number of governorships lost by the President's party has been 6.2, with Republicans (7.4) suffering more than Democrats (4.8). For example, in 1970 Republicans had a net loss of ten governorships, and in 1974 six, while in 1978 the Democrats had a net loss of five governorships.[9] This presidential-year impact is a major reason for states holding their gubernatorial elections in or changing them to off-presidential election years.

Fourth, there are also variations in the success rate of incumbents based on the type of state involved. For example, Nelson and Jones, in their study of the 1946-1976 period, found governors of industrial states more vulnerable than their counterparts in the less populated states. And Lammers and Klingman argued that durable governors, those serving more than eight years with a minimum of three elections, tended to be from smaller states.[10]

Fifth, incumbency success varies by the type of office held. Hinckley found incumbent governors seeking re-election less successful than were U.S. senators during the 1948-1966 period, and Bibby's analysis indicated that since 1960, incumbent congressmen have averaged more than a 90-percent success rate, while gubernatorial incumbents achieved an average 71-percent rate.[11]

Seroka, in his analysis of related findings, attributed this difference to the political executives' particular vulnerability to the "throw the rascals out" impulse.[12] More recently, however, there is evidence that governors seeking another term are more successful than U.S. senators.[13]

Sixth, the key campaign issues in races in which governors are defeated for re-election most often revolve around the governor himself or his administration. Between 1951 and 1981 there were 129 elections, both primary and general, in which an incumbent governor or a former governor was defeated. The key issues in these defeats included: intraparty conflicts in 41 of the cases (32 percent); scandals in 17 (13 percent) and political or administration incompetence in 10 (8 percent). These causes were not mutually exclusive categories but do point to the incumbent as the focal point in many of these defeats.[14]

The issues involved varied by region and party: In southern and western states <u>intraparty</u> politics was the issue, thereby affecting Democrats more, while in midwest and northeastern states <u>interparty</u> politics was more frequently the issue, thereby effecting Republicans more.[15]

Seventh, the increasing success of gubernatorial incumbents is associated with their being better known than others in the state's political system,[16] and with the growth of the public sector which[17] produces increasing resources available to an incumbent. These advantages, however, can be double-edged swords because the more visible governor who runs a more intrusive administration can be held responsible for any errors or oversights within that administration. As Tompkins notes, incumbency can thus "involve two forces at odds with each other: the initial advantages which come with the office, improving their prospects, and the subsequent burdens associated with service, which stimulate participation and erode the incumbent's ability to enhance their standings."[18] In Schlesinger's terms they "accumulate grievances" rather than support as they serve.[19]

Eighth, few incumbent governors are even seriously challenged for their party's renomination and when challenged there are few divisive primaries involved. However, in the McNitt and Seroka comparative study of the 1956-76 period they fared less well than did U.S. senators. They conclude that "incumbents have a stranglehold over politics in the United States," which, they argue, is tied to the strength and control of the incumbent over the state party organization.[20]

Studies on the impact of the re-election on a new or following administration are sparse in the literature. We hope this study begins to fill that gap.

THE 1982 GUBERNATORIAL ELECTIONS

The 1982 general elections included gubernatorial elections in thirty-six of the fifty states. Twenty-five incumbent governors ran for re-election in the thirty-six states (69 percent) and nineteen of the twenty-five were successful in their quest (76 percent). For the general election contests only, that is, excluding Governor Edward King (D) of Massachusetts, who was defeated in his attempt to secure his own party's renomination, the twenty-four incumbents in the general election were the largest number running since 1962, when twenty-four ran. Nineteen of those twenty-four incumbents won (76 percent), a rate which is among the highest of the even-year races sinces 1960. Only in 1964 when twelve of fourteen won (86 percent), 1978 when sixteen of nineteen won (84 percent), and 1974 when fifteen of eighteen won (83 percent), were the rates higher. Yet 76 percent was well below the incumbency win rates of U.S.

congressmen (92 percent) and U.S. senators (93 percent) in 1982.[21]

Voters in the other seventeen states selected new governors, six of whom unseated incumbents seeking re-election. Four of the ousted governors were Republicans and two Democrats, with a party shift occurring in five states (Arkansas, Nebraska, Nevada, New Hampshire, and Texas) and a factional shift in the sixth (Massachusetts).

Those who lost the governorship included King of Massachusetts who lost in his party's primary to former Governor Michael S. Dukakis (1975-79), whom King had defeated in the 1978 Democratic primary for the gubernatorial nomination. The other five lost in the general election: Frank White (R) of Arkansas to former Governor Bill Clinton (D), 1979-81, whom White had unseated in 1980; Charles Thone (R) of Nebraska to businessman Robert Kerry (D); Robert List (R) of Nevada to State Attorney General Richard Bryan (D); Hugh Gallen (D) of New Hampshire to academic and business consultant John Sununu (R); and Frank Clement (R) of Texas to State Attorney General Mark White (D).

As noted, two of these six incumbents lost to former governors whom they had defeated earlier, two lost to the incumbent of another important statewide elected office, the attorney general, and two lost to relative outsiders in the political system. This information suggests several points: one is that it is difficult to unseat an incumbent governor, since nineteen of twenty-five were successful in seeking re-election. In four out of the six states in which an incumbent lost, winning required the name recognition, known record and accomplishments, and political organization of candidates who had run and won statewide elections previously, and who, thereby, had held statewide office. In only two of the states where an incumbent was defeated were relative outsiders able to mount successful campaigns.

Secondly, it is significant to note that the two statewide offices held most often by those who defeated incumbents were those of governor and attorney general. The former is to be expected, the latter indicates, again, the rise in importance of the states' chief legal officers over the past decade. The former governors had stood at the top of the state's political career ladder, having taken the requisite steps to be there earlier. The attorneys general were on their way up this ladder and were "in line" to take that next step.[22]

Finally, to look at the half-empty cup, the results do support the proposition that it is difficult to unseat the governor when coming from outside the system, as only two of the six successful challenges were by outsiders. But their victories are no less significant to their states because these winners in essence broke in at the top of the career ladder, thereby upsetting other political ambitions, timetables, and careers in a ripple-like fashion.[23]

The nineteen re-elected governors included thirteen Democrats and six Republicans, which information, when added to fourteen new Democratic and three new Republican governors, indicates how substantial was the three-to-one Democratic (27-9) sweep of the statehouses in 1982. This was an off-year in American politics, so no explicit presidential politics were involved to overshadow these campaigns and elections. But the national situation was felt in terms of the declining economy and its effect on the state budgets, and to some extent in a mid-presidential term evaluation by the voters who obviously sought more Democratic leadership rather than Republican. For example, in the thirteen states of the thirty-six which had high unemployment rates (more than 10 percent as of August 1982), the Democratic candidates fared better in these races, winning eight of the seats (62 percent). For the seven incumbents in high employment states, two Democrats and five Republicans, the Democrats won their races, while one of the four Republicans lost his seat.[24]

The "Dean" of these governors was George Ariyoshi (D) of Hawaii, who has served since 1973 when, as lieutenant governor, he became acting governor because of the Governor's illness, and in 1982 was moving into his third term with this re-election.[25] Others moving into their third four-year terms were Richard Lamm (D) of Colorado and Ed Herschler (D) of Wyoming, while James Thompson (R) of Illinois also was going into his third term, the first of which (1977-79) was shortened as the state moved its gubernatorial elections from the presidential to the off-presidential cycle beginning with the 1978 election. Two others, Joseph Garrahy (D) of Rhode Island and Richard Snelling (R) of Vermont, were entering their fourth two-year terms with these victories. William O'Neill (D) of Connecticut was actually winning his first election for governor, having succeeded to the office as lieutenant governor when Ella Grasso (D, 1974-80) was forced to resign due to a terminal illness. (See Table 1, "The Re-elected Governors, 1982.")

Their road to the governorship was predominantly state based, since fifteen held state-elected positions as their "penultimate" or immediate past public position.[26] Included were five lieutenant governors, three attorneys general, two legislative leaders, and five legislators. One other, Harry Hughes (D) of Maryland, previously had been a state administrator and a longtime legislator. The other three

Table 1: The Re-elected Governors, 1982

State	Name and Party	Date of First Service	Present Terms Ends	Number of Previous Terms	Immediate Past Public Position	Profession	Birthdate	State of Birth
Arizona	Bruce E. Babbitt (D)	Mar 1978	Jan 1987	2[a]	Attorney General	Lawyer	06/27/38	California
Colorado	Richard D. Lamm (D)	Jan 1975	Jan 1987	3[b]	State Representative	Lawyer	08/03/35	Wisconsin
Connecticut	William A. O'Neill (D)	Dec 1980	Jan 1987	1	Lieutenant Governor	Businessman	08/11/30	Connecticut
Florida	D. Robert Graham (D)	Jan 1979	Jan 1987	1	State Senator	Lawyer	11/09/36	Florida
Hawaii	George R. Ariyoshi (D)	Oct 1973	Dec 1986	2[c]	Lieutenant Governor	Lawyer	03/12/26	Hawaii
Idaho	John V. Evans (D)	Jan 1977	Jan 1987	1[d]	Lieutenant Governor	Businessman	01/18/25	Idaho
Illinois	James R. Thompson (R)	Jan 1977	Jan 1987	2[e]	U.S. Attorney	Lawyer	05/08/36	Illinois
Kansas	John Carlin (D)	Jan 1979	Jan 1987	1	Speaker of State House	Farmer	08/03/40	Kansas
Maine	Joseph E. Brennan (D)	Jan 1979	Jan 1987	1	Attorney General	Lawyer	11/02/34	Maine
Maryland	Harry R. Hughes (D)	Jan 1979	Jan 1987	1[f]	State Administrator	Lawyer	11/13/26	Maryland
Oklahoma	George Nigh (D)	Jan 1963	Jan 1987	2	Lieutenant Governor	Businessman	06/09/27	Oklahoma
Oregon	Victor G. Atiyeh (R)	Jan 1979	Jan 1987	1	State Senator	Businessman	02/20/23	Oregon
Pennsylvania	Dick Thornburgh (R)	Jan 1979	Jan 1987	1	Asst. U.S. Attorney General	Lawyer	07/16/32	Pennsylvania
Rhode Island	J. Joseph Garrahy (D)	Jan 1977	Jan 1985	3	Lieutenant Governor	Public Service	11/26/30	Rhode Island
South Carolina	Richard W. Riley (D)	Jan 1979	Jan 1987	1	State Senator	Lawyer	01/02/33	South Carolina
South Dakota	William J. Janklow (R)	Jan 1979	Jan 1987	1	Attorney General	Lawyer	09/13/39	Illinois
Tennessee	Lamar Alexander (R)	Jan 1979	Jan 1987	1	White House Counsel	Lawyer	07/03/40	Tennessee
Vermont	Richard A. Snelling (R)	Jan 1977	Jan 1985	3	State House Leader	Businessman	02/18/27	Pennsylvania
Wyoming	Ed Herschler (D)	Jan 1975	Jan 1987	2	State Representative	Lawyer	10/27/18	Wyoming

Key: Source: The Book of the States, 1984-85 (Lexington, KY: The Council of State Governments, 1984), p. 49-50.
(a) Succeeded to governor's office on former governor's death. Elected to a full term November, 1978.
(b) Succeeded to governor's office on former governor's resignation due to ill health.
(c) Became acting governor when former governor became ill. Elected to a full term November, 1974.
(d) Succeeded to governor's office on former governor's resignation to accept a federal cabinet post. Elected to a full term November, 1978.
(e) First term was for two years, four years thereafter.
(f) Succeeded to governor's office in 1963 for a week on former governor's resignation to be appointed to the U.S. Senate by the new governor. Elected to a full term November, 1978.

used a federal position as their stepping stone: Lamar Alexander (R) of Tennessee coming from the position as White House Counsel, Thompson from his role as U.S. Attorney, and Richard Thornburgh (R) of Pennsylvania as an Assistant U.S. Attorney General. Most are lawyers (twelve) by profession, while five are businessmen, one a farmer, and one a public servant. Fifteen were natives of their states.

The Party Nomination

The first official step that any incumbent must take in order to gain another term is to become his party's nominee for the office. Of the twenty-five governors standing for re-election in their party's primary, convention, or caucus, eleven (44 percent) were unopposed, thereby freeing them from any divisive intra-party fight and allowing them to prepare for the fall general election campaign. Twelve others (48 percent) received the nomination in lopsided wins with victory margins of over 32 percent. Who challenged them? Businessmen, a retiree, a disk jockey, former and current legislators, a county executive, a farmer, a stock broker, and a rancher. (See Table 2, "The Gubernatorial Primaries: The Incumbent Governors.")

Only two incumbents were engaged in highly contested primaries: Ariyoshi of Hawaii, who defeated his lieutenant governor by a 9-percent margin, and King, who lost the Massachusetts Democratic nomination to former Governor Dukakis. Note again that these two contested primaries involved challengers who had run for and won statewide elections and had served in highly visible positions in their states' governments.

Clearly, an incumbent governor sits astride his or her party and if the nomination for re-election is desired, it will be given to him or her in most cases.

The General Elections

The nineteen incumbent governors who retained their chairs had varying degrees of difficulty in doing so in the general election contests. For some there was virtually no opposition from the other party candidate, which meant victory margins as great as 52 percent in Rhode Island, 42 percent in South Dakota, and 40 percent in South Carolina. At the other extreme were the highly contested races in Illinois (.001 percent), which was not decided officially until January; in Idaho (2 percent); in Pennsylvania (4 percent); and in Connecticut (6 percent). Generally, these victory margins indicate the strength of incumbency as a force for gubernatorial succession. And the strength of some of these wins illustrates Pomper's suggestion that "clear electoral wins are rare in gubernatorial contests"

The 1982 Gubernatorial Primaries: The Incumbent Governors

State	Governor (Party)	Challenger	Winner	Victory Margin[a]
Arkansas	White (R)	Former State Representative	Governor	72%
Arizona	Babbitt (D)	Retired Steel Worker	Governor	71%[b]
Colorado	Lamm (D)	Unopposed		
Connecticut	O'Neill (D)	Unopposed		
Florida	Graham (D)	Businessman	Governor	75%
Hawaii	Ariyoshi (D)	Lieutenant Governor	Governor	9%
Idaho	Evans (D)	Unopposed		
Illinois	Thompson (R)	Unopposed		
Kansas	Carlin (D)	Disk Jockey	Governor	58%
Maine	Brennan (D)	State Representative	Governor	54%
Maryland	Hughes (D)	County Executive	Governor	41%
Massachusetts	King (D)	Former Governor	Challenger	7%
Nebraska	Thone (R)	Farmer	Governor	32%
Nevada	List (R)	Stockbroker	Governor	37%
New Hampshire	Gallen (D)	Unopposed		
Oklahoma	Nigh (D)	Businessman	Governor	66%
Oregon	Atiyeh (R)	Businessman	Governor	75%
Pennsylvania	Thornburgh (R)	Unopposed		
Rhode Island	Garrahy (D)	Unopposed		
South Carolina	Riley (D)	Unopposed		
South Dakota	Janklow (R)	Unopposed		
Tennessee	Alexander (R)	Unopposed		
Texas	Clement (R)	Businessman	Governor	84%
Vermont	Snelling (R)	Unopposed		
Wyoming	Herschler (D)	Rancher	Governor	70%

Notes: a. Over closest opponent if more than two challengers in the primary.
b. Challenger died August 7, 1982, too late to have his name removed from the September 7 primary.

September 7 primary.

did not hold in 1982.[27] (See Table 3, "Politics of the 1982 Gubernatorial General Elections: Re-elected Governors.")

To no one's surprise, the most consistent issue in these campaigns was the incumbent governor--his record, style, alleged errors, and oversights. The fact of this emphasis had both a positive and a negative side. Obviously, with a strong and popular governor whose administration appeared to be unblemished, it was difficult for the opposition party challenger to make a very credible case as, for example, in Connecticut, Florida, Maine, and South Dakota. With no major errors evident, what is the need for change? Also, where a governor's leadership style was to avoid controversy and to let others carry the fight, as was true of Governor Nigh of Oklahoma, it was hard for a challenger to tag him with a negative administration label. But the successful challenges of incumbents in Arkansas, Massachusetts, Nebraska, Nevada, New Hampshire, and Texas indicate that such a case can be made and can work.

The other consistent issue in these 1982 contests concerned the economy and its impact on the state and the state budget. Had the governor done enough to protect the state and its citizens from the impact of the economic recession? As the chief fiscal officer of the state, had the governor taken the correct steps to keep the state's budget in balance, and to whose benefit or distress did he do so? South Carolina Governor Riley was accused of coping with the crisis in the state's budget by letting the state employees bear the burden on their backs. In Idaho, the fiscal crisis was the issue, diverting attention from all others, especially because Governor Evans was faced with a series of declining revenue estimates, which necessitated expenditure cutbacks. In Illinois, which was allegedly "better off" than the other hard-hit midwestern states, the issue devolved to questions of which taxes should or would have to be raised. Kansas Governor Carlin similarly faced the tax issue, but came out on the "right side," that is, backed by opinion polls, when he advocated a severance tax to help balance the state budget.

The economic situation in the country provided Democratic gubernatorial challengers an opportunity to attack the state's Republican administration for the problems of the national Republican administration. Challengers Stevenson (D) in Illinois and Tyree (D) in Tennessee attempted to tie their incumbent opponents to the Reagan administration policies, while the incumbents did their best to place distance between their national leader and themselves.

As happens too often in our political system, some of the challengers themselves became the issue, rather than the

TABLE 3: Politics of the 1982 Gubernatorial General Elections: Re-elected Governors

State	Candidates Democratic	Republican	Winner	Victory Margin	Campaign Issues General Election
Arizona	Babbitt, Governor	Leo Corbet, State Senate President	D	31%	a, b, c
Colorado	Lamm, Governor	John D. Fuhr, Former House Speaker	D	34	d
Connecticut	O'Neill, Governor	Lewis B. Rome, Former State Senator	D	6	d
Florida	Graham, Governor	L.A. "Skip" Bafalis, Congressman	D	30	d, e
Hawaii	Ariyoshi, Governor	D. G. Anderson, State Senator Frank Fasi (I-D), Former Mayor, Honolulu	D	19 (R) 16 (I-D)	d
Idaho	Evans, Governor	Philip E. Batt, Lieutenant Governor	D	2	a
Illinois	Adlai E. Stevenson, III, Former US Senator	Thompson, Governor	R	.001	a, d, f
Kansas	Carlin, Governor	Sam Hardage, Businessman	D	9	a, e
Maine	Brennan, Governor	Charles L. Cragin, Lawyer	D	24	d
Maryland	Hughes, Governor	Robert A. Pascal, Ann Arundel County Executive	D	24	b, d, e
Oklahoma	Nigh, Governor	Tom Daxon, State Auditor	D	24	a, d, e
Oregon	Ted Kulongoski, State Senator	Atiyeh, Governor	R	26	a, d, e
Pennsylvania	Allen E. Ertel, Congressman	Thornburgh, Governor	R	4	N/A
Rhode Island	Garrahy, Governor	Vincent Marzullo, Businessman	D	52	d (no issues)
South Carolina	Riley, Governor	William D. Workman, Jr., Retired Newspaper Editor	D	40	b, d
South Dakota	Mike O'Connor, State Senator	Janklow, Governor	R	42	a, b, d
Tennessee	Randy Tyree, Mayor, Knoxville	Alexander, Governor	R	20	d, e, f
Vermont	Madeleine M. Kunin, Lieutenant Governor	Snelling, Governor	R	11	N/A
Wyoming	Herschler, Governor	Warren A. Morton, Former House Speaker	D	26	d

Source: Congressional Quarterly Weekly Report (November 6, 1982) pp. 2817-2825 and state analysts reports.

Key:
a. Economy and state finances
b. Leadership style
c. Executive v. legislative roles
d. Incumbent's record
e. Challenger's own problems
f. Incumbent's tie with Reagan administration

incumbents they sought to unseat. Usually when the challenger becomes the issue it is a negative and major reason for his or her defeat. The following examples illustrate this cause of defeat: In Florida, the Republican challenger's public statements, record as a U.S. representative, and lack of knowledge of Florida state government were significant issues; in Kansas, the Republican challenger's personality and background hindered him; and, in Tennessee, the Democratic challenger's alleged receipt of major campaign funds from a political, sensitive source evoked memories of the state's most recent scandal-ridden and discredited Democratic administration.

There were other issues in these races but none were as consistent across all states as the three mentioned above: incumbency, economy, and the challenger. The Arizona contest included debate over the respective institutional accountability and responsibility of the executive and legislative branches, that is, who gets the credit and the blame for Arizona's problems. Challengers in several states attempted to raise other issues in the political campaign but were too often unsuccessful in the face of these three major issues. Put another way, the agenda was usually set by the incumbent and the economic situation, with the challenger restricted in his or her ability to shift it unless it was the challenger himself who became the issue.

Several re-election campaigns were not campaigns at all, as in Rhode Island where there was no credible candidate or issues and in Oklahoma where it was "one of the quietest gubernatorial campaigns in years." In Maine, Governor Brennan rarely ever mentioned the challenger's name, and few issues were raised, while in Connecticut the challenger was frustrated by Governor O'Neil's aloof "Rose Garden Strategy" of campaigning. Wyoming's campaign with no real issues of substance tended to degenerate into foolishness at times, as when the rival camps argued over the actors used in political advertisements.

The use of the political debate was a part of numerous races, and with differing results. The opening debate may have proved to be the key to Governor Thompson's re-election victory in Illinois, as he overruled his campaign strategists' advice and came out swinging, while the style of his challenger, Stevenson, seemed to remove the mantle of "statesman" from his shoulders. At the other end of the spectrum was Hawaii where the debates were cancelled.

Between these extremes, there were Arizona, where the debates did not do much to stimulate interest or enthusiasm, but did provide a forum for wider audiences than usual; Maine, where Governor Brennan ignored the challenger's attempt to set the agenda; Oregon, where Governor Atiyeh called for the debates despite his campaign strategists' entreaties, and won; and South Dakota, where Governor Janklow was not hesitant to debate his underfinanced and media-poor candidate.

Debates were clearly part of the political landscape in these state elections. They served as much as candidate forums to display style and credibility as they did knowledge of issues. Of interest are those governors whose gut political instincts led them to debate over the carefully thought out political strategies of their staffs and consultants. Gut politics won in each case.

The Costs of Retaining the Governorship

Governors' races are increasingly expensive, especially those in states where a new governor is selected. For example, in the 1982 races in which a new governor won, none of the seventeen races cost less than $1 million, and three cost more than $22 million. In contrast, five of the nineteen successful incumbent races cost less than $1 million and the two most expensive were between $7 and $8 million. Of course, these figures are only the officially reported costs of cash outlays by the candidates' organizations; the actual cost can never be known. (See Table 4, "1982 Campaign Expenditures: Re-elected Governors.")

Incumbent governors had not only the power of incumbency working for them but also financial resources, as thirteen of the nineteen outspent their challengers. Of the more than $47 million spent in these nineteen races, incumbents officially spent nearly $29 million to the $18 million their challengers spent, a 61 to 39-percent difference. Governor Garrahy of Rhode Island not only swamped his token opposition at the ballot box by 76 to 24 percent, but also he outspent him 96 to 4 percent. Governor Riley of South Carolina similarly defeated his weak opponent 70 to 30 percent in the voting booth and 82 to 18 percent in expenditures. Other lopsided campaigns included those of Governor Babbitt of Arizona, who won a 63 to 32-percent victory with a 75 to 17-percent expenditure difference, and Governor Lamm of Colorado, who won at a 67 to 33-percent rate and spent at a 71 to 29-percent rate. So political money was added to their considerable political power as incumbents to produce lopsided wins.

At the other extreme, there were six states in which the challenger outspent the incumbent governor, yet still lost. In Wyoming the challenger spent twice as much as the governor in a losing effort; Herschler beat his opponent at the ballot box 63 to 37 percent while being outspent 31 to 69 percent. Governor Carlin of Kansas, while winning at a

Table 4: 1982 Campaign Expenditures, Re-elected Governors

State	Major Candidates	Primary Election Percent of Total Vote	Primary Election Percent of Total Spending	Primary Election Cost per Vote	Percent of Total General Election Vote	Percent of Spending, Primary and General Election	Overall Cost per General Election Vote	Total Campaign Expenditures All Candidates – 1982
Arizona	w Babbitt (D)	86.0	N/A	N/A	63	75	3.73[a]	
	Corbett (R)	61.7	66.8	3.04[a]	32	17	1.65	2,262,750[c]
Colorado	w Lamm (D)	no primary, candidates			67	71	1.30[a]	
	Fuhr (R)	selected at party assembly (caucus)			33	29	1.08	1,142,933
Connecticut	w O'Neill (D)	no primary, candidates			53	30	1.67[a]	
	Rome (R)	won in party conventions			47	36	2.25[a]	3,152,543
Florida	w Graham (D)	84.4	99.5	2.55[a]	65	66	1.64[a]	
	Bafalis (R)	86.4	96.6	4.26[a]	35	32	1.46	4,222,742
Hawaii	w Ariyoshi (D)	53.6	85.8	11.59[a]	45	61	17.39[a]	
	Anderson (R)	97.0	99.7		26	19	9.55	
	Fasi (ID)	N/A – Independent			29	14	6.14	4,036,608
Idaho	w Evans (D)	Unopposed			51	36	2.82[a]	
	Batt (R)	63.8	55.8	3.13[a]	49	46	3.71[a]	1,306,804
Illinois	w Thompson (R)	No contested primaries			50	63	2.85[a]	
	Stevenson (D)	candidates slated by committee			50	38	1.74	8,000,000[b]
Kansas	w Carlin (D)	78.8	99.7	4.12[a]	54	38	2.84[a]	
	Hardage (R)	36.8	47.4	8.12	45	62	5.52[a]	3,028,520
Maine	w Brennan (D)	76.8	94.5	3.77[a]	62	48	1.94[a]	
	Cragin (R)	38.1	20.6	5.77	38	52	6.46[a]	1,663,327
Maryland	w Hughes (D)	65.3	68.5	1.87[a]	62	56	2.05[a]	
	Pascal (R)	84.1	100.0	4.66	38	32	1.96	2,553,942

54 to 45-percent difference, was outspent at a 38 to 62-percent rate. So political money cannot always overcome the other political powers that incumbents have.

The cost of getting votes at the polls varies considerably. For the winning incumbent governors the cost ranged from $17.39 in Hawaii to $.74 in South Dakota. Some of the losing challengers paid dearly for their too few votes. For example, it cost one of the losing challengers in Hawaii $9.55 per vote in achieving his 26 percent of the total vote. In Wyoming, the Republican challenger spent $9.16 per vote in order to win 37 percent of the vote.

Running for governor is an extremely expensive proposition for winners and losers alike. It appears that incumbents, although sometimes outspent by their challengers, are generally more effective in translating their spending into votes on election day.

THE NEW ADMINISTRATION

Changing the Guard and Structure

The problems a re-elected governor faces regarding appointments, processes, and style are generally his alone: They cannot be blamed upon a predecessor. Further, he has lived with the organization of his office and with state government processes and organization for a term. Therefore, to induce change or not is his responsibility. And when he has been re-elected handily, as Governor Garrahy of Rhode Island was, there may be no actual discernible impact of the campaign and election on his administration.[28]

However, some re-elected governors did take their re-election and the prospects for a new term and a new administration as an opportunity to consider and to attempt to carry out some changes in their leadership style. As noted by Harder in the Kansas study, this is the one time a governor can make such changes, without having them interpreted as indicators of weakness in his administration by his adversaries.

Were these changes in leadership style due to a serious planned review and analysis, or did they just flow from perceived needs? The Illinois governor's office staff and Governor Thompson were particularly alert to the dangers of inertia and insensitivity that often haunt second- and third-term governors. They knew the third term would be different from the first (1977-1979), which was basically an extension of his successful 1976 political campaign. And the new term could not be a copy of the second (1979-1983), as it was used to create a record upon which the third term campaign would be mounted in 1982--especially since now he will be the longest serving governor in the state's history by the end of this term.

Governor Thompson's re-election, however, was clouded by the closeness of the win--5,074 votes of the nearly 3.9 million cast, and challenges filed by the Democratic challenger. The election was not decided officially until January 7, 1983, inauguration occurred three days later, and the legislature convened January 12. The rapid pace of events left Thompson with little time to plan and initiate change. Further, he began his third term with difficult fiscal problems to address, which will probably last throughout the full term. The need to think through the possibility of change was there, but the time involved and the problems being faced did not allow it. (See Table 5, "Significant Dates in the 1982 Gubernatorial Re-elections.")

South Dakota Governor Janklow also recognized the dangers of complacency and stagnation which could affect himself and his administration. To counter such dangers he established an internal review process beginning in late November, which involved each cabinet-level appointee undertaking a self-analysis of his or her agency. They were to answer questions such as "Where have we been?" and "Where are we going?" which were then presented at a December cabinet review.

Governor Carlin of Kansas called for a planning process for his second term immediately after his re-election. He, his principal staff advisors, and two political scientists from the University of Kansas were involved in the process. The latter developed a planning document that was based on the assumption that the governor would wish to be viewed as a "statesman," projecting the ability to engage in positive political development.

Other states were probably similar to South Carolina, where little "agonizing reappraisal" was undertaken because of Governor Riley's satisfaction with his approach and style, and in Florida, where there was a period of administrative introspection after which they decided not to change very much.

If there is to be change, these studies suggest there are several options to follow.

The first option is to keep things as they are, with the rationale that you were just re-elected so what you are doing must be right. This was the approach in Wyoming where Governor Herschler retained his entire governor's office staff, most all agency heads, and made only one major appointment--a new attorney general, something he has done for each of his three terms. Oklahoma Governor Nigh saw no

Table 5: Significant Dates in the 1982 Gubernatorial Re-elections

State	Election	Inaugural[a]	Convening of Legislature[b]	Submission of Budget[b]
Arizona	2 November 1982	8 January[c] 1983	10 January 1983	14 January 1983
Colorado	2 November 1982	11 January 1983	5 January 1983	18 January 1983
Connecticut	2 November 1982	5 January 1983	5 January 1983	4 February 1983
Florida	2 November 1982	4 January 1983	4 January 1983[d]	16 November 1982
Hawaii	2 November 1982	6 December 1982	19 January 1983	31 December 1982
Idaho	2 November 1982	8 January 1983	10 January 1983	14 January 1983
Illinois	2 November 1982	10 January 1983	12 January 1983	2 March 1983
Kansas	2 November 1982	10 January 1983	10 January 1983	31 January 1983
Maine	2 November 1982	5 January 1983	8 December 1982	7 January 1983
Maryland	2 November 1982	20 January 1983	12 January 1983	19 January 1983
Oklahoma	2 November 1982	10 January 1983	4 January 1983	4 January 1983
Oregon	2 November 1982	10 January 1983	10 January 1983	1 December 1982
Pennsylvania	2 November 1982	18 January 1983	4 January 1983	4 February 1983
Rhode Island	2 November 1982	4 January 1983	4 January 1983	4 February 1983
South Carolina	2 November 1982	10 January 1983	11 January 1983[e]	11 January 1983
South Dakota	2 November 1982	3 January 1983	4 January 1983[f]	7 December 1982
Tennessee	2 November 1982	14 January 1983	4 January 1983	31 January 1983
Vermont	2 November 1982	6 January 1983	5 January 1983	18 January 1983
Wyoming	2 November 1982	3 January 1983	11 January 1983	1 January 1983

Notes:
a. Office of State Services, National Governors' Association, "Gubernatorial Elections in the States and Territories - 1982," 19 October 1982.
b. *The Book of the States, 1982-83* (Lexington, KY: The Council of State Governments, 1982), pp. 210-211, 276-279.
c. Set by winner
d. Organization session.
e. Organization session meeting for no more than three days.
f. Organization session meeting for no more than 15 calendar days.

reason for change, and while some may be asked to resign later, no wholesale changes were expected. In Hawaii what looked like some strategic shifts were not, as three department heads retired voluntarily. These changes were not dramatic and created no major administration policy shifts.

Arizona's Governor Babbitt continued his policy of little change by retaining his key people for reasonably long tenures, especially as he was very satisfied with their performances. He also may have been reacting to criticisms of his first-term appointments as being part of an empire of personally loyal, non-threatening sycophants, and of going out of state too often for key appointments.

The second option is to make some minor adjustments to your administration to make it work even better. In Maine, Governor Brennan decided to create an office of intergovernmental relations within the governor's office to improve state-local relations, and to fine-tune his administration rather than overhaul it. Kansas Governor Carlin reorganized his immediate office by creating two management positions: a chief of staff responsible for policy, press relations, and constituent services; and an executive assistant to handle scheduling, appointments, and clerical operations.

Third-term Governor Lamm of Colorado had to make appointments to major positions to replace seven appointees who resigned because of long service rather than dissatisfaction with performance or policy. But he startled state government observers by appointing the separately elected state treasurer to serve as his chief of staff, a position the treasurer had held in the mid-1970s. This unique arrangement lasted almost a year, but the treasurer decided to resign because the details a chief of staff must address were thought to be too great a burden for a person who is holding another office.

The third option is to make some changes in order to highlight particular new directions to be undertaken in the upcoming administration, using the re-election, its mandate, and the new term as justification. In South Dakota, Governor Janklow signaled an emphasis on education by appointing the secretary of labor as secretary of education and cultural affairs, and by putting emphasis on highways over railroads in his choice of the new secretary of transportation. He also sent a message throughout state government that he was trying to avoid complacency by replacing several other secretaries and his own chief of staff. Governor Hughes, the re-elected governor of Maryland, similarly accepted cabinet resignations, created a new department of employment and training, and gave his new lieutenant governor broader responsibilities.

Governor O'Neill of Connecticut, who succeeded to office as lieutenant governor upon the resignation of his predecessor, Ella Grasso, in late 1980, called for the resignation of all 134 appointed personnel the day after the election, his first election to the governorship. While this was a broad sweeping stroke undertaken with limited "touching base" with others, only one-third of the executive assistants and one-quarter of the agency heads and commissioners were actually replaced, while a considerable number of former Governor Grasso's holdovers were retained. At the same time, O'Neill made several appointments which would replace voluntary resignations, replace others because of their managerial incompetence, and reward political friends and supporters.

The fourth option is to undertake major shifts in direction by changing personnel, processes, and structure so the new administration is new in fact. Obviously, few governors would attempt this approach as it might be interpreted as a self-generated condemnation of the first term. However, Governor Alexander of Tennessee did undertake such a major endeavor as he moved from the "caretaker" role of his first term to that of the "program promoter" he envisioned for his second term. To do so he sought to streamline state government by reorganizing the executive branch through executive order and proposed legislation. He made significant shifts in his cabinet by appointing eight new people and selecting them with an emphasis upon the private sector in order to utilize professional managerial expertise. He reorganized the structure of his policy advisory, support, and implementation systems to assist him in having new policies effected. These changes made the re-election of a governor appear to be more like the transition of an incumbent governor leaving and a new governor coming in, with all the attendent messages and signals attached.

Gubernatorial Leadership Styles

But there can be more than just structural and personnel changes involved. Does a governor change his own style of leadership when a re-election provides the opportunity? And if a governor does so, what do the changes suggest?

First, what leadership styles did these governors have? Governor Atiyeh of Oregon saw his job as that of an elder statesman who was "running the company," by doing "what I think is right or in the best interest of the state." This style meant for him no risk-taking as governor. Similarly, as noted, Governor Alexander was viewed in his first term as a "caretaker" of Tennessee state government. And Governor Hershler was seen as incremental and reactive in Wyoming.

Others, such as Governors Graham of Florida and Riley of South Carolina, were perceived as detail men with both the positive aspects of being involved and knowing a great deal and the negative aspects of being too immersed and unwilling to delegate responsibilities. Riley also seeks to achieve mutual adjustment of these aspects in order to resolve problems. Governor Lamm of Colorado overcomes the structural weaknesses of his office by relying on exposure in the press and the use of task forces and blue ribbon groups to help set the agenda. It is a well-known fact that Hawaii's Governor Ariyoshi used a task force and committee approach to assist in his leadership responsibilities.

An emphasis on management seemed to pervade the other studies where use of managerial processes and structures was the key. Several governors such as Babbitt of Arizona and Carlin of Kansas used variations on the "spokes of the wheel" approach, in which many were involved in the process with the governor at the hub of the wheel. In Maryland, Governor Hughes paid close attention to the budget process and used it as the major instrument in shaping policy, using detail to achieve goals. Reliance on a mini-cabinet approach inherited from the previous Governor David Boren, and consolidating it by creation of a Governor's Cabinet, allowed Governor Nigh to attempt to "tame the [bureaucratic] dragon rather than cutting off each of its heads" in Oklahoma. His goal was to avoid controversy. Both Governors Brennan of Maine and Janklow of South Dakota were perceived as being strong program managers which helped Brennan's credibility in Maine but may have left a deficit on the personnel management side for Janklow.

A wide variety of approaches to providing gubernatorial leadership was in evidence, much akin to the varieties we have charted in the American presidency over the years. Some are agressive leaders, others are not; some use the organizational vehicles at hand, others must create other ways to lead; some go too deeply into the details of running a government, others let it run itself; and, some seek to be the focal point of leadership, others diffuse such a focus.

With the previous term possibly viewed as a time of learning, did these governors change their styles and approaches, and if so how, or did they stay with what works for them? Many stayed with what they had, saying that "if it ain't broke, don't fix it" in Oklahoma, "to do as he had been doing" in Maryland, or to "fine tune" the existing operating systems in Maine.

The changed, or hoped for changed, gubernatorial leadership styles are most instructive in terms of measuring a governor's learning capacity from his first term. Some changes appeared to be minor but to the governor were significant. Governor Graham in Florida began to move away from his "detail man" approach by going "one-on-one" with agency heads, using performance objectives and goals as standards and the budget as a planning tool. Governor Janklow in South Dakota redressed a deficiency in his first administration by placing greater emphasis on personnel management over programs management, and Wyoming Governor Herschler, pushed by the fiscal situation in his state, moved away from his earlier focus upon public relations and intergovernmental affairs toward an emphasis on planning and priority setting.

The two governors who sought the greatest change in style, Carlin of Kansas and Alexander in Tennessee, both wished to shed their old "caretaker" images and become policy and program advocates. Reorganization was one step they took; for Carlin it was his own staff support system that moved from a "spokes of the wheel" to a central management structure and a desire to have his lieutenant governor to become an active participant in the administration, especially in the policy process; for Alexander it was not only a revamped policy support system, but also a reorganized state government. In both states the governors were moving to a bolder style of leadership and needed stronger policy and central management systems to undergird their new direction and goals.

Therefore, while there was something old and something new to the new administrations, the something old being attached to what already works, the something new in these states is clearly better central management capacity to buttress the governor's leadership. The re-election transition in these states is one of new style with better processes and organization.

The Inauguration as Politics and Symbol

Inaugurations--the pomp, the social, the political, the address--can often send messages across the state as to the direction in which a new administration will be heading. However, the inaugurations in these states where a governor was re-elected were noticeably quiet affairs, seemingly devoid of symbolism and excitement compared to those in which a new governor is inaugurated to lead a new administration.

In part this difference can be attributed to the fiscal problems facing the states where the message was the extent of the fiscal crisis and the "urgent agenda" rather than the re-inauguration of the governor, as in Illinois. Oregon's Governor Atiyeh deliberately chose to have a "non-event," low-key inaugural with no fanfare or pomp, to keep with the tenor of the economic situation. Governor O'Neill addressed the issues, restating his campaign pledges, and blamed the national economy for Connecticut's plight, but did not indicate where the needed money was to come from, a point not missed by the legislature. The symbolism of these inaugurals was to indicate just how distressing the economic situation was in the states.

Other governors such as Hughes of Maryland, gave little or no indication of the future or changes in direction, and, in general, seemed to indicate that it would be business as usual. Governor Babbitt gave only a brief, low-keyed but upbeat address that presented nothing new, but gave only confident optimism for Arizona's future, while Governor Lamm spoke to the challenges facing Colorado. Florida's Governor Graham deliberately sought to re-emphasize the priorities of the first administration, using a policy-oriented, less emotional approach.

Politics seemed to be the theme of two of the inaugurals. In Maine, Governor Brennan used his address to stress the dire implications of the retroactive provision of the successful state income tax indexing referendum, which could seriously affect the state's budget. He had won the election, the referendum had also passed, and by challenging it he was creating what was called "the governor's tax increase," a potential political issue for his future. In South Carolina, the future political ambitions of the newly-elected lieutenant governor and the attorney general for the 1986 gubernatorial race led to a series of controversial maneuvers which overshadowed the inaugural itself, and from which re-elected Governor Riley was able to remain aloof.

In sum, there was considerably less to these inaugurals than meets the eye, as they served the purpose of formally inducting the governor back into office but did little else for the state. There were some messages sent out, but the main signals were status-quo oriented. If there was to be change, the signals would come from elsewhere or they would come later.

The Re-elected Governors' Legislative Relations

Soon after the inauguration, or even before in some states, the governor must present both the state budget for the next fiscal year and his legislative programs. He must also adapt his style of relating to the legislature and its leadership, which can largely determine the success of the gubernatorial programs in running the legislative gauntlet.

First, there are some states in which the governor's legislative style and approach showed no signs of change. Governor Lamm has had a record of problems with the Colorado legislature. Some of these problems stem from the fact that the Colorado governorship is structurally weak and faces a strong legislature, but some are tied to Lamm's occassional lack of diplomacy. Therefore, he has used his own visibility and popularity in addition to task forces and blue ribbon commissions to help achieve his goals.

In Oklahoma, Governor Nigh's style has been to avoid conflict and let the legislature "take the heat" on issues. He works on consensus building, defers to the legislative leadership, and then acts, or reacts. "Sometimes it is popular to be an anti-legislature governor, but Nigh won't be among those. He likes working with the legislature. When he vetoes a measure, it is his vote on the measure just as a legislator has an opportunity to vote."

These two governors' styles of legislative relations worked within their own context, and since they were just re-elected, why change?

In two other states, Arizona and South Carolina, circumstances just didn't allow the governor much leeway to seek new ways. Babbitt of Arizona, who beat the President of the Senate in the governor's race, still faced the nine-term House majority leader, Burton Barr. Barr is perceived as the single most powerful political force in the state and exercised that power in the House, which was dubbed "89 people surrounded by Burton Barr." Thus it is a question as to who really holds the veto power in Arizona. For South Carolina's Riley, the newspaper headline captured the sense of the situation: "No second honeymoon for Riley." He suffered several major defeats in the legislature, and only a few successes. The mandate he received in the 1982 election provided little political capital and few resources.

In three states, there were clear attempts to change the style and approach of legislative relations in order to better these relations and thereby to be able to achieve greater accomplishments. Carlin of Kansas became his own legislative leader and liaison when he met with his party caucus and the legislative leaders, all part of his new "statesman"-like approach to the office.

Governor Graham of Florida, especially concerned with his legislative relations during his first term, moved to a new softer approach, reducing the stridency which characterized much of his first term relations with the legislature. Further, he learned from his first term not to present an elaborate agenda for action, which in his case served to confuse rather than direct. His 1983 legislative agenda contained only six or so proposals for consideration.

Governor Alexander in Tennessee, like Carlin, became his own legislative leader, evidencing his shift in leadership style from "caretaker" to "program promoter." However, even after his landslide win, he still was unable to create the coalition necessary to match his new program-promoting style with legislative success during the first legislative session.

The message from these studies seems to be that a governor can use his win as a mandate for change and be able to carry out some change within his own office and in the executive branch, but that he has trouble in carrying this mandate and desire over into another working political and governmental system, the legislature.

In sum, though, the general theme is that there is not much change from one term of an incumbent governor to another. While there are some re-elected governors who do undertake to bring about change in their style and administration, the main finding from these studies is that these governors go with what has worked for them previously. The re-election is seen as a referendum on them and their administration, not as a mandate or an opening for change.

CONCLUSION

The 1982 gubernatorial re-elections seem to be part of a pattern that has developed over the course of this century. More governors who are able to seek re-election do so, and most are successful. The campaigns are fought over their records, conditions in the state, and to a certain extent, the persons who are challenging them.

Those who win are more likely to be of the opposite party to that of the president, and their road to re-election is eased by not facing major challenges to renomination by their party. They must and do spend considerable amounts of money to ensure continued control of the governor's chair, but a more important weapon is the fact that they are incumbents. Major challenges to them are mounted by those who have sought and won statewide offices in the past, such as former governors and attorneys general.

These incumbent governors most often are able to post rather easy victories in the general election, often of landslide proportions. This occurence can be read both as a referendum on how well the governor has performed in the past and therefore should continue in the same manner as before, or as an opportunity to rethink styles, processes, and policies for a revitalized, new administration.

Despite the opportunity afforded the re-elected governors, most stayed on the same course, viewing the re-election as a referendum. Several governors did use the opportunity to review the earlier administration and to make changes as appropriate to their goals. Few undertook major changes, but rather looked to fine-tuning what was already in place.

The message to those legislators, administrators, media, and citizens with an interest in who is in the governor's chair is that the way to predict the second term of an incumbent governor is to analyze the first.

NOTES

*Portions of this chapter appeared in *Publius*, and in *State Government* 57:3 (1984).

[1] For a sample of what these governors said, see Thad L. Beyle and Robert Huefner, "Quips and Quotes from Old Governors to New," *Public Administration Review* 43:3 (1983): 268-70.

[2] National Governors' Association (NGA), *The Critical Hundred Days: A Handbook for New Governors* (Washington, D.C.: NGA, 1975); *The Governor's Office* (Washington, D.C.: NGA, 1976); *Governing the American States: A Handbook for New Governors* (Washington, D.C.: NGA, 1978); *Transition and the New Governors: A Critical Overview* (Washington, D.C.: NGA, 1982).

[3] NGA, *Transition and the New Governors*, p. v.

[4] NGA, *Transition and the New Governors*, p. 5.

[5] Clark D. Ahlberg and Daniel P. Moynihan, "Changing Governors--and Policies," *Public Administration Review* 20 (1960): 195-205 (New York); Norton B. Long, "After the Voting Is Over," *Midwest Journal of Politics* 6 (1962): 183-200 (Illinois); David J. Allen, *New Governor in Indiana: the Challenge of Executive Power* (Bloomington, Ind.: Institute of Public Administration, Indiana University, 1965); Dale E. Carter, "When Governors Change: Symbolic Output and Political Support," Research Report No. 5 (Institute of Governmental Affairs, University of California, Davis, 1968)(California); Thad L. Beyle and John Wickman, "Gubernatorial Transition in a One-Party Setting," *Public Administration Review* 30 (1970): 10-17 (Kansas and North Carolina); Peter N. Kidman, "Gubernatorial Transition in West Virginia" (Ph.D. diss., University of West Virginia, 1972); Leonard K. Bradley, Jr., "Gubernatorial Transition in Tennessee: The 1970-71 Experience" (Master's thesis, University of Tennessee, Knoxville, 1973); Bernard Caton, "Gubernatorial Transitions in Virginia," *Newsletter*, Institute of Government, University of Virginia, 4 (1978): 9540-72; Diane Blair and Robert Savage, "The Rhetorical Challenge of a Gubernatorial Transition: Constructing the Image of Statecraft," (Paper delivered at the 1980 Conference of the International Communications Association, 1980) (Arkansas).

[6] Stuart R. Ringham, "The Governor-elect to Governor: Transition in the American States," (Ph.D. diss., University of Iowa, Iowa City, 1972).

[7] Kenneth Warner, "Planning for Transition," State Government 34 (1961): 102-103.

[8] Charles Gibbons, "Transitions of Government in Massachusetts," State Government 34 (1961): 100-101; Wayne F. McGown, "Gubernatorial Transition in Wisconsin," State Government 44 (1971): 103-106.

[9] Ohio Legislative Service Commission, (OLSC) "Problems in the Transition of Government," Staff Research Report No. 57 (Columbus, Ohio: OLSC, 1963); Wisconsin, Department of Administration, The Executive Office Transition (Madison, Wisc.: Department of Administration, 1970); Arkansas Legislative Council, Pre-Inaugural Staff, Office and Other Allowances for Governors in Arkansas and Various States (Little Rock, Ark.: The Council, 1971).

[10] Gibbons, "Transition of Government in Massachusetts," p. 100.

[11] McGown, "Gubernatorial Transition in Wisconsin," p. 106.

[12] NGA, Transition and the New Governor, p. 1.

[13] Ahlberg and Moynihan, "Changing Governors," p. 197.

[14] Beyle and Wickman, "Gubernatorial Transition in a One-Party Setting," pp. 15, 11.

[15] Long, "After the Voting is Over," p. 190.

[16] Beyle and Wickman, "Gubernatorial Transition in a One-party Setting," pp. 14-15.

[17] Blair and Savage, "The Rhetorical Challenge of A Gubernatorial Transition."

[18] Ahlberg and Moynihan, "Changing Governors," p. 195.

[19] Long, "After the Voting is Over," p. 196.

[20] Beyle and Wickman, "Gubernatorial Transition in a One-Party Setting," p. 14.

[21] Long, "After the Voting is Over," p. 188.

[22] Quoted in Beyle and Huefner, "Quips and Quotes from Old Governors to New," p. 268.

[23] ABC News, The 1982 Vote: What Happened (ABC News 1983), pp. 177-179.

[24] John F. Bibby, "State House Elections at Midterm", in Thomas E. Mann and Norman J. Ornstein, The American Elections of 1982 (Washington, DC: American Enterprise Institute, 1983) pp. 114-115.

[25] Quoted in Beyle and Wickman, "Quips and Quotes from Old Governors to New", p. 268.

[26] Long, "After the Voting is Over," pp. 192-94

[27] NGA, Transition and the New Governor, p. 76.

[28] Quoted in Beyle and Huefner, "Quips and Quotes from Old Governor to New," p. 268.

[29] NGA, Transition and the New Governor, p. 89.

[30] Beyle and Huefner, "Quips and Quotes from Old Governor's to New," p. 269.

[31] Ibid.

[32] Jack W. Germond and Jules Witcover, "Blanchard faced the music early," The Columbia Record (S.C.), 16 June 1983.

[33] Richard Neustadt, Presidential Power , (New York: Wiley and Sons, 1960).

[34] NGA, Governing the American States, p. 193.

[35] NGA, Transition and the New Governor, pp. 29-30.

1. POLITICAL MONEY AND GUBERNATORIAL PRIMARIES*

MALCOLM E. JEWELL

The study of money and politics begins with a simple question: Does the candidate who spends the most in campaigns usually win the election? There is reason to think that campaign spending should be more closely related to votes won in primaries than in general elections. In many general elections one candidate starts with an advantage because of the strength of one party in the state or district, and this advantage may be too large to be overcome by the minority party, even if it spends more money in the race. In primary elections, however, no candidate has a partisan advantage.

The effect of campaign spending on state gubernatorial primaries is an important topic that has been almost completely ignored by political scientists, perhaps because of the difficulty of collecting accurate data on such spending. This is a study of the impact of campaign spending in those gubernatorial primaries that were contested in 1982.[1] In the 36 states holding gubernatorial elections, there were 16 primaries that were uncontested and 3 others that were virtually uncontested. Data have been collected on campaign spending in 48 of the remaining 53 primary races. (Data are missing for both party primaries in Oklahoma, the Democratic primary in Alabama, and the Republican ones in Illinois and South Carolina.)[2]

Most states require primary candidates to file a financial statement just before the primary and again shortly after the primary. In most cases the latter statement is used in this report, except where the post-primary report came so late that it appeared to include significant amounts of spending by the winners for the general election. Since there are variations among states in legal requirements (such as requiring or not requiring that the previous year's spending be included), the total reported in one state may not be comparable to that reported in another. Because the reporting requirements are the same for each candidate within a state, however, the impact of spending on each candidate's share of the primary vote should not be distorted.

THEORIES OF MONEY AND POLITICS

Before examining the relationship of campaign spending to election results, we should consider what that relationship may mean. In order to win an election, candidates must develop name recognition and make a favorable impression on the voters. The less well-known they are, the more they must campaign and spend. The incumbent governor has name recognition and may have a favorable image, but governors believe that they must campaign extensively if they are seriously challenged. Although non-incumbents may have some recognition through holding other public office, they must rely primarily on media advertising and personal campaigning to make an impact on the voters. A statewide campaign, especially one that relies heavily on the media, is expensive--much more so, of course, in some states than in others.

The amount of money spent in a campaign is a good measure of the amount of campaigning that is done, although of course it does not measure the skill of campaign tactics or the effectiveness of television advertising. The amount spent on a campaign depends generally on two things: how much the candidate needs to spend, and how much can be raised. It is also true that the more a candidate needs to spend, the less he or she is likely to be able to raise. The incumbent, or any major candidate who is believed likely to win, finds it easier to raise money, partly because contributors like to donate to probable winners. The candidate who is virtually unknown, and needs the most expensive campaign, finds money raising very difficult.

If the candidates with the largest financing, and thus the most extensive campaigning, win the most votes, this does not mean simply that elections can be "bought." Candidates who are well-known, who have proven records in office, and who are skillful campaigners might win with limited campaign efforts, but these qualifications help them to attract enough money for large-scale campaigns.

The amount an incumbent spends on a campaign depends to some degree on how seriously the incumbent is challenged. For that reason the amount spent by non-incumbents might be a better predictor of election results in a race with an incumbent. This has been the finding of research on congressional general elections.[3] Research on gubernatorial general elections, however, suggests that spending by both candidates affects outcomes although the impact declines at the upper limits of spending.[4]

RELATIONSHIPS BETWEEN SPENDING AND VOTES

In most gubernatorial primary elections in 1982, the candidate who spent the most money won, but there were some exceptions. Table 1 summarizes the spending record of the winning candidates in the primaries. It shows the percentage of the vote and the percentage of total spending by the winner; it also shows how much the winning candidate spent for each vote he received. It identifies those winners who were incumbents, and it indicates whether the winner spent more campaign funds than any of the losers.

In 36 of the 48 contested races for which data are available, the winning candidate was the one who spent the most money. In 29 of these 36 cases, the winner's proportion of total spending was greater than his proportion of the vote. The most direct relationship between campaign spending and winning was in the South, where the winner spent the most in all six races. In the two states with runoff elections, the voting percentage is for the first race, not the runoff. In Georgia, however, Joe Frank Harris, who spent most and won the runoff, placed second in the first primary.

All of the 11 incumbents who won in the primary also were the top spenders in their races. One incumbent who was defeated in a primary, Democrat Edward King of Massachusetts, was the leading spender in that race. (Several incumbents were unopposed, and incumbents were renominated in two states, Illinois and Oklahoma, where spending data are unavailable.)

Another way of comparing campaign spending and electoral outcomes is to measure the statistical relationship between the percentage of votes won and the percentage of campaign funds spent by each candidate. The simple correlation between these two variables is .91, but the use of percentages may exaggerate this relationship.

A more precise way of relating spending to voting is to measure the magnitude of spending by each candidate, and by all other candidates. In

Table 1

Electoral and Spending Record of Winners in 1982 Gubernatorial Primaries

State	Party	Name	Incum-bent	Percent of Total Vote	Percent of Total Spending	Dollars Spent Per Vote	Spent Most Money
Alaska	D	Sheffield		39.7	62.5	52.17	X
Alaska	R	Fink		51.3	42.5	13.64	
Arizona	R	Corbett		61.7	66.8	3.04	X
Arkansas	D	Clinton		41.9	54.5	3.43	X
Arkansas	R	White	X	82.8	95.6	30.67	X
California	D	Bradley		60.8	64.8	1.58	X
California	R	Deukmejian		52.3	42.8	3.63	
Florida	D	Bafalis		86.4	96.6	4.26	X
Florida	R	Graham	X	84.4	99.5	2.65	X
Georgia	D	Bell		60.2	86.8	32.74	X
Georgia	R	Harris		24.2	32.6	13.94	X
Hawaii	D	Ariyoshi	X	53.6	85.8	11.59	X
Idaho	R	Batt		63.8	55.8	3.13	X
Iowa	D	Conlin		48.0	37.2	2.49	
Kansas	D	Carlin	X	78.8	99.7	4.12	X
Kansas	R	Hardage		36.8	47.4	8.12	X
Maine	R	Brennan	X	76.8	94.5	3.77	X
Maine	R	Cagin		38.1	20.6	5.77	
Maryland	D	Hughes	X	65.3	68.5	1.87	X
Maryland	R	Pascal		84.1	100.0	4.66	X
Massachusetts	D	Dukakis		53.5	43.1	3.82	
Massachusetts	R	Sears		49.7	21.7	3.69	
Michigan	D	Blanchard		50.1	31.4	2.92	X
Michigan	R	Headley		34.1	33.8	5.21	
Minnesota	D	Perpich		50.4	18.1	.48	
Minnesota	R	Whitney		59.9	81.0	4.95	X
Nebraska	D	Kerrey		71.2	83.9	2.05	X
Nebraska	R	Thone	X	62.6	77.3	2.80	X

State	Party	Name	Incumbent	Percent of Total Vote	Percent of Total Spending	Dollars Spent Per Vote	Spent Most Money
Nevada	D	Bryan		53.2	72.1	12.51	X
Nevada	R	List	X	70.6	96.0	16.05	X
New Hampshire	R	Sununu		31.9	27.7	5.73	
New Mexico	D	Anaya		56.9	46.2	5.12	X
New Mexico	R	Irick		54.6	42.6	6.17	
New York	D	Cuomo		52.9	31.0	2.42	
New York	R	Lehrman		80.0	95.0	15.55	X
Ohio	D	Celeste		42.3	32.4	3.65	
Ohio	R	Brown		53.6	43.9	3.12	
Oregon	D	Atiyeh	X	81.9	99.7	1.60	X
Oregon	R	Kulongoski		60.2	44.6	.67	X
Pennsylvania	R	Ertel		57.6	96.8	.26	X
South Dakota	D	O'Connor		58.8	67.8	.90	X
Tennessee	D	Tyree		50.0	74.0	34.60	X
Texas	R	Clements	X	91.9	100.0	16.33	X
Texas	D	White		45.3	41.7	3.07	X
Wisconsin	D	Earl		45.1	44.3	.88	X
Wisconsin	R	Kohler		67.3	79.4	1.13	X
Wyoming	D	Herschler	X	85.0	98.9	1.22	X
Wyoming	R	Morton		74.3	99.8	4.82	X

order to give some weight to the variation in the size of the electorate by state, each of these totals was divided by the square root of the total primary vote. (This is done because it costs more to campaign in large states but there are also some economies of scale: Per-vote costs are usually larger in smaller states.) The more each candidate spends, and the less spent by opponents, the higher the candidate's vote should be. In a multiple regression equation these two spending totals explain 46 percent of each candidate's percentage of the vote.

What is the relative importance of incumbency and spending in explaining voting outcomes? Do incumbents usually win only because they can raise more money? Adding incumbency to the regression equation improves our ability to explain elections, and measuring other major office-holding improves it even more. If a variable measuring different levels of candidates' political experience is added to the spending variables, the regression equation explains 61 percent of the vote. In other words, incumbency and other forms of political experience and spending by the candidate and by the opponents all have independent effects on the outcome of gubernatorial primary elections.

VARIATIONS BY STATE

While correlation and regression analysis can show the general impact of campaign spending, we must look at individual states in order to understand variations in the effects of spending on election results. There were 13 gubernatorial races in which the leading candidate (the incumbent in eight cases) spent over 90 percent of the campaign funds. Generally, that candidate won between 70 and 85 percent of the vote. The opposition was weak and poorly financed, but it seems likely that the winners spent more than was necessary to assure election. In Kansas, for example, Governor John Carlin spent $426,000 to defeat his only opponent who spent less than $1,500. Maine Governor Joseph Brennan outspent his opponent $213,000 to $12,000.

In three Republican gubernatorial primaries in southern states, the leading candidates outspent their opponents by huge margins. Arkansas Governor Frank White spent $320,000 compared to $15,000 for his opponents; Florida Congressman L. A. Bafalis outspent his opponent $1.3 million to $47,000; and

Texas Governor William Clements spent about $3 million in his race. It seems obvious that these southern Republican candidates spent such large amounts not so much to win landslides in the primary but to lay the groundwork for their fall campaigns. Because turnout in southern Republican primaries is usually so low, the cost per vote of the leaders is very high. In Arkansas, for example, Governor White spent $30.67 for each vote that he got in the primary.

The New York Republican primary is one example of a race in which spending had a major impact on the outcome. Lew Lehrman spent about $7 million in his campaign, roughly 20 times as much as Paul Curran, his only opponent. Before the state party endorsing convention, Lehrman had already spent almost $3 million, most of it on a media blitz, and it was obvious that he was willing and able to outspend any opponent. This was apparently a major reason why the Republican party endorsed Lehrman, and why Curran had great difficulty in raising enough money to make an effective challenge in the primary.

There are several examples of closer primary races in which the winner was also the top spender. Michigan Democrat James Blanchard won with half of the vote in a large field where his closest competitor only gained 17 percent. Blanchard's 31-percent share of spending was almost as much as was spent by the next two candidates combined. One other candidate in that race spent over $550,000 (15 percent), however, to win only 4 percent of the vote. In the Michigan Republican primary the two top candidates spent two-thirds of the funds and got almost two-thirds of the vote, though the winner spent a few thousand less than the second-place finisher. In the New Mexico Democratic primary the winner, Toney Anaya, outspent his closest opponent 46 to 35 percent, but outpolled him 57 to 34 percent. Another candidate in that race spent 15 percent only to drop out of the race in the closing weeks.

There are some interesting examples of 1982 races in which the top spender did not win. Democratic Governor Edward King of Massachusetts outspent Michael Dukakis by about $3.2 to $2.4 million, but lost the primary by about 83,000 votes. King was damaged by scandals in his administration and the opposition of liberal interests, and former governor Dukakis had an unusually strong grassroots organization and of course strong name recognition. In the Republican primary a political newcomer, John Lakian, spent almost $1 million, twice as much as was spent by his two opponents combined. Lakian had won party endorsement in part because he was able to finance most of his campaign. But newspaper stories that questioned the accuracy of Lakian's campaign literature about his background and record undermined his efforts and he polled only 27 percent in losing to John Sears, a well-known, veteran politician.

In California, Republican Lieutenant Governor Mike Curb outspent Attorney General George Deukmejian $5.5 million to $4 million, but lost the primary by 146,000 votes. Both candidates were well-known and had adequate funds to spend. One of the major primary upsets of the year occurred in New York, where Democratic Mayor Edward Koch had the advantage of name recognition, a colorful personality, party endorsement, and a campaign fund of some $3.6 million. Lieutenant Governor Mario Cuomo spent about $1.6 million, but had a strong grassroots organization and powerful support from labor, ethnic, and liberal groups in beating Koch by over 70,000 votes.

The contrasting patterns in the Republican and Democratic primaries in Minnesota illustrate dramatically the difficulty of generalizing about the impact of money on politics. In each primary one candidate outspent the other major candidate by a margin of 4 to 1, but only in the Republican primary did the high spender win. Lou Wangberg narrowly won the endorsement of the Republican Independent Party, but he proved to be ineffective in organizing his campaign and raising funds (only $213,000). His opponent, Wheelock Whitney, was a maverick with little name recognition or electoral record, but he spent $917,000, mostly on a media campaign, and beat Wangberg 60 to 34 percent. (Harold Stassen spent $2,400 and finished third.)

In the Democratic-Farmer-Labor (DFL) primary, Attorney General Warren Spannaus had the advantage of party endorsement and a campaign fund that enabled him to spend $577,820. His opponent, Rudy Perpich, spent only $128,000, but he was a former governor who was well-known for his colorful style and who was able to utilize a number of economic and social issues in the campaign. Incidentally, Perpich spent only 48 cents per vote, significantly less than any other winning candidate in the country who had substantial opposition.

Differences in reporting requirements among the states make any interstate comparison of spending imprecise; nevertheless, it is interesting to see how large the variations are in the amount each winning candidate spent per vote received:

* The median in 48 primaries was $3.67.

* In five states the figure was less than $1.

* In 31 states it was between $1 and $6.

* In nine states it ranged from $6.17 to $16.33.

* In three states more than $30 was spent.

The highest figure ($52.17), was spent by the winner of the Democratic party in Alaska. The high spenders were mostly in states where the per-vote costs are high because of low populations (Alaska, Hawaii, and Nevada) and in southern Republican primaries where candidates were starting early on the November election. Two other examples were the closely contested Georgia Democratic primary ($13.94) and the New York Republican race where Lehrman spent $15.55 per vote.

CONCLUSIONS

The following conclusions can be drawn about money and politics in 1982 primaries:

1) In races that are won in a landslide, the winner usually spends a very high proportion of the total, much more than is necessary to win. In some cases, particularly southern Republican races, much of this spending appears aimed at the general election.

2) Money is particularly important for candidates who lack a record in politics and are not well-known but are able to finance very expensive campaigns.

3) In races among well-known, strong candidates, money is seldom decisive. Both candidates usually have substantial funds, and where there is a significant imbalance in funding the underdog sometimes wins.

NOTES

*This chapter is reprinted from State Government 56,2 (1983), pp. 69-73.

[1] This analysis of campaign spending is part of a larger study of gubernatorial primaries supported by the National Science Foundation under Grant No. SES-8105701. The findings and conclusions are those of the author and do not necessarily reflect the views of the NSF.

[2] The data on campaign spending were gathered from state agencies where available. In a number of states I am indebted to political scientists who tracked down the information for me, and particularly to Thad Beyle, who coordinated some of the tracking efforts.

[3] Gary C. Jacobson, Money in Congressional Politics (New Haven: Yale University Press, 1980).

[4] Samuel C. Patterson, "Campaign Spending in Contests for Governor," Western Political Quarterly 35,4 (1982): 457-77.

2. THE COSTS OF BECOMING GOVERNOR*

THAD L. BEYLE[1]

Over the past decade there have been significant changes in the costs of running a gubernatorial campaign--for both successful and unsuccessful efforts. The reasons are many, including the decline in effectiveness of the political party structure in the states, the rise in use of the mass media in campaigns, and the increasing importance of the governorship as a position in itself and as a stepping stone to other offices and careers. Candidates are willing to spend more for winning the office, and they do.

No longer can a candidate sit back and work with the party organization and the party regulars to deliver the votes needed for winning. Going from county to county to meet with the local politicos may solidify some votes and bring together part of the winning coalition. But this effort takes time, hits too few people, and does not deliver enough votes.

The new campaign technology with opinion polls, political consultants, media advertising through major media markets, direct mail persuasion and fund raising, telephone banks, and rapid air travel throughout the state all come with high price tags. For example, out of the $20.7 million spent on the 1979 Louisiana gubernatorial campaign, $9.8 million (47 percent) was spent for producing and placing mass media advertising and $2.5 million (12 percent) for consultants and other professionals. Pollsters alone cost $690,000 (3 percent).[2]

This chapter will examine the costs of becoming governor in recent years and will focus particularly on the 1982 gubernatorial races. While Malcolm Jewell looked at the effect of campaign spending on state gubernatorial primaries, we will look at the total campaign costs involved, both primary and general elections. Finally, we will compare the results of the primary election analysis with those of the general election analysis.

TRENDS IN SPENDING FOR GUBERNATORIAL ELECTIONS

Comparative costs of gubernatorial campaigns over time are very difficult to obtain. Campaign reporting requirements at the state level are of relatively recent vintage so comparisons over time are scant and difficult. Figure 1, "Trends in Gubernatorial Campaign Expenditures: Selected States, Actual Dollars," presents what data have been found. There are problems of considerable magnitude in these data: They vary by the campaigns covered (primary and/or general), the candidates included (all candidates, the two major party candidates, or just the winner), and the years covered. With these caveats in mind we can see the general trend is for increasing actual dollar campaign expenditures for winning the governor's chair. For the two states, California and New York, where trend data is more available than for other states, we see the trend has been relatively consistent since the 1960s, with a rather stark jump in the 1982 figures. Ohio and Massachusetts also show a sharp rise in 1982.

However, to be accurate in such a comparison, we must take into account the changing value of the dollar over this time period. In effect, we must control for inflation in the dollar's value. To do so each of the state's reported gubernatorial campaign expenditures figures was normalized to the equivalent of the 1967 dollar.[3] The results are presented in Figure 2, "Trends in Gubernatorial Expenditures: Selected States, Adjusted to 1967 Dollars." Clearly the slopes of the individual state trend lines are reduced, except in the case of Virginia in 1981, where there was no Democratic primary to increase the cost of the race, as was true also for 1973. The trend is approximately the same, a general upward spiral in the cost of gubernatorial elections in these states. While the earlier-noted sharp rise in the early 1980s elections is not as pronounced using 1967 dollars, it is still apparent and significant for several of the states.

While the data are skimpy, there are some suggested patterns where a trend line over several elections is involved.

<u>Incumbency</u>. Seeking to retain the governor's chair in a state is associated with escalated expenditures in several cases: California (1966 and 1978); New York (1978); and Ohio (1978). Of

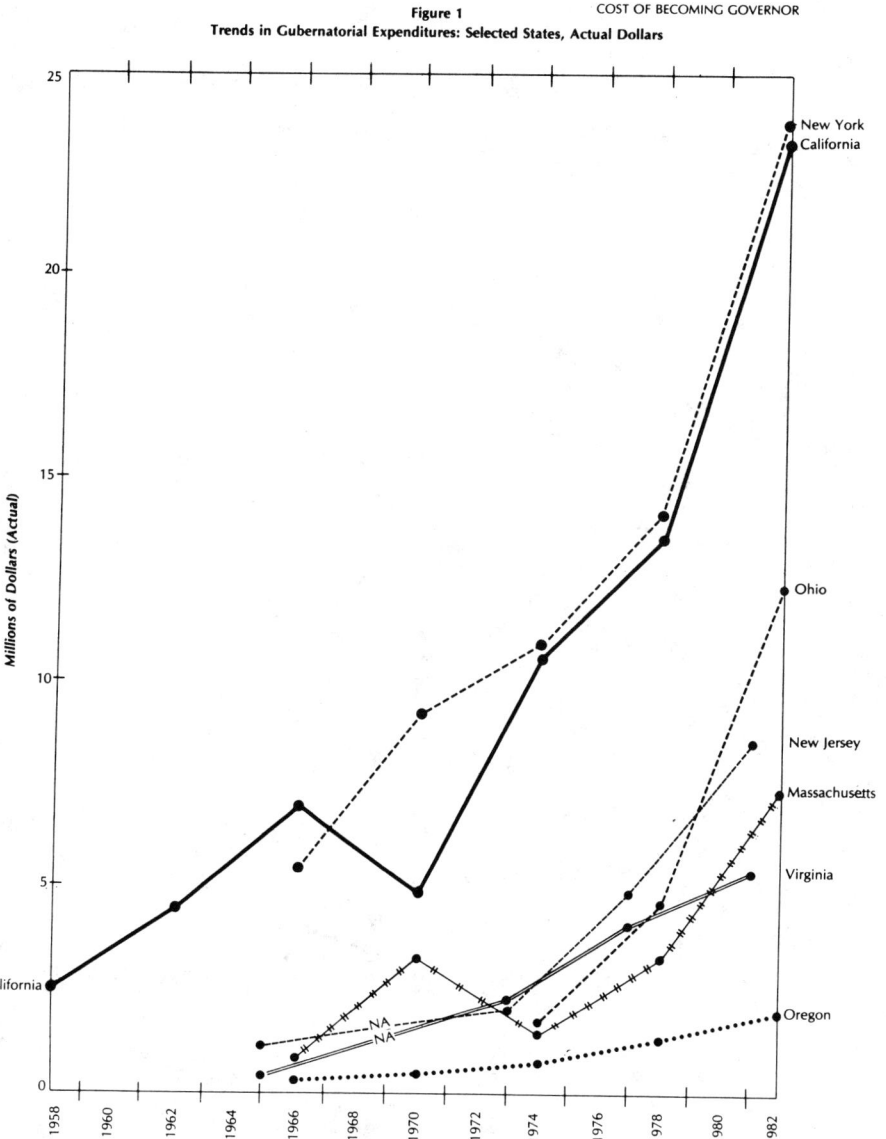
Figure 1
Trends in Gubernatorial Expenditures: Selected States, Actual Dollars
COST OF BECOMING GOVERNOR

Figure 2
Trends in Gubernatorial Expenditures: Selected States, Adjusted to 1967 Dollars

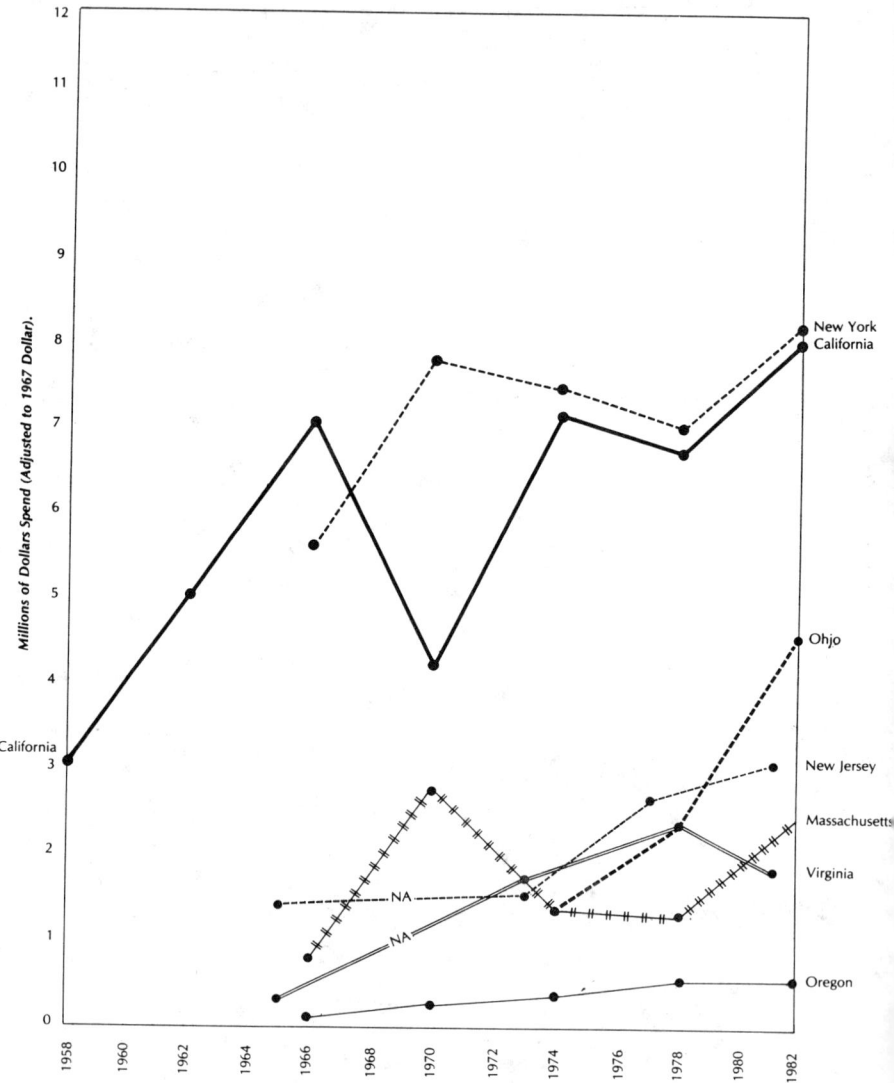

COST OF BECOMING GOVERNOR

Notes for Figures 1 and 2

Sources:

California:
- 1958-1978: The California Fair Practices Commission, *Campaign Costs: How Have They Increased and Why?* (Sacramento: 1980), p. 2.
- 1982: Elections Division, State of California.

Massachusetts:
- 1966: David W. Adamany, *Campaign Finance in America* (No. Scituate, MA: Duxburg Press, 1972), pp. 36-37. Major party candidates only.
- 1970: Office of Campaign and Political Finance, Commonwealth of Massachusetts.
- 1974: Herbert E. Alexander, *Financing Politics* (Washington, D.C.: C.Q. Press, 1976), p. 233.
- 1978: Rhodes Cook and Stacy West, "1978 Gubernatorial Contests: Incumbents, Winners Hold Money Advantage," *Congressional Quarterly*, 37:34 August 25, 1979, pp. 1756-57.
- 1982: Office of Campaign and Political Finance, Commonwealth of Massachusetts, Letter, February 18, 1983. (Unaudited Figures).

New Jersey:
- 1965: Adamany, pp. 36-37. Major party candidates only.
- 1969: Not available per letter, Election Law Enforcement Commission, State of New Jersey, January 26, 1983.
- 1973: New Jersey Election Law Enforcement Commission, *Public Financing in New Jersey: The 1977 General Election for Governor* (Trenton: 1978), p. 44. General election expenditures only.
- 1977: Ibid. p. 43, all general election expenditures and primary election expenditures by the two major party winning candidates.
- 1981: Letter from Scott A. Weiner, Executive Director for the Commission, March 15, 1982.

New York:
- 1962: Robert Marcus, "Campaign Spending: Is Up the Only Direction?," *Empire State Report* (November 1982), p. 20. Major party candidates only.
- 1966: Adamany, pp. 36-37. Major party candidates only.
- 1970: Herbert E. Alexander, *Money in Politics* (Washington, D.C.: Public Affairs Press, 1972), p. 27.
- 1974: Alexander, *Financing Politics*, p. 235. Figures is an estimation which represents only the expenditures of the two major Democratic primary contenders (Carey and Samuels) and the major party candidates in the general election.
- 1978: Marcus, p. 20. Major party candidates only.
- 1982: State Board of Elections, State of New York, Albany.

Ohio:
- 1974: Herbert Alexander, *Campaign Money* (New York: The Free Press, 1976), p. 267.
- 1978: Rhodes and Cook.
- 1982: Secretary of State, Ohio.

Oregon:
- 1966: Alexander, *Money in Politics*, p. 29.
- 1970: Ibid.
- 1974: Elections and Public Records Division, Office of the Secretary of State, Oregon.
- 1978: Rhodes and Cook.
- 1982: Elections and Public Records Division, Office of the Secretary of State, Oregon.

Virginia:
- 1965: Adamany. Major party candidates only.
- 1969: Not available.
- 1973: Richard W. Hall-Sizemore, "Money in Politics: Financing the 1977 Statewide Elections in Virginia," *University of Virginia Newsletter* 56:12 (Charlottesville: Institute of Government, 1980), p. 46.
- 1977: Ibid.
- 1981: Letter from Larry Sabato, University of Virginia, August 3, 1982.

Dollar Amounts:		Actual	Adjusted (1967 dollars)
California:	1958	2,655,292	3,066,862
	1962	4,542,195	5,014,583
	1966	6,940,654	7,141,933
	1970	4,882,356	4,198,826
	1974	10,563,509	7,162,059
	1978	13,481,678	6,902,619
	1982	23,397,385	8,235,880
Massachusetts:	1966	849,900	874,547
	1970	3,415,018	2,936,915
	1974	1,917,497	1,300,063
	1978	2,794,366	1,430,715
	1982	7,718,602	2,716,948
New Jersey:	1965	1,405,600	1,487,125
	1969	NA	NA
	1973	2,150,767	1,617,377
	1977	4,867,455	2,681,968
	1981	8,320,457	3,095,210
New York:	1966	5,476,000	5,634,804
	1970	9,200,000	7,912,000
	1974	10,756,663	7,293,018
	1978	13,793,829	7,062,440
	1982	23,558,518	8,292,598
Ohio:	1974	1,889,471	1,281,061
	1978	4,637,235	2,374,264
	1982	12,968,577	4,564,939
Oregon:	1966	215,000	221,235
	1970	415,518	357,345
	1974	799,667	542,174
	1978	1,172,202	600,167
	1982	1,933,574	680,618
Virginia:	1965	297,400	314,649
	1969	NA	NA
	1973	2,301,300	1,730,578
	1977	4,250,500	2,342,026
	1981	5,200,000	1,934,400

the states for which comparative data are available, only in the 1970 California contest, in which Ronald Reagan won re-election, did the incumbent seeking re-election participate in an election that was less expensive than his previous gubernatorial election effort. In Massachusetts the last two elections have seen an incumbent governor defeated in his own party's primary, with the same two actors involved each time: Michael Dukakis and Edward King. In 1978, King defeated then Governor Dukakis, and in 1982 Dukakis returned the favor. The 1978 race was slightly more expensive than the earlier 1974 race in which Dukakis was first elected, while the costs of the 1982 contest nearly doubled the 1978 race.

Long Tenure. The costs of a gubernatorial election tend to be greater when a long-sitting governor retires and the seat is essentially up for grabs. Such is the case in California where expenditures rose in 1966 when Ronald Reagan defeated two-term Governor "Pat" Brown; in 1974 when Jerry Brown followed two-term Governor Reagan; and in 1982 when George Deukmejian followed Jerry Brown's second term. New York (1982), when Mario Cuomo succeeded Governor Hugh Carey (1975-1983), and Ohio, when Richard Celeste followed Governor James Rhodes (1963-71, 1975-83), also follow this pattern of more expensive campaigns following the retirement of a long-term governor.

Party Shift. There is also a tendency for those elections in which partisan control of the governor's chair shifts from one party to another to cost more. This tendency was true in California (1966, 1974 and 1982), New Jersey (1981), Ohio (1982), and Oregon (1974 and 1978). However, it was not true in New York (1974) when Hugh Carey (D) beat Malcolm Wilson (R) who, as lieutenant governor, became governor when Nelson Rockefeller resigned in 1973; Massachusetts (1974) when Dukakis (D) followed Francis Sargent (R 1967-75); and Virginia (1981) when Charles Robb (D) followed John Dalton (R 1978-1982). On balance, based on this small sample, the generalization can be made that it is likely to be a more expensive contest when a party shift occurs.

These are not mutually exclusive patterns as there is overlap between them, especially when the contest follows a retiring governor's long tenure and is one in which a party shift occurs (California 1966, 1974 and 1982 and Ohio 1982).

TOTAL COSTS OF RECENT GUBERNATORIAL ELECTIONS

Fifty state comparative campaign expenditure data on gubernatorial elections have been available only since 1977. During this period there were 92 gubernatorial elections, 58 of which were won by Democrats and 34 by Republicans. Incumbents sought re-election in 60 of these contests, winning 43, losing in the general election in 13, and failing to obtain their own party's renomination in four others.[4] Table 1 presents the costs of these elections. The total amount spent by all candidates was more than $389 million actual dollars, and more than $160 million in 1967 dollars.

Comparing across these years we can again see how the costs are increasing. In both pairs of election years in which the same states held gubernatorial elections, 1977 and 1981; 1978 and 1982, the average election costs increased: between 1977 and 1981 from $2.5 million to $3.6 million or a 46-percent increase; and, between 1978 and 1982 from $1.4 million to $1.8 million or a 26.5-percent increase in average contest cost. The least expensive gubernatorial campaigns were in a presidential election year, 1980.

Interestingly, on an individual basis, spending the most money does not insure winning the governorship, although in two of every three elections (62-30), the winner was the one who did spend the most. Table 2, "Most Expensive Gubernatorial Campaigns: 1977-82, 1967 Dollars," indicates who the individual big spenders were, both winners and losers. Most all big spending campaigns were in the larger, more urban multi-media market states: California, New York, Texas, Illinois, Ohio, and New Jersey.

But other states have seen expensive gubernatorial elections. The so-called "Great Louisiana Campaign Spendathon of 1979 was one of the most expensive non-presidential elections ever held."[5] It still is. In a state where parties are weak, six major candidates tried to get into the second primary. A political consultant viewing the campaigns likened it to a nuclear arms race--"If one candidate had it, everyone else thought he had to have it too."[6]

Then there is the 1980 Rockefeller campaign in West Virginia, where incumbent Governor Jay

Table 1

Total Cost of Gubernatorial Elections: 1977-1982

	Number of Races	Total Campaign Costs, actual dollars	Total Campaign Costs, 1967 dollars	Average Cost per election, 1967 dollars
1977	2	$ 9.1 million	$ 5.0 million	$2.5 million
1978	36	99.7	51.1	1.4
1979	3	32.7	15.0	5.0
1980	13	35.6	14.4	1.1
1981	2	20.0	7.3	3.7
1982	36[a]	192.3	67.7	1.9
	92	389.2	160.5	

[a] Data for Illinois ('82) represents the estimate of expenditures from an AP wire story printed April 29, 1983 in The Champaign-Urbana News-Gazette. Final reports not filed until June 30, 1983.

Table 2

Most Expensive Gubernatorial Campaigns: 1977-1982, 1967 Dollars

	Party	State	Year	Amount Spent Actual Dollars	1967 Dollars
Winners:					
Rockefeller[a]	(D)	WV	'80	$11.6 million	$4.7 million
Clements	(R)	TX	'78	7.6	3.9
Carey[a]	(D)	NY	'78	6.9	3.5
White	(D)	TX	'82	8.9	3.1
Deukmejian	(R)	CA	'82	7.6	2.7
Treen	(R)	LA	'79	5.9	2.7
Brown[a]	(D)	CA	'78	4.8	2.5
Cuomo	(D)	NY	'82	5.3	1.9
Thompson[a]	(R)	IL	'82	5.0	1.8
Celeste	(D)	OH	'82	4.9	1.7
Losers:					
Lehman	(R)	NY	'82	$13.9 million	$4.9 million
Clements[a]	(R)	TX	'82	13.5	4.8
Bradley	(D)	CA	'82	7.0	3.1
Lambert	(D)	LA	'79	4.8	2.4
Butcher	(R)	TN	'78	4.7	2.4
Duryea	(R)	NY	'78	4.4	2.3
Coleman	(D)	VA	'81	4.3	2.2
Hill	(D)	TX	'78	3.6	1.8
Florio	(D)	NJ	'81	4.9	1.8
Younger	(R)	CA	'78	3.4	1.7
Eckerd	(R)	FL	'78	3.3	1.7

[a] Incumbent governor

Rockefeller spent $11.6 million--all but $250,000 from his own funds. The television campaign alone cost $4.5 million, $1.3 million of which was spent on Pittsburgh and Washington, D. C. channels received in West Virginia.[7] There were also extensive radio and billboard advertisements, and rallies and picnics in most of the 55 counties in West Virginia. The latter provided free food and entertainment--even country and western bands from Nashville--to thousands of voters.[8]

On the losing side of the ledger, the $13.9-million 1982 campaign by Republican Lewis Lehrman in New York was probably the most ever spent on a statewide office, and certainly the most spent by a candidate on a losing campaign. Much of the money went for paid media advertising with a heavy blitz toward the end of the campaign. Rather than create a voter backlash against so much being spent, the blitz was credited for his later but unsuccessful surge.[9]

Money isn't everything in gubernatorial politics, but it can buy most anything else that is. As the reports on the Louisiana, New York, and West Virginia campaigns suggest, the most important expenditures as measured by money spent are for media advertising, political consultants, and public opinion polling. These are the major building blocks of what Sabato calls "party substitutes," where the candidate constructs his own "instant organization."[10]

THE 1978 GUBERNATORIAL ELECTIONS

In the 1978 gubernatorial elections, 65 percent of the big spenders and sixteen of the incumbents running for re-election won. According to researchers Cook and West, these campaigns "generally demonstrate a correlation between spending, incumbency, and winning."[11] They also warned about the lack of uniformity across the states: "Because each state has its own (financial reporting) system, the only accurate comparisons can be made between candidates in a single state."[11]

Another analysis of the 1978 election expenditures suggested "that other things being equal, a 10-percent increase in the proportion of campaign spending by a candidate yields a 5-percent increase in the percentage of the general election vote for governor."[12] However, all things were not equal and Patterson found that there was a difference by the party of the candidates involved. Democrats, numerically dominant as governors that year, were able to use this incumbency factor in lieu of spending as much money as the Republicans. However, there was a point where spending by Democratic candidates had diminishing returns, that is, additional spending did them little good in terms of gaining additional votes. On the other side, Republicans, many fighting against incumbents and stronger Democratic strength, "benefit from increased spending whatever the level of expenditure."[13] Interestingly, he found no support for the hypotheses that it costs more for candidates to reach voters with their appeal in sparsely populated states or that competitive races are more expensive independent of the effects of partisan strength and incumbency on these elections.

THE 1982 GUBERNATORIAL ELECTIONS

More than 200 candidates vied for the 36 governorships open in 1982. Democrats won three out of every four seats (27-9), and there were 11 states in which a party switch occurred: Nine went from Republican to Democratic and two from Democratic to Republican.[14]

Twenty-five incumbent governors sought re-election; 19 were successful. Governor King (Massachusetts) lost his bid in the Democratic Party primary after having won the pre-primary convention; Governors White (Arkansas), Thone (Nebraska), List (Nevada), Gallen (New Hampshire), and Clements (Texas) lost in the general election. Of the 19 successful incumbents, 14 won by a landslide (more than 10 percent ahead of nearest opponent),[15] two others won by a somewhat comfortable margin (between 6 and 9 percent),[16] while the other three were victors in very competitive races (less than 5 percent between two top candidates.)[17]

Out of five former governors who sought to reclaim their chairs, four were successful.[18] Only former Governor Martin Schreiber in Wisconsin (1977-79) failed in his quest, losing to eventual winner Tony Earl in the Democratic primary.

In sum, there were incumbent or former governors running in 28 of the 36 gubernatorial campaigns. Each obviously had either positional and/or name recognition advantage to take into the campaign, and a public record, both good and bad, allowing the voters an evaluative handle for deciding whom to vote for or against. Despite their obvious advantages in position, name recognition, and known public records, incumbent and former governors spent considerable money in their campaigns. Of the more than $192 million spent on these races, governors and former governors spent nearly $58 million (30 percent); 16 were the top spenders in their contests. Thus we must add the ability to raise and spend money for campaign purposes to their previously mentioned advantages.

Two-thirds of the candidates who spent the most money in the campaign for governor won (24 of 36), but as Jewell noted for the 1982 primaries there were some exceptions.[19] Table 3, "Winners' Electoral and Spending Record: 1982 Gubernatorial Elections," summarizes the results of these elections and includes the following information on the winners: party and incumbency, percent of the vote, percent of expenditures, dollars spent per vote, and whether the winner spent the most money in the campaign. It also shows how expensive each state's gubernatorial campaign was for all candidates reporting.

There is considerable diversity in the cost of gubernatorial campaigns across the 36 states in 1982. The range is from a high of $23.6 million in New York, where the losing candidate Lewis Lehrman nearly tripled winning Democratic candidate Mario Cuomo's campaign expenditures, to about a quarter of a million in South Dakota where Governor William Janklow easily defeated his Democratic challenger. The average cost per contest was a little over $5 million.

The cost of obtaining votes in these elections varied widely from $36.18 spent per vote in Alaska to the $.98 spent in South Dakota with an average of $3.45 per vote across all 36 states. For winning candidates, Alaska Democrat Bill Sheffield led at $26.24 per vote, with Governor Janklow at $.74 per vote spending the least. For losing major party candidates, Republican Leo Corbet in Alaska spent at the rate of $17.75 per vote on the high side and Republican Vincent Marzullo in Rhode Island at $.25 on the low side. The size of Alaska and the difficulty of campaigning in that state obviously mean any serious statewide candidacy is bound to be expensive.

Table 3

Winners Electoral and Spending Records: 1982 Gubernatorial Elections

State	Winner	Party	Total Expenditures (All Candidates)	WINNER Percent of Total Vote	Percent of Total Spending	Dollars Spent Per Vote	Winner Spent Most Money
Alabama	Wallace[a]	D	$ 3,509,600	60	42	2.32	
Alaska	Sheffield	D	6,113,881	46	33	26.24	*
Arizona	Babbitt[b]	D	2,262,750	63	75	3.73	*
Arkansas	Clinton[a,c]	D	3,584,467	55	47	3.83	*
California	Deukmejian	R	23,397,385	49	33	2.06	*
Colorado	Lamm[b]	D	1,142,933	67	71	1.30	*
Connecticut	O'Neill[b]	D	3,152,543	53	30	1.67	
Florida	Graham[b]	D	4,222,742	65	66	1.64	*
Georgia	Harris	D	6,475,316	63	46	4.06	*
Hawaii	Ariyoshi[b]	D	4,036,608	45	61	17.39	*
Idaho	Evans[b]	D	1,306,804	51	36	2.82	
Illinois	Thompson[b]	R	8,000,000[d]	50	63	2.85	*
Iowa	Branstad	R	2,183,131	53	45	1.78	*
Kansas	Carlin[b]	D	3,028,520	54	38	2.84	
Maine	Brennan[b]	D	1,663,327	62	33	1.94	
Maryland	Hughes[b]	D	2,553,942	62	56	2.05	*
Massachusetts	Dukakis[a,c]	D	7,718,602	60	40	2.54	*
Michigan	Blanchard	D	9,985,103	52	25	1.58	*

			Total Expenditures (All Candidates)	WINNER			
State	Winner	Party		Percent of Total Vote	Percent of Total Spending	Dollars Spent Per Vote	Winner Spent Most Money
Minnesota	Perpich[a]	DFL	4,411,877	59	23	1.00	
Nebraska	Kerrey[c]	D	2,131,916	51	41	3.19	
Nevada	Bryan[c]	D	2,825,374	54	45	9.93	*
New Hampshire	Sununu[c]	R	1,207,898	51	53	4.35	*
New Mexico	Anaya	D	2,782,481	53	44	5.68	*
New York	Cuomo	DL	23,558,518	51	22	2.01	
Ohio	Celeste	D	7,650,877	60	64	2.48	*
Oklahoma	Nigh[b]	D	2,325,199	62	54	2.29	*
Oregon	Atiyeh[b]	R	1,933,604	63	65	2.04	*
Pennsylvania	Thornburgh[b]	R	4,924,592	52	73	1.93	*
Rhode Island	Garrahy[b]	D	423,029	76	96	1.70	*
South Carolina	Riley[b]	D	651,799	70	82	1.14	*
South Dakota	Janklow[b]	R	254,564	71	57	.74	*
Tennessee	Alexander[b]	R	6,979,265	60	57	5.42	*
Texas	White[c]	D	22,421,471	54	40	5.36	
Vermont	Snelling[b]	R	414,073	55	45	2.03	
Wisconsin	Earl	D	1,880,919	57	41	1.01	
Wyoming	Herschler[b]	D	825,770	63	31	2.42	

[a] Former Governor
[b] Incumbent Governor
[c] Defeated Incumbent Governor
[d] Is an estimate from an AP wire story printed in the Champaign-Urbana News-Gazette, April 29, 1983. Final reports not filed until June 30, 1983.

We now turn to a statistical analysis of some of these data in an attempt to sort out the relationship between campaign spending and winning the governorship in 1982.

The simple correlation between the percent of the votes won in the general election and the percent of the total campaign funds spent by the winner is .54, considerably lower than Jewell found for these two variables in the primaries (.91). Thus, while 82 percent of the variance in the percentage of the candidates' primary vote is explained by his or her primary campaign expenditures, only 29 percent of the variance in the candidates' general election vote is explained by his or her percentage of the total campaign expenditures. Campaign spending explains even less of the variance in the winner's vote (less than 4 percent) when only those 15 states with a competitive general election are included in the analysis.[20] It takes more than just spending additional funds to win a close election. These findings parallel Patterson's for the 1978 elections.[21]

Does incumbency make a difference in these relationships? The simple correlations between incumbency and the winner's percentage of the vote (.09) or the winner's percentage of the campaign expenditures (.27) are not high when all 36 governors' races are involved. These simple correlations do rise (.33 and .55, respectively) when only those 15 states in which there was a competitive election are analyzed.

However, placing these three variables--winner's percentage of the vote, winner's percentage of campaign expenditures, and incumbency--in a multiple regression equation adds very little to the general election analysis both overall ($R^2 = .29$) and for the 15 most competitive contests ($R^2 = .11$). Again, there is more to explaining the gubernatorial winner's percentage of the general election vote than to know what percentage of the total campaign expenditures was his and whether he was an incumbent or not.

OF PRIMARIES AND GENERAL ELECTIONS

There are several possible explanations for the differences between the primary and general election results.

First, in a primary all candidates are attempting to create a political organization which is highly individualized for their own candidacy; in the general election the major candidates are party designees for governor. Whatever organization the party has, and this varies greatly across the states, the gubernatorial candidate is at the head of the ticket for all state and local contests. In the primary, campaign funds must be used to create an individual's name, identification, and image; the general election funds are used similarly but also comingle with other monies and activities in the effort to enhance the party's identification and image. This would suggest a more direct relationship between primary spending and the vote than overall campaign spending and the general election outcome.

Second, there are different electorates involved in the two types of elections. Of the 36 states with gubernatorial elections in 1982, 29 had closed primaries in which only declared party members could vote, six had open primaries in which the voter decides in which party's primary he or she will participate, and one had a blanket primary where voting is permitted for candidates of more than one party.[22] Therefore, the primary electorate in most of the states was made up of members of the party in which the candidates were seeking the gubernatorial nomination, while the general election is open to all qualified voters. Money spent in the primary in most states is to reach the individual party member-voter to obtain support for a particular candidate within the party; money spent in the general election is to reach all voters including party members, to obtain support for the candidate and others running on the party's ticket. Again, this suggests a more direct relationship between political money and a candidate's vote in the primary than in the general election.

Third, the primary voter is answering two questions: Who can best lead our ticket as a gubernatorial candidate and who will be best as governor of our state? The general election voter is answering only the second question. Thus, the nature of the campaigns is somewhat different as individual candidates try to out-duel on their personal abilities, experience, and attributes to get the party nod in the primary; in the general election the question is not only which party's candidate is best, but which party can best govern.

When the voters perceive the need for a change in who controls state government, it most often will occur in the general election when a party shift occurs. In 1982, there were 11 such party shifts, the most notable in the Midwest where Michigan, Minnesota, Nebraska, Ohio, and Wisconsin all moved from a Republican to a Democratic governor. Illinois came within 5,100 votes of doing so. The economy, unemployment, and factors other than which candidates spent the most money in their campaigns were highly significant in these shifts.

In states that are primarily one-party, such a shift can occur within that dominant party's primary when the control of the party shifts from one faction to another through the selection of the gubernatorial candidate. The last two Democratic primaries in Massachusetts are examples. In some other states, as in the South, for example, winning the Democratic primary is tantamount to winning the general election so that the primary serves in effect as the general election.

In summary, the differences in the statistical relationships between primary and general elections are tied in part to differences in how the two campaigns are conducted and what the outcome of each means, the different electorates involved, and the nature of the voting decision in each election--which can include whether voters desire to achieve change in who runs state government or who will lead their party.

CONCLUSION

The costs of running for and winning the governorship have increased greatly over the past decade and will undoubtedly continue to do so in the future. The mass media approach to the potential voter, with the use of political polls and political consultants, has changed the way candidates and potential candidates approach an electoral campaign and certainly how they view the role of the political party. As Arterton has observed: "Parties can be useful to their candidates to the degree that they control means for reaching voters or provide services and resources to their candidates that may be difficult for them to duplicate elsewhere."[23] In a few words, working through the party is only one of several approaches to reaching the voters, and often not the primary one.

As technology continues to advance and even newer, more expensive means are developed to ensure that the individual voter is contacted or touched by a campaign in the search for the necessary majority or plurality, the costs of the campaigns will rise apace. The pressure to spend will most certainly be there. Whether the political party will be a part of this new spending or will be able to use it is, at this point, an unanswered question and one that will be most interesting to trace in upcoming elections.

NOTES

*This chapter is reprinted from State Government 56,2 (1983), pp. 74-84.

[1] I wish to thank Gloria Ambrosia, a graduate student in the Public Administration Program at UNC, for her research assistance in developing this article.

[2] Herbert Alexander, "Financing Gubernatorial Election Campaigns," State Government 53 (Summer 1980): 140-43.

[3] U.S. Department of Commerce, Bureau of the Census, Statistical Abstract of the United States, 1981 (Washington, D.C.: U.S. Government Printing Office, 1981), p. 458. The 1967 dollar equivalents are 1977 = .551; 1978 = .512; 1979 = .459; 1980 = .405; 1981 = .367; 1982 = .352.

[4] By year the data are:

Year	Races	Democratic Winner	Incumbent Running	Incumbent Winning	Incumbent Losing	
					G Election	Primary
1977	2	1	1	1	0	0
1978	36	21	22	16	5	1
1979	3	2	0	0	0	0
1980	13	6	12	7	3	2
1981	2	1	0	0	0	0
1982	36	27	25	19	5	1
Total	92	58	60	43	13	4

[5] Public Affairs Research Council of Louisiana, The Great Louisiana Campaign Spendathon (Baton Rouge: PARC, 1980), p. 1.

[6] Ibid.

[7] Don Baker, "West Virginia's Deep Pockets: Rockefeller Lays Out $30 for Vote," The Washington Post, 29 November 1980.

[8] "Rockefeller Campaign: $29 a Vote," The New York Times, 6 December 1980, p. 11.

[9]Robert Marcus, "Campaign Spending: Is Up The Only Direction?" *Empire State Report* (November 1982): 20.

[10]Larry Sabato, "Gubernatorial Politics and the New Campaign Technology," *State Government* 53 (Summer 1980): 149.

[11]Rhodes Cook and Stacy West, "1978 Gubernatorial Contests: Incumbents, Winners Hold Money Advantage," *Congressional Quarterly*, 25 August 1979, p. 1755.

[12]Samuel C. Patterson, "Campaign Spending in Contests for Governor," *Western Political Quarterly* 35, 4 (December 1982): 463.

[13]Ibid., p. 472.

[14]Moving from Republican to Democratic controlled states were: Alaska, Arkansas, Michigan, Minnesota, Nebraska, Nevada, Ohio, Texas and Wisconsin. Shifting from Democratic to Republican control were: California and New Hampshire.

[15]Garrahy (RI) 52% spread between top two candidates; Janklow (SD) 42%; Riley (SC) 40%; Lamm (CO) 34%; Babbitt (AZ) 31%; Graham (FL) 30%; Atiyeh (OR) 26%; Herschler (WY) 26%; Brennan (ME) 24%; Hughes (MD) 24%; Nigh (OK) 24%; Alexander (TN) 20%, Ariyoshi (HI) 19%, and Snelling (VT) 11%.

[16]Carlin (KS) 9% spread between top two candidates and O'Neill (CT) 6%.

[17]Thornburgh (PA) 4% spread between top two candidates; Evans (MT) 2%; and Thompson (IL) less than 1%.

[18]Wallace (AL 1963-67); 1971-79); Clinton (AR 1979-81); Dukakis (MA 1975-79), and Perpich (MN 1976-79).

[19]All references to Jewell concern his chapter in this book, "Political Money and Gubernatorial Primaries."

[20]A competitive election is defined as one in which the winning candidate wins by less than a 10-percent margin. (r = .19). Those 15 states with competitive elections were: Alaska, where the winner's margin over his nearest opponent was 8%;

Arkansas 10%; California 1%; Connecticut 6%; Idaho 2%; Illinois, less than 1%; Iowa 6%; Kansas 9%; Michigan 7%; Nebraska 2%; New Hampshire 4%; New Mexico 6%; New York 3%; Pennsylvania 4% and Texas 8%.

[21] Patterson, p. 474.

[22] Council of State Governments, The Book of the States, 1982-83 (Lexington, Ky.: Council of State Governments, 1982), p. 110.

[23] F. Christopher Arterton at a Yale University conference, "The Communications Revolution and American Politics," April 1983. Quoted in Richard Reeves, "Technology Provides Possibility of More Party Power," The News and Observer (Raleigh), 5 May 1983, sec. A, p. 5.

3. ARIZONA GUBERNATORIAL POLITICS: 1982

RUTH S. JONES

In 1982, while 63 percent of the seats in the Arizona legislature were given to Republican candidates, Democrat Bruce Babbitt was elected to his second full term as Governor of Arizona with 62 percent of the vote. Thus, understanding Arizona gubernatorial politics in the 1980s is a matter of understanding something about Bruce Babbitt, his policies, his politics, and his personal political style.

His own description of the job is that "being governor isn't a job of giving philosophical speeches, arguing abstractions. It's a question of doing something, pragmatic problem-solving."[1] Although he prefers a reasoned, cooperative mode of action, he is not adverse to hard-ball politics. "If there's a problem, I'm willing to antagonize anybody who tells me there's not a problem. But I like to solve it by sitting down at the table, twisting arms and bringing people in as part of the solution."[2] He is, in academic parlance, an active-positive executive. He seeks out areas of challenge and systematically crafts programs of action; he relishes the competition, conflict, and publicity of the position.

Supporting this aggressive, problem-solving approach to being governor is an obvious sense of personal confidence: confidence to set the agenda and formulate programmatic solutions to state problems, to work successfully with an overwhelming Republican legislature to initiate policies that will maintain the momentum of a booming sunbelt state, to maintain personal contact with and public support of many diverse groups throughout the state, and to select and direct an extremely young, energetic, and personally loyal staff of executive branch personnel.

Road to the Governorship

Although Bruce Babbitt seems to exude personal and political confidence, he has not always been in control of his political fortunes. He is, by birth, the scion of a pioneer family who built a thriving cattle and mercantile industry in northern

Arizona. He was socialized in a milieu of political activism with the frontier ethos of individualism and pragmatic action. His formal education as a cum laude geology major from Notre Dame and a Marshall Scholar in geophysics in Newcastle, England, was a logical extension of his boyhood interest in natural resources and the environment, developed by growing up with the Grand Canyon in his backyard. Subsequently, with a law degree from Harvard and experience as an ACTION volunteer in Venezuela, he served as a VISTA community specialist and returned to Arizona to direct the Maricopa Legal Aid Society, and then became involved in a variety of social service and minority-related programs in the state. After a brief stint with a prominent Arizona law firm, Bruce Babbitt sought and was elected to the position of attorney general of Arizona in 1974 and made headlines by his pursuit of white collar fraud and antitrust prosecutions.[3]

On March 4, 1978, amid increasing rumors that he was positioning himself for a U.S. Senate race, the Attorney General received word of the sudden death of Arizona Governor Wesley Bolin. Under the Arizona state Constitution, and given recent political events, he, Babbitt, was next in line of succession to be governor. Consequently, at age 39, without a campaign and without serious consideration of the office, Bruce Babbitt became Governor of the State of Arizona.[4]

With the 1978 gubernatorial primary less than six months away, the new incumbent governor was faced with a totally new set of political alternatives. His decision was to present his new position as one of a caretaker governor by making few changes, but he also took on the tasks and trappings of the office, and shortly declared himself as a candidate for the office. Although the Democratic nomination was not simply his for the asking (there were other prominent Democrats who had been preparing to make the race before Babbitt had become the incumbent), ultimately Babbitt entered his first gubernatorial election contest and was elected governor in his own right in November 1978.

The First Term

As the Governor's first State-of-the-State address suggested, there were a series of issues, politically and philosophically compatible with the Governor's interests that were already under discussion, which he was eager to champion and which therefore made up the agenda for his first term. As one of his aides recalls, "There was a backlog of issues waiting for us to seize. We just organized them and ran." Thus, by the time the 1982 campaign was underway, the Governor had seen a new groundwater code developed, the growth of state expenditures reduced, an alternative health program to Medicare established, a new program to manage state-owned urban lands established, numerous anti-crime measures enacted, and the economic climate of the state--relative to other states--greatly improved. During his four years as governor, the state had successfully addressed many issues critical to its development, and continued to experience population growth and generally favorable industrial and commercial development.

Looking back with a clear sense of accomplishment, Bruce Babbitt might have felt he was in a most enviable position for making his 1982 re-election bid. However, decreased revenues and increased demands for state services provided major themes for the 1982 Arizona gubernatorial campaign just as they did for so many other states. For Arizonans who had internalized the vision of perpetual bounty in the Valley of the Sun, fiscal hard times were inconsistent with their sunbelt image. Facing such realities as a decimated copper industry or the fact that Arizona's unemployment rate hovered around 10 percent throughout 1982, was unique, unsettling, and uncomfortable for politicians and voters alike.

THE 1982 CAMPAIGN

The economic stability and health of the state clearly dominated the campaign. However, two other themes were also prominent. Because the Republican candidate, Leo Corbet, was a highly respected, five-term state Senator who had served as president of the upper chamber since 1979, one repeated theme was executive vs. legislative institutional accountability and responsibility. Who deserved the credit for the state's progress and who deserved the blame for the state's problems? As Babbitt sought to run on his record, Corbet responded that the legislature in fact had provided the impetus for whatever program the Governor might be claiming as a product of his leadership. Where problems existed, Babbitt pointed to the failure of the legislature to act and Corbet countered that the Governor had actively opposed, frequently vetoing, appropriate legislation without providing a responsible program of his own.

A second theme, advanced largely by the Republican candidate, was described as a "style wars of party stars."[5] The style confrontation placed the Republican candidate's emphasis on homegrown interests, a laid-back style, a parochial loyalty to Arizona against the Democratic candidate's well-known erudition, global experience, and perceived political ambitions.

> Where Babbitt is scholarly and intense, Corbet is aw-shucks loose and witty. The representative of the self-proclaimed 'party of the people' hails from a wealthy northern Arizona dynasty, while the Republican's father worked on the railroad. Where Babbitt may be most comfortable at a wine-and-cheese tasting after the symphony, Corbet is happier downing a six-pack after pitching a softball game . . . Babbitt is Harvard and Newcastle, Corbet is University of Arizona. The governor dreams of the White House. The senator longs for a great weekend. . . .[6]

Corbet repeatedly stressed that his single objective was to improve the welfare of Arizona for Arizonans, implying that the Governor had his sights set on Washington and was using Arizona as a personal stepping stone. Babbitt's response, as captured in a pre-election interview, was that such charges had been around since he first entered politics but that he had "no intention of leaving this state, period. . . . I love what I do and I'm here to stay."[7]

In contrast to the acrimonious Republican primary where old party factions re-emerged and old wounds were opened, Governor Babbitt faced only token opposition in the Democratic primary. In fact, the only name in opposition on the primary ballot was that of Steven Jancek, who died before the September election. Nevertheless, Jancek received 14 percent of the vote, which was readily interpreted as an anti-Babbitt vote. It was no secret, and even the Governor acknowledged that not all Democrats were ecstatic at the idea of four more years of Babbitt at the party's helm. Factions within the party ebb and flow, but they persist; and the primary provided an opportunity for fellow Democrats to express their displeasures with the Governor. Corbet, on the other hand, had gained the unofficial party pre-primary endorsement in a much publicized, behind-the-scenes orchestration by party leaders, only to be involved in an acrimonious primary campaign which he eventually won with 62 percent of the vote.

Ultimately, although for quite different reasons, both candidates ran personal rather than party-oriented general election campaigns. On all other dimensions the two campaigns were markedly different largely because Babbitt had ample campaign money and Corbet did not. The costs of gubernatorial campaigns have increased in Arizona as elsewhere. In 1978 when Bruce Babbitt waged his first campaign for Governor, he was, in fact, the incumbent Governor and the best funded gubernatorial candidate in the field. His total primary and general campaign spending accounted for two-thirds of all spending in the entire campaign and he spent just over $500,000 to win 54 percent of the vote at a cost of $1.86 per vote. In 1982, his total primary and general election spending accounted for 75 percent of all campaign expenditures reported in the gubernatorial campaign. He spent over $1.7 million to win 62 percent of the vote at a cost per vote of $2.85.[8]

The Governor's well-financed campaign provoked controversy among Republicans and Democrats alike. Republican party leaders were unhappy because Babbitt, having made clear his intention to run for re-election, had long been amassing a campaign war chest to signal that he would be able to wage a very expensive campaign if necessary. By mid September he had collected over $1 million compared to just over $300,000 for Corbet. Furthermore, Babbitt posed formidable early opposition to Republican candidates. Given his popularity in the state, many contributors who otherwise might have helped finance a strong Republican challenge, in fact, were early contributors to the Babbitt campaign. To the chagrin of party leaders, there was an official "Republicans for Babbitt" committee, which included many top names in the business community and which actively sought Republican money for the Governor's campaign.

Democratic candidates who mounted their campaigns later than the Governor also found that many of their potential benefactors had already contributed to the Governor's campaign and were not inclined to give generous support to additional candidates. The fact that Babbitt was the overwhelming favorite in the gubernatorial campaign but continued to spend sizeable amounts of money campaigning created resentment among some Democrats, especially state legislative candidates in close races, who felt that the Governor's largess could have been used to better advantage in other, that is, their own, campaigns. On the other hand, all Democratic candidates clearly benefitted from the massive phone banks, voter canvass, and get-out-the-vote campaigns that were financed primarily by the campaign committees of the Governor and Senator DeConcini. The two best financed Democrats in the state indirectly did assist their fellow Democrats, but such efforts did not erase feelings that the ballot was that of Steven Jancek, who died before the Governor, in particular, did less than he could have done for the ticket, and more than was necessary for himself.

The Governor received both direct and indirect support from labor, but he also was widely supported by the business community through prominent groups such as the "Business for Babbitt" organization. And, although he received visible amounts of money from PACs throughout the state (and even a little out-of-state money), his primary source of campaign funds was individual Arizonans. Moreover, a review of his contributor lists reveals that contributions were rather evenly divided between those who gave sums over $100 and those who gave smaller amounts.

Senator Corbet, after a divisive primary that was only publicly "healed" as the general election campaign got underway, had a great deal of difficulty raising money. Although he received money from a variety of PACs, his primary source of funding also was individual contributors. Caught in the political "Catch 22" familiar to many candidates running against favored incumbents, Corbet could not campaign vigorously because he was underfunded and he could not raise the money he needed for a more vigorous campaign because his campaign seemed to be going nowhere. Twenty-three months after the November election, the Corbet

Committee had not filed its post-election campaign report--supposedly because there was still a sizable campaign deficit. Even a well-publicized fundraiser in April 1983, did not erase all the debts that his estimated three-quarters-of-a-million-dollar campaign incurred.

The third gubernatorial candidate, Sam Steiger, the Republican Congressman turned Libertarian, spent only a token amount and focused his campaign on obtaining the five percent of the vote that was needed to secure a place for the Libertarian party, as an official political party, on the 1984 election ballot.

The Campaign Issues

In a practical sense, the campaign for governor never really got off the ground. Ballot issues and newly redistricted Congressional and state legislative races sparked far more citizen interest than did the 1982 gubernatorial campaign.

The Republican candidate tried to capitalize on the uncertainty surrounding the state's 1982-83 budget and to paint Babbitt as a liberal, pro-labor, anti-business candidate. However, Babbitt had positioned himself well to fend off such attacks. In October, the Joint Legislative Budget Committee released a report that predicted a minimal deficit for the 1982-83 fiscal year of $70 million. This was perhaps the strongest gun in the Republican arsenal and Corbet repeatedly tried to use it to his advantage. Babbitt's stock response was that the JLBC's figures were overly pessimistic, and that his own analysis provided a more accurate and brighter picture. He also noted that he had already taken steps in the summer to guard against any shortfall by directing state agencies to reduce spending by almost 10 percent and by reallocating revenues so that Arizona's budget would continue to operate in the black. In this battle of budget statistics and complex, creative financing, Corbet was able to pick up only minimal ground.

As one of the first governors to support the concept of President Reagan's "New Federalism," and as an articulate advocate of controlling entitlement programs and taxing social security and medicare benefits as well as medical insurance and employee benefit programs, Babbitt displayed other credentials that appealed to many conservative Arizonans--regardless of party.

Democratic governors in right-to-work states traditionally walk a tight rope where labor issues are concerned; the fact that major labor and business leaders were active in his campaign was evidence that Babbitt had been able to maintain an appropriate labor-management balance. Babbitt had in fact vetoed anti-labor legislation, which he described as unnecessarily harsh and polarizing, but then he turned around to support a modification of the industrial compensation law that was to reduce premium wage rates an average of 40 percent. Under the banner of cooperation-in-time-of adversity, Arizona labor and management had been drawn together on many political issues, and, although in no way a situation the Governor created, this cooperative effort to improve the state's economic outlook certainly did not work against the "balanced treatment" image that Babbitt sought to project where labor issued were concerned.

His success with this tactic reflects a more general strategic posture that Babbitt has adopted over the years. As a self-avowed centerist, he is viewed by many fellow Democrats as a Republican in Democratic clothing. Babbitt says he is not a Republican because he believes that "the historical goals of the Democratic Party are in the main, solid." According to Babbitt, a successful Democrat on the domestic front is one who recognizes that the pie isn't growing and can figure out "how to address the traditional constituency of the party without simply advocating that we spend more money for more programs."[9] Success oriented, Babbitt has been accused of playing left field in Washington and right field at home, but his partisan and ideological orientations were certainly not his points of vulnerability during the 1982 campaign for the Arizona governorship.

The well-publicized activities of the Governor working through the Office of Economic Planning and Development to improve the climate for business and industry in the state were not lost on the business community. In fact, Babbitt received credit from all sectors for the fact that the state had moved from ranking 28th in a 1977 Business Week poll on the business attractiveness of the state to being

8th in 1982. The fact that so many prominent members of the business community were identified with the "Business for Babbitt" group or were among the financial backers of the Governor supports the notion that, although many might have wanted him to do more for business, Babbitt was certainly not viewed as anti-business by the business community itself.

With the failing state economy and a potential budget deficit as the primary issues in the campaign, neither candidate presented a comprehensive set of new policies and programs but instead offered suggestions for doing more with less. A variety of secondary issues were discussed, including toughening anti-crime laws, revising educational standards, raising the drinking age, changing the structure of the Corporation Commission, and promoting energy conservation. The two televised debates in which all the candidates for governor participated did not do much to generate interest and enthusiasm in the campaign but did provide a forum for the candidates to replay the leadership, style, and budget themes to larger audiences than usual.

The Election

In spite of the immediate economic problems facing Arizona, the recent trend for the state has been one of tremendous population growth and commercial and industrial expansion. Obvious social and economic changes in the sunbelt state have been accompanied by political change as well; most strikingly, an increase in Republican voter registration. In 1960, 32 percent of the registered voters were Republicans and 66 percent were Democrats. By the 1982 election, the Democratic edge had been sharply reduced and the two parties were almost evenly matched in registration: 44.5 percent Republican; 46.9 percent Democratic, and 8.6 percent Libertarian.

Although voter turnout as a percentage of registered voters is generally high (78 percent in 1980), only 54 percent of all eligible voters were registered in 1982.[10] With partisan registration virtually even and with Democratic supporters traditionally lower in election day turnout, the Governor clearly needed Republican votes to win. In his first gubernatorial campaign against a much more ideologically conservative Republican, but with a 10 percent Democratic registration advantage, he won with 54 percent of the vote. The fact that he led in the polls by 40 points, received the editorial endorsement of all four of the state's major papers, and garnered the largest number of votes of any statewide candidate running in 1982 as he carried every county in winning 62 percent of the vote (in contrast to 33 for Corbet and 5 for Steiger), measures the success of the Babbitt organization's efforts to cultivate bipartisan support throughout the state. Although the election outcome was never in doubt, the magnitude of the victory was impressive.

POST ELECTION

Other than the predictable but anticlimactic election night celebration and the statements of a magnanimous winner, the election was followed, with one exception, by business as usual for the Governor and his staff. That one exception was provided by the fiscal status of the state, and its impact on the 1982-83 state budget.

Campaign rhetoric not withstanding, the budget picture had gotten worse and by late November the Joint Legislative Budget Committee was predicting a $180-million deficit if no cuts were made. Even the Governor's budget analysts were predicting a $25-million deficit beyond the $68 million in cuts that had been ordered in late summer. With all the relevant legislative leaders on hand to signal agreement, if not happiness, with the plan, the Governor called a press conference to announce that he would request the legislature to amend the Arizona tax code to require corporations and some individuals to pay their taxes earlier. In effect, he called for a program of accelerated tax payments that would provide a one-shot infusion of revenue to the state. "It's time to lay aside our differences and draw together . . . . We're going to have to retrench and accept that our earlier optimism was misplaced," said Babbitt.[11] At the same time, the Governor asked the legislature formally to revise the 1982-83 budget consistent with the budget cuts he had administratively ordered earlier in the year. But in spite of the gloominess of the budget scene, both the Governor and the legislative leadership reiterated that there would be no tax increases for either fiscal 1982-83 or 1983-84.

Formal revision of the 1982-83 state budget consumed most of the policy attention of the executive branch between the election and the Governor's inauguration in January. This was due, in part, to the policy vacuum which had been created by the success the governor had enjoyed during his first term of office. By 1982, most of his original agenda was either well in motion or had been successfully implemented. After the election, as throughout his campaign, the Governor was in need of issues that his administration could seize and pursue as they had during the first term. So obvious was the policy-issue void that a weekend retreat for brainstorming was suggested as a means by which the new administration might come up with new marching orders, or at least learn which drums to beat and at which cadence to herald the coming year.

Babbitt's Gubernatorial Style

The staff and the people hired and appointed by Babbitt are overwhelmingly young, energetic, ambitious people. The Governor's management style, perhaps reminiscent of FDR, appears to be to reward individual motivation with a degree of autonomy but always to maintain a short leash; to play one set of ideas, staff, or interests against another while maintaining final control over decisions for himself. The Governor has been criticized for being expedient when it comes to selecting and removing personnel, but his overall record has been one of retaining key people for reasonably long tenures. As he looked forward to his second full term, there were relatively few changes in his overall staffing decisions. "I'm generally very satisfied with the performance of my Cabinet group. They're really outstanding. But the price you pay for outstanding people is that some of them want to move on."[12]

During his first administration, when many fellow Democrats felt that the Governor was too busy solidifying his personal electoral base, there was criticism that too many Republicans were being appointed to state commissions, boards, and the like. Similarly, the youth of the Governor's appointments (very few of them over forty years old) brought charges that he wanted to build an empire of personally loyal, non-threatening sycophants. And the lack of any hesitancy in recruiting talent from out of state brought comments such as that from a Democratic state Representative who, upon the announcement of a particular appointment complained that, "the man on the ninth floor has done it again--he's gone out of state . . . to make an appointment," and suggested a moratorium on all gubernatorial appointments.

The Second Term "Agenda"

Over twenty thousand invitations were issued for the Governor's inauguration on the Capitol Mall and more than 2,500 were in attendance to hear the Governor's brief, low-keyed but upbeat inaugural address. Sprinkled with a little familiar Thomas Jefferson, "We are all Republicans. We are all Democrats," and a little Hubert Humphrey, "The moral test of government is how it treats the children, the elderly and the needy," he reminded Arizonans that they were in a position to lead the technological revolution just as New York and Massachusetts led the Industrial Revolution a century ago. To achieve this goal, he asserted, requires us "to draw together a pattern of continuing restraint in governmental expenditures, a positive regulatory climate, strong support for our universities and tax policies that encourage productive investment."[13] In short, there were "no new packages, no new ribbons" but a confident optimism for the state's future.

Similarly, in his subsequent State-of-the-State speech to the legislature, Governor Babbitt underlined the importance of the pending budgetary considerations by referring to the fact that Arizona's unemployment rate was 10.8 percent, that construction industry employment had dropped 32 percent from traditional levels, and that many of the copper miners had experienced their second Christmas season without pay checks. He again issued a call for the legislature to adopt the accelerated tax program and urged careful and prudent consideration of the Executive Budget he would submit, which he described as "cut beyond the fat into muscle and bone."

As it had during the campaign, education took a prominent place in the Governor's message to the legislature. He made several specific proposals such as requiring higher admission requirements for math and science at the state universities, extending the school year by one week, and requiring computer literacy for teacher certification, but the total projected expenditure was a modest $500,000. To the consternation of the education community, he also urged that the automatic 7-percent increase currently enjoyed by the public school funding program be decreased to a 4-percent increase.

The Governor proposed continued efforts to finance prison expansion and to upgrade juvenile offender and criminal justice programs. In the area of Health and Human Services he gave greatest priority to shoring up and energizing the Arizona Health Care Cost Containment System. In the area of Natural Resources and the Environment, he urged a systematic consideration of expansion for the state's water-based recreational opportunities and the management and maintenance of the state park system. He urged that the state continue to explore policies and administrative procedures for handling toxic materials. His final notes were an appeal for county home rule as a means of alleviating the fiscal crises facing many county officials and for the establishment of an independent Office of Consumer Advocacy that would represent the consumer, particularly in utility rate increase discussions.[14]

It was not a gourmet menu for either politics or government, and it contained no surprises. Given the problems of budget deficits and shrinking revenues, it was not a time to propose new, expensive programs. The tone was somber but upbeat; the message had enough substance for news copy but not enough controversy to draw battle lines, set opposing alliances in motion, or divert energies away from the task at hand, that of creating a workable state budget.

The Legislature Reacts

As the new legislative session began, there were only five continuing standing committee chairmen in familiar positions; there was a phalanx of new members, especially in the Senate; the former president of the Senate, Babbitt's unsuccessful opponent, had been replaced, but the House majority leader was back for his ninth term as majority leader. Acknowledged by friend and foe alike as the single most powerful political force in Arizona, Majority Leader Burton Barr held the pivotal role for all budget negotiations. The Governor, well aware of the importance of Barr to success with the legislature, described Barr as "the center of gravity, the impetus for change," and suggested that the legislature had been aptly characterized as "89 people surrounded by Burton Barr."[15]

While the legislature first disposed of the accelerated tax proposal and the revised 1982-83 budget, it was becoming clear to all concerned that new sources of revenue would be essential if the Governor's $1.7-billion budget for 1983-84 was to be realized without massive cuts in all state programs and services. With the Republicans only one vote shy of a veto-proof legislature, the budget battle that ensued was hard fought and involved constantly shifting coalitions. By late February, the Governor began paving the way for a tax increase when he spoke to the Democratic caucuses in the legislature. In late March the Governor asked the legislature to approve a half-point increase in the state sales tax (an increase that would expire at the end of 1984) and to earmark all revenue increases for the use of state (not county) government.

The call for a tax increase did not surprise the legislative leadership, and Majority Leader Barr, after some partisan rhetoric, confessed that it had been "obvious that there will be a shortfall in state revenue and that we'll have to raise the tax."[16]

Ultimately, the Governor and the legislative leaders, all of whom had pledged no new taxes, engineered a tax increase. The Senate Republicans split openly on the tax issue and, with the Governor marshaling Democratic votes and the Republican leaders building a coalition from a very ideologically fragmented legislative party, a sales tax of one, not one-half, percent was enacted in the waning hours of the 1983 session. Because the proposed tax increase was likely to raise more revenue than a balanced budget would require, the Governor proposed to give some funds back to the day care programs he had cut, some back to state aid to public school and prison reform programs, and to aid the Arizona Health Care Cost Containment System. Legislators, of course, had different ideas about where any extra revenue should be placed. Consequently, while the issue of a tax increase dominated the activities of the legislature, the bargaining chips were primarily those of possible new expenditure allocations.

The Future

As the weary legislators adjourned the session and went home to catch their breath, reflect on the events of the spring, and begin recapturing and restructuring the non-political dimensions of their lives, the Governor and his staff remained on duty to oversee the implementation of the new budget and a few new programs and to plot the course for the future--the future of Arizona and the future of Governor Bruce Babbitt.

The future of Arizona is basically a bright one. The general assumption is that the economic hard times that have recently plagued the state are momentary and that, in the long run, the growth and expansion of the state's economy will continue. The problems that accompany rapid growth are ones the Governor no doubt will welcome.

The future of Bruce Babbitt is less certain, more unpredictable, but obviously potentially very exciting. His potential for higher office has been touted since he first entered electoral politics. In an interview printed in the National Journal in January 1983, Babbitt was quite candid in saying:

> Would I like to be President? Yes. Any competent politician who gets elected to the national Congress or governorship looks himself in the mirror every couple of weeks and says, 'Am I presidential?' It's there. It's a fact. I deal with it this way. I want to be competent, very good, partake very vigorously in national debate. If lighting strikes, fine. If it doesn't, I will be fully satisfied. I don't foresee a scenario where Bruce Babbitt goes out and runs in presidential primaries. But I'm not a wallflower. My decision point is one that every governor has--at what point do you decide that you want to run for Congress or the Senate? The problem with being governor is you can't be governor forever. It's an executive position. Every time you make a decision, the recipients forget. You're running against the clock, and governors self-destruct. Then what do you do?[17]

Indeed, what do you do? Babbitt's name is in the forefront of discussions as plans are formulated for the Senate race in 1986, when Babbitt's current term as governor ends and when the dean of the Arizona Congressional delegation, Senator Barry Goldwater, will retire. Babbitt's name is among those touted as potential vice-presidential candidates in 1984 although Babbitt has said that, "Yes, [that possibility has] crossed my mind, and it's exited very rapidly. There's no probable scenario in which that's going to happen. The West just does not factor in the composition of a Democratic ticket. From time immemorial, the ticket has been a Northerner and a Southerner."[18]

Fortunately for Governor Babbitt and for the State of Arizona, these political decisions may not be made for some time. In the meantime, the Governor, who has written books on topics such as art, the Grand Canyon, and geology, has become a spokesman for the Democratic Governor's Western Policy Conference. The Governor, who has served on the Trilateral Commission and chaired the Nuclear Regulatory Oversight Commission, who embraces the concept of New Federalism and yet characterized Interior Secretary James Watt as displaying "an acute sense of schizophrenia in managing federal land," will continue to be Governor in the aggressive, global style that served him so well during his first administration.

Once, when asked about his alleged political ambitions beyond the governorship, Babbitt said that he had learned a "profound lesson" in 1978 when he was suddenly thrust into the governor's role. "The big decisions in life tend to get made for you, rather than by you."[19] And while that may indeed be one of the basic lessons of political life, there is another one that Bruce Babbitt has learned equally well: He who hesitates is lost. Hesitation is certainly not consistent with the open, aggressive political style the Governor has pursued thus far; there is no reason to believe that it will become part of his repertoire in the future. To the contrary, one suspects that if called, he would come, if nominated he would run, if elected, he would serve.

NOTES

[1] "Babbitt vs. Corbet," *Arizona Today's Business*, October 1982, p. 8.

[2] Ibid., p. 28.

[3] Thomas Ropp, "The Babbitt Choice," *Arizona*, 27 March 1983, pp. 6-9 and 26.

[4] Arizona has no lieutenant governor. Under the rules of succession, the second highest elected state official is first in the line of succession. When Governor Raul Castro resigned to become President Carter's ambassador to Argentina, then Secretary of State Wesley Bolin was therefore elevated to the office of governor and his longtime assistant was appointed to fill his unexpired term as secretary of state. Because she had been appointed rather than elected, the highest ranking <u>elected</u> official in the state when Governor Bolin died was Attorney General Bruce Babbitt, and consequently he assumed the duties of the governor.

[5] David M. Brown, "Style Wars: Harvard Political Ambition versus Home-grown Interest and Care?" *Arizona Today's Business*, October 1982, pp. 8-10.

[6] John Kolbe, "Incumbency: Babbitt uses it Skillfully," *Phoenix Gazette*, 30 October 1982, sec. A, p. 4.

[7] "Babbitt vs. Corbet," p. 28.

[8] See Thad L. Beyle, "Gubernatorial Campaign Costs Entering the 1980's," a paper presented at the Annual Meeting of the Midwest Political Science Association, Milwaukee, Wisconsin, April 30, 1981; and Thad L. Beyle, "The Cost of Becoming Governor," *State Government*, Summer 1983, p. 82.

[9] Thomas Ropp, p. 26.

[10] U.S. Department of Commerce, *News*, 18 April 1983, Table 4.

[11] *Capitol Times*, 1 December 1982, p. 1.

¹²John Kolbe, "State May Lose Key Officials," *Phoenix Gazette*, 6 November 1982, p. 1.

¹³Joel Nilsson, "New Beginning," *The Arizona Republic*, 9 January 1983, sec. A, pp. 1 and 12.

¹⁴For the complete State-of-the-State message, see the *Capitol Times*, 12 January, pp. 5, 6, and 15.

¹⁵Babbitt vs. Corbet," p. 8.

¹⁶*Capitol Times*, 30 March 1983, p. 1.

¹⁷Jerry Hagstrom, "Don't Return to Old Ways, Arizona's Democratic Governor Warns His Party," *National Journal*, 1 January 1983, p. 23.

¹⁸John Kolbe, "State May Lose Key Officials," sec. A, p. 4.

¹⁹Ibid.

4. THE LAMM LANDSLIDE IN COLORADO: INCUMBENT POPULARITY AND A DIVIDED OPPOSITION

RODNEY HERO

The 1982 gubernatorial election in Colorado was a historic but predictable and unexciting one. Richard D. Lamm (D) was elected to an unprecedented third consecutive term, and his margin of victory was the largest ever in a Colorado gubernatorial election. The size and ease of the victory may be surprising given that Colorado is a competitive two-party state. But along with competitive parties there have been high levels of independent identification. The result of the combination of widespread independence and strong party competition has been a greater emphasis on candidate characteristics and issue stands than on party affiliation.[1] It thus appears that Lamm's ability to project an image of competence, honesty, good government, and an affinity with the state, which Coloradans have found and continue to find highly appealing, help to explain his resounding victory. Also, the voting public apparently recognized few, if any, specific pressing problems facing the state for which the governor could be held directly or solely responsible. Moreover, internal division damaged Republican hopes. Yet not all Democrats fared as well as the governor.

The Setting

The national recession had affected Colorado much less than it had most other states and the state had had considerable population growth for some time. Therefore, state economic conditions were not a major issue in the election. The fiscal impact of the Reagan Administration's "New Federalism" initiatives raised some concerns but their underlying principles seemed generally compatible with the views of most Coloradans. In short, national issues were inconsequential and the state setting was basically a tranquil one, politically. This setting provided a propitious backdrop for an incumbent governor seeking re-election.

Colorado's major parties use a "caucus-primary" system to nominate their candidates. Candidates who receive at least 20 percent support at the party's state assembly (caucus) are placed or "designated" on the party's primary ballot according to their level (above the 20 percent) of support.² Lamm, not surprisingly, faced no opposition in seeking his party's renomination and thus had the luxury of concentrating on only the general election. The situation for the Republican nominee was different.

The Republicans

The eventual Republican nominee, John Fuhr, had to overcome the well-financed campaign of Phil Winn. Winn, a former state Republican Party chairman and a developer, resigned his post as federal housing commissioner to seek the governorship. Winn began his campaign early and it was widely assumed, at least early on, that he would be the Republican nominee. Winn had the support of numerous business and real estate interests, and he raised and spent almost as much money in his bid for the Republican nomination as Lamm did in his successful general election campaign. The Fuhr campaign received relatively little media attention during this period.

The Winn campaign faltered, however, because of several early mistakes. One was his statement that, never having held elective office before, he did not really know how state government worked. Second was his suggestion that there might be a need to raise taxes to make up the shortfalls caused by national government spending reductions. This possibility concerned Republican Party supporters. Third was his statement in support of making Martin Luther King's birthday a state holiday at the same time that Republicans in the state legislature were seeking to defeat such a bill. Not only were Republican legislators annoyed by the substance of Winn's proposal but also they contended that it indicated insensitivity and a lack of understanding of the political process. Winn was able to assuage some criticism by contending that his critics had overreacted to his symbolic gesture and by stressing his basic agreement with his fellow Republicans on the need for reduced government and less tax burden. The damage, however, was not undone entirely.

Fuhr, a former state legislator and Speaker of the House, ran a low-key nomination effort that emphasized courting party caucus delegates. Early indications were that his approach was effective.

Fuhr was the winner of a straw poll of GOP officials taken in mid-April, two months before the party's state nominating caucus. Despite this level of support, observers several times noted a "lack of enthusiasm" for Fuhr and, indeed, for the several other Republican candidates. This lack of enthusiasm was attributed to several factors. Despite his well-financed and highly visible campaign, Winn was not especially popular among the Republican rank and file. Fuhr, while well-respected, was not particularly dynamic and his "behind-the-scenes" nomination campaign generated little interest among the larger public. And it seemed that many Republicans shared the view that Lamm hadn't been all that bad for a lot of Republicans. Republican enthusiasm was difficult to muster in the absence of a particularly objectionable opponent. In any case, the Fuhr campaign steadily built momentum, although many observers still considered Winn the favorite going into the Republican State Party Assembly in June.

Fuhr received the greatest delegate support at the Party Assembly by a wide margin; Winn received 38-percent support but two other candidates fell short of the 20-percent support required to be placed on the ballot. After an early start and the investment of much time and money, Winn's support was disappointingly low. Immediately following the caucus vote, Winn, surprisingly, withdrew. The need for the September primary was thus obviated and Fuhr was the Republican nominee. Two grey-haired, native midwesterners were thus the major party nominees in the general election. Three minor party candidates were also on the ballot.

Observers have suggested that the nomination stage of the election process damaged Republican chances. Certainly, Winn's withdrawal lessened the potential of greater division but a somewhat divided party simply lessened the already slim possibilities of defeating a popular two-term incumbent. Also, vast campaign resources had been consumed in the nominating stage, particularly by the Winn campaign. Therefore, relatively few resources remained for the general election. Finally, partly as a result of the way the nomination process had developed, Fuhr was perceived as less moderate than he actually was. This perception seemed to lead numerous moderate Republicans away from their party's nominee.

The Democrats

Lamm's first formal presentation in the election year was his 1982 State-of-the-State message. In that message and other public statements shortly thereafter, Lamm stressed the need for the maintenance and improvement of the state's infrastructure, promotion of the right kind of growth, and public/private cooperation. He sought to portray himself, it seems, as the good steward and the prudent manager of a state blessed in its physical beauty and fortunate in its relative economic prosperity. To preserve the state's quality of life, Lamm called for continued planning. But in a state where the term, "planning," might have undesirable connotations, it was necessary to qualify and justify the concept. Thus, planning was discussed as a necessary, appropriate, and reasonable tool. Lamm quoted Peter Drucker, who said that "long range planning does not deal with future decisions but with the future of present decisions." Here and in other pronouncements Lamm projected a progressive, but not necessarily a liberal image, and adroitly combined liberal and conservative views consistent with state interests.

Evidence early in the election season indicated Lamm's popularity. A Denver Metro-area poll of January 31, 1982, conducted by the Denver Consulting Group and published in the Denver Post, found that about 68 percent of those polled perceived that Lamm was doing an "excellent" or "good" job. The poll noted a high regard for Lamm not only among fellow Democrats; 58.8 percent of self-identified Republicans rated Lamm's performance good or excellent. A similar poll of May 20 in the Denver Metro area found that 61.4 percent of those questioned rated Lamm's performance as good or excellent. This poll also showed that, matched against either Winn or Fuhr, Lamm was the overwhelming choice.

THE GENERAL ELECTION: THE CANDIDATES AND THEIR SUPPORT

The Lamm Candidacy

As the general election campaign began in earnest, Lamm had several distinct advantages. Public polls indicated high regard for his performance. Private polls, conducted for the

Governor's campaign by Peter Hart and campaign volunteers, indicated high (98 percent) name recognition and a generally "good feeling" about the incumbent Governor. In the words of one close Lamm associate, there was a high "comfort level" with their Governor among most Coloradans. The Lamm campaign strategy was to reinforce this feeling.

The Lamm campaign was well-organized. It drew on large numbers of volunteers, many of whom had not been involved in previous Lamm campaigns and worked fairly closely with the party organization. There was frequent consultation with the state party organization, and in many of the state's counties the party organization and the Lamm organization were virtually synonymous. While many close Lamm associates played leading roles, the campaign was not merely a personal effort.

Financial support was abundant and came from a wide array of groups. For example, the AFL-CIO Political Action Committee contributed over $10 thousand, and the Communications Workers of America contributed a similar amount. On the other hand, the business community also gave substantial support. For instance, one oil billionaire, a business partner of Lamm's campaign treasurer, gave $25 thousand; the campaign treasurer, a developer, also gave large contributions, as did fellow developers. Lamm received considerably more money, generally, and more large contributions in 1982 than he had in 1978, partly because he had stronger support in the business community in the latter election.

Lamm received the endorsement of most of the state's major newspapers. Lamm was said to have performed ably and to have studied carefully state problems and set an agenda to deal with them. A third term would allow Lamm to pursue that agenda and thus reap what he had sown. He was also praised as an able and ardent defender of the state in its relationship with the national government. His well-publicized disagreement with former President Carter over water projects was said to be indicative of his willingness to protect and defend state interests. An assertive stance toward the federal government is common in Colorado governors.

While Lamm's support, as has been suggested, was very broad-based, he did not receive the endorsement of several groups. First, leaders of several Chicano organizations urged fellow Chicanos not to support Lamm. This stance is traceable to several factors. On numerous occasions Lamm had contended that stricter federal laws were needed to stem the flow of immigrants to the United States, a position which annoyed many Chicano leaders. Mexican Americans were also dismayed that the Governor had allowed a bilingual education bill to become law without his signature. In the minds of these Chicano leaders, this law greatly diluted earlier state legislation. The Governor's assertion that his choices were limited to the diluted bill or to no bilingual program at all did not satisfy the group. Lamm was also criticized for having appointed too few Mexican Americans to administrative and advisory positions.

The Colorado Realtors PAC had contributed to but had not endorsed Lamm in 1978. This group endorsed Fuhr in 1982. They claimed that Lamm had snubbed them by not addressing the group's annual meeting for several years. Observers have suggested, however, that the primary reasons that the realtors PAC did not support Lamm were his stance on certain tax policies and his initiation of a set of planning guidelines for state agencies called the "Human Settlements Policies." Realtors argued that the policies stifled market forces and impeded growth. Republicans in the state legislature argued vehemently that the planning guidelines usurped legislative authority and were therefore unconstitutional. After a short time, and in response to the criticisms, Lamm rescinded the guidelines.

Finally, the Colorado Association of Public Employees was not entirely unified in its position and was critical of Lamm for several reasons. First, the Association contended that too often Lamm had appointed individuals from out of state to till important positions. Second, they were critical of the extent to which the Governor sought to use private contractors, rather than the state administrative apparatus, to accomplish tasks. Third, the Association criticized Lamm for his support of an amendment to the state constitution which would have allowed the governor more appointments and would thus have removed those positions from the civil service. Despite these criticisms and the position of the Association's leadership not to endorse Lamm, other members of the Association said that they disagreed with their leaders, and they supported Lamm.

Lamm's television ads sought to reinforce the Governor's favorable image. They showed the governor joyously jogging and enjoying the state's beauty and quality of life, and implied that the governor had helped maintain and secure this beauty and quality for the future. The commercials closed by suggesting that Lamm had created a "partnership with Colorado...let's keep it together."

The Republican Challenger

In contrast to the Lamm campaign, the Fuhr campaign had few strengths. Its major asset was the candidate himself, who was highly respected and well thought of. But Fuhr had not held public office for eight years and his low-key nomination effort had drawn relatively little public attention. He therefore suffered from low name recognition. To begin to match Lamm's name-recognition level and popularity would have required that Fuhr raise a vast amount of money. He was, however, unable to do so; in fact, Lamm outspent Fuhr by about two and one-half to one. Fuhr's relatively meager resources were provided primarily by Republican party organizations such as the state and national party. Not only were these resources insufficient, they also indicated the shallowness of Fuhr's support.

Because Fuhr had relatively little money, his ads were televised much less frequently than were Lamm's. The ads showing Fuhr, a veterinarian, ministering to man's best friend and shaking hands with people may have had their intended effect of making people feel good about the candidate. However, they had little ostensible effect in making people feel like voting for the candidate.

THE GENERAL ELECTION: ISSUES AND DEBATES

The backdrop of the election tended to enhance the already favorable Lamm position. The state had enjoyed low unemployment--about half the national average--and general economic prosperity for some time. While there were some indications that the national recession might lead to revenue shortfalls, that possibility did not play a major role in the campaign. It was not clear whether there might be such a shortfall, and if so, how large it might be. The possibility of such a shortfall was downplayed by Republican legislators as much as by anyone. Other potential contentious issues such as air pollution and rising crime seemed unimportant.

A series of debates were held around the state. In those debates Fuhr generally took the offensive and criticized Lamm on several grounds. Fuhr argued that Lamm had initiated several useful studies of state problems but had failed to act on those problems. This inability to act on problems, Fuhr contended, was the result of Lamm's lack of leadership. Lamm's approach to leadership was one of press releases and vetoes, said Fuhr. Another frequent criticism was that Lamm was not a good manager. Whatever the validity of this criticism, it seemed too nebulous to damage the Governor. Fuhr also criticized Lamm at various points for inattention to increasing unemployment, for not getting along as well as he might with the business community, and for neglecting the tourist industry. At other times he suggested that two terms were enough for one governor and that Lamm was establishing an "imperial governorship."

Lamm often simply ignored Fuhr's various criticisms and took a "high road" approach, seeking to appear thoughtful and even philosophical. Rather than an environmentalism and anti-business tone, Lamm stressed the need to continue policies that provided a "creative tension" between preservation and development and protected against economic boom and bust. In this way Lamm tempered and took the ideological edge off most of the issues. Lamm's response to criticism of his leadership was more direct, however.

Lamm pointed to what he argued were some important vetoes and asked whether, as governor, he, Fuhr, wouldn't have also vetoed bills which would have: repealed the mine reclamation act, delayed air pollution control, and allowed lobbyists to increase their spending. Fuhr's response to Lamm's specific question was equivocal. Fuhr asserted, however, that Lamm's rejoinder missed the main point: that proper leadership and greater skills of compromise would have obviated the need for vetoes in the first place. Fuhr's criticisms had little effect, however. In other instances where Fuhr contended that Lamm had not acted decisively on problems, Lamm was able to cite some proposal which, in most instances, had been blunted by the Republican legislature. Lamm contended that the problem had generally not been one of leadership, but of followership. In short, there were a few sparks in the campaign debates but none really exposed any major differences between the candidates nor generated great public interest in the election.

As the campaign progressed it became clear that Lamm would win re-election easily. A <u>Denver Post</u> poll of October 3 showed Lamm leading Fuhr 62 percent to 25 percent among those most likely to vote. That same poll showed that 80 percent of Democrats, 70 percent of the Independents, who outnumber major party identifiers in Colorado, and 43 percent of Republicans favored Lamm. A similar <u>Post</u> poll taken just two days before the election indicated some erosion in Lamm's support but most of that erosion went to the undecided ranks rather than to Fuhr and was the result of changes among Republicans and Independents. Lamm led by healthy margins in all five of the state's congressional districts.

THE ELECTION OUTCOMES

The election produced the landslide that had been predicted. Aided by a higher-than-expected voter turnout, Lamm won over 67 percent of the vote and carried all but five of the state's 63 counties. Most of those who had been undecided in the days just before the election apparently voted for Lamm. (See Table 1.) Examination of the results suggest that to the extent that Lamm lost support from the previous (1978) election, increased support from other groups more than compensated for those losses. For example, it appears that Lamm lost little support among Mexican Americans and that his stance on immigration, which led to criticisms from some Mexican American leaders, may have gained him support among other groups.

Table 1

<u>The Lamm Vote</u>

Year	Percent of Vote	Number of the 63 Counties Carried
1982	67.5	58
1978	58.7	46
1974	53.2	30

Other relevant election outcomes should also be noted. The incumbent state treasurer, a Democrat, was re-elected by a sizable majority. The secretary of state's and the attorney general's positions were both won by Republicans. The partisan makeup of the state legislature remained essentially the same with Republicans retaining control of both houses but falling short of a hoped-for veto-proof legislature. However, some of the most extreme and conservative Republican House members, who had often been among Lamm's major critics, had been defeated in their party's primaries. Despite Lamm's impressive victory, then, the overall results of the general election were mixed.

Another ballot issue was an amendment to the state constitution to abolish the "Governor's call." The "Governor's call" permitted the Governor to determine what issues, other than fiscal questions, the state legislature could consider in even-numbered years. This provision had been criticized by state legislators for some time as an inappropriate encroachment upon legislative authority. The campaign over this issue received little public attention and the Governor made no concerted effort to defeat the proposal. The Governor apparently felt that this provision did not make a great deal of sense constitutionally and that it had been as contentious as it had been beneficial from the standpoint of both formal and informal gubernatorial power. In any case, the Governor may have been too preoccupied with his own re-election to concern himself with a ballot issue. The ballot issue carried, and the Colorado governor can no longer determine the legislative agenda in alternate years.

THE (RE)-NEWED ADMINISTRATION

The day following the election, Lamm made the surprising announcement that State Treasurer Roy Romer had been appointed as his (Lamm's) chief of staff. That is, Romer would serve both in the Cabinet as the state treasurer, a position to which he had just been re-elected, and as Lamm's chief executive aide. Romer had served as Lamm's chief of staff in 1975-76 and had previously been a state legislator. A former political advisor would serve as deputy chief of staff in the new Lamm administration.

The stated reason for this arrangement was that it would help the Governor achieve a top priority: putting into place some of the suggestions made by a "blue ribbon" panel of businessmen and government officials who studied state problems for two years. Romer had been a co-chairman of that panel. Some political observers perceived the arrangement as an effort by Lamm to form a strong front among the three Democrats holding statewide office--himself, the Lieutenant Governor, and the Treasurer--as insulation against a new Republican attorney general and the secretary of state. The state legislature has Republican majorities in both houses and Romer's previous legislative experience and relationship might prove helpful here as well. One political analyst suggested that the new arrangement puts Romer in a stronger position to seek the governorship should he choose to do so at some future point.

This novel administrative arrangement was quickly criticized by the state Republican Party chairman who questioned its legality and appropriateness. The chairman argued that Lamm had misled voters in not announcing beforehand his intention to appoint the state treasurer as chief of staff, and questioned whether one person could adequately handle both positions. Romer's response was that the treasurer's position required knowledge and judgment, not time. Outside Republican Party circles this administrative approach does not seem to have raised many objections.

Romer relinquished the chief of staff responsibilities on December 1, 1983. He and other administration officials perceived that the chief of staff role too often required attention to relatively minor administrative matters and thus dissipated energies that might better be focused upon issues of larger and major importance. Romer remains a close advisor to Lamm and has concentrated on issues such as state education, growth and development, and transportation (especially in the Denver metropolitan area).

Other administrative changes followed Lamm's re-election. No fewer than seven cabinet officials and other aides resigned. Among the resignees were the directors of the Department of Natural Resources and the Department of Regulatory Agencies, the head of the Office of State Planning and Budgeting, and the chief executive assistant. Long service in state administration and a resulting desire to pursue other career opportunities, rather than dissatisfaction with their performance on Lamm's part, led to these resignations. In conversations with the deputy chief of staff, it was suggested that the new appointees may not have the same level of political experience or constituency base as did their predecessors; otherwise, their skills appear generally comparable.

THE NEW ADMINISTRATION'S AGENDA

The immediate task facing the new Lamm administration was how to deal with a looming budget deficit initially estimated at $102 million; later estimates placed the deficit at $120 million. After some bickering, agreement was reached on addressing the deficit problem. About half of the shortfall was made up through budget reductions and the remaining portions from transfers from state trust funds and some temporary tax increases. The budget projections for 1984 indicate a potential deficit of more than $40 million; Lamm has suggested the necessity of tax increases but the Republican legislature seems reluctant to support such action at this point. Beyond this immediate crisis, Lamm's perspectives and goals for the immediate and long-term future of the state are familiar.

Lamm, in his 1983 State-of-the-State address, discussed the extent and nature of the economic problems facing the state. He suggested that government "can and should play only a limited role in the creation of jobs," and that government should "work with the private sector to develop and promote an environment which will stimulate job creation in the state." He added that the "government role may be limited, but it is important" and that despite existing financial difficulties, a status quo budget would not do. There are, Lamm contended, numerous state responsibilities for such functions as education, law enforcement, and other facilities, which are "not bureaucratic luxuries" but public necessities that must be dealt with "in good times or bad."

Lamm also stressed the need to attend to the "new economy of Colorado," and proposed several activities. First, he discussed the growing importance of "high tech" in the state's present and future economy and called for the creation of an Advanced Technology Institute to encourage this development. Second, Lamm contended that the state needed considerable capital investment to meet its infrastructure needs. Colorado's infrastructure needs are, Lamm asserted, somewhat unique in that there is a need to replace or repair existing systems as well as for new construction to meet the demands of growth. Third, he argued that the state must provide other mechanisms "essential to the new economy." Lamm claimed that "proper control of hazardous wastes is the most critical environmental problem" facing the state, and he called for legislative action to provide state agencies with adequate authority to protect public health and the environment from the dangers of hazardous wastes as well as to ensure that the state's industries have adequate facilities to manage wastes properly.

Other items on Lamm's legislative agenda for the first year of his third term can be mentioned. Lamm reiterated the need for the establishment of a Department of Public Safety to deal with various organizational and substantive problems with the state's public safety policy. Other initiatives supported: health-care cost containment; a consumer advocate for the Public Utilities Commission; statutory authority for the Office of Energy Conservation; greater efforts to reduce air pollution; funding for an already authorized incentive pay system for state workers; and quick state ratification of a new Equal Rights Amendment should Congress initiate such an effort. Subsequent messages to the state legislature specified these in greater detail and suggested appropriate funding mechanisms. Those funding mechanisms generally stressed a "user fee" approach. A number of Lamm's proposals have subsequently enjoyed legislative success.

Lamm's inaugural address spoke to the various challenges facing the state, most of which already have been noted, and suggested that "the process of developing solutions must include at least four ingredients": cooperation; a need to examine basic assumptions; better skills and knowledge ("a renewed emphasis on education is required and must be geared to the future"); and hard work.

CONCLUSION

Lamm has been a popular governor by positively stressing the state's "quality of life" and by studying and proposing those efforts that are necessary to preserve that quality. He has been praised for his foresight but criticized for his lack of accomplishment. Perhaps both assessments are correct. However, in a state in which the chief executive is relatively weak in terms of formal powers and faces a rather strong state legislature, which has been dominated by the opposition party for most of Lamm's administration, the criticism for lack of accomplishment may need qualification. Lamm has not always been as diplomatic as he might have been in dealing with the state legislature. This is the result, one suspects, of frustration resulting from the tension between a progressive, if fiscally conservative, personality on the one hand, and the limited powers of the Colorado governor, particularly in budgetary matters, on the other. Lamm has thus often relied on his public visibility and popularity along with various task forces, blue ribbon panels and the like to establish and promote an agenda for state government. The apparent underlying assumption that more open processes and greater information and knowledge will lead to desirable outcomes and tangible legislative victories has not always been borne out. Considering the circumstances, however, the symbolic and substantive accomplishments are impressive.

Richard Lamm entered his third term with great popular support, a carefully developed agenda of unfinished and related new business, and what is likely to be a more agreeable state legislature with which to work. It therefore seems that Lamm, who has continuously denied any ambition to seek a United States Senate seat or other higher office, and his administration will have generally propitious circumstances in which to pursue their goals for the state of Colorado.

NOTES

This discussion is based on several sources:

1) Close monitoring of the <u>Denver Post</u> from January 1982 to March 1983;

2) Interviews with the Governor's present deputy chief of staff, David Miller, who formerly served as a speech writer and who was involved in the re-election campaign;

3) Interview with the executive assistant to the governor during Lamm's second term, John Lay;

4) Monitoring the Colorado Springs <u>Gazette Telegraph</u> from July to March 1983.

The author would like to thank Mr. Miller and Mr. Lay for their time and for sharing their insights. They are not, however, responsible for the interpretation presented in the paper; that is my own.

[1] See, Kathleen M. Beatty, "Colorado: Increasingly Unpredictable", <u>Social Science Journal</u> 18,3 (October 1981): 31-40.

[2] Candidates not receiving the minimal (20 percent) level of support can still be on the ballot but must do so through petition. The same applies to third parties unless the party received 10 percent of the vote in the previous election.

5. CONNECTICUT:

THE GOVERNOR FILLS HIS OWN SHOES

SARAH MCCALLY MOREHOUSE

I. THE POLITICAL CLIMATE

The cartoon which appeared in the Capitol newspaper depicts a triumphant Governor O'Neill easing into his comfortable slippers exclaiming, "This time I'm filling my own shoes." He was referring to the fact that he was elected to fill the shoes he inherited as lieutenant governor from Ella Grasso who died soon after she turned them over to him in December of 1980. The Governor's two-year incumbency formed the basis for the electoral calculations made by his political rivals as well as himself. His calculations were fortified by a strong Democratic party organization which he had cultivated for many years. This organization habitually backs a governor who wants to run. In addition, the state is "leaning Democratic," electing only one Republican governor in the last eight contests and maintaining an average 56 percent Democratic voting loyalty.

However, Governor O'Neill faced his first campaign for major office burdened by a series of problems that were partially a natural consequence of serving out the last two years of a two-term administration. He conceived of himself as a caretaker and did not try to alter the direction of spending or taxing. A grand jury investigation of the awarding of contracts within the Department of Transportation resulted in the resignation of the transportation commissioner appointed by Governor Grasso. The public perception of O'Neill's governorship was non-existent. He was apparently reluctant in the first year of his administration to try to turn press coverage to his advantage. All of these factors gave his rivals hope that they could beat him in the gubernatorial election. The Democrats were counting on the sluggish economy to remain stable and not take a turn for the worse. Connecticut's economy reacts to the national trends but at a slower rate and with buffers to moderate the peaks and troughs of economic cycles. Hence, the Connecticut economy was moving in a lateral direction and was not a major campaign issue.

The steady economy, however, hides many contrasts. The state remains number two in the nation on the per capita income list. Despite this indicator of wealth, more of its residents slipped below the poverty level in the last decade, bringing to 8 percent those who live in poverty.[1]

Even more surprising than the contrasts between the wealthy and poor in Connecticut is the way the state raises and spends it revenues. The second wealthiest state in terms of per capita income does not have an income tax! Instead, revenues are collected by means of twenty-nine different state taxes plus hundreds of fees. The sales and use tax brings in 35 percent of the state's revenues. The corporation tax brings in 11 percent more, a capital gains and dividends tax 6.2 percent, and a gasoline tax 4.8 percent. From there on, revenues are collected from a variety of sources.[2] Most of these taxes are regressive in that they take proportionately more from a poor person than a wealthy one.

States are often compared in terms of spending per capita. The second richest state in the nation is 26th in terms of state and local spending. Connecticut is 31st in terms of money spent on education, 41st in terms of spending for health and hospitals, 42nd in spending for highways. The state treats its poor more generously, rising to 13th place in welfare spending per capita.[3] This spending pattern reveals that with the exception of providing for its poor, which is none too generous, the people of Connecticut are content with frugality. But this frugality comes at a future high price.[4]

Federal aid cutbacks have compounded the state's problems. Budget balancing becomes harder each year. Connecticut's existing sales tax rates already rank among the highest in the nation. The 1982-1983 fiscal year was projected to end $62.3 million in the red, although this was not known until after the election. This made the fourth straight year of deficits. Connecticut was $40 million short in 1982, $66 million short in 1981, and $1 million behind in 1980.

Taxes were the biggest issue in Connecticut as the gubernatorial election began to heat up. Shrinking services, growing deficits, and regressive taxes all needed to be addressed by the candidates who threw their caps into the ring.

II. PARTY CONVENTIONS PICK THE NOMINEES

In Connecticut, the convention system remains strong and it is rare for a candidate for statewide office to be unseated in a primary election after winning the endorsement of a majority of the convention delegates. State law provides that the winner of the party endorsement may only be challenged in a primary by someone who receives 20 percent of the vote in the convention (on at least one ballot). The party norms against running in the primary are strong. Traditionally candidates at the convention make a commitment to abide by the endorsement if they should fail to get it. Only twice since the challenge primary system was installed in 1955 have these informal norms broken down. In 1978 the Democratic lieutenant governor challenged incumbent Governor Grasso; after barely winning 20 percent in the convention, he won one-third of the primary vote. In 1970, Thomas Meskill, the future governor, won a Republican primary by over 70 percent against a challenger. No candidate for any other state office had ever challenged the endorsee in either party until 1982 when there was a Democratic contest for secretary of the state which was won, not surprisingly, by the endorsee. Convention rules make it difficult for a challenger to get 20 percent, because they allow vote changing at the end of a ballot, and there are pressures to shift votes to the winner.

The endorsed candidate can count on money from state headquarters and from most of the town committees, plus man hours, telephone banks, and use of town party offices. It is, therefore, of the greatest advantage to receive the endorsement and the money and privileges which flow from it. And the endorsement is automatically bestowed upon an incumbent governor who wants to run.

A. The Democrats

For Governor O'Neill, the decision to run for a full four-year term had to await his recovery from double-bypass heart surgery which he had undergone in December of 1981. He had time to reflect on the first year and what he had accomplished as governor following the death of Ella Grasso. The state had been in the thick of yet another fiscal crisis. The legislature was unruly, unwilling to heed the wishes of a leader-by-circumstance, an unelected governor who had no mandate from the voters. Legislators were looking for ways to challenge the Governor for the 1982 election.

The Governor had never run independently outside of his East Hampton district from whence he emerged in 1967 to the state legislature. He was elected to serve as majority leader from 1975 to 1978. In addition to this he was Democratic state chairman for the same time period. An attempt by Governor Grasso to oust him as the state chairman failed in 1976. He had built a strong political base as he performed the dual functions of party chieftain and legislative leader. In 1978, he captured the Democratic nomination for lieutenant governor, proving that he had more clout than eight other contenders. After the Grasso-O'Neill ticket was victorious in 1978, he was the loyal soldier, staying in the shadows while the Governor basked in the limelight. All that changed when the Governor fell ill with cancer and resigned on December 31, 1980. Bill O'Neill suddenly became the head of the political power structure in the state.

In February 1982, his doctors gave him a clean bill of health and on March 5, O'Neill declared that he would seek election to his first full term. In an interview, the Governor described his course of action:

> I had a lot of political connections within the party structure, and that's immediately what I attempted to take advantage of. They responded very, very well. I started immediately by making the announcement and inviting people to the residence for the announcement, which was a good place to do it because of the prestige (I think) of the governor's residence. The party organization, which is the Democratic State Central Committee--They were all invited. Then the Democratic chairman in each and every one of the towns and the vice-chairman--They were invited. The mayors and the select men of the Democratic Party and the Democratic legislators, of which, of course, I had been one for twelve years. So I had a built-in constituency within the Democratic Party and that's really who I attempted to appeal to immediately for the nomination. That was successful.[5]

The challenge within the Governor's own party came from the Speaker of the House, Ernest Abate. Abate admitted that he did not have the political organization backing. He did not even consult the state party chairman. Abate knew that he could never get a majority of the votes in the Convention, so he took a long shot and tried to get the twenty percent needed to challenge the Governor in a primary. "If I could get by the twenty percent, I believed I could win the primary. The polls told me that Bill O'Neill's public support is--was then, is now--very shallow, that people are indifferent about Bill O'Neill. I felt I had enough commitments for substantial financial contributions, campaign contributions, that I could have gotten into the kind of high exposure media campaign that I wanted to get into. And I think it would have made a difference. I believe I could have won the primary.[6]

Abate's strategy was to challenge the Governor openly, hoping to get the maximum publicity out of each charge. He hoped to win the 260 delegates necessary by proving himself in command of the issues. He attempted to discredit the Governor and his administration and to link them with mismanagement, abuse of office, and alleged illegal handling of funds. Abate charged that O'Neill had diverted $28 million in federal reimbursement funds from the state's general fund to a "discretionary" category over which he alone had control. He cited indications that the money went to pay consulting contracts in the State Department of Transportation, which was under investigation by the Office of Chief State's Attorney for alleged corruption. O'Neill's strategy was to deny his challenger any debates, joint appearances, or gubernatorial platforms from which to build the statewide recognition factor he so badly needed. The object was to neutralize Abate.

The strategy succeeded. The Democratic convention held on July 16-17 gave Abate only 14 percent of the delegate's votes. The party organization controlled the organization and leadership. When it was clear that the Governor had the votes to stop a challenge, they allowed Abate to second his own nomination as a means of addressing the assembled delegates prior to the first ballot. It was an extremely well-received address, but it did not change the vote of any delegates. After spending $295,000 on his challenge, Abate was prevented from going any further. Abate lost the challenge due to one of the oldest unwritten laws of politics: It is nearly impossible to successfully challenge an incumbent governor who has made no major errors.

B. The Republicans

Republican State Conventions have been less tightly controlled over the last twenty-five years, rarely awarding the endorsement by more than 70 percent of the vote. The 1982 nominating contest was no exception, with four contenders in the field for nearly a year before the Convention. The contenders were all state senators with varying degrees of party experience. They did not attack each other personally as the contest for delegates proceeded. Each hoped that he could sway to his side more easily those committed to another if he did not attack their camp and solidify their loyalties.

Lewis B. Rome started his career in politics as Mayor of Bloomfield in 1965 from whence he was elected to the state senate, becoming majority leader in 1973. In 1978 as minority leader, he sought the party's gubernatorial nomination, but fell short in the convention to a Congressman, who was backed by the party chairman, Frederick Biebel. Under pressure from Biebel and other party leaders, Rome reluctantly agreed to abandon a primary fight and take second place on what Biebel dubbed the Republican "dream ticket." The Sarasin-Rome team was buried in a landslide for Governor Ella Grasso (41 percent to 59 percent).

Rome did not decide to run for governor until September of 1981, several months after his opponents for the nomination had been building their campaign organizations. He said he was pressured by party leaders to run. He was the candidate quietly favored by the state party leadership and was eventually backed openly by the party chairman a week before the Convention. Rome thinks of himself as a healer in the party. He says he tries to follow a middle course between Lowell Weicker and Fred Biebel, leaders of two strong personal factions.[7]

The other major contender for the nomination, Richard Bozzuto, was also a state senator and had been minority leader 1979-1981. He sought the U.S. Senate nomination in 1980 but lost to James L. Buckley, a former senator from New York, by only seven votes at the convention. He challenged in the primary and was solidly beaten. He was not favored by the party leaders, and in fact, it may have been his growing momentum for the nomination which prompted them to pressure Lewis Rome to run. While Rome is a reserved team player, Bozzuto is a gusty protagonist. Bozzuto hurled himself into the race, set up a superior organization and spent over $500,000 in the attempt to capture the endorsement. (This was over $200,000 more than Rome, the eventual winner.) Severin/Aviles was his pollster and he spent $46,000 sampling the electorate. One of his strategies was to use extensive radio and newspaper advertising in February and March.

Buzzuto had plans to rebuild the Republican party, claiming that it was the "minority" party in the state insofar as there were many more Democrats and self-styled Independents. He said that the present leadership represented a clique who had been in power for twenty years or more and for whom elite control meant more than winning elections. "Party control of the state is not important because they always maintain good contacts with Democrats as well. So they can manage to have their needs attended to by Democrats or Republicans, so it doesn't make any difference who has dominant control over the state."[8]

Two other senators ran for the endorsement. Russell (Rusty) L. Post hired a Washington Campaign Planning firm to assess his chances for the governorship and to draw up a plan to achieve it. The 200-page game plan was delivered July 1, 1981, and Post set about following its dictates. After eight months he had garnered only 20 or so delegates out of the 933 who were to attend the convention and withdrew on July 16 leaving the race to the three remaining contenders. An articulate legislator who is best known for his support of the bottle bill, Post had a patrician manner, a Yale establishment mein that he counted on parlaying into support in Fairfield County. However, contributions to his campaign had slowed to a trickle in the second quarter of the year.

In one sense, Gerald Labriola, the friendly baby doctor, played the most crucial role of all. He held the balance of power, and eventually threw the endorsement to Lewis Rome. However, this is not the role that Dr. Labriola intended to play. Originally his strategy was to win the necessary 20 percent of the delegates in order to challenge in a primary. When he realized, shortly before the convention, that he would not receive that percentage, his strategy changed to that of deadlocking--holding the balance of power by preventing either of the two frontrunners from receiving 50 percent until he became the compromise candidate, second choice of a majority. Labriola's calculations may have been appropriate for other state systems, but not Connecticut, where power comes from experience and apprenticeship in the party. Labriola claimed his appeal lay in the fact that he was a "fresh face," "not the usual politician," a doctor who would take good care of the state. Apparently being chosen Freshman Senator of the Year in his first term did not give him the clout he needed to deadlock the Convention, and his supporters left for one or the other of the major contestants.

As the day of the Convention approached, both Rome and Bozzuto claimed that they had the necessary votes to win the endorsement on the first ballot. There was a skirmish over the choice of chairman, with both candidates accepting a compromise; the chairman, however, had openly backed Rome. Bozzuto apparently wanted to avoid a procedural defeat on the floor of the Convention. The Rules Committee voted to have the candidates nominated in the order determined by drawing lots. This also went against Bozzuto who lost the draw.

On the first roll call, for which each of the 933 delegates stood in front of a mike and reported his or her choice, the count was Rome 414 (44 percent), Bozzuto 392 (42 percent), and Labriola 122 (13 percent). The balloting had taken over three hours. Under the Convention's rules, delegates can switch their votes before the closing of a ballot. Labriola's supporters began to switch to either Rome or Bozzuto. The 6 Labriola delegates from Waterbury switched to Bozzuto, the choice of the rest of the delegation. At that moment, Labriola entered the Hall and released his delegates, saying, however, that he favored Rome. His delegates divided, with approximately 70 going to Rome and 50 to Bozzuto. Hence the final vote was close: Rome garnered 52 percent and Bozzuto 48 percent. It was no surprise that Labriola consented to run as lieutenant governor. A Rome-Labriola alliance had been rumored for months before the convention, but was strenuously denied by Labriola himself. The remainder of the underticket was chosen by the endorsee, as is customary in the Republican party. Extending an olive branch, Rome asked Bozzuto to select the candidate for attorney general. These choices are, of course, ratified by the Convention.

The question that remained, as the delegates packed up and went home, was the possibility of a primary challenge by Bozzuto. For two weeks the answer hung in the balance. Traditionally, the convention choices are not challenged. Bozzuto had a hard decision to make, since he came so close to winning. In weighing his chances, he had his 1980 U.S. Senator primary defeat to consider as well as sizable campaign debt. He had spent much more than his opponents for the nomination, and his final campaign finance report (December 31, 1983) showed that he was $113,000 out of pocket for the campaign. On August 5, Bozzuto announced that he would not contest the primary. He said it was a personal choice. Both Republican Congressmen as well as Senator Weicker endorsed Rome. Again, this action is customary in Connecticut where a party endorsement is taken seriously. Thus the gubernatorial campaign began without a primary for the head of the ticket in either party.

III. THE CAMPAIGN

Both gubernatorial candidates were bland team players, quiet, reserved political veterans of the state legislature, and persuaders and conciliators rather than flamboyant innovators. The polls indicated at the start that the Governor had a sizable lead over Lewis Rome. The O'Neill strategy was to run a low-keyed campaign and hope incumbency and traditional partisan advantage would carry him into office. (Of the 1,644,498 registered voters, the breakdown is 40 percent-D, 27 percent-R, and 33 percent unaffiliated.) This turned out to be a successful game plan; Governor O'Neill campaigned as little as possible and maintained a low profile. Lewis Rome could never convince the voters that there was need for a change in administration.

A. Organization

Both candidates chose good friends with political experience as directors of their campaigns. For O'Neill, the friends stemmed from 1967 when they found themselves in the state legislature for the first time. George W. Hannon, John D. Mahaney, and William O'Neill were all from working-class families when they took seats in the House of Representatives. James A. Wade, counsel to the House Democrats and a Yale-educated lawyer, joined them. The four Irishmen have worked together on many a campaign since. Wade directed the Governor's campaign, Hannon raised the money, and Mahaney was a part-time adviser. The lines between their operation and the Governor's office were blurred. O'Neill used his office staff, for example, to prepare for the first gubernatorial debate and his key aides were all there to cheer him on. Several members of the Governor's staff traveled with him as he hit the campaign trail, including the chief of staff, a hold-over from Ella Grasso, as well as his press secretary.

For Rome, it was another triumverate. Ed Simpson, Joe Burns, and Jo McKenzie have been Republican party stalwarts since they worked on Governor Thomas Meskill's campaign in 1970. Since a Republican governor has not won since, they were all the more determined this time. Before the Convention they garnered delegates for their candidate. After the convention they devised the broad strategy and helped raise the money. Simpson had worked on Rome's 1978 campaigns for governor and lieutenant governor, and was closest to Rome. Burns was chairman of the Ford for President campaign and became head of Rome's strategy committee. Jo McKenzie was formerly state party chairman. Carl A. Cella was the actual day-to-day manager of the campaign.

The size of the campaign staffs differed. O'Neill hired only four and his payroll was about $1,400 per week. Rome's payroll amounted to about $3,000 per week. Not all of that difference can be attributed to O'Neill's gubernatorial staff help. The Governor chose to spend more money on media, spending $602,261 for coverage to Rome's $414,433, and $97,100 on polling to his opponent's $18,500.

B. Money

The incumbency factor played a large role in terms of raising money for the Governor's campaign. James A. Wade said that some 4,000 individuals and PACs contributed. O'Neill raised his money in large measure through 125 small cocktail parties where donations were under $500 apiece. These parties were given by supporters and state officials and attracted an average of 150 people. They proved to be both financially and politically successful, and they fitted O'Neill's style of person-to-person contact. In addition, many of those on O'Neill's contributor list were state commissioners. State contractors also appeared on the list, proving the well-known hypothesis that it is easier for an incumbent to raise money because of the potential contacts and appointments he has. Rome charged that state officials were pressuring builders, architects, and engineers to give to the O'Neill campaign.

The comparison between the amounts of money raised through party committees reveals that the Republicans had a great advantage. Rome received $113,500 from the State Central committee compared to O'Neill's $20,500. The U.S. Senate Republican committee also gave Rome $5,000. Labor PACs gave O'Neill somewhat more money than business PACs gave Rome ($27,250). However, O'Neill received a $5,000 contribution from insurance PACs, and received more local committee funds than did Rome ($73,994 to $55,744).

In terms of overall campaign spending incumbent Governor O'Neill only slightly outspent his Republican challenger Rome. Of the $2.2 million spent by the two partys' nominees, O'Neill spent 51.6 percent or about $1,150,000 to Rome's 48.4 percent or about $1,075,000.

The involvement and impact of national figures on the gubernatorial contest was minor. Because the race for the Senate between Lowell Weicker and Toby Moffett was more heated and a great deal more colorful, our two mild-mannered contestants for governor suffered in the shadows of the national figures chosen with the desires of the senate combatants in mind. Former Vice President Mondale and Senator Kennedy both came to Connecticut to stump for Toby Moffett. Since O'Neill is not of the liberal Democrat persuasion and did not need help in the race in his own backyard, his participation in the events was minimal. Howard Baker, Senate majority leader, came in October to a GOP fund-raising dinner and helped net $50,000 for the Rome campaigning. Vice President George Bush and Secretary of Commerce, Malcolm Baldridge, came to aid Rome's fund-raising efforts. Noticeably missing was the President himself.

C. Different Campaign Styles: The Incumbent and the Challenger

Lewis Rome accused the Governor of using a "Rose Garden strategy" by campaigning as little as possible. The Governor was busying himself cutting ribbons in housing projects around the state and hailing them as "something that government has done right." One typical Friday, O'Neill helped lay a cornerstone for a housing project for the elderly in Glastonbury, dedicated a similar project in Hamden, broke ground for a new high-technology company in Trumbull and announced plans for a new factory in Seymour. His announcement of the new plant, which was to employ 300 people, got a page-one banner in the local paper. When the state selected six cities for job-creating urban enterprise zones, it was the Governor, not the two legislators who initiated the program, who made the announcement.

Rome started the day about 4:00 a.m. and returned home at 10:00 p.m. He began by seeing off New York commuters at Fairfield County stations and greeting workers at factory gates. He invited reporters into his campaign van, accepting as many as showed up in the pre-dawn hours. He tried to compensate for the lack of money needed to bring him name recognition by his energy and coverage, particularly in Fairfield County where he needed a high turnout of Republicans to do well. But he also needed issues and confrontations. While he charged the O'Neill administration with corruption and incompetence, the Governor continued to cut ribbons and break ground.

D. Debates and Issues

O'Neill agreed to four debates to be held around the state. He insisted that they must be public forums, not television studio productions. Rome wanted as many debates as possible, and made a strong bid for six, one in each congressional district. He also wanted television debates that would gain the widest audience.

Rome looked forward to the debates because polls had shown that voters who knew both candidates preferred him. He hammered away at the scandal in the Department of Transportation. He cited errors by the State Department of Education in calculating the amount of aid due to school districts. O'Neill always answered that he had dealt with the problems by accentuating the positive. He cited jobs as the big issue—adding that Connecticut is in much better shape than the national average. He mentioned job retraining as a way to keep firms in the state. The Governor mentioned that he had brought about the reorganization of higher education and the modernization of Bradley International Airport. Stressing that Connecticut is a "darned good state," the Governor said he should be elected to keep it what it is.

The state's most enduring political issue, the income tax, was neutralized by both candidates because both promised not merely to oppose an income tax but to veto any bill establishing one. Yet, in each debate the income tax surfaced. Neither candidate faced up to the simple fact that there was a projected $200-million deficit in the budget for the 1983 fiscal year. (By spring, this gap had reached $250 million.) New taxes would be required. Neither Mr. O'Neill nor Mr. Rome proposed specific solutions.

E. The Media

As noted earlier, O'Neill outspent Lew Rome by nearly $200,000, or by a 6 to 4 ratio. Although Connecticut is a compact state, reaching all its voters, particularly by television, is difficult. Residents of Fairfield County watch New York television stations and the reception from the three major commercial television stations in Hartford and New Haven is poor. But, it costs too much to put campaign commercials on major New York stations (an aide said it would cost about $26,000 for one spot—ten times the cost in Connecticut). Because Lew Rome did not have that kind of money, he relied on local radio stations instead of

New York television to reach the voters in Fairfield County. In addition, he spent several days a week campaigning there because the area has a large proportion of Republican voters.

O'Neill's campaign message that the state was in good shape was simple and consistent. It ran through all his public appearances, his brochures, and his television and radio advertising. Occasionally, U.S. Senator Christopher Dodd or former Senator Abraham Ribicoff did the talking, emphasizing the same theme.

Rome sought to make mismanagement an issue in one of his commercials. Mr. Rome's integrity was stressed while arrests of former officials of the state's Department of Transportation rolled up the screen.

F. The Polls

While Carl Cella said on October 15 that Rome planned to spend $50,000 on polling, the total figure paid to Lance Terrance was more like $18,500. O'Neill spent nearly five times as much, paying $97,000 to Century Research. Both candidates referred to their polls frequently. O'Neill usually confirmed the independent polls taken by the University of Connecticut's Institute for Social Inquiry. Rome repeatedly said that the Courant-Connecticut Poll, as it was called, overstated the vote margin between the two.

Two New York Times Polls taken in early and late October, as well as four Courant-Connecticut Polls, were in essential agreement on the gubernatorial race. They predicted the incumbent would win by a substantial margin. (The two polls differed sharply at one point on the margin between Lowell Weicker and Toby Moffett for the U.S. Senate.) The Courant-Connecticut Polls taken between late July and late October showed O'Neill's strength "soft" but remarkably stable. Rome seemed unable to gain the public recognition needed to enable him to cut into the Governor's margin which remained in the 20 to 30 percentage range throughout the polls. When the last Connecticut Poll tried to locate that portion of the people likely to vote, the poll showed the same margin--the Governor 21 points ahead among the "most likely voters." Rome said his last polls showed that he had narrowed the gap to a "single digit" situation.

No matter how inaccurately the polls predicted the vote, they must have had an effect on the ability of Mr. Rome to raise funds. About two weeks before the election he said that he had found it much more difficult to raise money than he had anticipated. He had originally hoped to raise $1.5 million, and had to settle for $1 million. Because of this reduction he could not engage the "media blitz" over the New York television stations he had hoped would help him narrow the gap.

IV. THE VICTORY

When the votes were counted, the Governor beat the challenger by seven percent, 53.7 percent to 46.3 percent. Rome did better than the two previous Republican challengers, Steele and Sarasin, who had not reached 41 percent of the vote. Rome carried Fairfield County by 8,000 votes, not enough to give him the statewide lead he needed. The cities of Bridgeport, Norwalk, and Stamford went Democratic. Turnout was not quite as high as in the gubernatorial election four years before. A low turnout traditionally hurts Democrats as it probably hurt Toby Moffett who lost to Lowell Weicker by four percent. It did not have much effect on the Governor's contest. In fact the low turnout was probably a reflection of the low-key campaign. And the low-key campaign was deliberate.

The results proved that an incumbent governor who has not made major errors can count on being re-elected. Rome could not convince the voters there was need for change. While he said repeatedly that the spectacular Senate race kept him from getting the issues out in the open, there is no assurance that the results would have been any different. Although the last two U.S. Presidents, Gerald Ford and Jimmy Carter, had thrown out the notion of the advantage of incumbency in national politics, it is alive and well in Connecticut.

The 1982 elections test and confirm several hypotheses about political parties in strong party systems. The victory of Governor O'Neill can be interpreted as a party victory. The Governor said at the outset that he would go through the party apparatus, and that he would be successful because of it.

In strong party systems, the party leaders make pre-primary endorsements which are usually not challenged. This was true in Connecticut. The Governor had token opposition in the party convention and closed out a challenge in the primary. On the Republican side, Rome, the candidate favored by the party leaders, won the endorsement. Bozzuto, the other serious contender, did not challenge in a primary, claiming personal reasons, but he was advised to withdraw by the party leaders and he knew that they would aid the endorsee. As the hypotheses predicted, he did not challenge.

In both the Democratic and Republican races, the party aided its candidates. The incumbent party, however, had the advantage. The Governor was the central figure at 125 cocktail parties around the state, attended by Republicans as well as Democrats. Republican money went to his campaign treasury via these parties. Everywhere he went, the press followed. He announced building programs, cut ribbons, broke ground. The incumbent governor had the resources to win the election. This confirms the hypothesis that it is uncommon for an incumbent to lose.

There is an additional hypothesis which states that the coalition which helps elect a governor continues into the governing process and aids him in the fulfillment of his policy promises. This hypothesis remains to be tested.

V. PREPARING FOR THE NEXT TERM

A. Appointments

At an impromptu news conference in his capital office on the afternoon following the election, Governor O'Neill said he would ask for the resignations of all state workers in appointed positions.[10] The letters that were mailed out of the Governor's Office the next Monday requested resignations from 134 state commissioners, deputy commissioners, executive assistants, and members of the Governor's staff.[11]

The Governor said that he spoke to "only two or three people altogether" concerning the personnel decisions.[12] The person who figured most prominently was James A. Wade, his campaign manager and close friend. Also included were the other two friends who helped him run the campaign: George Hannon, fund raiser, and John D. Mahaney, advisor. The Governor did not consult General Assembly leaders nor Lieutenant Governor Joseph J. Fauliso. Surprisingly enough in such a politicized state, the Governor did not consult Democratic State Chairman, James M. Fitzgerald. This may have been because the recently exposed grand jury investigation of the awarding of contracts within the Department of Transportation contained testimony which affirmed that the chairman had requested consideration of engineers who had donated to the party. While this practice is not illegal, the Governor may have wanted to stay clear of the impending controversy.

After all of the requested resignations and all of the consultations, what were the results? They were in line with the Governor's traditional reluctance to make changes unless forced by circumstances. For 24 major cabinet positions, the scoreboard looks like this:

Grasso holdovers 12
O'Neill holdovers 4 (3 replacements: 1 forced resignation)
New appointments 6 (2 replacements: 4 forced resignations)
Board Appointees 2 (Education)
                    24

Of the ten appointments O'Neill made both before his election as well as after, only five were because he initiated a change in policy direction in the departments involved. After his election, O'Neill made only six new appointments, two of them (Insurance and Agriculture) replacing voluntary resignations. Two commissioners, of Income Maintenance (Welfare) and Human Resources, were asked to resign largely because they mismanaged a program providing fuel bill money.

The most significant new appointee was Stephen B. Heintz, a talented young administrator from the Office of Policy and Management, who was put in charge of the huge and troubled Income Maintenance Department. Five retiring commissioners were paid as consultants to assist the new commissioners as they took over their departments. For instance, Ronald E. Manning, whose resignation was accepted, contracted with the state to be paid $5,800 for an undetermined time period to help James Harris assume control of the Human Resources Department.

Several former legislators were chosen for deputy commissioner posts. The appointments mixed talents and politics. They revealed that the Governor felt most at home with loyal friends. Edwin X. "Doc" O'Dea, Waterbury's Democratic Town Chairman, willingly recounted the events that led to his appointment as State's Deputy Commissioner of Motor Vehicles. "'I became deputy commissioner for one reason--the governor wanted to recognize the city of Waterbury,' he said of his new $36,000 a-year position. 'We produced for him. We produced financially for him, and we produced votes for him,'"[13]

O'Neill eventually chose to retain most of the commissioners, deputies, and executive assistants appointed by his predecessor. Statistics from the state personnel office show O'Neill replaced only about one-third of the executive assistants and about a quarter of the agency heads and commissioners. "'Some people think I made a mistake, but I don't think so at all,' O'Neill said of his decision to keep so many Grasso holdovers. 'They've done a pretty darn good job in almost all instances. We didn't change political affiliations here; we just changed governors.'"[14]

B. Party

The Party that backed the Governor throughout his nominating campaign and right through the election with unquestioned loyalty came under a cloud during the last days of 1982. The statement of former Transportation Commissioner Arthur Powers to a state grand jury investigating the awarding of contracts raised questions about the relationship between the Democratic Party and the award of no-bid, multi-million-dollar engineering contracts in the state DOT. Powers said he received calls from many prominent Democrats including state party chairmen and aides to the Governor. The Governor took several steps to correct the situation. He told his executive aide and the Democratic chairman not to call DOT on behalf of engineers seeking state jobs. He called a news conference to announce the change in DOT's method of selecting and paying engineers.[15]

The Governor rewarded the party by giving it some of the proceeds from an inaugural fund raiser as well as a $25,000 surplus from the campaign.

It is surprising that George Hannon was not given the party chairmanship. Perhaps the cloud hanging over the party was not to his liking. Some speculated that he would be skillful in handling such issues as contracts and would take the heat off the Governor's aides. To date, Hannon is a fund raiser for the Democratic National Committee; James Wade is continuing as party counsel. James Fitzgerald, Grasso's choice, is still party chief.

As of March 31, 1983, the Democratic fund-raising machine was chugging on unhindered. The flow of money from consulting firms continued unabated in spite of the fact that new Department of Transportation procedures have effectively curtailed the amount of work any firm can receive and despite the Governor's claims that he has depoliticized the process.

C. The Inaugural Address

The Governor was escorted to the swearing-in by more than 300 members of the Foot Guard and Horse Guard. His inaugural address sparked little debate. With the budget for the current fiscal year running $46.5 million in the red instead of in the black as he had promised and a $200-million shortfall for the next year, O'Neill blamed the state's fiscal problems on the national economy. He pledged to keep a tight rein on spending while saying as he had before that tax increases were inevitable. He repeated campaign pledges to provide a $17-million economic development program to promote high-technology businesses and to allocate $30 million in borrowed money to assist housing development. He noted that he was creating a task force to study the state's infrastructure—roads, bridges, buildings, and dams. He promised legislation dealing with the disposal of solid wastes. Senate Majority Leader Richard Schneller said that the Governor dealt with all the major issues except one: Where do we get the money?

A. The Governor's Budget and Tax Package

The major problems Connecticut faced had not been addressed during the election campaign. Shrinking services, growing deficits, and regressive taxes remained on the agenda. The Governor had promised that he would not propose an income tax and that he would veto it if the legislature passed one. The budget and tax package were due on February 9.

The Governor had an ally in the Bipartisan Commission on State Tax Revenue and Related Fiscal Policy. The Commission was appointed by the Governor and the legislative leaders in March 1982 to make a study of present and alternative revenue systems for the state and to report back on January 1. The Commission's Final Report was good news for the Governor because the principal recommendation was to extend the 7.5-percent sales tax to cover several areas previously exempt.

The Commission was sharply divided, however; and seriously considered the personal income tax coupled with reductions in other taxes. A minority report entitled "Dissenting View: Fairness for the Eighties" was signed by ten members.

If Governor O'Neill had an ally in the Commission, he had a trusted and highly competent aide in his chief fiscal advisor, Anthony V. Milano who serves as head of the Office of Policy and Management, a staff agency reporting directly to the Governor. Milano was on the Bipartisan Commission and hence had an insider's view of its deliberations.

On February 9, the Governor presented a $3.57-billion state budget that recommended extending the state sales tax to gasoline, professional and personal services, children's clothing, meals under $1.00, and fertilizer and seed bought for non-farm use, and imposing a new tax on interest income. The $277.9 million to be raised thereby was needed to eliminate the projected deficit in the 1982 fiscal year and finance the spending increases for the 1983-1984 budget. On the spending side, there was an increase of 10.7 percent over the 1982 spending levels, the biggest single increases to pay for state employee salaries and benefits and Medicaid and education grants. The most controversial pullback came in the Guaranteed Tax Base grant, the state's biggest aid-to-education program. GTB was projected to grow by about $90 million, but O'Neill included only a $13-million increase.

B. The Legislative Reaction

In Connecticut, party cohesion in the legislature remains high. In 1975-1976, over 60 percent of the roll calls produced cohesion levels above 80 percent for both parties in the House. In the Senate, the parties were internally more divided: The Democrats scored 47 percent and the Republicans 56 percent on the same measure of cohesion. For the same time period, the percentage of party votes (a majority of voting Democrats taking a stand against a majority of voting Republicans)$_{16}$was 73 percent in the House and 59 percent in the Senate. The party caucus is a major instrument of leadership. The Governor had comfortable majorities in both chambers (House: 88-D; 63-R. Senate: 23-D; 13-R).

Achieving party unity among the Democrats over the tax package proved difficult. Democratic Party leaders in both chambers favored tax reform, including a personal income tax. Richard Schneller, Senate majority leader, was placed in the position of having to support his governor on the patchwork tax extension program even though he opposed it. The President Pro Tempore of the Senate was also an advocate of the income tax. On the House side of the Capital, the Speaker, Irving Stolberg, as well as the chairman of the finance committee, favored the income tax. The majority leader and his deputy favored the Governor's program. It was estimated that 13 to 15 of the Senate Democrats as well as 50 to 60 House Democrats wanted an income tax. The leaders promised to try to get the tax package passed by April 1 in order to help balance the 1982 budget before the next fiscal year.

In view of the divisions within the Democratic Party, it was not surprising that progress on the budget was exceedingly slow. The Governor was accused of remaining aloof. He only met with the legislative leaders twice in March to promote his tax program. As the session progressed toward a June 8 deadline, he made it clear that he would not budge on the income tax question. At an agonizingly slow pace the General Assembly ground out two tax packages that raised revenues for the deficit in 1982 as well as spending increases for 1983-1984 and a budget of $3.6 billion.

In the end, the Governor got what he asked for. Furthermore, he achieved his budget and tax program with well over 80-percent support from his party in both the House and Senate. Only toward the end of the session did he enter the process and "thump the table."

The state has yet another package of patchwork taxes, depending primarily on the regressive sales tax. Another budget has passed and the same problems remain: shrinking services, growing deficits, and regressive taxes.

VI. The Impact of the Election on the Governor's Administration

The people of Connecticut expect the political parties to take the lead in nominating, electing, and governing. When Governor O'Neill invited all Democratic office holders and party leaders to the Governor's Mansion to announce his bid for the nomination, he assumed that the party would back his nomination and election. His opponent Lewis Rome, backed by the Republican leaders, was able to prevent a challenge to his own nomination by a close rival.

In the election campaign, each candidate chose political organizers who had managed campaigns before or who were associated with the party. Each was given money by his respective party. After the campaign, each sponsored a fund raiser to put money back into the party coffers.

The financial advantages of incumbency were obvious by an examination of the Governor's campaign finance statements. State commissioners as well as contractors doing business with the state appeared on the lists. It is doubtful whether any reform will change the way the political game is played in Connecticut. Contractors will continue to give to the party and most of them will eventually receive contracts. No exact link can be determined between these two events. Commissioners will continue to give to the campaign of their governor. There is nothing that prevents individual donations, nor the ability of the governor to scrutinize those gifts. A strong party needs money, and those who give the most expect something in return.

Because the party is strong, legislators are expected to go along with the program of the governor. His support is useful to them upon occasion and his opposition relegates them to the back bench. The budget of the Governor was put to the test and survived a challenge from the liberal wing of the party which wanted an income tax. This wing could have deadlocked the Governor's party. The Governor has been criticized for not meeting regularly with the leaders as well as the rank and file legislators in caucus. When the Governor finally tried a new type of collegial decision making with the income tax liberals, they came around to support his tax package. Thus party loyalty can still be garnered in this state. Occasionally it is reinforced by threatening to eliminate projects which will benefit legislators' districts, although this heavy-handed approach is used sparingly.

After all the shouting was over in Hartford, one ponders how far removed from the desires of the people are their decision makers. Was public opinion clear on the major issues that so troubled the legislator? Were there clear messages from the citizens on the matter of taxation? A poll conducted by the Institute for Social Inquiry at the University of Connecticut addressed itself to taxes and the state budget. Presented with the statement, "We would be better off if Connecticut had an income tax and other taxes were reduced," the sample split: 43 percent agreed and 47 percent disagreed.[17]

Thus the struggle in which the Governor and the legislature were enmeshed, was reflective of the populace. The Governor reflected the 47 percent of the population who disliked the income tax. The leadership in the legislature mirrored the 43 percent who considered it a better bet than the present structure. The electorate could not give a clear message--it was not surprising that their elected representatives could not agree. In the end, the compromise that was reached was worked out within the Governor's party after agonizing hours of negotiating with the income tax proponents and the budget cutters. The fact that this compromise was accomplished speaks to the ability of the Connecticut party to build coalitions in the electing and governing process.

NOTES

[1] Richard L. Madden, "Census Report Shows Increase in State Poverty," <u>New York Times</u>, 12 December 1982, sec. 11, p. 1.

[2] State of Connecticut, <u>Economic Report of the Governor: 1982-1983</u>, p. 97.

[3] These statistics were for 1980 and were taken from: Council of State Governments, <u>The Book of the States: 1982-1983</u>, 24 (Lexington, Kentucky: 1982), Table 8, p. 366.

[4] "The Crisis is Here," <u>Hartford Courant</u>, 20 March 1983, sec. B, p. 2.

[5] Interview with Governor William O'Neill, December 13, 1982, State Capitol, <u>Transcript</u>, pp. 2-3.

[6] Interview with Ernest Abate, July 21, 1982, Law Office, Stamford, CT, <u>Transcript</u>, pp. 10-11.

[7] Interview with Lewis Rome, July 15, 1982, at his Law Office in Bloomfield, CT.

[8] Interview with Richard Buzzuto, July 13, 1982, at BSD Insurance, Waterbury. <u>Transcript</u>, p. 6.

[9] Marc Gunther and Larry Williams, "O'Neill Leads Rome in Campaign Funds," <u>Hartford Courant</u>, 15 October 1982, sec. A, pp. 1 and 12.

[10] Matthew L. Wald, "O'Neill, Having Won Top Post on His Own, Expects to Make Changes in Connecticut," <u>New York Times</u>, 4 November 1982, sec. B, p. 16.

[11] Richard L. Madden, "O'Neill Stresses He Is In Charge," <u>New York Times</u>, 14 November 1982, sec. 11, p. 1.

[12] Larry Williams, "Governor Accepts More Resignations," <u>The Hartford Courant</u>, 23 November 1982, sec. A, p. 10.

[13] Barbara T. Roessner, "Patronage a Handy Way to Pay Political Debts," <u>Hartford Courant</u>, 9 May 1983, sec. A, p. 1.

[14] Ibid., sec. A, p. 11.

[15] Clifford Teutsch, "O'Neill Forbids Calls to DOT," <u>Hartford Courant</u>, 4 January 1983, sec. A, p. 1.

[16] Wayne R. Swanson, *Lawmaking in Connecticut: The General Assembly* (New London: Connecticut College, 1978), p. 36.

[17] Connecticut Poll #31, (March 13, 1983) Institute for Social Inquiry, University of Connecticut.

6. THE INCUMBENT WINS: THE POLITICS OF GUBERNATORIAL RE-ELECTION IN FLORIDA

RICHARD K. SCHER

On election day, November 2, 1982, Governor Bob Graham won an overwhelming victory over his Republican opponent, and by so doing remained chief executive of Florida for a second four-year term. Graham was only the third Florida governor to retain his incumbency. Until the late 1960s Florida governors were unable to succeed themselves because of a constitutional prohibition. However, in 1956 LeRoy Collins won a four-year term following a special election two years earlier: He was the first to succeed himself. Reubin Askew next accomplished this feat in 1974 against weak Republican opposition. But in 1966 Haydon Burns, who also had to run in a special election, and Republican Claude Kirk, who sought re-election in 1970, both failed in their attempts.

Florida, then, has had limited experience with governors who succeeded themselves. It may be that in the future two-term governors will become the norm in this state, but the history of the office indicates that it has had something of a revolving-door quality. Floridians have been accustomed to watching governors come and go, and indeed one of the favorite pastimes of political pundits has been to watch the parade of candidates waiting to succeed the most recent lame duck.

The consequences of this kind of gubernatorial politics have been serious for the state. It has hindered continuity in policy development and underscored the fragmented character of state politics generally. Most important, it has not permitted governors to have a second chance to correct errors or redirect their priorities to provide more effective leadership. Most administrations were, essentially, unique moments in time, divorced from those coming before and those following. Bob Graham, in contrast to most of his predecessors, had an opportunity to examine, evaluate, and, where needed, fine-tune his administration. This chapter examines Graham's first administration, and assesses the impact that it and his second campaign had on planning for and beginning his second term.

THE GOVERNOR'S OFFICE IN FLORIDA

From a purely structural standpoint, the office of governor in Florida must be considered relatively weak. Schlesinger originally ranked it forty-seventh among the states in his survey, but there have been some changes in recent years that have strengthened it, one of which permits two successive four-year terms. In a recent update of the ranking, Florida's governorship now ranks about midway among all the states in terms of its formal powers. Nonetheless, it must be said that any Florida governor wishing to provide strong leadership has an uphill battle, and cannot rely on the attributes of the office to help him very much. Analysis of the office, based solely on structural considerations, can of course be very misleading. However, Florida has had only a few strong governors in the twentieth century. They were remarkable men whose talents and capabilities enabled them to transcend the liabilities of the office. Most have not been able to do so.[1]

Space does not permit a full discussion of the problems facing anyone wishing to occupy the Florida governorship.[2] Four matters are so important, however, that they deserve at least brief consideration. The first involves election in a very fragmented political system. The traditional problem for the would-be governor has been identifying a constituency. Localism and sectionalism have acted to prevent establishment of a statewide coalition: For example, a successful campaign aimed at uniting Florida's diverse urban centers was not mounted until 1956, when LeRoy Collins managed it. Indeed, given the normally crowded field in gubernatorial primaries, the major task of the candidate was simply insuring that he could make the run-off. But creating a faction and an organizational structure strong enough to do this in a disorganized political system was generally problematic.[3]

A second major difficulty confronting the successful gubernatorial candidate was simply learning how to be governor. In spite of the regular turnover in the office, Florida never established any real structures or mechanisms to aid in the transition process. Indeed, the usual pattern was that incumbent governors stepped aside for and stayed out of the way of the incoming occupant. Most governors apparently felt that it was inappropriate for them to try to influence in any way what their successor would do.[4] There was, then, in general, only the most minimal communication between outgoing and incoming governors, and in cases of personal or political animosity between them, sometimes there was none.

As a result, Florida governors had no way to prepare for the job; they had to learn while in office. Moreover, with a four-year term, and for much of this century only two regular legislative sessions during their tenure, mistakes could be costly. Also, many incoming Florida governors knew very little about the actual mechanics of the governorship. Only Park Trammell (1913-1917) had occupied a state executive position before his inauguration, which gave him some prior knowledge. Almost universally, governors expressed amazement at the number, variety, and complexity of the tasks that faced them upon assuming office. But with no transition machinery, there was virtually no way for them to know what awaited them. For example, when Bob Graham began organizing his first administration in 1978, he and his aides had a plan for setting up the office. What they discovered, however, was that there was not even a manual or guidebook available in the Capitol for discussing matters such as correspondence, legislative relations, appointments, and so forth. Essentially, they had to proceed in the dark.

A third problem awaiting the governor has been the weight of the political culture and tradition of the state. While there are many aspects of this problem that have affected governors, perhaps the most important is that which tended to limit strong leadership and centralization of authority. We will see in a moment how this aspect became institutionalized in the Cabinet system. On a more abstract, but no less real, level, Floridians have not been sympathetic to the idea of strong gubernatorial leadership. Whether this lack of sympathy was a result of a reaction to the constitution of 1868 (which provided during Reconstruction for a very powerful governor), the development of public attitudes and beliefs favoring a "rugged individualism" philosophy and <u>laissez-faire</u> political/ economic ideology, or something else, is not clear. But the tradition militating against strong leadership has been felt in the governor's office, especially by those few incumbents who wished to use the office to lead the state forward. Indeed, most of those who tried actually found that their popularity declined significantly while in office, and they ended their tenure as lonely men. Many of the more popular governors just accepted the traditional, relatively low-key, essentially managerial role of governor, and did not bring an activist, policy-oriented stance to the office.[5]

Floridians' desire to avoid a strong executive was actually built into the structure of state government in the form of the Cabinet. It has actually been an extreme form of a divided executive, and it is the fourth major problem confronting the governor in Florida. The Cabinet has consisted of the governor, attorney general, secretary of state, comptroller, treasurer, commissioner of agriculture, and superintendent of public instruction (later called commissioner of education). This structure is different from cabinets in other states, however, because it has performed in a variety of ways as a collegial board or decision-making unit. For example, until 1967 it served as a state budget commission; it continues to act as a parole board and state board of education, among others. Very importantly, governors have been only one of seven members. They have not always been able to dominate the Cabinet. Moreover, even while governors could not succeed themselves in office, members of the Cabinet could. Thus, a number of Cabinet members literally spent decades on it, creating their own independent constituencies and fiefdoms. While the Cabinet did not always oppose governors, it did have the effect of limiting gubernatorial control over important areas of state politics. It also underscored the balkanization of the state's politics at the very highest levels of state government. Combined with the other problems facing the Florida governor, the Cabinet structure served to limit, especially in administrative terms, his effectiveness.[6]

THE FIRST GRAHAM ADMINISTRATION

Bob Graham surprised a number of observers of Florida politics by winning the governorship on his first attempt. His father, Ernest Graham, had sought the office in 1944 after a distinguished career in the Florida Senate, but had not been successful. Bob Graham served ten years in the Florida legislature (four in the House, six in the Senate), and established, by Florida standards, something of a reputation as a progressivist/ liberal. He was particularly regarded as a friend of education, and although his economic philosophy was essentially conservative, he favored tax reform and delivery of more effective and comprehensive social and other state services for citizens. He was also considered "friendly" towards civil rights issues.

When Graham decided to enter the Democratic gubernatorial primary in 1978, he had to confront a number of other political heavyweights, including Robert Shevin, the state attorney general; Bruce Smathers, secretary of state and son of former U.S. Senator George Smathers; Hans Tanzler, mayor of Jacksonville; Jim Williams, lieutenant governor in the second Askew administration; and former governor Claude Kirk, who switched parties to run as a Democrat. Graham essentially had two problems in his candidacy: name recognition, and a reputation as a wealthy young man who knew relatively little about the problems of "everyday" people in the state. To counter these difficulties, Graham campaign strategists designed a series of "workdays," in which Graham actually took such unglamorous jobs as bellhop, waiter, steelworker, and hospital orderly. It was a gimmicky but effective idea; he received widespread media coverage, and apparently many Floridians believed the workdays to be a serious attempt to learn about the state and its people (Graham even continued to schedule the workdays during his first administration).[7]

The primary and runoff proved to be a slugfest between Graham and Shevin; it was the first time in Florida history that two candidates from the urban, southern portion of the state had squared off. Shevin actually was first in the initial primary with thirty-five percent of the vote, and Graham received twenty-five percent. However, the stridency and negative tone of Shevin's campaign ultimately hurt him. Graham, moreover, was seemingly the only candidate willing to discuss issues, especially tax reform (in general, all the candidates were agreed on economic development, budget restraint, and a tough stance against crime). His image as an intelligent, youthful, vigorous man also helped, and he handily defeated Shevin in the runoff with fifty-four percent of the vote. In the general election Graham easily won over Republican drugstore magnate Jack Eckerd, with fifty-six percent of the total vote. More than $12 million was spent by all the candidates in the primaries and general election; it was the most expensive campaign in Florida history.

Upon taking office, Graham laid out an elaborate agenda for the state and the legislature to tackle. His priorities included tax reform (especially in the area of property tax relief and revision of the gas tax laws); improvement of the state's transportation facilities, including a shakeup of the unwieldy Department of Transportation (a traditional headache for Florida governors); energy self-sufficiency and environmental protection; economic development, especially in the creation of new jobs; improvement of the state's lackluster educational system; and a more aggressive war against crime, including drug smuggling. It was, by all accounts, one of the most ambitious agendas ever established by a governor of this state.

Graham's initial efforts to bring his plans to fruition met with only mixed success. There seemed to be two reasons for this. First, he had considerable difficulty dealing with the legislature, particularly the Senate, traditionally an independent and balky body. He may have misjudged the amount of cooperation he could expect from his former colleagues. But additionally, there were some personnel problems in the governor's office which exacerbated friction with the legislature. Some of the Governor's own staff, including legislative liaisons, were not well-received by legislators. Justifiably or not, many legislators felt they were pushy, arrogant, and unwilling to cooperate, compromise, or bargain with them. Some apparently felt that the governor's staff was unwilling to recognize their own role and interest in the process of policy formation.

But whatever the reasons were, in his first two years Graham's relations with the legislature were marked by considerable acrimony, and his legislative "batting average" on key issues was not high. Perhaps the most stinging defeat came on revision of the gas tax in 1981. The legislature's rebuff was so great that one Florida newspaper, the prestigious St. Petersburg Times, called him "Governor Jell-O" for his inability to lead the legislature effectively. Other political observers also feared that Graham's performance as governor might not live up to his early promise.

A second reason why Graham's initial legislative record seemed to disappoint many of his partisans was that early in his administration a series of catastrophic events struck the state, and were of sufficient magnitude that they distracted the Governor from pursuing his policy agenda. Indeed, as Graham himself frankly noted, they occupied so much of his time, thought, and energy that they forced him to reduce the amount of attention he could give to his other gubernatorial tasks, including working with legislators. These events included a truck strike that seriously affected distribution of gasoline across the state during a peak tourist season; two devastating hurricanes which required massive evacuation programs and state assistance for cleaning and repairing damaged areas; the collapse of the Sunshine Bridge in Tampa Bay; a severe race riot in Miami triggered by the acquittal of white policemen alleged to have murdered a black businessman, and for which Graham had to call out 5,000 national guard troops; and, most important, the huge influx of Cuban refugees for whom Graham had to mobilize local and state emergency facilities. Any governor, of course, is always confronted by unseen and unanticipated crises, but Graham seemed to have had more than his share, especially during the first two years when he was still seeking to chart the initial course of his administration.

Interestingly, however, it was his handling of these crises which began to improve Graham's record. His prompt action to insure continued supplies of gasoline and to aid hurricane victims won considerable praise. But his response to the Miami riots and boatloads of thousands of Cuban immigrants attracted national attention. Particularly in the latter instance, Graham resisted considerable pressure within the state not to accommodate the Cubans. At the same time, Graham successfully demanded federal assistance for the immigrants, even eventually going to court to insist that the federal government recognize its responsibilities in what appeared to be as much a national as a state problem.

Graham's response to the crises seemed to give his administration a second wind. Rather than being victimized by circumstances, he gave the impression of being able to master them. At a minimum, the vigorous leadership he showed worked to his political advantage. He gained considerable prestige statewide, and his reputation began to change from that of uncertain, even ineffectual, leader to one of strength and activism.

Additionally, Graham made a number of changes within his office designed to improve relations with the legislature. He replaced legislative liaison staff with individuals who were more willing to communicate with legislators, make commitments and bargains, and generally be more sensitive to their needs. Members of the budget office were also changed to include individuals who could deal effectively with legislators on budget and other fiscal matters. Considerable rancor had developed between legislators and the Governor's budget office during budget deliberations, and this added to the difficulties Graham had in enacting his programs.

Graham also sought to solidify his renewed support within the larger Florida community. He travelled extensively throughout the state, especially in rural areas where he was not well-known, and in populous urban centers. He additionally tried to maintain the support of blacks and women through political appointments and public endorsement of the doomed Equal Rights Amendment. Perhaps most significantly, he reaffirmed close ties with powerful interest groups in the state, especially major agricultural and business groups such as the Florida Farm Bureau, citrus and cattle groups, the state Chamber of Commerce and prestigious Council of 100, an organization of leading commercial, business, and industrial interests in the state.[9]

The effect of the crises, changes within the governor's office, and political fence-mending was to enhance Graham's prestige and stature. His legislative record in the last two years of his first term was substantially better on major issues than in the first two. Of particular note were significant commitments to education, environmental protection, economic development, and the war on crime. In perhaps his most important achievement, Graham was able to shepherd a sales tax increase through the legislature during an election year (1982), even in the face of a substantial statewide recession.

GRAHAM'S FIRST ADMINISTRATION: AN ASSESSMENT

Let us now attempt to assess the quality or character of Graham's first four years in office. In their study of Florida gubernatorial politics during the twentieth century, Colburn and Scher substantially modified Barber's typology of leadership to provide a more complete, multidimensional analysis of gubernatorial effectiveness.[10] Governors were evaluated in terms of their ideological preferences on economic, racial, and social service issues; their personal appeal, character, psychological satisfaction, and style; their administrative and legislative records; their policy proposals; and public ethics.

Following this framework provides an interesting view of the first Graham term. Essentially an economic conservative, Graham has nonetheless sought to use the power of the state to enhance Florida's economic health by actively recruiting business and industry both domestically and internationally in order to create jobs and diversify the state's economy. Moreover, he has tried to create more equitable systems of taxation, particularly in creating property tax relief and allowing local options for sales tax revenues. In race relations and other civil rights issues Graham has consistently taken progressive positions. In the social service area Graham has been criticized for increasing funding for crime prevention and penal institutions at the expense of other social programs, but at the same time Graham has been sensitive to the needs of the elderly and the poor. He has also consistently sought to improve the state's educational quality. Graham, in sum, would probably not be considered a "liberal" by national standards in terms of his ideological preferences. But within the context of Florida politics, Graham appears as a very progressive governor who is anxious to move the state forward.

In the personal qualities which form an important part of leadership, Graham emerges as dedicated and professional. While neither especially charismatic nor gregarious in public, he nonetheless projects an aura of sincerity, warmth, and concern, which have rendered him a popular figure. And his serious (but not cold), business-like style complements his quiet, reserved public demeanor. On the traditional Barber categories of character and psychological satisfaction, Graham emerges as "active-positive." His approach to the governorship is that of problem solver and activist policy architect, and he appears to relish his job, even with the frustrations inherent within it.

In carrying out administrative and legislative tasks Graham shows considerable change from the first half of his term to the second. Administratively, Graham initially tried to oversee as many details as possible. He was convinced that to make state government work effectively, he had to personally define goals and supervise performance. He insisted that agency and department heads work directly for him (not even permitting policy statements without pre-clearance), and did not hesitate to intervene directly into bureaucratic affairs to "keep tabs" on what state agencies were doing or how well they were performing.

While Graham continued the practice of goal-setting and careful monitoring of administrative behavior and procedures, he learned how to delegate some of the tasks to his staff. Bureau chiefs were still aware of his personal willingness to intervene, and Graham tried to insure that none "go into business" for themselves. Nonetheless, by delegating some of the monitoring and supervisory tasks, Graham gave himself more time for planning. His emphasis became less on personally implementing laws and programs than on seeking alternatives from state agencies which could aid him in policy formulation and execution.

Changes in Graham's legislative relations have been more publicly visible than the shift in administrative style (as they usually are), and they have been no less important. As noted earlier, most of the changes consist of appointing personnel who are more willing to work closely with legislators in formulating programs and in accommodating their interests. While a member of the legislature Graham was considered something of a renegade, and perhaps initially he felt he could deal with legislators from that same perspective. He learned, however, that he had to pay closer attention to its traditional norms and styles, as well as to individuals, if cooperation were to be possible.

Space does not permit a full assessment of Graham's policy proposals. The real question that this matter involves is the adequacy of his plans: that is, have they really addressed state needs, are they realistic, and are they aimed at future, or only present, concerns? Obviously these are complex matters requiring detailed analysis. Nonetheless, even a cursory examination suggests that Graham has been one of Florida's more forward-looking governors in terms of his policy proposals. His willingness to start overhauling a creaky tax structure (which included, at the beginning of his second term, a successful revision of the gas tax), continued support for energy conservation and environmental protection, and added resources for education are evidence for this assumption.

What distinguishes Graham from some of his predecessors in terms of his policy proposals, moreover, is his willingness to persist in making them. The tradition among Florida governors was to create a "laundry list" of desirable programs (usually in campaigns, the inaugural address, or the State-of-the-State speech opening legislative sessions), but then to avoid following through with specific proposals, or even to withdraw them in the face of opposition.[11] Graham has shown a willingness to follow through on his "laundry list," and, in the case of tax reform, education, and crime prevention, to actually seek more changes once the initial ones were put into effect.

Finally, Graham has also sought to run an administration exemplifying high ethical standards. Concerning his own personal integrity there has never been any question. And even a scandal in the State Highway Patrol towards the end of his first term in no way reflected on his own ethics or the standards he tried to bring to the whole administration.

In sum, then, the first Graham administration emerges as a vigorous, progressive one in which the Governor learned how to become more effective as time went on. There have been, of course, criticisms. Complaints have been heard that, in an effort to secure legislative cooperation, Graham has made deals which belie his progressive image. The 1979 execution at Raiford Prison of John Spenkelink, and Graham's willingness to sign more death warrants, have provoked outrage in some quarters. Some have argued that he has sought to raise taxes too fast and too high, and that further expansion of state services is not necessary; others have felt that Graham has played too much to the business community in an effort to maintain its support, and has not been sufficiently attentive to the state's poor citizens. And allegations have been made that he has not kept his future political ambitions very well-hidden. This is not the place to evaluate the validity of these criticisms, and of course any governor, especially an activist one, is a ready target for them. But it remains to be seen whether or not Graham or his aides take them seriously, and if they will have any impact on his second administration.

GRAHAM'S SECOND GUBERNATORIAL CAMPAIGN

It was no secret that the Republican Party, both at the state and national levels, was looking forward to the 1982 general election in Florida. Republicans had captured the governorship once before (1966) and also a senatorial position (1968). And while that state party had had organizational problems in the ensuing years, which prevented it from consolidating its gains and capitalizing on a rapid increase in Republican voter registration, it nonetheless was optimistic about its chances. Ronald Reagan easily won the state in 1980, and at the same time another Republican U.S. senator, Paula Hawkins, was elected. Polls taken by Democratic and Republican organizations in 1981 indicated that both Senator Lawton Chiles and Governor Bob Graham were potentially vulnerable to Republican challengers. The state Republican Party had a war chest of $1.1 million before serious fund raising even began, nearly triple the Democratic total. Moreover, national Republican strategists targeted Florida as a crucial state in the establishment of a permanent Republican powerhouse in the southeast. Accordingly, they decided that vigorous, well-financed campaigns would be mounted against both Chiles and Graham.

There was never any real doubt that Graham would seek re-election, but by 1981 it became clear that it might not be an easy task. It was already certain that Republicans were making Florida a high-priority state. And while Graham was becoming more assertive in his leadership, there was still the gas tax defeat and controversy over his willingness to welcome 150,000 Cuban refugees and commit state resources to assist them. Nonetheless, Graham and his staff felt they had a few points in their favor. His legislative record had begun to improve, in spite of the gas tax problem. Property tax reform had proved popular with the public, as had the increased efforts to fight crime, protect the environment, and provide additional resources for the elderly, schools, and universities. His own personal popularity remained high. Moreover, Florida was facing a severe recession, and it was felt that rising unemployment (blamed primarily on President Reagan's economic policies) would drive many Democrats who had voted for the President and Paula Hawkins back into the Democratic fold. Also, Graham's own standing in the Democratic party was solid; he had no real opposition, and renomination was not expected to be a problem. Finally, as of early 1981 it was by no means clear whom the Republicans would be able to find to run against Graham, even though they wanted to make the contest a nationally visible one.

The Graham strategy was to start early and to organize effectively so that a serious campaign could be mounted.[12] Accordingly, an organization was established which was essentially built by the same people who had run Graham's first campaign. A number of these individuals had actually entered the Graham administration: Gary Smith, the first campaign director, had become chief of Graham's staff; Kathy Kelly had become appointments secretary; and Steve Hull served as press secretary both in the first campaign and in the governor's office.

Hull remained in the office, but Smith, Kelly, and a few others left to create the second campaign organization. Thus, the second Graham campaign was not run directly from the Governor's office, even while some of the personnel had served in both. In part, this arrangement permitted campaign/political and executive/political activities to be separated. However, the structural division also reflected diversity within the Graham camp about how the campaign was to be run. Some, particularly those who left, wanted an aggressive campaign which directly confronted Republican opposition. Others favored more of an "executive" campaign in which the emphasis was less on active politicking than on creating an image of the Governor's being "in charge."

In the end, a kind of compromise was reached. During the early primary season obvious forms of campaigning were to be minimized. It was felt few mistakes could be made by this strategy. The emphasis became that of showing Graham acting as governor. Workdays were planned, and television slots were created in which Graham could demonstrate the kind of job he was doing as governor, emphasizing his accomplishments in tax reform, economic development, and crime prevention.

On the other hand, the Republican threat was never far from the minds of Graham's campaign strategists. Accordingly, a "worst case" scenario was designed to combat a strong Republican challenge. Plans were worked out for a vigorous campaign to begin late in the summer, and efforts began early to attract funds from important contributors in Florida, including those who might have been expected to support a Republican nominee. In short, a sophisticated campaign was readied to counter a substantial Republican challenge.

THE REPUBLICAN CAMPAIGN

It never materialized. Republican hopes, which looked so promising in 1980 and 1981, were never realized. The problems, which were the classic ones of Republicans in Florida, began early. While funds, at least initially, seemed ample, there was no campaign on which to spend them, because Republicans could not even find a candidate to oppose Graham. (The same problem arose in the senatorial contest against Chiles; Republicans even approached Eastern Airlines President Frank Borman and golf star Jack Nicklaus to run, but both declined.) Finally, state Republicans and President Reagan prevailed on Congressman Skip Bafalis to run against Graham.

Bafalis was no newcomer to Florida politics. He had served in the state legislature, and in 1970 opposed Claude Kirk's attempt for renomination in the Republican gubernatorial primary. In 1972 he was elected to the U.S. House of Representatives from a large district running from Port Charlotte on the west coast of the state to West Palm Beach on the east. During his tenure in the state legislature he had established solid conservative credentials, and in the U.S. House he became an ardent supporter of President Reagan's policies. He was a man with a certain patrician air about him, from the cut of his clothes to his Boston accent. He moved easily in conservative, wealthy circles, and enjoyed the company of the social upper crust. Nonetheless, Bafalis was a solid campaigner, very effective in personal appearances as well as on television, and he had been uninterruptedly re-elected to the House from his district. While he had a consistently conservative voting record, only one major piece of legislation bore his sponsorship: an amendment to the provisions of the inheritance tax laws benefitting wealthy families.

From the start matters went badly for Bafalis. His first difficulty was in finding a lieutenant governor running mate. No one seemed to want to join him, and it was not until just twenty-four hours before the qualifying deadline that a relative newcomer to Florida politics, the police chief of Ft. Lauderdale, Leo Callahan, agreed to run. Callahan, however, almost immediately became ill, and went to Houston for heart surgery. He was never able to campaign for the ticket.

Bafalis' next problem was name recognition. Just three months before the general election, forty-five percent of those Floridians polled had never heard of him; the same poll showed Graham ahead of him by forty-five percentage points.[13] Moreover, even though Bafalis had to face a Republican challenger in the primary, a lawyer from Winter Garden, the contest seemed not to stir the public's interest, and he remained something of an unknown.

Meanwhile, Graham continued his own primary effort against two weak opponents. He scarcely recognized their existence, instead concentrating on his own accomplishments and plans for the future. He travelled extensively throughout the state, seeking endorsements and shoring up support in areas he felt he might prove weak, particularly in panhandle, northern, and central areas of the state.

THE GENERAL ELECTION

Both Graham and Bafalis handily won their primaries in early September, each receiving more than eighty percent of the vote.[14] The end of the primary signaled a change in the Graham strategy, although less so in Bafalis's. While previously Graham defended his record and conveyed a "gubernatorial" image, his campaign began to attack Bafalis directly, attempting to put him on the defensive, pointing out errors in his public remarks ("'Skip-the-Facts' Bafalis" became a favorite way of referring to his opponent), and attempting to point up his own record as governor in contrast to Bafalis's lack of experience and accomplishments.

More important, he continued to seek support, and money, from important segments of the Florida population. By the end of the campaign, Graham had collected over $2.5 million. The vast majority of the funds came from a diverse collection of groups, including accountants, lawyers, agriculture, alcoholic beverages, construction, dog and race track owners, manufacturing, insurance, health professions, real estate, and utilities. He took only a token $4,000 from the Democratic party. Graham even received substantial contributions from traditional Republican sources, business and banks. The effect of this, of course, was to cut off the flow of cash to Bafalis.[15]

Bafalis was indeed having money problems, among others. His attacks on Graham for presiding over a "crime wave," for being a free-spending, high-taxing liberal, and for mishandling the Cuban migration problem seemed to fall on deaf ears. His own proposals for fighting crime and cutting government spending were vague and poorly developed. He was embarrassed for criticizing Graham's new sales tax and other tax proposals while at the same time casting an unneeded vote in support of President Reagan's tax hike; at almost the identical moment Bafalis voted in Washington to increase taxes, Graham in Florida called for a two percent cut in the state budget because of falling revenues.

He also seemed to lack knowledge of state government, even asking reporters about the function of the state Cabinet. But there were two more embarrassing moments as well. The first was his discovery, just before the primary, that his campaign manager had been indicted in 1975 for "dirty tricks" in a 1970 campaign in Indiana. The indictment was later dropped, but Bafalis had to admit publicly that he knew nothing of the whole matter. In October, a West Virginia mining company in which Bafalis held an interest became the subject of a federal tax investigation, along with several of its other owners. Bafalis was not implicated, but media coverage began to focus on the problems of his coal company, and not on the message he was trying to convey to Floridians.

As Bafalis's campaign became more hopeless, his money began to disappear. Graham had cut off many of the state sources, and the national Republican organization, seeing the inevitable defeat, by the latter part of October refused to commit any more of its resources, either funds or visiting political celebrities, to him. He was not able to pay for television ads for much of October.

Bafalis raised a total of $1.5 million, but by the end of the campaign had less than $100,000 in reserve. Graham, in contrast, had $1.3 million in cash reserve.[16]

In the end, Graham simply had too much support for Bafalis to handle. His personal popularity, as well as his strategy of defending his tax policy, supporting education and services for the elderly, economic development, protection of the environment, and fighting crime proved effective with voters. Moreover, Bafalis was never able to gain the offensive because Graham was too well-organized, and had secured endorsements, money, and support from all segments of the Florida population. On election day Graham received 65 percent of the vote, Bafalis 35 percent. The Republican challenger was unable to win even his home county.[17]

THE CAMPAIGN AND THE SECOND ADMINISTRATION

For Graham and his staff, the meaning of the overwhelming victory in November was very clear. The entire thrust of the campaign had been to present the Governor's record to the citizens of Florida and allow them to pass judgment on it. That he won so convincingly was seen in part as a personal triumph. But more important, it was interpreted as a desire by Floridians to continue the same set of priorities that had existed in the first term.

Graham and his staff were too politically mature, however, to view a victory, even a substantial one, as a "mandate." On the other hand, they assumed that the programs and policies Graham had pursued were also the ones the citizens wanted. The results of the election, then, were critical for defining plans for the new administration. Indeed, perhaps its greatest effect was in creating a renewed sense of purpose, confidence, and assurance in both the Governor and his staff. This is most clearly seen in the decision to call a special legislative session shortly after the inauguration to revise the gas tax laws, a matter on which the Governor had been defeated previously. It was a risky strategy, but it proved to be a very successful one this time.

Graham and his staff wanted to exploit the considerable political momentum built up by the election and, later, by the gas tax victory. Accordingly, relatively few changes of priorities or programs were contemplated for the next four years. No task forces or blue-ribbon study commissions (common devices used by governors to build support for new proposals) were appointed. Rather, Graham and his staff were determined to re-emphasize earlier priorities and agendas. His second inaugural speech was a more policy-oriented message than was the somewhat more emotional one four years earlier, but in the second as well as in the State-of-the-State speech opening the 1983 legislative session, many of the same themes struck in the first administration were restated: continued improvement of education, tax reform, economic development, and crime prevention.[18] Added to these was transportation--repair and construction of state roads and bridges--and improvement of mass transit facilities. It had been one of Graham's early priorities, but had essentially disappeared in the press of other matters. As noted earlier, traditionally in Florida these major addresses were used by governors to lay out their vision of the future, and sometimes they had little to do with specific proposals made. On the other hand, Graham has shown a willingness to persist in his priorities, and there is every reason to think that, unless major events occur which force a drastic change in plans, they will form the basis of his second administration.

This is not, however, to say that there will be no differences from the first term. Staff members who had left his office to run his campaign did not, in many cases, return. While major restructuring of the governor's office did not occur, new personnel will naturally create a different tone. Moreover, Graham and his staff were aware of mistakes made previously, and they have sought to make changes to prevent their recurrence. They are especially concerned that relations with the legislature proceed in a less strident fashion from the initial experience of the first term. Accordingly, those positions in the governor's office requiring legislative contact have been staffed with individuals experienced and competent in legislative negotiations. Moreover, Graham recognized an important change in his own legislative role which could enhance his effectiveness. Early in his first term, he claimed, he presented too elaborate an agenda for legislators to deal with. This proved confusing to them, and prevented a focus for action. He learned that it was better to present a half dozen or so high priority items, and begin consultation with legislators on them as soon as possible, in order to maximize chances for success.[19] He began his second administration by following this strategy.

In terms of his own administration role, Graham has also refined his earlier views. No longer does he expect to be personally involved in every administrative detail. On the other hand, he has reaffirmed his administrative interests. He intends to go "one on one" with agency heads whenever possible. More important, however, will be increased use of performance objectives and goals. His feeling is that effective administration and implementation of existing programs can be just as important as the introduction of new ones, and potentially cheaper for the state. Accordingly, staff in the governor's office have been given increased roles for supervising administrative activity. Moreover, more emphasis will be given to the use of quantifiable agency objectives and computer analysis to assess performance. All of these changes are designed to provide Graham with better information about program effects, and to permit more options in budget and policy planning. Finally, Graham intends to utilize the budget office more fully as a planning and evaluation tool and to insure that it works more smoothly with the legislature than in the past. And through the appointment of new personnel, Graham hopes, as did many of his predecessors, to create a more smoothly functioning Transportation Department.

In approaching his second term as governor, Graham apparently did not contemplate a significant change in his own role or style. He sees himself as a "people's governor," in that he seeks to represent as many segments of the population as possible. To some extent this role conception is not exactly congruent with his rather quiet demeanor and cerebral approach to the office. Nonetheless, Graham seeks to reconcile these differences by spending time travelling about the state, meeting with diverse groups in his office, and continuing his workdays. He feels this approach has served him effectively in his first administration: It is his intention to make it work in the second, as well.

MOVING FROM THE FIRST TO THE SECOND TERM

Does the Florida experience provide any insight into the nature of moving from an incumbent governor's first to second terms? Obviously, this is not the same thing as a transition from one individual or party to another. But neither is it a "non-event." The Governor and his staff were able to make a reasonable interpretation of the campaign victory and use it to help plan for the inauguration and its aftermath. Moreover, the period between the campaign and second inauguration was a time of assessment, planning, and renewed vigor in the Graham office. The fact that Graham and his aides determined that the new administration would continue the previous agenda, and work to complete unfinished business from the first term, did not mean that there was no activity, or that nothing of political consequence occurred.

Perhaps, in the end, Governor Graham's own assessment of the period between his second election and inauguration is best. This time, he indicated in an interview, is what the governor chooses to make it. It can be a time of activity or restraint, of renewed commitment or substantial alteration in direction. The decisions made during it will clearly influence what happens during the next four years. Thus, even though it may not be as dramatic as a change from one individual and party to another, it nonetheless emerges as a critical portion of the total political composition of a two-term gubernatorial administration.

NOTES

Data for this study come from a variety of sources, including published books; newspaper accounts (especially that of the Miami Herald, notable for its coverage of state politics); interviews with former and present members of the state government, including Governor Bob Graham, as well as individuals knowledgeable about state politics and/or the Graham administration (all of whom except the Governor were promised anonymity); and documents made available to the author. The author wishes to express his thanks to those who assisted in the preparation of this study, or who commented on drafts. They are not, of course, responsible for its errors. Very special thanks go to Governor Graham who, in spite of the press of other matters, was most generous with his time and candor during his interview with the author (Tallahassee, May 31, 1983).

[1] Joseph A. Schlesinger, "The Politics of the Executive," in Politics in the American States, 2d, ed. by Herbert Jacob and Kenneth N. Vines (Boston: Little, Brown, 1971), pp. 210-237. An update and expansion of Schlesinger's work can be found in Thad L. Beyle, "Governors," in Politics in the American States, 4th ed. by Virginia Gray, Herbert Jacob and Kenneth N. Vines (Boston: Little, Brown, 1983), pp. 180-221, 454-459.

[2] For a complete survey, see David R. Colburn and Richard K. Scher, Florida's Gubernatorial Politics in the Twentieth Century (Tallahassee: University Presses of Florida, 1980).

[3] Cogent analyses of Florida's unique political system can be found in V.O. Key, Southern Politics (New York: Alfred A. Knopf; 1950); Manning J. Dauer, "Florida: The Different State," in The Changing Politics of the South, ed. by William Havard (Baton Rouge: Louisiana State University Press, 1972), pp. 92-164; Neal R. Pierce, The Deep South States of America (New York: W.W. Norton, 1972); Jack Bass and Walter DeVries, The Transformation of Southern Politics (New York: Basic Books, 1976); and Manning J. Dauer, ed., Florida's Politics and Government (Gainesville: University Presses of Florida, a University of Florida book, 1980). See also Colburn and Scher, Florida's Gubernatorial Politics, for a discussion of the relationship between a fragmented political system and the politics of the chief executive in Florida.

[4] Colburn and Scher, Florida's Gubernatorial Politics, pp. 57-58.

[5] Colburn and Scher, Florida's Gubernatorial Politics, pp. 291-295.

[6] See Key, Southern Politics; Dauer, "Florida: The Different State"; Manning J. Dauer and William Havard, The Florida Constitution of 1885 - A Critique, (Gainesville: University of Florida Studies in Public Administration, no. 12, Public Administration Clearing Service, 1955); and Colburn and Scher, Florida's Gubernatorial Politics, chapters 4 and 5.

[7] Graham, Bob, Workdays, ed. by Lawrence Mahoney (Miami: Banyan Books, 1978).

[8] A brief but cogent analysis of this episode can be found in the Miami Herald, 1 September 1982, sec. A, p. 1.

[9] For a view of the relationship between Graham and the Florida business community, see Otis White, "Business Likes Bob Graham Enough to Want Four Years More," Florida Trend (September, 1982): 64-68.

[10] Colburn and Scher, Florida's Gubernatorial Politics, pp. 1-8, 275-296.

[11] See Colburn and Scher, Florida's Gubernatorial Politics, chapter 6, for examples of this practice.

[12] Information about the second Graham campaign came primarily from the Miami Herald and anonymous interviewees.

[13] Miami Herald, 8 August 1982, sec. A, p. 1.

[14] Miami Herald, 8 September 1982, sec. A, p. 1.

[15] Miami Herald, 24 October 1982, sec. D, p. 1; Miami Herald, 4 November 1982, sec. A, p. 22; See also Otis White's article in Florida Trend magazine, cited in note 9 above.

[16] Miami Herald, 24 October 1982, sec. D, p. 1.

[17] Miami Herald, 4 November 1982, sec. A, p. 22. These figures are corroborated in "America Votes," CQ Weekly Reports, (November 6, 1982): 2819.

[18] *Miami Herald*, 2 and 3 January 1979, sec. A, p. 1; *Miami Herald*, 3 and 4 January 1983, sec. A, p. 1.

[19] *Miami Herald*, 22 October 1983, sec. A, p. 1.

7. HAWAII:

PLACID REAFFIRMATION

DANIEL W. TUTTLE, JR.

Political history continues to weigh heavily upon the contemporary political scene in Hawaii. Never was it more evident than in 1982 as Hawaii approached its seventh gubernatorial campaign period. Even as the territorial Republican Party had dominated the political life of the Islands from 1900-1954 (always winning control of the legislature and seldom experiencing defeat for the few other elective offices),[1] incumbent Democratic Governor George R. Ariyoshi in 1982 was determined to maintain the new Democratic status quo, which dated from 1962, and to win re-election to a third term. A capsule of this history provides background and facilitates an understanding of Ariyoshi's successful campaign and of the transition from his second to his third four-year period of incumbency.

BACKGROUND TO ELECTION 1982

The election of 1954 ended more than a half-century of Republican control of Hawaiian politics. Until this election, Republicans, representing largely the modern developers of the Islands, held a firm grip on political life. Although the Democratic Party had co-existed with the Republican Party during this period, it had never enjoyed control of the elective territorial legislature. An early indicator of change came in 1946, when Democrats did achieve a tie for control of the thirty-member House of Representatives. However, even in that year, a Republican was elected as speaker. Democrats were able to win occasional victories in contests for county offices, and, of course, had nominal control of the executive branch because Democratic presidents made appointments of territorial governors. Notwithstanding, the Democratic Party, until 1952, was poorly organized and easily outclassed at the polls by the well-organized and well-financed Republicans. The period 1900-1954 was clearly an era of domination by the Republican Party.

Background to the first-time Democratic legislative victory in 1954 was intensely dramatic and reflected, in large part, social change in the wake of World War II. Young men of Japanese extraction persisted in seeking the opportunity of serving their country in the military. They did so with distinction. After the war, they were determined that they would become active in politics and, encouraged by others such as John A. Burns, they gravitated toward the Democratic Party, in which they joined young persons of other ethnic extractions.

There were other factors that aided the Democratic cause. At their 1952 territorial political convention, a divided Democratic Party (divided largely because of the issue of Communism) forged a unified organization. Furthermore, passage of the McCarran Act in 1951 permitted the naturalization of persons of Oriental extraction, and these new citizens were added to the voting rolls. The 1952 State Party Chairman John A. Burns, who was later governor, put it bluntly: The Democratic Party should court two largely uncommitted groups, namely persons of Japanese ancestry and members of the International Longshoremen's and Warehousemen's Union which had, from its inception, been at odds with the Republicans. The Burns approach was, in a sense, an oversimplification, but the application and implementation of this philosophy did provide a massive new basis of support for Democrats. The 1952 Democratic territorial platform was brief and to the point. It was readily saleable to the electorate, focusing as it did upon tax reform, land reform, added support for education, and recognition of labor.

The 1954 Democratic victory came sooner than most Democrats had expected, due largely to young, well-qualified candidates, an appealing program, an enlarged electorate, and a slate that was ethnically well-balanced. Democrats that year won 22 of the 30 House seats and 5 of the 7 Senate seats at stake (giving them a 9 to 6 majority).[2] In a broad sense, Republicans have yet, even in 1983, to adjust and to recover from their unexpected first-time legislative defeat in 1954.

Democrats repeated their legislative victory in 1956 and 1958, but suffered a setback in the mid-year Statehood Election (1959), in which they lost control of the state Senate, and Republicans won the governorship and one U. S. Senate contest. However, in 1962, Democratic ascendancy was confirmed as John A. Burns snapped back form his 1959 defeat and won the governorship, defeating incumbent Republican William F. Quinn. Later, in 1970, Democrats won the one U.S. Senate seat they had lost in 1959, and periodically succeeded in electing legislative majorities and winning county mayoralty, and council elections. They elected Burns three times and in 1974 gave the governorship to Burns's chosen successor, George R. Ariyoshi. As of 1982, the GOP held on to the only one of the four county mayoral positions (the result of a special election), and had captured only small minorities on the county councils. Republicans held no top-level posts. Democrats, therefore, could note at least twenty years of total control as an answer to fifty years of earlier Republican domination.

ELECTION 1982: THE SETTING

As the 1982 election campaign period loomed on the horizon, the State Republican Party and others took advantage of erratic Democratic efforts to effect decennial legislative reapportionment and challenged the nominally bipartisan reapportionment committee's plan in federal court. There a three-person federal court, including Hawaii District Court Judge Samuel P. King (son of former territorial governor Samuel Wilder King and, himself, the territorial GOP chairman in 1954) found in favor of the plaintiffs and rejected the State's reapportionment plan.

This led to a court-drawn (masters) plan, which replaced a combination single/multi-member district scheme with a single-member district plan for both houses. (The plan also used population rather than registered voters as a base, large numbers of military notwithstanding.) Republicans rejoiced. Party officials proudly proclaimed that the single-member apportionment plan would aid their cause and they set about trying to find candidates to fill the ticket while incumbent Democrats hurriedly scrambled to adjust. Republicans also broke with general precedent and, at their spring state convention, endorsed State Senator D. G. Andy Anderson as "the candidate" for governor and indicated that no other candidates were desired.

Such efforts were, however, more technical than dynamic. Even as claiming a Democratic label thirty years earlier had been unpopular, so few in 1982 rushed to espouse the Republican label tainted by history. The GOP state organization was still floundering and under-financed. Traditional sources of financial support had years earlier found it more productive to give the lion's share of their contributions to Democrats. Little effort had been made to lure and encourage new, young, or dissident faces. Were it not for the dominant role enjoyed by Democrats for a score of years, an outside observer might well have noted that the recent series of Democratic landslides were in jeopardy in 1982 because internal Democratic problems were erupting at the top level, namely in and around the governorship. Two-term incumbent Governor George R. Ariyoshi wanted a third term. Former three-term Honolulu Mayor Frank F. Fasi, a lifelong Democrat who had twice lost by narrow margins to Governor Ariyoshi, indicated that, in spite of his 1980 primary defeat for mayor, he would again challenge Ariyoshi, this time probably as an Independent Democrat so that he could be assured of reaching the general election. Furthermore, even as Fasi was mapping and assessing his strategy, incumbent Lieutenant Governor Jean S. King decided that she would not seek re-election but would instead run for governor and oppose Ariyoshi in the Democratic primary. With the announcement that King would challenge Ariyoshi in the primary, speculation mounted that Fasi might drop his plan to run as an Independent and enter what could be a serious three-way primary contest. However, by the filing deadline it was clear that Fasi would run on an Independent Democratic ticket, with Maui businessman Randy Piltz as a lieutenant governor running mate, and that King would alone offer a serious challenge to the incumbent governor.

The general background setting for the 1982 Hawaii campaign period was placid, but uncertain. Pre-campaign polls had suggested that crime was viewed as a prime concern of the general public. However, the economic picture was darkening and less than clear. After a brief delay, effects of the national recession were becoming obvious, but tourism had begun slowly to improve after a marked decline in 1981. Traditional basic industries, sugar and pineapple, were clearly in difficulty and recognized as declining aspects of the Hawaii economy. Although seeming to improve, tourism growth had not been sufficient to correct abnormally low hotel occupancy rates on the Islands of Hawaii and Kauai. Sluggish inter-island air traffic coupled with competitive price cutting had left two of the three inter-island air carriers in grave financial difficulty. There was, in fine, a general business slowdown in the Islands, but unemployment rates were well below the national average. Yet, pockets of unemployment were severe, especially in the construction fields, and several basic labor contracts required concessions from employees.

Although periodic reports noted a slowdown in general excise tax (sales tax equivalent) collections, incumbent political leaders, including Governor Ariyoshi, repeatedly pointed out a continuing surplus in the state's general fund and stated that, pursuant to 1978 constitutional amendments, year-end rebates would be made as they had been a year earlier. Moods within the business community varied. Some were optimistic that Hawaii would escape the full impact of the Mainland recession. Others were fearful that the economic lag would worsen and that a slowed rate of growth for tourism would not compensate for declines in the sugar and pineapple industries.

In summary, except for the plight of construction and airline workers, the general public was not overly concerned about the economic future. This lack of concern was, perhaps, due in large part to relatively low rates of unemployment. However, the specialized business public was more concerned and fearful, and some blamed state government for failing to develop a climate that would attract new business and thereby build a more divers economy. A few observers were distressed about the slow growth of Neighbor Island economies (islands other than Oahu). However, even before the public political campaign period got underway, Governor Ariyoshi was able to assert and to reiterate that the Hawaii economy was very sound, that the unemployment rate was among the lowest in the nation, and that the Hawaii treasury still enjoyed a surplus, whereas many other states were faced with deficits and increased taxes. Early and late in the campaign, he insisted that no tax increases were in the offing.

The social setting in 1982, although strikingly different from that which was evident when Democrats won their first victory in 1954, remained generally calm and preoccupied with personal undertakings. As an area, Hawaii had really never been more affluent. However, crime figures had mounted, home ownership remained out of reach for more young people, and immigration of diverse peoples from the Mainland USA, Asia, and the South Pacific posed special problems for both private and public social services and for the public schools. The standard and mode of living for persons in areas outside metropolitan Honolulu differed markedly from the city dwellers. Thoughtful observers periodically noted that new arrivals in Hawaii, whether from the Mainland or from points to the West of Hawaii, were being less readily absorbed into the society than in earlier years. However, among the many latent social problems facing the Islands, only the issue of crime could be pinpointed and recognized by the general public (or so the politicians seemed to believe). Other matters were more complex and, therefore, difficult for politicians to address.

THE PRIMARY CAMPAIGN

There was no question about it. The Democratic gubernatorial contest was the feature race of the 1982 Hawaii primary election; the Democratic struggle for the lieutenant governor nomination was secondary. However, the upcoming drama did not fall into place until the filing deadline on July 10. There were no serious top-level races on the Republican, Independent Democratic, or other tickets. As noted earlier, after weeks of rumors, incumbent Lieutenant Governor Jean S. King decided at the last minute to challenge Governor George Ariyoshi. Mindful of the possibility, Ariyoshi had been campaigning unofficially since May, and his campaign strategy was well in place. However, this situation did not deter King. She squeezed all of the mileage that she could out of the deadline for filing, which occurred in her office. In announcing her candidacy, King bluntly stated: "If you'd been sitting where I've been sitting and seeing what I've been seeing for the last three and one-half years, you'd be running for governor, too."[3]

Later, as Ariyoshi appeared in her office to file formally for re-election, King directly confronted him before television cameras and challenged him to a debate. Ariyoshi politely declined to discuss the proposal, saying that this was not the time or place for such conversation. King supporters hailed the beginning of a dramatic campaign; Ariyoshi backers groused that in provoking the episode, King had shown poor taste and had sought to embarrass the Governor. As the campaign progressed, it became obvious that the early King strategy had backfired. Yet, there was still an opportunity for her to tell the voters exactly what she had "seen" to cause her to challenge Ariyoshi.

Early pyrotechnics notwithstanding, the King campaign was a disappointment. She repeatedly challenged the governor to debate the issues, openly stressed that she was abiding by voluntary campaign spending limits, criticized Ariyoshi's mass spending and the sources of his support (developers, architects, engineers, and builders, for example), pushed a 4-percent hotel room tax, supported elimination of the 4-percent general excise tax on food, favored county revenue sharing, and opposed the death penalty. These positions distinguished her from the Governor, but the only wrongdoing alleged was "cronyism," "barnacles and rust," and campaign abuse by state workers who were said to be distributing Ariyoshi literature during office hours. The King call for administrative reorganization was only occasionally mentioned and attracted a sparse public. Her criticism that Ariyoshi was seeking a third term in spite of a new two-term constitutional limitation did not take either, perhaps because it did not apply specifically to Ariyoshi.

Governor Ariyoshi, by way of contrast, repeated and repeated via television and the press the virtues of his eight-year record in office. He rarely appeared with King on the same platform and, even then, did not engage in any verbal exchange. He vowed fiscal responsibility, pledged no tax increases, and pointed up the excellent economic health of Hawaii. In the process, Ariyoshi won the endorsement of most labor unions--seventeen in all--including the large International Longshoremen's and Warehousemen's Union, the Hawaii Government Employees Association, and the Hawaii State Teachers Association. He also had the endorsement of longtime U. S. Senator Daniel K. Inouye. A confident incumbent did not bother to respond to any of King's statements.

The King campaign was obviously handicapped by the lack of campaign funds. Ariyoshi had no such problems. As a result, King relied upon low-cost media such as peripheral television spots and radio, which had limited success, and personal appearances. Ariyoshi used a well-produced thirty-minute, prime-time, made-for-television campaign film and prime-time television spots. His extensive grass-roots organization became operational (mostly for later usage). King had a loyal, but small band of organizational personnel. The Ariyoshi campaign employed national campaign advisors Joseph Napolitan, Matthew Reese, a local public relations firm (Seigle), and local pollster Ray Soon (Hawaii Opinion, Inc.). King employed one campaign advisor, Paul Sullivan, a former Carter White House staffer, who coordinated modest public relations efforts. Ariyoshi outspent King by a wide margin, $1.5 million to $248,000.

The Democratic contest for lieutenant governor featured young incumbent State Representative John Waihee, resigned State Senator Dennis O'Connor, and former State Representative and Senator Bernaldo Bicoy. O'Connor, who received early publicity due to a successful court battle to obtain a place on the ballot as a resigned mid-term state senator, chose to remain neutral in the gubernatorial contest. He was the early favorite. Waihee, first, and then Bicoy supported Ariyoshi, knowing that he would not openly return the favor. Both O'Connor and Waihee were able to raise and spend substantial sums of money ($251,352 and $307,457, respectively) and to mount rather extensive media campaigns. Bicoy was less fortunate ($94,000).

The renomination of Ariyoshi was no surprise. In winning the Democratic nomination on September 18, he polled 54.0 percent to King's 44.6 percent; 1.4 percent went to minor candidates. Notwithstanding, King's showing was considerably better than the 33.0 percent (among intended Democrats) indicated by the last Honolulu Advertiser's Hawaii Poll, published on September 12. The size of King's vote could well have presaged general election difficulty for Ariyoshi had he faced only one rather than two opponents.

The Democratic nomination of John Waihee for lieutenant governor was a bit more surprising to most observers. By polling 45.2 percent of the vote, he upset the favorite Dennis O'Connor by 1.9 percentage points, thanks, in large part, to his Neighbor Island strength. Bicoy was able to muster only 9.1 percent of the vote.

The 1982 Democratic tandem team of Ariyoshi and Waihee was generally considered to be strong and balanced. Their cause in the general election campaign was aided by a serious three-way race, which was uncommon for Hawaii. Opposing the Ariyoshi-Waihee ticket was the Republican team of D. G. "Andy" Anderson and Pat Saiki, both former state Senators, and the Independent Democratic duo of Frank F. Fasi (Honolulu mayor from 1968 to 1980) and Randy Piltz (a Maui businessman).

THE GENERAL ELECTION CAMPAIGN

The 1982 Hawaii primary election was held on a Saturday, as usual, and on Monday things started to happen. Independent Democrat Fasi proposed to Republican Anderson that a three-way poll be conducted, with the gubernatorial team that polled third dropping out of the governor's race. Anderson made a counter proposal for an Anderson-Fasi poll, but basically seemed to feel that the Fasi proposal was a transparent effort to get Anderson to drop out. There were, apparently, several meetings, but, in final analysis, nothing came of efforts in the direction of Fasi-Anderson reapprochement. Although Anderson and Fasi forces talked about "Anybody but Ariyoshi," neither camp was prepared to make the sacrifice. The Ariyoshi group was, of course, forced to campaign on the basis that "drop-out," even at the last moment, was possible.

The Governor's campaign was a Napolitan-Reese "formula" campaign plus statewide techniques formulated for Governor John A. Burns in his 1966 campaign for re-election. This strategy called for a one-half hour campaign film, as noted earlier, entitled "The Truth About Governor Ariyoshi," to be shown again and again on prime-time television, a "good news" set of press releases from the various departments of state government, direct mail and telephone campaigns, packaged television spots and newspaper advertisements, and a mass gathering of campaign workers at Aloha Stadium (39,000 attended in 1982). In addition, Ariyoshi made hundreds of small group appearances, meeting with some 15,000 people in this manner. Local elements of the campaign were masterminded by former State Representative and former Party Chairman Robert Oshiro, with businessman Frank Hata heading the fund-raising efforts. Dan Ishii and Gary Caufield served as day-to-day coordinators. Fund raising was, of course, critical and, in this instance, it was very successful. By the end of the campaign the Ariyoshi-Waihee effort would spend more than $3,000,000, about double the combined spending of Anderson and Fasi.[4]

Fasi, weakened by his 1980 defeat for re-election to a fourth term as Honolulu mayor, waged a technically good, if underfinanced, campaign. Very early in the year, he had conducted daily radio talk shows, and he continued those until his campaign was officially underway. Thereafter, he utilized call-in radio and television shows in prime time. He merged the media well and sought to pinpoint his issues. However, even though for the first time he used Mainland campaign experts (California's Joe Cerrell, with Andy Cohen on the scene), mistakes crept in. For example, a direct-mail appeal to unregistered voters asking them to register and vote went to many who were already registered, including Governor Ariyoshi. Further, a former aide to Fasi as

Honolulu Mayor was sentenced to prison for income tax evasion during the campaign period.

Anderson hired West Coast consultant Stuart Spencer early, and combined his talent with local advisor, Doug Eagleson. Although Anderson was able to raise and spend more money than Fasi, his media efforts were disconnected and never quite succeeded in portraying him as "a governor." Full-page newspaper advertisements tried to show him as a winner, using opinion poll results, but seemed less than convincing to most observers. A lawsuit filed against him as a businessman during the campaign season did little to assist the Anderson cause.

Fasi's substantive campaign was pungent, but, even though he was less volatile than usual, he still appeared to employ a shotgun approach. He sought to emphasize as issues, crime, jobs, economic conditions, cost of living, and favoritism in state jobs. Anderson issued several position papers, but always seemed to echo the Fasi critique. Anderson, along with Ariyoshi, refused to appear with Fasi on a League of Women Voters television debate, and, as a result, the debate was canceled. Otherwise, Anderson criticized the Governor for using state business lists to obtain campaign donations, and for directing poor prison administration. Meanwhile, the Governor stated and restated his record and stressed a "Special Place" theme. Newspaper endorsements (both statewide dailies) touted Ariyoshi's record concerning growth, energy, housing, money management, education, aid to the elderly, and plans for the future.

Most organizational endorsements, including labor union support, went to Ariyoshi. One major union, the Carpenters' Union, endorsed Fasi, and COPE (AFL-CIO) remained officially neutral, even though most affiliates backed Ariyoshi. The Anderson-Saiki duo gained little organizational aid; even an endorsement by the University of Hawaii student newspaper proved controversial.

There was little reason for suspense on general election night in 1982. If neither Fasi nor Anderson withdrew, an Ariyoshi victory seemed assured. And, as mentioned earlier, neither withdrew. Accordingly, Ariyoshi won a third term and with his running mate John Waihee received 45.2 percent of the vote. The Independent Democrats Fasi and Piltz received 28.6 percent. Although the Ariyoshi-Waihee plurality was impressive, the fact remained that Ariyoshi became a minority governor. Democratic legislative majorities became the greatest in their party's history, as Democrats won 43 of the 51 House of Representatives seats and all of the contested Senate posts, which gave them a 20-to-5 Senate majority.

THE DEMOCRATIC VICTORY

Although Democrats won their greatest victory in 1982, it was largely the force of contemporary history, divided opposition, and technical factors such as reapportionment, that allowed them to claim such a prize. Governor George Ariyoshi wanted the election to be a referendum upon his eight-year administration, and he got a plurality vote of confidence. The depth of the modern Democratic Party enabled this group to capitalize upon the new single-member districts, a plan which, as noted earlier, ironically had been sought fervently by the GOP. Whereas the Democratic victories of 1962 and 1966, in particular, had reflected a vote for change, their 1982 victory was clearly a vote for maintenance of the status quo, for the "new establishment." Had Fasi and Anderson been willing to forge a fusion ticket in opposition to Ariyoshi, such a ticket might well have defeated Ariyoshi-Waihee. However, the fact of the campaign disputes their voiced goal, namely the defeat of Ariyoshi. The ambition of each was obviously greater than the desire to unseat Ariyoshi. Republicans badly miscalculated the effect of reapportionment to single-member districts, and they automatically lost two incumbent state senators in the persons of Anderson and Saiki. National factors and trends had no appreciable influence on the Hawaii electoral outcome in 1982.

It would be easy to label the Ariyoshi re-election as a personal triumph amid a historic Democratic Party victory. Of course, in a sense, this is true. However, astute observers must note that earlier Ariyoshi primary victories for governor were by razor-thin margins, and his 1982 win rests upon a plurality rather than a majority vote. The zest for the Democratic Party today derives largely from the desire to retain imcumbency and to maintain the status quo rather than from new programs and organizational effectiveness. By the same token, the GOP in Hawaii is in a state of collapse at a time when few citizens seem inclined to devote time, effort, and money to party activity. Meanwhile, more than a quarter of the electorate, dissident Democrats and Republicans who supported Fasi in 1982, are completely cut adrift.

In summary, the force of contemporary history and a measure of present-day political disorientation handed Ariyoshi and his Democratic colleagues a 1982 victory that was easier than they thought, albeit costly in terms of campaign dollars (about $20 per vote for governor). Background factors present before the election remain, and the voters decided in favor of the status quo.

ACCEPTANCE OF A THIRD TERM: MINIMAL CHANGE

After the inaugural ceremony on December 6, 1982, and until mid-January 1983, political Hawaii rested. Then, shortly after the convening of the state legislature, Governor George R. Ariyoshi, on January 24, delivered his State-of-the-State address. Once again, the Governor spoke proudly of past accomplishments and appeared optimistic about the future. His address forecast no dramatic change from the past eight years. He did advance a number of proposals, indicating that he would:

1. Appoint an Agriculture Industry Development Commission;

2. Appoint two business committees, an alternative economic development group, and another to consider whether Hawaii is anti-business (as alleged in a Forbes article of January 31, 1983);

3. Ask the legislature to establish a High Technology Development Corporation;

4. Ask the legislature to fund another Tax Review Commission;

5. Consider having the state government operate (or contract) aircraft to assure that Hawaii products get to Mainland markets promptly.

The Governor's address was generally hailed as workmanlike and, in certain instances, intriguing. However, some observers were disappointed that it largely endorsed the status quo and relied heavily upon the appointment of commissions and committees to study change rather than upon making direct-action assignments to line departments. In essence, the address was a reiteration of the Governor's well-known administrative style, which in the past has depended upon task forces and committees. His address gave no hint of any pending administrative changes.

Approximately one month later, Governor Ariyoshi announced several pending top-level personnel changes. Personnel Director Donald Botelho would retire and, pending senatorial approval, be replaced by James Takushi, a member of the Labor and Industrial Relations Appeals Board and former Personnel Director. In turn, former Kauai Mayor Eduardo Malapit, who chose not to seek re-election, would replace Takushi. Hideto Kono, director of the Department of Planning and Economic Development would retire and be replaced by his deputy, Kent Keith, a young Harvard-trained Rhodes scholar. Adjutant General Arthur Ishimoto would also retire and be replaced by Alexis T. Lum. Such changes were less than dramatic and would appear to presage no major administrative policy shifts. Ariyoshi stressed that all retirements were voluntary and not sought by him, adding that there may be a few more cabinet changes in the future. Later, Ariyoshi nominated Supreme Court Justice Herman Lum to replace Chief Justice William Richardson, who had resigned to accept a Bishop Estate trustee position. Although Hawaii Democrats had little difficulty in organizing the Hawaii State Legislature (the Senate had been governed by a Democratic/Republican coalition from 1980 to 1982), the general political scene for the Governor rapidly became troubled. In sharp contrast to the economic optimism exuded by the Governor during the 1982 campaign, Ariyoshi in January and February began ordering sharp spending cutbacks in an effort to reduce a projected $225,000,000 budget deficit for fiscal years 1983-1985. Most departments obliged the Governor and sought to honor his orders. However, affected parties were less than happy, and the general public was left to ponder how quickly economic optimism could turn to pessimism. The Board of Education, when ordered to effect a third cutback, balked and announced that, rather than cut services further, they would close the public schools early. The Governor's response was curt and reflected a lot of background tension: ". . . school board members are 'lay persons' and they don't have the expertise to assess the state's financial problems and the executive's solutions."5 He asserted that the schools would not close early. The flap was later resolved, after the Superintendent of Education met with the Governor, and the Board found funds to transfer, thus assuring a full school year.

A Forbes magazine article of January 31, 1983, stressed that Hawaii government was anti-business and that state government discouraged business entries into the Hawaiian economy. Here again, the Governor's reply was curt, as he termed the piece "yellow journalism." However, as noted earlier, Ariyoshi did pledge to appoint a special business committee to investigate the allegations. Meanwhile, the Hawaii business community took more direct action. Herbert Cornuelle, Campbell Estate trustee and former chief executive officer of the Dillingham Corporation, moved to form a Hawaii Business Roundtable to create a "coalition of awareness." In general, the Hawaii business community noted that the Forbes article exaggerated the situation, but that bureaucratic excess and negative attitudes toward newcomers did constitute a problem for Hawaii business. Defeated gubernatorial candidate Fasi, never noted for shyness, observed that the State's budgetary woes and negative attitudes toward business had been stressed in his campaign. Anderson, the defeated GOP candidate, remained silent. Other episodes also puzzled observers. The State Salary Review Commission, after careful study, submitted its report on state executive salaries. Among its comprehensive proposals was one which would have

increased the governor's salary from $59,440 to $89,400. The
Governor promptly opposed the entire plan. Alleged favoritism in the admission of relatives and friends of prominent
state politicians to the University of Hawaii Law School cast
further doubt upon the behavior of Democrats. Earlier, during
the campaign period, an aspiring Democratic legislator, a law
student at the University, had mobilized a number of fellow
law students to assist him, and they had registered out-of-
district voters within his district, apparently using
fictitious addresses. The episode cost the Democrats one
certain House seat,[6] but had no apparent effect on the
gubernatorial race. Later, toward the end of March, the
public was advised that a recently developed $5,000,000-state
park was deserted and rapidly deteriorating. Freed from the
possibility of facing another election, these developments,
nonetheless, could not be very satisfying for the Governor.
Even as the 1983 State Legislature, stacked with many
neophyte Democrats, is shackled with a fiscal situation that
defeats creativity, the Governor's administration is
beginning to find that continued guardianship of the status
quo, however gratifying the power, can become tedious and
even difficult.

EVALUATION AND THE FUTURE

The 1982 Hawaii election that handed the third term to
Governor George R. Ariyoshi appears to have done little to
change the contemporary Island political scene. The newness
and proclivity to effect socio-economic and political change
that characterized the state during the 1950s and 1960s is no
longer clearly evident. Governor Ariyoshi, who became the
trustee of the earlier Burn's twelve-year administration,
appears determined to stay the course of new orthodoxy,
living out an earlier campaign theme of "Quiet and
Effective." As Governor, most would characterize him as
workmanlike, prudent, and personally honest, but given to
myopia concerning human frailty within an administration and
a political party that has been long in office. He serves as
the guardian of an exciting political heritage.

The Democratic Party and the Governor's administrative
family are not devoid of youth, but it is a youth attracted
more to the "goodies" of political success than to idealism
and willingness to work between gubernatorial elections.
Democrats today are inclined toward the earlier GOP syndrome,
namely reveling in the glory of past accomplishment. As a
result, many problems, even those that are well-known and
publicized, are avoided and relegated to study sometime
tomorrow.

As indicated earlier, political opposition for Democrats
is in a state of over-extended delay. The Republican Party
in 1982 suffered its most crushing defeat in the wake of more

than twenty-five years of setbacks. Pat Saiki, candidate for lieutenant governor, sought and won the Republican state chairmanship and will attempt the difficult task of resurgence. Dissident (non-establishment) Democrats are similarly disoriented. A pocket of free-thinking Democrats remains in the State Senate (members who engineered the 1980-1982 coalition), but there is little cohesion within these ranks.

Hawaii's political history, brief though it may be, tends to suggest political cycles of considerable amplitude. The Islands have demonstrated that they have no proclivity for sudden political jolts or swings. Island Republican leaders, as participants in national politics, have tended to favor the Tafts and the Goldwaters rather than the Eisenhowers or the Rockefellers. Hawaii Democratic leaders have been more comfortable with Lyndon Johnson or Russell Long types than with the Humphrey or Kennedy types. All of this suggests that political Hawaii has been and remains basically conservative, but selectively liberal, insofar as the long-labeled spectrum has meaning.

Governor Ariyoshi cannot be elected to another term, and it is difficult to foresee that Democratic majorities can increase in the future. (There are, or course, already several potential Democratic successors to Ariyoshi.) Thus, it would appear to be almost axiomatic that one day, in the not-too-distant future, Hawaiian politics will move away from the current plateau. Possessed of impressive power and personally removed from the question of succession, Governor Ariyoshi can do much to determine future directions for the state, whether by creative design or by unattended deterioration with respect to the political process. With declining months of tenure remaining, the implicit follow-up question must here remain unanswered. Until there is an answer, the lack of an alternative political party and an uncommonly apathetic public do not augur well for a dynamic political future for the nation's newest state.

NOTES

[1] Hawaii did not elect a governor until 1959, when statehood was secured.

[2] See Daniel W. Tuttle, Jr., Paper son Hawaiian Politics, 1952-62, (Honolulu: Department of Political Science, 1964), 29-35.

[3] Honolulu Advertiser, 21 July 1983, sec. A, p. 1.

[4] Ariyoshi reported spending of $2,680,000; Waihee, $605,830. Honolulu Star-Bulletin, 30 July 1983, sec. A, p. 3.

[5] Honolulu Star-Bulletin, 26 February 1983, sec. A, p. 1.

[6] Several persons have been indicted in this vote fraud case.

8. THE IDAHO RE-ELECTION: POLITICS AS USUAL

H. SYDNEY DUNCOMBE AND ROBERT H. BLANK

The most significant governmental development in Idaho during 1982 and early 1983 was not the 1982 elections but the onset and resolution of the state's worst fiscal crisis in sixty years. Idaho voters re-elected incumbent Democratic Governor John V. Evans, so there was no major transition in the executive branch of state government. There were no major upsets in the races for the other elective offices. The Republican majorities in House and Senate were retained, although slightly diminished. Thus, 1982 was a year of electoral status quo, with the most important developments in the realm of state finance.

IDAHO POLITICAL AND FISCAL BACKGROUND

Idaho voters are both independent and conservative. Traditionally, more than a third of Idaho voters split their ballots. Republican Secretary of State, Pete Cenarrusa, unopposed in 1982, regularly captures a 70-percent majority. Idaho voters tend to vote for incumbents, and it is no surprise that not a single incumbent was defeated in statewide and congressional races in 1982.

The preponderately conservative Idaho voters now are represented by an entirely Republican Congressional delegation of two Senators and two Representatives and by a state legislative delegation with a 5 to 2 Republican margin in the House and a 3 to 2 margin in the Senate. Idaho voters have shown their fiscal conservatism by approving a property tax initiative in 1978 modeled after California's Proposition 13 and an initiative in 1982 that raised the property tax exemption on residential property to 50 percent of market value or $50,000, whichever is less.

Idaho has personal income, corporate income, and sales taxes but rates tend to be relatively low. Before the 1983 legislative session, for example, Idaho had a three-cent sales tax, which was among the lowest rates in the nation. <u>The Book of the States, 1982-83</u> lists Idaho's per capita state taxes at $568.60, lower than all five surrounding states, and much below the national average of $662.95.[1] Idaho legislators and citizens take pride in avoiding debt, and Idaho's interest on state and local debt was the lowest of any state in the nation in 1979-80.[2]

The Idaho fiscal year begins July 1, and there are strong constitutional and legal constraints on running a deficit. In 1982, the state's fiscal crisis occurred during a gubernatorial election campaign and finally was resolved by action of the Idaho Legislature, which met from January through April, 1983.

THE 1982 FISCAL CRISIS AND ITS IMPACT ON STATE POLITICS AND GOVERNMENT

In 1982, state government in Idaho faced the most severe fiscal crisis in the past sixty years. Thousands of state employees had payless Fridays in the last seven weeks of the fiscal year that ended June 30, 1982. Gubernatorial holdbacks of 9 percent in August 1982, and 1-1/2 percent in October cut deeply into state programs, but even these cutbacks proved inadequate. The fiscal crisis in Idaho became a key political issue in the gubernatorial campaign, sparked partisan debate since the election, and cast a huge shadow over state program planning and administration.

Origins of the Crisis

In November 1978, the Idaho voters passed a one-percent property tax initiative modeled after California's Proposition 13. Faced with the loss of local government property tax revenue of up to 60 percent, the Idaho Legislature replaced the 1-percent limit with a property tax freeze and reduced public school tax levies.[3] To compensate public schools for lost property tax funds, the Legislature dramatically increased its appropriation to public schools.[4] Since the election of President Reagan, the state personal and corporate income tax base also has eroded as Idaho has moved to conform to federal changes in regulations and laws.

As long as Idaho's economy was prosperous, the tax base erosion caused no apparent problems. In the autumn of 1981, there were significant layoffs in Idaho's wood products and mining industries, and state tax collections began to fall behind estimates. In January 1982, the Legislative Revenue Projection Committee estimated FY 1983 revenue collections at $425.9 million for the state's general fund.[5] Despite a faltering economy, a several million dollar FY 1983 surplus appeared likely and the Legislature passed some supplemental appropriations raising the appropriation level to $442.1 million.[6] No one foresaw the sudden fiscal crisis that would occur in April as Idaho citizens filed income tax returns.

THE CRISIS HITS

The April revenue figures received May 6, by the Division of Financial Management from the Idaho State Tax Commission were worse than anyone imagined they could be. On May 8, the Division of Financial Management re-estimated revenues at $408.3 million. Instead of a several million dollar surplus, it was apparent that the state would be facing a $13.8-million deficit.[7] A $13.8-million deficit would require only a 3.3-percent cutback if applied to the entire fiscal year. However, on May 8 there were only seven weeks left in the fiscal year and a 24.5-percent reduction would be needed to bring state expenditures down to anticipated revenues. The Governor could not ignore the crisis because Idaho has a $2-million constitutional debt ceiling and laws which make clear that the Governor has an obligation to reduce allotments to keep the state from having a deficit.

On May 10, the Governor announced that employees paid from the state's general fund would receive a 20-percent pay cut for the remaining seven weeks of the state's fiscal year.[8] Employees were given Fridays off as an unpaid holiday and many state offices were staffed at minimal levels on Fridays for the remainder of the fiscal year. The Governor also requested that state agency heads reduce their costs within target figures developed by the Division of Financial Management. Agencies complied, and allotments were reduced $7.2 million.[9]

Revenues declined further in May and June, and the "payless Fridays" and allotment reductions were insufficient to prevent a deficit. Payroll accounting procedures were changed so that payrolls amounting to about $5 million were charged to FY 1983 instead of FY 1982. Encumbrances were cancelled and shifted to FY 1983. Tax refunds, which normally would have been paid in FY 1982, were deferred until FY 1983, thus raising net tax collections for FY 1982. The result was that revenues were raised to the $406.3-million level and expenditures pared so that there was a small ($246,500) balance carried over into FY 1983.[10]

The Nine Percent Cutback for FY 1983

When the April revenue report was released by the State Tax Commission on May 6, 1982, it was evident that reductions would need to be made in FY 1983 expenditures as well as in FY 1982 costs. The Idaho Legislature had appropriated $464.7 million from the state's general fund based on revenue estimates which had totaled $465.1 million.[11] General fund revenues had increased from $388 million to $406 million from FY 1981 to FY 1982 and it was obvious that they would not reach $465 million in FY 1983. In June 1982, the Governor estimated FY 1983 revenues would be $421 million and on June 14 he issued Executive Order 82-13 requiring state agencies to submit a plan to reduce general account expenditures by 9 percent.

The Governor and the Division of Financial Management gave state agencies six weeks to plan for the 9-percent holdback. State agencies had time to involve division directors and program administrators in the reduction process and the impact of each cut was carefully identified. Agency reduction plans were reviewed by the Division of Financial Management and the Governor; the amounts of the approved reductions were embodied into Executive Order 82-17 of August 3, which decreased agency allotments.

Some state officials asked for exemption from the holdbacks. An official of the Department of Corrections stated that staff shortages and prison overcrowding might result and cause an increase in prison escapes.[12] A court official asked for exemption on grounds that a high proportion of the costs of the judicial branch were salaries set by state law.[13] The Governor's August 3 Executive Order contained a number of full and partial exemptions from the holdback. The Judicial Branch received only a 2.8-percent reduction, the Department of Corrections 3.3 percent, and the Department of Revenue and Taxation 2.6 percent. Public schools were entirely exempt from the holdback order.[14] Under Idaho law, any holdback in public school funds would have triggered a property tax increase in the fall of 1982 and the Governor was reluctant to raise this issue two months before the election.[15] The result of the exemption process was that with $19.3 million in public school funds entirely exempt and some other agencies partially exempt, the net effect of the cutback was $20.1 million rather than the $42 million proposed in June.

The Gubernatorial Campaign and October Holdback

The budget-balancing approach of Governor John Evans became a major issue in the gubernatorial election campaign. An advertisement sponsored by the Idaho Republican Party claimed that $13.8 million in FY 1982 obligations were transferred into FY 1983 and that the deficit for FY 1983 would be $70.8 million.[16] The advertisement concluded, "Let's Return Fiscal Sanity to Idaho--Elect Phil Batt." Governor Evans fought back, stating:

> I didn't run this state into a deficit. I balanced the budget and I did it morally, ethically and constitutionally. I think that he [Batt] misinterpreted this issue for political purposes. I was

insulted and outraged when I heard he was claiming this in his television ads.

The candidates differed also on the way to deal with the 1983 fiscal crisis. Governor Evans stated that he had ruled out holding back $19.3 million in funding for public schools because it would have driven up local property taxes by an equal amount. He attacked the Lieutenant Governor for suggesting the holdback and recommended closing the loopholes in the state tax system and broadening the sales tax. The Lieutenant Governor said he did not favor an increased property tax but said the solution lay in cutting budgets and, perhaps, a temporary increase in the sales tax.

When the gubernatorial campaign entered its final weeks, Governor Evans was faced with a new fiscal crisis. The U.S. Supreme Court refused to review a case involving a multi-state and multi-national payment of Idaho corporation income taxes. With the last chance of preventing a $6 to $7-million loss in corporation income taxes gone, Governor Evans ordered a 1-1/2-percent holdback of funds from state agencies.[18] Public schools were exempt from the holdback, leaving a net reduction of $3.2 million. Most state agencies had anticipated further holdbacks and quickly prepared plans for 1-1/2-percent additional savings. The 1-1/2-percent holdback was not implemented through an executive order, which made specific allotment reductions (as was done in May and August holdbacks) but agencies were expected to reduce expenditures by 1-1/2 percent. The 1-1/2-percent holdback may have been politically helpful to Governor Evans because the Governor was shown to be taking the responsible position of cutting costs in the face of declining revenues. As election day neared, most observers felt the gubernatorial election would be very close.

ELECTION RESULTS AND THE QUESTION OF MANDATE

Governor Evans won re-election by a narrow (50.6 percent) majority over his Republican challenger Phil Batt. Despite the debate over whether or not the 1982 budget was balanced by Evans, the budget issue does not appear to have been decisive. There is evidence that Batt's support of right-to-work legislation and attempts by several PACs to exploit Evans's veto of that bill in the last session sparked heavy union turnout in labor-oriented counties, which Evans carried by an almost 2 to 1 margin.[19] This issue was exemplified by the publication by a group called B.R.I.M.S.T.O.N.E. of a comic, "The Adventures of Big John," which portrayed Evans as a puppet of out-of-state union bosses. Although Batt disavowed any connection with the publication and acknowledged it could cost him votes, he apparently did not publicly use his influence[20] to stop the distribution of about 250,000 copies in Idaho. The comic offended many independent voters and the backlash may have cost Batt the election.

In other elective offices, the Democratic Treasurer and Auditor and the Republican Secretary of State and Superintendent of Public Instruction were re-elected. The Republican Lieutenant Governor, who was defeated in the campaign for governor, was replaced by the Republican Attorney General. The Attorney General was replaced with a Republican candidate who will probably carry on most of the former Attorney General's policies. The incoming Lieutenant Governor of Idaho, David Leroy, has developed an internship program for his office and hopes to make some major research and policy studies during his four-year term.

Despite some changes in individual members of the legislature as well as in the legislative leadership, the partisan and ideological composition of both houses remained virtually the same as before the election. The legislature continues to be highly conservative in economic and social issues and heavily Republican. Although the Republicans lost five seats in the House, they maintained a better than five-to-two edge with a 51 to 19 margin. In the Senate, the Democrats picked up two seats but fell well short of their stated goal, capturing a majority in that house. Instead, the Republicans held a relatively comfortable 21 to 14 advantage after the election. From the gubernatorial perspective, however, the inability of the Republicans to attain a "veto-proof" two-thirds majority in both houses was a positive note in an otherwise normal Republican Legislative sweep.

Given the closeness of the gubernatorial contest and the maintenance of the partisan status quo in other statewide offices, the 1982 election cannot be interpreted meaningfully as either a mandate for change or a vote of confidence in the officeholders. As usual in Idaho electoral politics, the public's perceptions of the candidates personally rather than their particular stands on the issues probably had much to do with the results.

THE FISCAL SITUATION DETERIORATES IN NOVEMBER AND DECEMBER, 1982

After the election, the Governor was faced with new fiscal and economic problems. Idaho's unemployment rate reached the highest level (11.1 percent) in more than 22 years.[21] Idaho tax collections continued much below the previous year and by mid-November the Division of Financial Management had revised its general fund revenue estimates to $405 million.[22] Considering the August and October holdbacks and a small amount of FY 1982 reappropriations, the spending authority of state agencies stood at $441.7 million or more than $36 million greater than revenue estimates.

The Governor and his budget staff took the leadership in alerting state legislators to the seriousness of the fiscal situation. The Administrator of the Division of Financial Management had a series of regional meetings for legislators and the public throughout the state and listed six alternatives for raising the needed funds.

On November 29, the Governor announced that higher unemployment had prompted a reduction of the general fund revenue estimate by an additional $10 million to $395 million.[23] The Governor stated that the latest estimates "further underscore the need for a special session of the Legislature before the end of the year."[24]

The Idaho Legislature met in organizational session for several days in early December without taking action on the fiscal situation. On December 14, the Governor recommended a 10-percent surcharge on personal income taxes and other measures.[25] The Republican Speaker of the House reacted by suggesting the Governor was putting too much weight on tax hikes rather than budget cuts.[26] On December 18, the Governor proposed a special legislative session. Republican legislative leaders turned down the plea and, without assurance of cooperation, the Governor did not call the special session. On December 21, Republican legislative leaders were reported considering massive reductions that would eliminate 1,600 state jobs and reduce costs by $28 million.[27] Governor Evans promptly attacked proposals such as closing Lewis-Clark State College, eliminating the state's agricultural research program, and abolishing the state's Human Rights Commission.[28] December ended with the Governor and the legislature at odds without action to remedy the budget imbalance.

Solutions Are Proposed--January to February, 1983

In late December, Governor Evans proposed his own budget-balancing plan in his FY 1984 Executive Budget. The plan recommended a one-cent sales tax increase effective March 1, 1983, a corporation tax increase, an income tax surcharge, the filing of quarterly income tax payments by corporations, and two measures intended to eliminate loopholes in the corporate income tax.[29] Having previously committed himself to refrain from triggering a property tax increase, the Governor rejected suggestions that the 9-percent August holdback and the 1-1/2-percent October holdback be applied to public schools.

In January the Legislative Revenue Committee met and estimated $374.3 million available for FY 1983.[30] With spending authority at $441.7 million, the legislature was estimating a budget gap of $67.4 million. House Speaker Tom Stivers first proposed selling up to $50 million in

long-term exempt bonds and making up the remaining
$20-million shortfall through fund transfers and program
eliminations.[31] When this plan was criticized, House
Republican leaders developed a new plan which involved some
budget reductions for the current fiscal year, some
transfers from other funds, a sales tax increase, and the
issuance of tax anticipation notes.[32] Under this plan
public school foundation payments were to be cut sufficiently in FY 1983 to balance the budget. At the start of
the FY 1984 (in July 1983), the state was to issue tax
anticipation notes to repay public schools and prevent the
automatic triggering of the property tax increase. The tax
anticipation notes were to be repaid from a sales tax
increase that would run from March 1, 1983, to June 30,
1984.

The Republican plan embodied in H.B. 130 passed both
houses and was approved by the Governor with two exceptions.
The Governor vetoed a $6.4-million reduction for public
schools and a 1-1/2-percent reduction in funds for other
state agencies. The Governor made the vetoes at a time when
there were signs of economic recovery in Idaho and the
governor felt that the one-cent sales tax increase and other
funds would keep the 1982-83 general fund in balance. As of
July 1983, it was apparent that the Governor was correct in
his estimates. The 1982-83 year closed with a surplus. The
serious fiscal crisis that began in May 1982 appeared to be
over.

Administrative Implications of the State's Fiscal Situation

The cutbacks of May, August, and October, 1982 and the
threat of further cutbacks in FY 1983 and FY 1984 have had
an overwhelming impact on program planning in Idaho. With
10.5-percent cutbacks already made, and an additional
cutback possible for FY 1984, state agency directors are not
putting much time into planning new programs. They are
trying to protect and preserve existing programs. According
to one official, agency heads are more active in protecting
their turf and preserving their budgets than ever before.
This is a time of great fiscal uncertainty and no program
administrator can be sure that his or her program will be
spared elimination or substantial reduction.

In this atmosphere of great fiscal austerity, it is
possible for courageous administrators to make politically
sensitive administrative changes that save money. The
Department of Administration, for example, has used this
period to replace state custodial personnel with private
maintenance contracts.

The two areas of state government in which there is
increased emphasis are industrial development and tourism.

Governor Evans, his opponent (Phil Batt), and both candidates for lieutenant governor emphasized the need for Idaho to bolster its tourist economy and to attract new industry and population growth in Idaho. The recession and state fiscal crisis seem to have produced strong support for industrial and economic expansion by most Idaho political leaders.

CONCLUSIONS

Incumbent Governor John V. Evans was re-elected in Idaho in 1982 and none of the other statewide incumbent officials were defeated for re-election. The Idaho Legislature continued to have a 5 to 2 margin in the House and a 3 to 2 margin in the Senate. The 1982 election brought very few of the problems and changes one typically finds in Idaho during an election year.

The most significant governmental development in Idaho in 1982 and the first half of 1983 was the most severe fiscal crisis in sixty years. An eroding tax base and a recession affected by declining demand for wood products brought a sharp decline in Idaho tax revenues. To complete the 1982 fiscal year with a surplus, Governor Evans needed to impose drastic expenditure reductions in May 1982, including requiring payless Fridays for many state employees for the last seven weeks of the fiscal year.

The fiscal crisis continued in the 1982 fiscal year with the Governor needing to impose a 9-percent expenditure reduction in August and another 1-1/2-percent reduction in October. The fiscal crisis was not resolved until March 1983 when the Legislature passed a one-cent increase in the state's sales tax to repay tax anticipation notes which the state would need to issue to balance the FY 1983 budget. The cutbacks during 1982 have encouraged state officials to shift their attention from planning new programs to preserving and protecting existing programs. The fiscal crisis seems also to have increased support for expanding the state's industrial and tourist economic base.

NOTES

[1] The Council of State Governments, *The Book of the States, 1982-83*, (Lexington, Kentucky: The Council of State Governments, 1982), p. 409.

[2] Ibid., p. 365.

[3] The Idaho 1979 Legislature limited property taxes by limiting 1979 property taxes certified in September, 1979 to the amount certified in September, 1978. The freeze has continued but in 1981 and 1982 local governments in Idaho may certify up to a 5-percent increase over the amount certified in any of the previous three years.

[4] Appropriations for the public school foundation increased 102 percent from FY 1978 to FY 1983 while all general fund appropriations increased 67 percent. During this period, public school foundation appropriations increased from 33.8 percent to 40.8 percent of total general fund appropriations.

[5] For the projections see H.C.R. 29 in *Idaho Session Laws*, 1982, p. 948.

[6] Idaho Legislative Fiscal Office, *Legislative Fiscal Notes*, June 22, 1982, p. 1.

[7] Idaho Division of Financial Management, *Idaho Outlook*, July, 1982, p. 2.

[8] Reported in The *Idaho Statesman* (Boise), May 11, 1982. On May 13, Governor Evans issued Executive Order 82-11, which reduced the work week of employees paid from the general fund to thirty-two hours and designated Friday as the day which most employees would not work.

[9] Governor John V. Evans, Executive Order 82-12, May 18, 1982.

[10] Governor John V. Evans, *FY 1984 Executive Budget in Brief*, p. 4.

[11] The revenue estimate was revised upward from $463.4 million to $465.1 million during the legislative session as additional revenue measures were passed. The revised revenue estimates and appropriation amounts are found in Idaho Legislative Fiscal Office, *FY 1983 General Account*, March 24, 1982, p. 1.

[12] The Idaho Statesman (Boise), 17 July 1982.

[13] The Idaho Statesman (Boise), 15 June 1982.

[14] Idaho Division of Financial Management, FY 1983 General Account Holdback, 3 August 1982, p. 1.

[15] Idaho Code, Section 33-1001 (4) provides that if the full amount appropriated by the legislature is not transferred to the public school income fund, an increase in property taxes would result.

[16] Idahonian, (Moscow), 26 October 1982.

[17] Idahonian, (Moscow), 16 September 1982.

[18] Idahonian, (Moscow), 19 October 1982.

[19] Ladd Hamilton, "The Kiss of Death in Right-to-Work," Lewiston Morning Tribune (Lewiston), 4 November 1982.

[20] Matthew Collin, "State Finances, Labor Law Dominate Governor's Race," Idahonian (Moscow), 29 October 1982.

[21] Idahonian, (Moscow), 5 November 1982.

[22] Idahonian, (Moscow), 18 November, 1982.

[23] Idahonian, (Moscow), 29 November, 1982.

[24] Ibid.

[25] Idahonian, (Moscow), 14 December 1982.

[26] Ibid.

[27] Idahonian, (Moscow), 21 December 1982.

[28] Idahonian, (Moscow), 23 December 1982.

[29] Governor John V. Evans, FY 1983 Executive Budget in Brief, p. 5.

[30] Idaho Legislature, House Concurrent Resolution No. 4, January, 1983. This included a $3.5 million transfer into the general fund as well as $370.8 million in general fund revenues for FY 1984.

[31] Idahonian, (Moscow), 11 January 1983.

[32] The plan was embodied in H.B. 130.

9. THE 1982 ILLINOIS GUBERNATORIAL ELECTION:

HISTORIC ON MANY "COUNTS"

BOYD KEENAN

Illinois voters gave Republican Governor James R. Thompson an unprecedented consecutive third term on November 2, 1982. But the margin of victory over Democrat Adlai Stevenson III was a mere 5,074 ballots (of nearly 3.7 million cast), and the challenger's recount request was not rejected by the State Supreme Court until three days before the January 10 (1983) inauguration.

As in other Great Lakes and midwestern states, the 1982 Illinois campaign centered on issues arising from economic recession. The Democratic challenger argued that Illinois was faring worse than its neighbors. The Republican incumbent contended that the state was weathering fiscal crises with less misfortune than others in the region. But three weeks after the election, new data forced Governor Thompson to acknowledge that the future would yield economic woes approaching in severity those that challenger Stevenson had predicted. And, as this is written, the Governor has just completed a complex legislative battle--centered on tax increases--more controversial than any faced in his earlier administrations.

These ingredients of the 1982 Illinois election, then, will place it in the history books: (1) the only election providing a governor with a consecutive third term; (2) the closest election in terms of vote margin; and (3) intense debates over economic distress. A fourth aspect, one not actually a factor in the ultimate election of a governor, may stand as even more significant in the broader social sphere. This is the record-breaking turnout of black voters in Chicago.

Though not fully understood at the time, this closest gubernatorial race in Illinois history may be the first manifestation of what could become a new black "movement." Some believe the election may have significant long-range impacts, both state and national. From the moment that early election night returns showed Thompson trailing Stevenson in Chicago's black wards by much wider margins than predicted, astute observers suspected something "big" was happening in Illinois's largest city. Until that point, few questioned major pre-election polls, which indicated a decisive or even a landslide victory for Thompson.

As weeks passed after the election, various political actors and analysts devised theories about why Stevenson, a former U. S. Senator who voluntarily left that chamber in 1980, came within less than 6,000 votes of the Governor, prompting the most dramatic "long count" since Illinois became a state in 1818. Spokesmen in the challenger's camp welcomed the close vote as vindication of his largely-unheralded efforts. (His campaign performance had been so unimpressive that both major Chicago dailies, including the Democratic-leaning Sun-Times, endorsed Governor Thompson.) Leadership in the Chicago Democratic organization, including then-mayor Jane Byrne, took credit for delivering voters for Stevenson, particularly in the black wards on the city's south and west sides. Independent black leaders argued that voter registration campaigns in these wards were the source of Stevenson's surprising showing.

Nearly six months later, in April of 1983, former Democratic Congressman Harold Washington was elected as Chicago's first black mayor. The character of that election and the primary that preceded it proved beyond all doubt that Thompson's earlier close call resulted in large part from the voter registration drives and from the highest turnout of blacks in the history of the state, and perhaps of the country. Before examining the election and the early months of the third Thompson administration in detail, it is necessary to review the state's political and governmental milieu, as well as backgrounds of both candidates and major issues of the campaign.

THE ILLINOIS MILIEU

Through past decades many observers have argued that Illinois is the state most representative of the nation's politics as a whole. The state is often described as the heart of the heartland. From the Illinois-Wisconsin border on the north to the state's southern tip--381 miles in distance--virtually every imaginable social and political setting can be found. Illinois has also long offered the classic picture of the massive Democratic city struggling against the Republican countryside. Chicago, perched in the northeastern corner of the state, remains as Illinois's dominant Democratic stronghold.

But complex social and demographic forces are changing the political face of America's fifth largest state, which had a 1980 population of nearly 11,500,000, ranking behind California, New York, Texas, and Pennsylvania. Generalizations still valid a year ago about both state Republican and Democratic party characteristics are not being challenged. For example, the heart of the Democratic strength traditionnally has been in Chicago and other smaller industrial cities with large numbers of low-income white ethnic and black voters in uneasy alliance. Since the 1982 guberna- torial election, speculation has grown that this alliance may be weakening.

Continuing shifts in population patterns, which intensified after World War II, are affecting both Democratic and Republican parties in ways that even the most knowledgeable analysts admit cannot be fully understood. But the population drift away from the city of Chicago remains the most significant shift. The 1980 census revealed that this movement continued during the 1970s, with the Chicago population placed at 3,005,072, down 10.7 percent since 1970.

A majority of those who left Chicago in the 1970s were white, and some of them have moved into suburban communities outside of Chicago but still in Cook County. But even Cook County's total population, now at 5,253,655, shows a decline of 4.3 percent from 1970. More instructive in understanding present Illinois politics are 1980 census figures for five "collar" counties that surround Cook County. All show population growth of more than 10 percent since 1970, with three recording gains exceeding 30 percent. One of these, DuPage Country, directly west of Cook, is now the state's second largest county, with a population of 658,835, up 33.9 percent since 1970. Population in the non-Chicago portion of Cook County and the five collar counties totals 4,098,552 (1980 census), representing a suburban vote substantially larger than Chicago's.

Some ex-Chicago residents, particularly those staying in Cook County, have taken along their Democratic party preferences. But a large percentage of those moving into the collar counties have become Republicans.

Long ago the term "downstate" was applied to virtually everything outside Cook County in Illinois. In most recent gubernatorial races it has been convenient for the media to cast the contest as between Democratic Cook County forces and downstate Republican elements. But many circumstances now illustrate the inadequacy of this generalization. For instance, Governor Thompson is himself a native and resident of Chicago.

Illinois voters apparently like to share their governorship among various sections of the state and between the two major parties. When Thompson first sought the office in 1976, Democrats and Republicans were tied in providing eighteen governors apiece since statehood was granted.

Prelude to 1982 Election

Thompson first captured state-wide attention as U. S. attorney for northern Illinois in the early and mid-1970s. In this office he successfully sought conviction of several prominent Illinois political leaders on a variety of charges. Best known of these individuals was the late former Governor, Otto Kerner, who was forced to resign from the U.S. Court of Appeals in 1974, following conviction on charges associated with Illinois racetrack scandals. (Kerner, a Democrat elected in 1960 and 1964, resigned from the governorship early in 1968 to accept President Johnson's appointment to the federal bench.)

Thompson first sought elective office in the 1976 gubernatorial election and defeated Democrat Michael J. Howlett, former secretary of state and state auditor, by the greatest margin in history. (The latter was winner in a primary contest with incumbent Dan Walker.) In a year when Democrat Jimmy Carter barely lost the state to Gerald Ford, the 1.4-million Thompson landslide was described by one journalist as an "incredible political feat in a state that has known few runaway elections for governor."[1] In this election Thompson cast himself as a moderate Republican on most issues, but his reputation as an effective prosecutor was usually prominent in campaign materials.

In 1976 Thompson lost Chicago to Howlett by only 160,000 votes, far from the plurality a Democrat needs in the city to carry the whole state. (In 1982, Stevenson's margin over Thompson in Chicago was 464,525 votes, and the latter still managed to squeak through at the state level by 5,074 votes.) The 1976 election also saw Thompson carry twenty of Chicago's fifty wards. Less than a month later came the death of Chicago's legendary mayor, Richard J. Daley. Both Chicago and the entire state began new political eras.

Upon being inaugurated in 1977, Thompson was somewhat of a rarity in another sense. He became one of only twelve Republican governors in the country, and the triumph brought national attention. Thompson '60s inauguration also began an administration that was to be unique in Illinois history. A new state constitution, placed in effect in 1970, provided that the governor taking office in 1977 would serve only a two-year term, thereby removing gubernatorial contests from presidential election years.

In 1978, Thompson won re-election to a full four-year term, defeating Michael Bakalis, former superintendent of public instruction and state comptroller. Though Thompson's 1978 victory margin fell short of the earlier 1.4 million, it still represented a larger plurality than that achieved by any other Illinois governor.

In 1980, at a time when it was clear that no midwestern state would escape the effects of economic recession, Thompson was elected chairman of the thirteen-state Midwestern Governors' Conference. He closed his term as chairman in the summer of 1981 by planning and presiding over the group's twentieth annual conference, whose theme was "Reconstruction of the Midwestern Economy." That event and Thompson's leadership are significant here because they provided an opportunity for him to examine possibilities for economic recovery at the regional level more than one year before he was to use the same theme in his next re-election campaign. His claim that he had been more successful than his midwestern counterparts in times of economic decline was to become central to his 1982 campaign.

The Challenge of a Famous Name

By mid-summer of 1981, a half dozen Democratic hopefuls, including Stevenson, were viewing the gubernatorial nomination. Having freed himself from Senate responsibilities at the end of 1980, Stevenson apparently spent the summer months of 1981 pondering his chances. A Chicago Tribune columnist put it this way:

> Adlai Stevenson is communing with the northern sky in Canada while deciding if he intends to run. That matches the idyllic portrait of Stevenson that has been painted before.[2]

Stevenson was slated by his party's state Central Committee in November of 1981. Running without opposition in the March 1982 primary, he became the Democratic nominee. In selecting Stevenson as their gubernatorial nominee, Democrats confronted Thompson with probably the most illustrious name in modern Illinois politics. The nominee's father, Adlai Stevenson II, was governor from 1949 to 1953 and was the Democratic Party's unsuccessful nominee for the presidency in both 1952 and 1956. Adlai III served in the Illinois General Assembly and as state treasurer before election to the U. S. Senate in 1970.

PRIME ISSUE: THE ECONOMY

Even before his slating--about fourteen months in advance of the general election--Stevenson sounded his own theme of economic recovery for the entire campaign:

> The state is in trouble. The deteriorating economic condition of the state is the main issue.

It's reflection of a failure of leadership. The governor can't escape all responsibility for the condition of the state.³

Thus for more than a year the state's economy dominated virtually all exchanges between Thompson and Stevenson. Such exchanges assumed an intensity perhaps unmatched in Illinois history. Stevenson's theories appeared to chart a mixed course between President Reagan's conservatism and the standard liberalism of the Democratic party. From the beginning, he personalized his comments on the economy: "The state is going through the throes of industrial transformation and he [Thompson] doesn't understand it."⁴

Thompson answered such changes by repeatedly characterizing finances in Illinois as the soundest among midwestern states. He often noted that his state had maintained aid to education and most other services without increasing the income tax or losing its AAA bond rating. Stevenson countered late in November of 1981 with the claim that "the state government is already on the verge of insolvency."⁵

In mid-January 1982, on the even of Thompson's own State-of-the-State address, Stevenson charged that the Governor had "presided over an economic decline unprecedented for Illinois and unmatched by any other state."⁶ In response, a spokesman for the Governor maintained that Stevenson's assessments were in error, based not on a comparison with other midwestern states with similar problems but on national averages: "Illinois may be limping because of the national economy and recession, but it certainly hasn't been crippled to the extent that other comparable state economies have been."⁷

As Thompson presented his fiscal 1983 budget a few days before the 1982 primary, Stevenson warned that the Governor's budget would end up $750 million in the red, partly because the Governor's economic projections were too optimistic. (A year later, in the spring of 1983 after his defeat of Stevenson and when he was urging tax increases, the Governor's critics in the legislature were to recall that his budget submission in 1982 was accompanied by counsel that they end the "raise the income tax debate.")

There was not a single "economics" issue. There were distinct aspects of the question, and challenger Stevenson fashioned a number of these aspects into themes which became central to his campaign attacks. With increasing frequency through the campaign, Stevenson sought to associate Thompson with "Reaganomics." Again and again Stevenson asserted that President Reagan's policies were leading Illinois into deeper recession and that Thompson was the President's major "cheerleader."

No doubt the Governor himself was aware of the likely negative impacts from linkage with President Reagan. The media frequently speculated upon Thompson's perceived efforts to put "political space" between himself and the President. For instance, at a Republican Governors' Conference late in 1981, the Governor had grabbed headlines by urging Defense Secretary Casper Weinberger to seek ways to shift "a relatively few billion dollars, from military to domestic spending."[8] Thompson argued that the defense of the nation is more than military hardware and that by weakening the economy "we are weakening our national defense internally."

The Governor appeared to be attempting to reassert his own moderate Republican image without being disloyal to Reagan. He often addressed the problems of blacks, the elderly, and the disabled. His administration, he said, had provided increased grants to the needy, more home care for the elderly, more money for education, more funds to fight child abuse, tougher laws, and more prisons.

In early February of 1982, after Reagan responded to pressure from Thompson and other governors by promising to seek supplemental appropriations for state unemployment insurance and employment services, the Chicago Tribune applauded Thompson. Describing his approach in dealing with a President of his own party, an editorial declared:

> It is a nicely-judged blend of praise and exasperation. Mr. Thompson keeps saying loudly how much he admires President Reagan's new federalism, while tactfully calling attention to some of the devastation it may create.[9]

However, in that same month, Stevenson charged that Thompson was "not man enough to call for tax increases during a campaign year."[10] According to the Democratic nominee, "Thompson is pushing everything off beyond the next election." In his 1982 budget message, delivered on March 3, 1982, Thompson acknowledged that outside economic forces were taking their toll in Illinois:

> Our basic economic strengths--agriculture and heavy industry--are battered by national and international pressures and forces against which no governor and no legislature can guard or protect, though we have so far withstood recession better than our neighbor states.[11]

During the early months of 1982 there was general agreement in the media and among pollsters that Stevenson was clearly the front-runner and that the weak economy was damaging Thompson's efforts. The Governor's campaign aides now acknowledge that a conscious effort was made to keep the Governor and President Reagan apart when the latter was in Illinois. On only one occasion--at a farm equipment exhibition in a central Illinois field, far from Chicago media--did the two make a joint public appearance during the campaign period. (The President was in the area to make a major campaign address in Peoria in behalf of a fellow Republican, U. S. Representative Robert H. Michel.)

CAMPAIGN HIGHLIGHTS

Thompson's image apparently did not improve until late August or early September of 1982. In addition to unfavorable publicity, which dogged him through the spring and summer months, unemployment in Illinois rose a full percentage point in July to 12.3 percent. The governor was quoted in early August as realizing that he was trailing Stevenson in the polls. Thompson's own explanation for the Democrat's lead was that the latter had been free to tour the state for six months while the Governor was tied down with the General Assembly in the Springfield capital.

In early August, at about the same time the League of Women Voters of Illinois announced it would sponsor a series of four debates, Thompson's organizational efforts and personal attitude seem to have been infused with new enthusiasm. On August 8, he declared: "I've got to convince people they're better off with me as governor no matter what the national economy is. There's not much of an overt tie between me and Reaganomics."[12]

The Debates: Opportunity to Recoup

The debates, which were staged between August 30 and October 23, provided Thompson and his campaign staff an opportunity to revive a lagging candidacy. Aides saw the events as forums where he could regain his popular image as a forceful governor. But leaders in the Stevenson campaign organization, mindful of their candidate's reputation as a lackluster speaker, were also eager to use the debates to his advantage. According to press accounts, Stevenson's advisors believed Thompson, a former prosecutor, would hurt himself by being overly aggressive in his attacks.

Ironically, those in the Thompson camp apparently perceived as a problem their candidate's reputation as a dynamic orator. Since there was a common perception that Thompson was more effective as a speaker than Stevenson, expectations might place an added burden on the Governor to perform more ably than his challenger.

Thompson aides now acknowledge that, before the first debate held in Peoria, they attempted to dissuade him from "hitting too hard" on Stevenson. The latter was seen by many at that time as an atypical lofty politician who would remain "above the battle." The Governor's advisors were fearful that Thompson's aggressiveness might give Stevenson an opportunity to exploit this perception.

In this debate, to the initial chagrin of his aides, Thompson departed from his prepared statements and challenged Stevenson's statements and tactics. In turn, the Democratic nominee responded with uncharacteristic emotion, hurling what some felt were intemperate charges. Thompson's assistants now identify this moment as the turning point of the campaign. "This took the statesman's luster off Stevenson, revealing him as like all other politicians, and he never got it back," one campaign leader argues. "We were wrong and the Governor's intuition was right."

A Tribune poll released on September 5, a week after the first debate, suggested that Thompson's deficit in the surveys was being erased. According to this poll, the Governor had pulled ahead of Stevenson by eight points. Several media representatives expressed the view--after the first two debates--that Thompson was attempting to play the role of underdog. But the observers felt that the Governor found it unnatural to contain himself in responding to Stevenson. One reporter put it this way:

> It appears that Thompson is more comfortable with an aggressive campaign style. Thompson loves the jousting, the ripostes, the parry and thrust. He sometimes can overdo it, as even he will admit, but the hand-to-hand combat is his style.[13]

Some thought the influence of the first debate may have been minimal because it was not televised. The second debate undoubtedly had greater impact because of wide television coverage. In terms of "style," most media representatives believed Thompson was even more effective than in the first debate:

> On the small screen, Thompson came on forcefully, eyes firmly fixed on the cameras, where the real audience was. Stevenson appeared to be ill-at-ease and rambling, his eyes often scanning the Radisson hotel crowd.[14]

Three days after this second debate, Stevenson acknowledged that he was "unhappy" and "disappointed" with major aspects of his campaign. "It's been difficult to get the state focused on my strategy for its economic renewal."[15] The admission seemed to symbolize the tone of the Stevenson effort in the remaining seven weeks of the campaign.

Two October debates remained (in deep southern Illinois and in a Chicago suburb), but all future major polls showed dramatic gains for Thompson. For example, a Sun-Times poll, conducted by the Gallup organization on the weekend before the election, found Thompson leading Stevenson by a 16-percentage-point margin. As discussed later, Thompson's actual victory by only about one-seventh of 1 percentage point challenges the credibility of present polling practices.

Media Treatment of Candidates

One of the most paradoxical aspects of the 1982 campaign was the treatment of Governor Thompson by the media. Though virtually all major state newspapers and most other media outlets eventually endorsed Thompson, the spring and summer months of 1982 probably marked the lowest point of the Governor's entire public career in relations with the media.

A series of media stories, centered on the Governor's personal and family affairs, appeared during this period. In their frequency and character they appeared to Thompson supporters to assume a bizarre flavor. They viewed the stories as digressions designed to embarrass the Governor at critical campaign points. Certainly they plagued the Governor as no other difficulties had in past campaigns, and it seems certain that they affected his popularity and standing in the polls.

Actually, the spate of stories had their origin as early as November of 1981, when the Tribune carried a series of articles on the Thompson family. The dwelt upon tax exemption privileges utilized by Mrs. Thompson in her antique business, tax deductions based on a rental apartment in the basement of the Thompsons' Chicago home, and refinancing of the home through a Chicago bank. (The Governor's spokesmen felt criticism of Mrs. Thompson was particularly unjustified, claiming that she had devised the antique management plan primarily to enable charitable organizations to benefit from a well-publicized sale at the Governor's capital mansion.) Even the articles themselves acknowledged that no illegalities were involved. Thompson, who was successful in proving that the stories were all based on information supplied by himself many months before, termed them a "smear."

March and April 1982 brought even more adverse publicity for the Governor. Jayne Thompson, wife of the

Governor and former practicing attorney, in late March indicated her interest in an available federal judgeship. Mrs. Thompson soon withdrew her name from consideration, but the episode brought negative media coverage.

Still other media presentations in April centered on personal gifts from individuals who had dealings with the state. Once again, Thompson and media critics agreed that information on all such gifts was supplied from records made available for public scrutiny far in advance of the stories. No legal improprieties were involved. Thompson described the attacks as "probably unprecedented in the history of Illinois."[16]

The intensity of the exchange between the Governor and the media was particularly striking in view of his almost unprecedented earlier popularity, including editorial endorsements, extending from his entry into public life. The author of Thompson's only major biography (not an entirely uncritical one) described him as "far and away the state's most successful user of media." This author also contends Thompson became a full blown "media darling" after he became U. S. attorney in 1971.[17]

Thompson was not alone in attracting adverse media attention during the months preceding the election. Probably just as bizarre, and perhaps more damaging over the long run in terms of voter impact, was an embarrassment suffered by Stevenson. Not known as a dynamic speaker, the former Senator himself apparently stimulated the episode by informally mentioning to a reporter that Thompson viewed him as a "wimp."

Other reporters, commentators, and cartoonists seized upon the term, and the entire state seemed preoccupied for a time with Stevenson's perceived wimpish ways. Thus, issues were neglected for several weeks as many columns of print and much air time were devoted to such matters.

THOMPSON VICTORY AFTER LONG COUNT

As already noted, Thompson won the election by a razor-thin margin. His vote totals were 23 percent lower in Chicago than the polls had predicted. He was also down 10 percent in Cook County suburbs and 3 percent outside the county. Pundits, pollsters, and most leaders in both parties were left in shock, bewildered and embarrassed. For historians interested in election predictions, the failure of professional pollsters to capture some hint of the heavy Democratic vote in Cook County will stand alongside the famed 1948 Truman-Dewey miscalculation.

The actual vote clearly resulted from registration drives in Chicago's black wards and an unprecedented turnout there. But why did the pollsters' methodology fail them? Some observers speculate that many polls relied too heavily upon telephone calls and that black family telephone listings are not reflective of true demographic conditions.

Even now, months later, no fully convincing explanations of the pollsters' failure have been provided. Of relevance, however, is a prediction made several days in advance of the election by the Cook County Democratic Committee chairman that his party workers would give the Democratic slate a history-making victory in Chicago. (One of the greatest ironies in recent Chicago political history is the fact that this white chairman suffered a major setback himself three months later when black mayoral candidate Harold Washington defeated incumbent mayor, Jane Byrne, the party machine candidate, in a primary contest.)

Through the first night of tallying ballots, neither candidate offered a prediction of the outcome. But the following day, with 98 percent of the vote tallied, spokesmen for both candidates claimed victory. At that time Thompson held a 35,000-vote lead over Stevenson. However, about 400 precincts, half in heavily Democratic Chicago, remained to be counted. Expecting these late Chicago returns to give him victory, Stevenson convened a "transition" team, and his aides reported plans to ask for a suite of capitol offices to prepare for the transition.

Resolution by Supreme Court

But all parties remained in limbo from election night until November 22, when the Illinois Board of Elections gave its stamp to tabulations showing Thompson winning by 5,074 votes. (Total ballots cast were 3,856,586. Two fringe parties, Taxpayers and Libertarians, drew 22,001 and 24,417, respectively. A total of 183,311 voted for no gubernatorial candidate.)

Under state law, Stevenson then successfully sought "discovery" recounts in at least 58 of the state's 102 counties. This process involved retabulation of the vote in up to 25 percent of the precincts in the selected counties. Next, on the basis of allegations of irregularities and miscounted ballots rising out of this limited recount, the challenger requested the Supreme Court to order a full-fledged statewide recount.

Finally, on January 7, 1983, two months and five days after the polls closed, a divided Illinois Supreme Court rejected the recount request. By a vote of 4 to 3, the Court said the allegations did not warrant a review. Thus, with the 1982 election finally behind him, one week into January, Governor Thompson prepared for his inauguration, scheduled three days later on January 10.

Significance of the Black Vote

Of course Thompson's victory would have more closely approximated the polls' predictions in the absence of the massive turnout of Chicago's black voters. It seems impossible to appreciate either the dynamics of the gubernatorial race or the challenge that Thompson faces in his third term without placing the black vote in distinct Chicago, state, and national perspectives.

The View from Chicago. Two days following the Thompson-Stevenson contest, a black <u>Chicago Tribune</u> columnist, Vernon Jarrett, wrote:

> Tuesday was a historic moment in the history of Chicago politics. Black voters went to the polls in greater percentages than voters in many white wards without the lure of an especially attractive--or repugnant--candidate or a specific crisis-oriented issue. I visited several precincts Tuesday, and I gathered that blacks came out in response to a general crisis-- Reaganomics.
>
> The pro-Stevenson vote was not due to the magnetism of Stevenson. He often appeared befuddled, and he lacked luster. Nor was there a pinpoint animosity against Governor James Thompson, the Republican. However, there was the awareness that Thompson is a Republican and the Illinois extension of President Reagan.[18]

Jarrett's denial of any "pinpoint animosity" against Thompson in Chicago's black wards is particularly striking in view of the extent of his loss of votes there when compared to his showing in his 1978 race. Six largely middle-class black wards on the south side are illustrative. In 1978, the Governor won 26 percent of the vote in those wards. But in 1982 he took only 8 percent. As noted earlier, Stevenson emerged from the 1982 contest with a 465,525-vote plurality in Chicago, winning an extraordinary 74 percent of the vote. Thompson's opponent in 1978, Michael Bakalis, received just 60 percent of the Chicago vote, and edged Thompson there by a modest 166,443 votes.

If, indeed, no strong personal animosity produced the heavy vote against Thompson in the black community, three other factors initially appeared as plausible explanations: (1) an affinity with Stevenson, which the polls never reflected; (2) the resentment stirred by Reaganomics; and

(3) the use of the gubernatorial election as a Democratic "test run" by the black community in advance of the Chicago mayoral primary in late February 1983. Events that unfolded through the year strongly suggest that the latter two factors were most critical. Harold Washington, now serving as Chicago's first black mayor but still a congressman and not yet a mayoral candidate at the time, identified Reaganomics as the key: "Ronald Reagan deserves the credit. Black people know where their interests lie, and it is not with Reagan or his supporters, like Jim Thompson."[19]

Some Chicago analysts believe an adequate interpretation must include other subtle factors. For example, for some months in advance of the gubernatorial race, Chicago's black community had been devising arrangements to identify its strongest candidate for mayor. It was apparently clear to black leaders long before the race for governor that Washington was the most popular possibility. But Washington, who had unsuccessfully sought the mayoralty in 1977, was a reluctant candidate.

It now seems likely that Washington was awaiting results of the gubernatorial contest to determine just how many of the newly registered black voters could be counted upon to turn out on election day. Though pressure had been mounting for Washington to accept the black community's draft, he delayed until about two weeks after the gubernatorial election to make a positive announcement. Then, of course, he went on to defeat incumbent Mayor Jane Byrne and State's Attorney Richard M. Daley, son of the city's late mayor, in the February Democratic primary. In April, he became mayor with a victory over Republican nominee Bernard Epton.

Many believe that support for the reluctant Washington had actually achieved the status of a "grass-roots movement" in advance of the gubernatorial race. If so, votes for Stevenson represented the most dramatic way for blacks to participate in the eventual election of Washington as mayor. From this perspective, Thompson's narrow victory became less disappointing to supporters who had expected a decisive win.

Statewide Perspectives

Chicago legislators have often voted as a bloc in the General Assembly on such issues as taxes, transportation, education, and other human services. No one knows what effect the election of a black mayor and the reorganization of the Chicago City Council will have in the Springfield capital. In the past, particularly during the Daley era, a Chicago mayor in a leadership role with the broader Cook County Democratic organization could deal from a position of strength with state authorities and downstate politicians.

Now, however, there is a strong possibility that the Chicago Democratic machine is dead. Chicago's black Democrats elected a mayor, but it appears that white leadership figures, former stalwarts in the machine, have seized control of the City Council. Possible implications of this situation for state politics are summarized by Professor Milton Rakove, who believes a long-existing system is breaking down:

> The state government in Springfield also is in a state of drift, headed by a governor who has barely got into office and who has little control of his party and who is saddled with a legislature dominated by Democrats who are also fragmented along racial and geographic lines. Who will speak for Chicago for the next two years?...Can Mayor Washington speak for Chicago, with a handful of black legislators and a black constituency that voted solidly for Adlai Stevenson in 1982?[20]

Rakove believes that race has replaced "ethnicity" and party identification as the dominant factor in Chicago politics. He argues that Chicago, formerly a city made up of ethnic groups and neighborhoods represented by ethnic politicians, has become a city of racial areas--black, Hispanic, and white. Politicians representing the latter groups, he says, have become responsive to those racial constituencies. If this is true, traditional labels of Republican, Democrat, and Independent could become relatively meaningless. Such a revolutionary change could have a major impact on political and governmental systems at the state level.

National Significance

It is clear that the election of Harold Washington as Chicago's mayor in April of 1983 captured much more national attention than the gubernatorial race six months earlier. His victory has been acclaimed by some as a momentous event in American politics with possible implications for the 1984 presidential election and beyond. Some have even identified Washington's election as the beginning of a "movement" whereby blacks and other minorities across the country will coalesce to present a united front "within the system."

For reasons noted above, these two elections--the 1982 gubernatorial contest and the 1983 Chicago mayor's race--will be linked by historians. Now recognized as the first statewide election in which this potential black "movement" manifested itself, the Thompson-Stevenson contest assumes more than historical significance. If Washington's Chicago victory should become, indeed, the stimulus for a vital black force in American politics, its roots will always be traced to the Thompson-Stevenson election.

From some perspectives, such an association may not be an enviable one for a Republican governor. But it would be wrong for Thompson to be identified as a major figure inspiring unprecedented reaction from the black community. That role is clearly reserved for Ronald Reagan. The dynamics typified by the phenomenal black registration drives were already largely developed by the time the gubernatorial election was staged. Thompson supporters with hopes for his continued leadership in Illinois or at the national level might well argue that his survival--in the face of such a powerful force--was a major achievement. Most Republican governors in the economically-distressed Midwest met defeat.

Also, Thompson's victory, narrow as it was, has left him--at the relatively young age of 47--as the nation's senior Republican governor among the large states. In 1983-84, he is also chairman of the National Governors' Association (NGA) and past chairman of both the Republican Governors' Conference and the Midwestern Governors' Conference. For many reasons, Thompson's third term will be scrutinized nationally more closely than were his first two terms.

CAMPAIGN EVALUATION

Once the shock of the election's closeness wore off and analyses revealed the dynamics associated with the heavy Democratic vote in Chicago, Thompson and his aides apparently were satisfied with their campaign efforts. One spokesman who had moved from a high-level administration slot into a leading campaign position believes that one key factor was most responsible: "We mobilized all the desirable forces of incumbency."

Others associated with Thompson's campaign echoed this sentiment. There was apparently a successful effort to blend the achievements of his two previous administrations into campaign rhetoric. Campaign strategists maintain that virtually 100 percent of materials used in media advertising came from film shot in "real life" governmental settings. The "everyday" Governor was brought into the campaign. According to spokesmen, two major types of successes from past administrations were emphasized: (1) Thompson effectively controlled budgets and taxes, and (2) he kept the state scandal-free. These successes were overlaid with an image of a "regular" politician but one who was totally clean.

Campaign staff members feel that the public perception of Stevenson as a weak leader, in contrast to Thompson's image as a vigorous governor, was a significant factor in the victory. They are confident that the surprisingly large Democratic vote in Chicago would have gone to any candidate slated by the party. Stevenson's debate performances and his own apparent creation of the "wimp" issue are perceived by the Governor's aides as playing into the overall Thompson strategy.

Probably because of the previous government experience of Thompson's top campaign assistants, reports of effective coordination between the Governor's statehouse office and campaign staff outnumber negative reports. One staff member commented: "From the very beginning we had no flailing around; the two offices were always aware of what the other was doing."

Political Support and Financial Contributions

Much of Thompson's success in winning three consecutive terms is attributable to his ability to gain support from sectors often reserved for Democratic candidates. For example, he has consistently attracted both endorsements and substantial contributions from organized labor.

During the 1978 campaign Thompson was endorsed both by the Illinois Teamsters (Joint Council 25), with a membership of 165,000 and the state's 125,000-member unit of the United Auto Workers (UAW). In the 1982 campaign the Teamsters favored him again, and their donation of $91,500 to Thompson was labor's largest in the campaign. Stevenson received what the media called a "tepid" endorsement from the UAW, but a union spokesman offered the governor a compliment: "Thompson's not the worst governor labor has ever had. He's pretty good."[21]

At the national level, Thompson was cordially received by AFL-CIO delegates at their annual convention several months before the election. But the Illinois AFL-CIO gave Stevenson a less than enthusiastic endorsement. A comparison of contributions illustrates Stevenson's difficulties with organized labor. Thompson received $293,589 from unions while Stevenson got $109,394.

Other examples of Thompson's good fortune in pulling support from unlikely groups are available. Perhaps most surprising, in view of the heavy black turnout for the Democratic nominee, was the support that came from various elements of the black community. This support included endorsements from the Chicago Defender, a prominent black Chicago newspaper, and Mohammed Ali, former world heavyweight boxing champion.

Both Stevenson and a portion of the media consistently charged that "big money" and "special interests" played the dominant role in Thompson's financial campaign. A Common Cause report issued several weeks after the election also was critical of the pattern of contributions to the Governor. The report cited gifts of $340,332 and $16,525 to Thompson and Stevenson, respectively, from the Illinois manufacturing sector.[22] The report also noted that the construction industry raised $460,617 for the Governor and only $44,390 for the Democratic ticket.

State reports indicate that the 1982 gubernatorial campaign was, at a total of $8 million, the most expensive ever staged in Illinois. According to state reports, Thompson and his running mate for lieutenant governor together received nearly $5.8 million. Contributions to Stevenson and his running mate totalled $2.3 million. (The Thompson ticket total is somewhat inflated because it includes $470,000 that the candidate for lieutenant governor raised to win the Republican primary. Stevenson's running mate faced no primary.)

The Matter of "Style"

Mention was made earlier of Thompson's apparent successful "style" in the debates. His personality and style were also frequently cited with respect to fund raising. The sometimes critical biographer quoted earlier declares that "one can describe his fund-raising prowess only as awesome."[23] Not entirely in a complimentary manner, he goes on to describe Thompson's 1978 efforts as "a dazzling display of personality campaigning."

A media preoccupation with Thompson's 1982 style was probably accentuated by Stevenson's lack of charisma. While Stevenson's appearances were often described as stiff and formal, much was made of Thompson's talents in tailoring his appeal to suit his audience. His performances in black Chicago churches and in southern Illinois communities were seen by some commentators as contrived. The Governor's informal manner, combined with a hearty laugh and a massive 6-foot, 6-inch frame, frequently inspired exaggerated caricatures by the media. This was particularly the case when used with depictions of the restrained Stevenson.

However, it would be difficult to find a media representative covering the race who does not view Thompson as an extremely effective campaigner. Illustrating this view are comments from a Chicago Sun-Times columnist, who authored perhaps the most brutal items on Thompson. Reviewing the Governor's television style in a sarcastic piece appearing immediately after the election, he quipped: "While Stevenson is uncomfortable on TV, Thompson plays it like a violin. And Thompson's commercials were among the slickest ever to be seen in this state."[24] He also declared:

> 'Landslide Jim' just slides by. Making him governor was not the point of the exercise. Making him president was. He had everything going for him. . . . He had the endorsement of every large and almost every small newspaper in the state . . . [but] Jim Thompson does not like being governor. Jim Thompson is bored with the governorship. He has been for years.[25]

While this column was one of the most critical printed about the Illinois Governor, it does reflect a concern that even some Thompson supporters voice occasionally. He is often perceived as enjoying the campaign more than the service as governor. Others of his admirers argue that his first two terms did not provide a challenge for a man of Thompson's capabilities. Given the difficulties now facing Illinois, it seems unlikely that anyone will ever be tempted to make this judgment about his third term.

THE THIRD TERM: EARLY MONTHS AND THE FUTURE

Two weeks after the November election, Governor Thompson announced that an unexpected drop in October tax revenues could force the state to make drastic cuts or increase taxes to avoid deficits. "I've talked with a number of governors in both Republican and Democratic states in the last four or five days and they've found the same phenomenon," the Governor said.[26] He emphasized that neither Democrats nor Republicans in state government had realized earlier there was a problem.

According to the Governor, the anticipated revenue decline of $107 million was flagged by neither the office of the state comptroller nor the Economic and Fiscal Commission. Democrats control both, Thompson pointed out. "If there was any flagging to be done, they would have done it."[27] But the Governor came under sharp criticism from some Democrats, who charged that he had waited until after the November 2 election to reveal the state cash crisis.

Even the <u>Chicago Tribune</u>, which had given the Governor one of his strongest endorsements, received "Mr. Thompson's jolting news" with some indignation. An editorial reminded readers that he and his aides had "poo-poohed Stevenson's arguments that Illinois was in bad shape" and might need new tax resources:

> They told the world--especially the voting world --that Illinois had everything under control because

they'd planned things so much better than other Midwest governments. But it is now obvious that everything wasn't under control. Not that there is any evidence that news of the October drop was covered up . . . . Yet it appears that the state's finances are more fragile than the governor had indicated.[28]

As the weeks passed, it became clear to Republicans and Democrats alike that expected revenue growth of $400 to $500 million a year would not be available. The underlying cause was unemployment; people out of work simply do not pay taxes. In December of 1982 the Tribune seemed to voice the sentiments of many state residents: ". . . the question of who is to blame for failing to foresee or warn of this crunch is important, but it can wait. A coherent tax structure cannot."[29] In early January the Illinois Economic and Fiscal Commission reported that it expected the state to receive $374 million less in fiscal year 1983 than the Thompson administration had predicted in October before the election.

First Tax Increase Proposal in Fourteen Years

In his third inaugural message, delivered January 10, 1983, Thompson pledged to deliver an "urgent agenda" to solve Illinois's fiscal crisis. On the heels of the revenue shortage disclosure, he seemed to demonstrate a sudden change in direction away from budget balancing and towards human concerns. He did not reveal at that point whether he would seek higher taxes.

The question of possible new taxes dominated the legislature and increasingly concerned most sectors of the state during the early weeks of 1983. Democrats, who controlled both houses of the General Assembly, generally favored a higher income tax and other revenue reforms. But most of them were unwilling to risk voter anger, particularly after the Governor's assurances before the election, unless Thompson himself would vigorously seek support for new taxes among his fellow Republicans. Daily the media highlighted the Governor's predicament.

In a year of many ironies for Thompson, perhaps the most significant irony of all soon became visible to everyone. No statewide tax increase had been approved since the income tax was enacted in 1969 with the support of a Republican governor, Richard B. Ogilvie. By most criteria, Ogilvie is still judged as one of the state's most effective governors. But after only one term he was defeated in 1972 by resentful voters. There is agreement among Illinois politicians that the income tax was almost totally responsible for his rejection. The "Ogilvie effect," a term coined to describe the probable treatment of voters for other politicians favoring new taxes, entered the Illinois political lexicon in 1972. It was resurrected by worried office holders in 1983 as they debated the necessity of greater revenues.

In mid-January, Democratic Senate President Philip Rock, himself a probable future candidate for the U. S. Senate or the governorship, declared that "an increase in the state's income tax is necessary if Illinois is not to go broke." What if Thompson failed to propose such a tax? "I told him I'd laugh him out of the chamber," Rock reported.[30]

Finally, in his February State-of-the-State message, Thompson asked the General Assembly to adopt a $2.1-billion tax package increase, including a 60-percent increase in personal income taxes. Without new taxes, Thompson staff aides warned, he would be forced to propose "draconian" budget cuts. The media saw the Governor as facing the toughest job of his career in efforts to persuade legislators that his $2.1-billion tax increase was necessary.

Through February, Thompson could muster no support among his Republican colleagues. And even Democrats desiring additional revenues, recalling the Governor's rosy picture of the state's economy on the eve of the election, vowed to resist pulling his "chestnuts" out of the fire. In the face of such attitudes, at the beginning of March, Thompson sent the General Assembly a "doomsday" budget which he himself termed "unacceptable" and "inadequate" to meet the needs of the state. While emphasizing that present revenues would force such an austere budget, the Governor pleaded with the General Assembly to pass substantial tax increases. At $13.9 billion, his doomsday budget offered several hundred million dollars less than the 1983 budget and less than any budget in recent years. It would require drastic cuts reaching into the very core of state government.

Also in March, Thompson--apparently in response to claims that his remedy of increased taxes was far out of proportion to the need--reduced his estimate of required new taxes from $2.1 billion to $1.8 billion. The Illinois Chamber of Commerce, among others, charged that his doomsday budget was merely "a stalking horse" for persuading the legislature to increase taxes. At the same time, the Illinois unemployment rate jumped sharply from 12.6 to 13.5 percent while the nation's official jobless rate held steady at 10.4 percent.

In mid-April, reportedly as the price for support from Republican leadership in the Senate, Thompson abandoned his plan for a permanent income tax increase and proposed a temporary "surtax" that would expire in four years. Until the last week in April most of the media assumed a moderate-to-pessimistic posture on Thompson's chances of persuading the required number of legislators to accept a substantial tax increase. About that time the Governor stepped up his own personal efforts to take the tax matter to the people. After a swing through southern Illinois, viewed as a center of anti-tax sentiment, Thompson was quoted as expressing confidence in his own abilities to influence the General Assembly through a public convinced that a higher income tax was necessary.

He continued to call for a $1.8-billion increase in state taxes until two days before the 1983 Memorial Day recess. At that time he again reduced his requested amount in an apparent effort to gain votes in the Senate. This time the Governor lowered his recommended tax increase to $1.5 billion. For a time it appeared that the Governor's supporters in the Senate might persuade enough of their colleagues to approve such a proposal. But on May 27, the last day before the recess, Governor Thompson and Senate leaders came up one vote short in efforts to put the $1.5-billion comprehensive tax plan to a vote.

Resolution in the General Assembly

Thompson continued the battle for higher taxes through June, midst legislative dynamics more complex than any he had faced in his previous terms. The split among Chicago Democrats, stemming from the City Council conflict between Mayor Washington's predominantly black forces and the faction led by the white Cook County Democratic chairman, made negotiations difficult for both the Governor and legislative leaders. Unlike most previous legislative sessions--particularly those during Mayor Richard Daley's reign--there was no single Democratic party leader in Chicago with whom the Governor could strike a deal to put Chicago votes on a tax bill. Instead, Thompson was forced to negotiate with individual Chicago legislators, as well as with those from other parts of the state.

As the June 30 mandatory adjournment date approached, the media increasingly warned that the doomsday budget was a real possibility. The plight of the state without a tax increase was likened to a fiscal abyss perhaps unmatched in any other state in recent years. Three days before adjournment, Thompson agreed to support a House proposal increasing taxes by only $1 billion. Partisan support from legislative leaders, plus Thompson's own efforts, led to passage of the measure.

Illinois personal income taxes rose from 2.5 to 3 percent, and corporate income taxes were boosted from 4 to

4.8 percent. A state sales tax rose from 4 to 5 percent, but an existing 2-percent tax on food and medicine was to be abolished as of January 1, 1984. Under the legislation the income taxes were scheduled to expire June 30, 1984, but the sales tax provisions were to remain.

Thus, instead of the $13.9-billion 1983-84 doomsday budget, which Thompson had battled against, the legislation provided the state with $15.7 billion. Representatives of some groups dependent upon state services felt the increases were inadequate. And some taxpayers (many within the Governor's own party) argued that Thompson had deceitfully won re-election on the pledge to hold taxes steady. But general response around the state seemed sympathetic to the position in which the Governor and legislators found themselves.

Thompson himself, though expressing regret that his higher tax increase proposals were not accepted by the General Assembly, appeared pleased with the last-minute action. "We will take the tax dollars and invest them in a better state," he said. "Tonight's vote was a vote of confidence in the future of this state."[31] He told a televised press conference that the night of the successful vote was "probably the most significant" in his six and one-half years as governor.

Lessons After Three Victories

After having won victories in three gubernatorial contests and having signed into law the largest tax increase in Illinois history, what are Thompson's most significant contributions to statecraft? Some of the Governor's aides and several detached observers, as well, believe Thompson's method of exercising power is most worthy of attention. While the governor has his share of political critics, relatively few of them have charged him with misuse of power. This appears striking in that the 1970 Illinois Constitution clearly provides for a "strong" governor. Some scholars and practitioners believe the office is entrusted with the greatest power of any governor in the nation. In addition to the absence of any constitutional limitation on terms, the Illinois governor is given strong budgetary control, including the item veto and an amendatory veto power probably unparalleled elsewhere. (Critics of the system claim it permits the governor to dip into the legislative process.) Aides believe Thompson's examples of responsible wielding of such immense power may provide helpful examples for other governors granted considerable constitutional authority.

Staff leadership in the Thompson administration appears particularly alert to the dangers of inertia that haunt second- and third-term governors. They recognize that the dangers of insensitivity become greater each year a governor remains in office. The Governor and his staff realized from the first that a third term would be different from the two preceding ones. They knew it could not resemble very much the Governor's first-term, which was the short two-year term imposed by the state's new constitution. In many ways the latter was simply a continuation of the 1976 campaign. Nor could the third term be simply a copy of the second term. Staff members report that they always assumed the 1979-83 administration would create a record upon which a campaign for a third term would be mounted.

But even before the unexpected "long count" of the 1982 election and the tension-filled first six months of 1983, there was no confidence that the third term would be followed by an attempt to win the fourth. Already, in addition to being the only Illinois governor elected for three consecutive terms, upon completion of his present term Thompson will have served the state longer than any other governor in this century.

In 1977, when he first burst upon the scene as perhaps the most colorful of a small band of promising Republican governors in the post-Watergate period, Jim Thompson, then only forty years old, was cited frequently as a potential national office holder. Such speculation has faded and reappeared through the years. The close call in the 1982 election dampened such talk for a time. And the tax battles during the first year of his third term so dominated the scene that little time was left for discussions of this sort.

However, in August of 1983, Thompson's installation as chairman of the National Governors' Association rekindled interest in prospects of a national leadership role. The media claimed that he had fought for the one-year term in an effort to gain national visibility. Acceptance of the chairmanship was seen by some as a symbolic moment for the Governor. Finally the "long count" and the 1983 tax battles were behind him. Thompson himself declared: "This is a changing time of my life. Six and a half years ago I was a raw rookie who didn't know much."[32]

Thompson and Illinois together face a period of almost unprecedented problems. The fiscal challenge, especially, seems certain to confront him during the remainder of his third term, particularly since the income tax provisions are temporary. This challenge stands in the way both of further personal aspirations and of history's assessment of his stewardship. If he is able to make visible progress through 1986, he will be in a position to claim the voters' attention for further service in Illinois or on the national level. But if he fails he is likely finished as a political leader.

NOTES

[1] Robert E. Hartley, *Big Jim Thompson of Illinois* (Chicago: Rand McNally & Company, 1979), p. 97.

[2] F. Richard Ciccone, "Sign Up Here for Governor," *Chicago Tribune*, 26 July 1981.

[3] Basil Talbott, Jr., "Adlai to Offer Himself as Candidate for Governor," *Chicago Sun-Times*, 10 September 1981.

[4] Jon Margolis, "Adlai Says He'd Serve Full Term as Governor," *Chicago Tribune*, 6 November 1981.

[5] David Axelrod, "Adlai Hits Thompson on School-Aid Finagling," *Chicago Tribune*, 24 November 1981.

[6] David Axelrod and Mitchell Locin, "Adlai: Thompson Has Caused Decline," *Chicago Tribune*, 13 January 1982.

[7] Ibid.

[8] Jon Margolis, "Thompson Pleads for Economy," *Chicago Tribune*, 24 November 1981.

[9] "Nice Save, Mr. Thompson" (Editorial), *Chicago Tribune*, 3 February 1982.

[10] Michael Briggs, "Pro-Reagan Stand Seen as Major Election Issue," *Chicago Sun-Times*, 22 February 1982.

[11] Daniel Egler and Mitchell Locin, "Thompson Plan Reduces Spending," *Chicago Tribune*, 4 March 1982.

[12] Mitcell Locin, "Thompson on the Trail--I Know Job I've Got to Do," *Chicago Tribune*, 8 August 1982.

[13] Philip Lentz, "Players' Roles a Bit Reversed in '82 Gubernatorial Contest," *Chicago Tribune*, 12 September 1982.

[14] Ibid.

[15] G. Robert Hillman, "Stevenson Vows Daily Blast at Foe," *Chicago Sun-Times*, 13 September 1982.

[16] Mitchell Locin, "Thompson Lashes Out, Defends Gifts, Funds," *Chicago Tribune*, 24 April 1982.

[17] Robert E. Hartley, *Big Jim Thompson of Illinois*, p. 189.

[18] Vernon Jarrett, "The Armies at the Ballot Box," Chicago Tribune, 4 November 1982.

[19] David Axelrod, "Revived Machine Facing Tough Tests," Chicago Tribune, 7 November 1982.

[20] Milton Rakove, "Chicago's New Political Base," Chicago Tribune (Perspective Section), 29 May 1983.

[21] David Axelrod, "Adlai Wind Tepid UAW Backing," Chicago Tribune, 16 September 1982.

[22] Philip Lentz, "Interest Groups Backed Thompson," Chicago Tribune, 3 May 1983. (Article cites report from Common Cause, which based figures on statements filed with Illinois Election Board.)

[23] Hartley, Big Jim Thompson of Illnois, p. 186.

[24] "'Landslide' Jim Just Slides By," Chicago Sun-Times, 4 November 1982.

[25] Ibid.

[26] Phil Lentz and Robert Enstad, "Thompson Calls Shortfall New," Chicago Tribune, 20 November 1982.

[27] Ibid.

[28] "Mr. Thompson's Jolting News" (Editorial), Chicago Tribune, 22 November 1982.

[29] "Mr. Thompson's New Powers" (Editorial), Chicago Tribune, 7 December 1982.

[30] Daniel Egler, "Tell it Like it is on Tax, Rock Urging Thompson," Chicago Tribune, 16 January 1983.

[31] Mitchell Locin, "Illinois Steps Back from Edge of Abyss," Chicago Tribune, 3 July 1983.

[32] Jon Margolis, "A 'New' Thompson will Lead Governors," Chicago Tribune, 2 August 1983.

10. THE RE-ELECTION OF A GOVERNOR AND THE AFTERMATH:

THE CASE OF KANSAS, 1982-1983

MARVIN A. HARDER

It is conventional wisdom that an unanticipated crisis is politically hazardous for a governor. If few good options are open when a crisis suddenly develops, a governor may be perceived by the voters as ineffectual. On the other hand, a crisis may also be an opportunity to accomplish what otherwise would be politically difficult or impossible.

Governor John Carlin of Kansas was confronted with an unanticipated crisis during the last eighteen months of his first four-year term in office. State revenues fell sharply below what had been projected by the Revenue Estimating Group. He responded by ordering a four-percent recision in the current operating budgets of state agencies. Faced with the prospect of further recisions and the consequent costs in reductions in services and in political support of those constituencies adversely affected, the Governor chose to become an aggressive advocate for the enactment of a minerals severence tax law. By defending the proposed tax as equitable and fair, he was able to counteract in degree the unpopularity that ordinarily accompanies support for new or increased taxation.

Governor Carlin probably won re-election because of his strategy and for reasons to be presented later. But there is a prior question: Why was Democrat Carlin able to win the governorship in Republican Kansas in the first place? To answer that question requires a brief excursion into the history of electoral politics in Kansas.

HISTORICAL PERSPECTIVE

There have been two eras in the history of electoral politics in Kansas. During the first era, from the admission of Kansas into the Union in 1861 to the middle of the decade of the nineteen fifties, the Republican Party was dominant. In most general elections, Republican Party candidates for district or statewide offices could expect to win about 58 percent of the total number of votes. Most election outcomes were predictable because party identification was the strongest influence in voting behavior. Republicans who were in the majority voted for Republican candidates except during those years when short-term influences, such as intense party factionalism or a severe economic recession, caused some Republicans to defect by voting for one or more Democrats. Democrats who won gubernatorial or congressional offices were only rarely re-elected to office. Most defecting Republicans did not change their party identification. The stability of the party balance or electoral power was not undermined by population changes, such as the immigration of southern blacks into northern industrial cities during the nineteen thirties, forties, and fifties or such as the immigration of middle class northerners into the sunbelt states of Arizona and Florida. The general election choices that voters were given were essentially selected by the elites of each of the major party organizations. The adoption in 1908 of the direct primary in Kansas deprived the party organizations of their legal monopoly of the nominating process, but the leaders continued to recruit the principal candidates for major offices.

During the 1950s the pattern of electoral politics in Kansas began to change. There was a gradual increase in split-ticket voting and corresponding decline in the influence of party identification on voting behavior. Issues and personalities became more important in affecting election results. General election outcomes were less predictable than they had been during the first ninety-five years of the state's history. Some Democratic victors were re-elected, so that the Republicans could no longer assume that every Democratic gain was destined to be short-lived. Party organizations continued to atrophy and more and more candidates were self-starters. Access to financial resources became more important in primary elections than party organizational support.

These changes are best illustrated by reviewing the history of gubernatorial elections in Kansas. The Republicans won every gubernatorial election during this first era except in 1882, 1892, 1896, 1912, 1922, 1930, and 1936. The two Republican defeats during the 1890s were to Populists supported by the Democratic Party organizations. The Democratic Party victories in 1882, 1912, 1922, 1930, and 1936 all resulted from Republican party schisms which were caused or aggravated by personality or issue considerations. None of the Populist or Democratic governors were re-elected and, except for 1912, neither of these parties, either separately or in fusion, won control of the Kansas Legislature. The exception, 1912, occurred because the Republicans fielded two sets of candidates in that year. The split between the Standpatters and the Bull Moosers allowed the Democrats to win many legislative seats by pluralities.

During the second era, every Democratic governor was re-elected. George Docking won re-election in 1958; Robert Docking was re-elected three times (1968, 1970, 1972) and John Carlin was re-elected in 1982. Moreover, the

Democratic percentage of State House and Senate seats was generally higher during the second than during the first era. In 1976, the Democrats won control of the Kansas House of Representatives and nearly won control of the State Senate as well.

It is appropriate to say that today the balance among Republicans, Democrats, and Independents, roughly 35, 32, and 33 (as percentages of the total number of registered voters), means that general elections in Kansas are regularly competitive. The Republicans remain advantaged, but they no longer enjoy the dominance which gave Kansas the image of being a strong Republican state.

How can we explain the erosion of Republican dominance beginning in the 1950s? A plausible explanation is that World War II, the advent of television, and the increased mobility of Kansans effectively destroyed the conditions of a closed society. Political socialization was no longer limited to the traditional influences of the small community. World War II caused many Kansans to live in places they otherwise would not have lived in and meet people they otherwise would not have met. The G.I. Bill accelerated this mobility and, through education, attitudes and beliefs changed. Television and the media generally contributed to the nationalization of Kansans. Old loyalties and prejudices were weakened if not jettisoned.

From the historical perspective the features of the 1982 general election in Kansas come into bold relief. What happened in 1978 and in 1982 that would have been extremely unlikely during the first era and during the early years of the second era in the history of electoral politics in Kansas?

THE GUBERNATORIAL ELECTION OF 1978

In 1978 John Carlin defeated Republican Governor Robert Bennett by breaking even with Governor Bennett in the total votes cast in the 104 non-metropolitan counties of Kansas and by winning enough of a margin in each of three metropolitan counties--Sedgwick, Wyandotte, and Shawnee--to offset Governor Bennett's winning margin of about 25,000 votes in the remaining metropolitan Johnson County. An analysis of the county-by-county vote in 1978 reveals that in most counties the distribution was similar to what one would expect. Carlin received his highest percentages in the upper quartile Democratic counties and his lowest in the upper quartile Republican counties. He won because he uniformly received more votes in each of the non-metropolitan counties than a Democrat generally obtains. That fact is prima facie evidence that Independents were more strongly supportive of Carlin than of Bennett. Though Carlin's promise to control utility rates is viewed by some analysts as the issue position that won the election for him, it is probable that the victory is as much attributable to Governor Bennett's image as to Carlin's issue. Unlike his predecessor, Governor Robert Docking, Governor Bennett did not allocate much time or effort to the performance of the governor's representative role. Campaigning was not an activity he enjoyed. He chose instead to give his attention to the other roles a governor is expected to perform.

THE GUBERNATORIAL ELECTION OF 1982

On November 2, 1982, the Democratic incumbent Governor John Carlin and his running mate, Thomas Docking, defeated Republicans Sam Hardage and Dan Thiessen, by a margin of 66,416 votes. Governor Carlin received 53.2 percent of the total number of votes cast for governor. Republican gubernatorial candidate Hardage received 44.5 percent of the total vote.

The differences between the last two sets of election results are more striking than the similarities. A county-by-county analysis reveals the following findings:

1. In 1982 Governor Carlin lost 13 counties he had carried in 1978. All are located west of Highway 81, the conventional boundary that separates western from central and eastern Kansas.

2. In 1982 Governor Carlin's percentage of the vote in 40 counties in western Kansas was less than he had received in 1978. In 13 counties east of Highway 81 his percentage of the vote also decreased. Most of these counties are located in central Kansas.

3. Offsetting the vote losses in western and central Kansas, Governor Carlin increased his margin by 5 percent or more in each of 34 counties, most of which are located in the eastern part of Kansas. The most spectacular increase, 28 percent, occurred in Johnson County, the number one Republican county in Kansas as measured by the traditional size of the Republican margin of actual votes. In 1978, Governor Bennett had received a margin in Johnson County of more than 25,000 votes, or 65 percent of the total vote. In 1982 Governor Carlin carried Johnson County, receiving 56 percent of the vote. Equally surprising, Governor Carlin carried such strong Republican counties as Brown, Marshall, Jackson, Jefferson, Franklin, Republic, Cloud, Mitchell, Morris, and Chase, which historically rank in the upper quartile of Republican counties. In certain traditionally Republican counties the vote was distributed as expected.

The Flint Hills counties of Greenwood, Elk, and Chautauqua; the adjacent counties of Woodson, Wilson, and Coffey; and the northern tier of counties bordering on Nebraska--Decatur, Norton, Phillips, and Jewell--the Republican gubernatorial candidate, Sam Hardage, 60 percent or more of their votes.

4. During the first half of the general election campaign most political analysts expected Hardage to carry Sedgwick County (Wichita) or at least to break even with the Governor. That expectation was based on three premises: First, Hardage is a Wichitan. Second, Wichitans had often complained about the domination of Kansas State Government by the "North-East Axis," Topeka, Kansas City, and the northeast quadrant of the state. Third, Hardage had conducted an effective media campaign before the primary election. But Governor Carlin actually increased his percentage in Sedgwick County by 2 percentage points.

5. During this same period there was also speculation that Governor Carlin would lose some of his previous margin in Shawnee County (Topeka). That projection was based on two premises: that support for Governor Carlin among state employees was soft; and that Hardage had carried Shawnee County in the primary election. In fact, Governor Carlin increased his Shawnee County margin by 6 percentage points.

6. Another primary election statistic was viewed as ominous for Governor Carlin. A primary opponent, a radio announcer in Wichita, had garnered more than 20 percent of the total primary vote. Analysts remembered that former Governor William Avery, defeated for re-election in 1966, had lost a considerable number of votes in that primary election to a relatively unknown candidate. But the results indicate that Governor Carlin's opponent's votes were only harbingers of the general election losses he experienced in Ellis and other western Kansas counties.

Why did Governor Carlin win and why did Hardage lose? The implication of the compound question is that the results cannot be explained by any one influence. Even in the absence of a post-election survey it is reasonable to assume that voters vote as they do for different reasons. Nonetheless, certain dominant influences can be inferred from campaign information and the election results. A summary of those judgments follows:

1. Governor Carlin's consistent and repeated advocacy of a severance tax placed him on the side of majority opinion on this issue. Pre-election polls indicated that about 58 percent of Kansas favored the adoption of the severance tax. Apparently, Governor Carlin's argument that the state's fiscal crisis left no alternative but to raise taxes, with

either a severance tax or substantial increases in the property tax, was persuasive for many voters. Though the advocacy of the severance tax cost Governor Carlin votes in Ellis, Barton, Russell, and other oil counties, it probably earned him the substantial increase in votes that he received in Johnson and many other counties.

2. Though difficult to measure, it is likely that Governor Carlin's pre-general election efforts to reach voters by organizing town meetings won votes for him. Generally, those who heard him regarded him as knowledgeable, articulate, and straightforward in his responses to questions.

3. Governor Carlin's strategy of naming Tom Docking as his running mate not only enlisted the popularity of the Docking name for him, but earned him the active support of many Democrats whose support for him was lukewarm. Tom Docking may also have neutralized Hardage's support in Sedgwick County.

4. It is also reasonable to argue that Hardage lost an election he might have won. Polls conducted soon after the primary election indicated that the two gubernatorial candidates were about even. That situation is usually advantageous to a challenger. But by the last two weeks of the general election campaign it was evident that Hardage was losing ground. Why?

The answers to this question are based on reports of individuals, newspaper stories, and editorials. In no order of importance Hardage either learned or was victimized by stories which alleged that his business associates did not like him, that he was often cold or unfriendly in his interpersonal relationships, that he claimed credits which he did not deserve, that he was uninformed about government in Kansas, that the airplane he purchased was built in Oklahoma, and that he was inconsistent in his positions on issues.

5. It is no secret that the Capitol Press Corps in Topeka generally disliked Hardage. They tended to be negative because of Hardage's alleged tendency to treat tough questions as evidence of personal hostility. Whatever the motives, there is little doubt that the stories and editorials in the Kansas City Times and Star were strongly pro-Carlin and anti-Hardage. Though the Wichita Eagle Beacon endorsed Hardage, some of the newspaper's stories probably undermined confidence in Hardage's ability to be a good governor.

6. There is little evidence that suggests any influence stemming from attitudes pro or con to the Reagan

Administration or stemming from the national economic downturn. Two Democrats won Congressional seats and three incumbent Republican congressmen easily won re-election. Moreover, the balance of Republicans and Democrats in the Kansas House of Representatives remained unchanged.

In general, the results of the gubernatorial election of 1982 reinforces the belief that in the second era of Kansas electoral politics, issues and candidate orientation are much more decisive influences on voting behavior than is party identification.

THE SECOND ADMINISTRATION

The story of Governor Carlin's re-election to a second four-year term would be incomplete without a report on the aftermath, the principal events that occurred during the first six months of the second term. There are at least two questions which are appropriate to those scholars and practitioners who are interested in gubernatorial politics: What kinds of changes, if any, did Governor Carlin make in the organization of his administration? How did the Governor's revenue program fare during the first legislative session after re-election? Both questions, though different, are related to the general question of the immediate effects of a re-election victory.

Initial Planning of the Second Term

Within days after he was re-elected, Governor Carlin convened his principal staff advisors to instruct them to begin helping him plan his second four years in office. Two political scientists at the University of Kansas were also invited to prepare a planning document. The latter developed a series of propositions and questions based on the assumptions that Governor Carlin would wish to earn the accolade of statesman, would want greater flexibility and latitude in the allocation of his time and energy, would desire to make changes in his staff organization and in cabinet-level positions, would be the guardian of his own political influence, and would be his own legislative leader. They defined a statesman image as that of projecting the ability to engage in positive political development.

During the time that planning document was formulated, and soon after, Governor Carlin reorganized his staff support operation. He created two management positions, chief of staff and executive assistant. To the first he appointed Bill Hoch, former press secretary, and made him directly responsible for policy matters, press relations, and constituent services. To the second he appointed Shirley

Allen, former patronage secretary and campaign director, and assigned her responsibility for supervising schedules, appointments, and clerical services. These changes are described by one of the principals as a move away from a "wagon wheel" structure toward central management. The objectives set by Governor Carlin, as expressed by one of his principals, were to control the costs of accessibility, to provide a better scrutiny of demands on the governor's time and energy, and to allow the governor "think time."

The Governor also requested preparation of a county data book, a loose-leaf notebook which would provide him basic demographic, economic, and physical facts about each of the 105 counties and which would include political information. Such a data book would provide him an opportunity to be prepared for extemporaneous remarks, a briefing which could occur enroute to a speaking engagement.

During the campaign and before the beginning of the 1983 Session of the Legislature the Governor made two kinds of planning decisions. He decided that he wanted the new Lieutenant Governor to be an active participant in his administration; specifically, to be a participant in the generation, evaluation, and execution of policy, to be a participant in a task force charged with making a comprehensive assessment of taxation in Kansas, and to be a participant in a high technology task force he soon appointed.

The other kind of planning decision he made was to recruit new cabinet-level appointees to fill anticipated vacancies and to transfer personnel from one assignment to another. The initial planning stage ended when the demands of the legislative session began. But the Governor's chief of staff indicated that planning of the second term would continue.

In analyzing the differences between the first and second terms of Governor Carlin, it is appropriate to ask a series of questions which have been suggested by various reports and articles written by analysts in other states. This approach may facilitate comparative analysis as well as provide potential help to the staff of the National Governors' Association, an organization which provides consultative services to all state governors.

1. Was the post-election period in Kansas a non-event? No. It was a time when the Governor began to reflect about the future of his administration (and perhaps his own political future) and a time in which he could and did make changes in his staff organization. He overtly encouraged aides and several advisors to help him plan the second term of his administration.

In other respects, the post-election period was a continuation of policies, programs, and processes that were developed or modified during the first four years of the administration. The fiscal crisis and its impacts upon the institutionalized processes of budget making and legislative program development absorbed the time and energies of the Governor and his staff. The policy agenda had been shaped in its essential character before the post-election period.

2. **Did the post-election period provide the Governor an opportunity to do what would have been difficult to do before election?** Yes, in two respects: He could address the problems of his time and the problems of formulating a plan for the rational use of his energies. He could also make changes in his cabinet without the risk of having those changes interpreted by his political adversaries as indicators of weakness in his administration.

3. **Were the staff organizational changes significant or relatively inconsequential?** They appeared to be significant, in the sense that staff operations were centralized and the responsibilities more clearly delineated.

4. **Was the role of the lieutenant governor changed?** Yes. The previous occupant of this office rarely came to his Statehouse office, a situation which indicated his relative non-involvement in the administration. The newly-elected Lieutenant Governor was assured before he agreed to be on the ticket (in Kansas the gubernatorial candidate chooses his running mate) that he would be given significant tasks to perform in the administration.

5. **Did the re-election produce changes in the patterns of relationships between the Governor and various components of the task environment?** This question is difficult to answer. What became evident during the 1983 legislative session is that Governor Carlin became his own legislative leader. He came to certain legislative caucases of House Democrats to explain his strategies and he negotiated with legislative leaders more frequently than during his first term in office. It was also evident in staff conversations with the Governor that he intended to honor his political obligations by giving priority in the allocation of his time and effort to groups that had been supportive during the campaign.

6. **Did the post-election planning conferences provide any indication of what would be the Governor's personal style during his second term?** It appears likely that Governor Carlin does not intend to serve his final term as Governor as a caretaker. The questions of issues priority is central in the planning dialogue. The impression of his staff is that he intends to remain a policy advocate and to continue

the town meetings method of advancing his views, a forum particularly suited to Governor Carlin's extemporaneous speaking skills.

The 1983 Legislative Session

The state's fiscal crisis was the central focus of the session. In September of 1982 Governor Carlin imposed a four-percent recision on the existing budgetary allocations to all state agencies. That action was necessitated by a significant decline in state revenues. Indeed, that problem was also the focus of the gubernatorial campaign in which Governor Carlin strongly and consistently argued that a mineral severance tax was both necessary and appropriate. That argument had been made during the previous legislative session. The House of Representatives passed a severance tax bill, but it was defeated in the state senate.

In his annual message to the Legislature in January 1983, Governor Carlin addressed problems and offered proposals in each of the categories of revenue, education, transportation, energy, agriculture, environment, economic development, public safety, aging, health, social services, local government, and public employees. But the revenues issues, particularly the severance tax and motor fuels tax, dominated the political dialogue. When an impasse developed late in the Session, Governor Carlin presented in person a special message to a joint session of the House and Senate in which he revised his initial revenue proposals by advocating a package of tax measures which included an additional income tax for Kansans in the higher brackets of income. The Republican-controlled House and Senate eventually enacted most of the measures the Governor recommended. Thus, Governor Carlin was able to achieve a substantial number of the fiscal objectives he outlined during the 1982 gubernatorial campaign.

CONCLUSION

For those who are interested and involved in the never-ending quest for a "science of politics," whether academics or practitioners, this case study of the re-election of a governor and its aftermath in Kansas illustrates the importance of combining two kinds of variables in seeking to explain significant political events. One kind involves environmental conditions which are neither subject to any public agent's direct control nor entirely predictable. The other kind involves the actions of public agents in anticipation of or in response to social, economic, and political development, actions which are often labeled by the somewhat ambigious term, leadership. Neither kind of influence alone could explain fully Governor Carlin's re-election, the post-election planning in the Governor's office, or the results of the legislative session which followed the election. And to a lesser extent, the case study illustrates the often heard observation that the past is prologue to the present, that the character of a political environment at any given time may have been shaped before any of the actors in a story entered the political arena.

The decline in the economy, which resulted in revenue shortfalls in Kansas, was not the result of the Carlin Administration's actions or inactions; it was an environmental condition that developed during his first term. But his response to it, particularly the advocacy of a severance tax, was his own decision. There were other options he could have elected. Governor Carlin was successful, as measured by the facts that he was re-elected and that subsequently the Kansas Legislature enacted a severance tax. But Governor Carlin was not the only actor whose decisions affected the result. His opponent in the gubernatorial election of 1982 also made decisions that contributed to the results. Thus, the re-election and its aftermath can only be explained as consequences of a variety of influences categorized for purposes of simplification as environmental and personality factors.

11. PREPARING FOR THE SECOND TERM:

THE GUBERNATORIAL EXPERIENCE IN MAINE

KENNETH T. PALMER AND ALEX N. PATTAKOS

POLITICAL BACKGROUND

Once one of the nation's most Republican states, Maine, has for the past thirty years become an increasingly Democratic stronghold. The state began to move toward the Democratic party in 1954 with the election of Edmund S. Muskie to the governorship. Muskie defeated a competent but unpopular Republican governor at a time when the Democratic party claimed only 15 percent of the seats in the state legislature. By Muskie's second two-year term (1957-59), Democrats had increased their share of seats in the lower House to slightly more than one-third of the membership. In subsequent years, the party developed a strong organization in most counties and proved able to elect legislators from rural as well as urban areas. The legislature was lopsidedly Democratic for two years after the Lyndon Johnson landslide in 1964. For about a decade following 1966, Republicans held narrow margins in both houses.

In the race for governor, a Democrat succeeded Edmund Muskie in 1958. Upon his death in office in 1959, he was succeeded by the state Senate President, Republican John Reed. Governor Reed managed to win election in 1960 and in 1962 on his own. He was, however, the last Republican governor in the post-World War II period. Reed was defeated in 1966 by Democrat Kenneth Curtis, who won re-election in 1970. Independent candidate James Longley succeeded Curtis in 1974 (winning narrowly over current U. S. Senator George Mitchell, a Democrat). Longley's successor was his attorney general, Joseph E. Brennan. Brennan won a three-way race in 1978 over the Republican floor leader in the state House of Representatives, a conservative clergyman running as an Independent, who tried to garner support from the Longley constituency. The legislature elected with Brennan had a Democratic House (77-73) and a Republican Senate (19-13). In 1980, the mid-point of Brennan's four-year term, Maine resisted the national Republican trend and saw the Democrats increase their margin in the legislature. In 1981, the line-up in the House was 84 Democrats and 67

Republicans. Moreover, in the Senate, Republicans had only a one-vote margin of control (17-16).

The evolving strength of the Democratic party in Maine is also revealed in recent party registration figures. Democrats began to outnumber Republicans in the mid-1970s. In 1978, Democrats counted 234,700 registrants (at the time of the party primary), while Republicans had 223,800 enrolled voters. By 1982, Democrats had gained nearly 13,000 additional adherents (making their total number in that year 247,200), but Republicans in 1982 had added only 600 new registrants over those in 1978. Spurred in part by the election of Independent Governor Longley in 1974, the numbers of Independent voters had grown rapidly. In 1982 they accounted for about one-third of the electorate. Much of this growth has come at the expense of the Republican party.

Democratic successes have come about largely because of the superior organization of the party and its ability to recruit candidates for top offices who have appeal to both Independents and Republicans. The Republican party seems to have been handicapped by a very conservative state party committee, which has often been out of touch with many rank-and-file Republican voters and with members of the Republican congressional delegation. Party primaries have frequently been divisive. The party nominees in both 1974 and 1978 were relatively conservative Republicans who had difficulty in the general election campaigns in widening their electoral base. Maine voters generally seem to prefer candidates who take a somewhat left-of-center position on economic questions and a rather cautious posture on social and cultural issues. Overall, Democrats have done much better in attuning their statewide campaigns to these preferences than have Republican candidates.

In recent years, Democratic campaigns have stressed the need for job creation and economic development in the state, in recognition of the fact that Maine remains one of the poorest states when measured by per capita income. However, the state was not especially affected in an adverse way by the first two years of Reaganomics nor by the 1981-82 recession. The state's rate of unemployment remained below the national average, and no serious layoffs plagued specific industries. Both in 1981 and 1982 the state government recorded budget surpluses, amounting to about 5 percent of its general fund. This favorable financial condition was achieved without the enactment of new taxes.

THE RE-ELECTION CAMPAIGN

Governor Brennan approached the 1982 campaign from a position of strength. The state's economy was relatively stable and the Democratic Party was steadily gaining support. A more immediate asset was a group of legislative and administrative accomplishments in Governor Brennan's first term that most observers regarded as impressive. The issues on which he had concentrated spanned a wide area. He had led a reorganization of the state Department of Agriculture and had redirected its functions from a primary emphasis on regulation to one of development and advocacy. He had also strengthened the state's child welfare services, giving particular attention to the problem of child abuse. In economic development, the Governor had campaigned successfully for a bond referendum which permitted a major expansion of the Bath Iron Works, a ship overhaul and repair facility that is one of the state's largest employers. Brennan was identified as well with new programs in energy and in environmental protection. He had formulated a state energy policy that stressed the development of Maine's renewable resources. He had also designed a small communities facilities program to enable eligible towns to build small wastewater treatment plants. Importantly, the Governor had been able to keep a pledge made during the 1978 campaign that no new taxes would be levied during his four-year term.

Because he had established a substantial record on which to run, Governor Brennan's 1982 campaign differed from his 1978 campaign in the way issues were developed. As noted earlier, Brennan ran for governor from the post of attorney general in 1978. In that position he had been intensely involved in a dispute between the State of Maine and two Indian tribes, the Penobscots and the Passamaquoddys. The Indians had brought a suit in federal court calling for the state to return to them 12.5 million acres of land that they claimed had been obtained in violation of the Nonintercourse Act of 1780, which required that land dealings with Indian tribes be approved by the U. S. Congress. The claim covered wide areas of eastern and northern Maine, and provoked much concern throughout the state. Brennan was seen to take a "hard line" stance in defense of the state. At one point he termed a suggested settlement by a federal task force as "really outrageous," and insisted on formal adjudication of the dispute.[1] While the Indians' claims were eventually settled out of court in late 1978, the dramatic nature of this controversy dominated much of the Brennan campaign. By contrast, in 1982, Brennan was able to focus on a variety of issues.

Another difference in the two campaigns for the governorship concerns the posture Brennan took toward federal system issues. Partly because of the way the Indian land claims case evolved, Brennan appeared in 1978 to be pitting himself against federal officials and the federal government. His was a strong stance in favor of Maine residents against possible federal efforts to take away their property. After his inauguration, Brennan became involved in national questions, but not on a state versus federal government basis. He generally spoke out on the liberal side in national debates. In this regard, he was the only governor to endorse Senator Edward Kennedy (D., Mass.) for president in 1980; and in February 1981, he was one of only two governors to vote against a National Governors' Association resolution supporting President Reagan's budget policies. While he opposed many of the President's specific actions, he praised Reagan for highlighting federalism issues and made state/local relations a major topic of discussion in his administration. In the spring of 1982, he convened a statewide conference on intergovernmental relations to address the state's concerns in this area. Finally, Brennan became very active in the National Governors' Association (NGA) in his first term. He was a member of the NGA Executive Committee, as well as four of its seven standing committees. In a related responsibility, he served as chairperson of the New England Governors' Conference toward the end of his term.

Governor Brennan faced one Democratic primary opponent in June, in a contest that mainly served to stimulate his campaign organization and thereby line up support earlier in the election year than it might have done otherwise. His primary opponent was Georgette Berube, a state Representative from Lewiston, who sought support from an assortment of groups that she believed were unhappy with one or more of the governor's specific programs. Included were the Maine State Employees Association, with whom there had been protracted and somewhat difficult contract negotiations, some Franco-American organizations, and proponents of retaining the Maine Milk Commission, an agency which the Governor favored abolishing. The Governor won with 77 percent of the vote in a relatively quiet campaign. Meanwhile, Republicans in their party primary nominated Charles Cragin, a Portland lawyer, as their gubernatorial candidate. Although a party activist and a veteran member of state commissions dealing with health care issues, Cragin had never held state elective office. He had run unsuccessfully in 1978 for the party's gubernatorial nomination, and the factor of name recognition seemed to enable him to win narrowly (38 percent of the vote) over two more politically moderate Republicans. Regarded as a conservative, Cragin was probably best known for his support of a state referendum to provide for indexing of the state income tax. The referendum issue appeared on the November ballot.

Within the Brennan organization, there was never any real doubt of the election outcome during the campaign. As one staff member explained: "Our polls never varied by more than three or four percentage points. The Governor was always ahead with about 60 percent of the vote." The general strategy was for Brennan to talk about his first term record, to discuss and defend his positions on various policy questions, but not to raise new issues. The governor also mentioned his opponent's name as little as possible. The candidates took part in three debates, but the principal issue that Cragin wanted to address, a plan for Maine's future, was generally ignored by the incumbent candidate.

Governor Brennan's campaign was operated largely by two longtime associates who had worked in his 1974 and 1978 campaigns. In 1982, they held state appointive positions, and worked on the campaign after performing their regular duties. One of them was responsible for fund-raising, scheduling, and polling; the other took charge of campaign expenditures, field offices, and advertising. Under them was a paid staff of six persons at the time of the primary election and sixteen persons during the general election campaign. The campaign had one office for the primary, and six offices (in the principal cities) operating during the fall campaign. In another twenty communities, the Brennan campaign shared an office with other Democratic candidates. The campaign maintained links with the state Democratic headquarters, but it was basically directed by Governor Brennan and his principal advisors. The governor himself determined the outline and strategy of the campaign. (State party headquarters in this state tend to be more involved in state legislative races than in statewide contests.)

Candidates Brennan and Cragin each raised about $500,000. for their campaigns. About one-third of Brennan's financial support came from three fund-raising dinners held in his behalf in 1981 and 1982. Senator Kennedy was the featured speaker at the 1981 event, but otherwise, national figures played virtually no role in the gubernatorial campaign. The remaining portion of the Brennan funds came primarily from small donations ($100 to $500). Approximately one-half of the money raised was spent on television advertising. The other principal expenditures were for fund-raising dinners and maintaining the paid campaign staff.

Because Maine is predominantly a state of small towns with populations under 10,000, Governor Brennan devoted much of his campaign time to meeting with voters at "coffees" held in private homes. The campaign staff would work with a local Democrat in arranging such meetings and getting out invitations. Thirty to forty people might attend these gatherings. The governor tried to apportion his time in the various parts of the state according to population, but he did manage to visit about 400 separate communities (out of nearly 500 in the state).

VICTORY FOR WHOM?

On November 2, 1982, Governor Joseph E. Brennan was re-elected by an unprecedented margin, carrying all of the state's sixteen counties. Indeed, Brennan's electoral strength increased in all counties over his 1978 showing, in some areas by well over twenty percentage points. What does such a margin of victory say about this election? In this regard, did the Governor's re-election signify a popular mandate to guide the future of Maine over the next four years? Or, was the election a moral and/or organizational victory for the Democratic Party, coming at a time when

Republicanism may have been associated, rightly or wrongly, with the ill effects of President Reagan's first two years in office? Or, was the victory related most closely to Joe Brennan the person? In other words, was his candidate appeal a sufficient condition to account for such an overwhelming expression of support?

To some observers, the re-election of Governor Brennan could be best characterized as a "nonevent."[2] For the most part, the "contest" was really not one at all, and it did not engender much excitement or concern about the outcome. Most observers of Maine state politics seem to agree that the Republicans did not field their strongest candidate in 1982. This is not to say that the Governor would not have been re-elected anyway, only that the nature of the contest, to the extent that there was one, left little doubt about the eventual outcome.

As we pointed out earlier, Brennan's campaign was well organized and orchestrated. Speculation about his opponent's strengths and weaknesses notwithstanding, the Democratic campaign machinery, and the Governor's organization in particular, was in much better working condition than its Republican counterpart. In fact, it even seemed to work harder. Yet, there is little evidence that his was a "party" victory. The Democratic Party in Maine is relatively weak when compared to other states, and the national organization was involved only peripherally in the Governor's campaign. Although national concerns about the impact of Reaganomics and New Federalism initiatives were raised periodically during the campaign, it would be unreasonable to suggest that a vote for Joe Brennan was, at the same time, a vote <u>against</u> the Republican Party and Ronald Reagan.

Although Maine politics can be described as relatively placid, this does not imply that the state is devoid of controversial issues that warrant the attention of those seeking elected public office. On the contrary, we have already pointed out that the governor's race in Maine is often single-issue oriented, which was even a distinguishing characteristic of Brennan's 1978 victory. In 1982, the gubernatorial race appeared to be less issue-oriented, or perhaps the multiplicity of issues raised during the campaign gave it a more "diffused" character. Interestingly, the principal issues confronting the state were organized around separate, if not parallel, referenda campaigns, even though all candidates for the governorship (there were actually four such candidates) were, of course, quizzed regarding their personal positions on these issues. Only the Republican candidate (Charles Cragin) was identified closely with any one of these referenda items, in his case, a measure to index the state income tax to the annual rate of inflation. In fact, his close alliance with this measure may have paradoxically contributed to his defeat, since Maine voters could (and did) accept the notion of tax indexing without electing him governor. A campaign strategy that was based primarily on such a single issue may have left his candidacy more vulnerable than he or his party could have anticipated. Clearly, unless a candidate's campaign is backed by a well-established party machinery, or unless the candidate's personal appeal, in and of itself, is a major drawing card, reliance on single issues is rarely enough to carry a candidate to victory. Generally speaking, few issues are so compelling as to warrant putting all of a candidate's eggs in one campaign basket. Broadening a candidate's policy appeal becomes even more important in cases where certain issues can be resolved directly by the voters through referenda, as was the situation in Maine in 1982.

In some respects, voter approval of tax indexing in Maine can be seen as a mixed message when one considers the strength of the Brennan vote. In effect, the voters had charged a "liberal" Democrat with the awesome responsibility for implementing a basically Republican policy initiative. Indeed, the implications were far-reaching, particularly when one considers the Governor's long-standing commitment to social justice and the "human" element of government service. The 1982 election, then, appeared to be two elections rather than one. Mainers seemed to want it both ways--to have their cake and eat it, too. To be sure, the extent to which the Governor can accommodate such yearnings will be a major challenge facing his second term.

Issue salience in political campaigns is often a two-edged sword.[3] Astute campaigners, of course, must do their "homework" on issues that may be raised during the campaign. The evidence in Maine supports the notion that Governor Brennan was very capable and careful in this regard. By the same token, candidates for elected public office also need to be "issue conscious," knowing when to articulate a position and when not to do so. One of Governor Brennan's campaign aides expressed the point that issues are more likely to hurt a candidate than to benefit him or her, especially if the candidate is an incumbent. Although we suspect that the Governor would not necessarily share this view, its message is still important. Overall, there appeared to be a perception that the nature of the Governor's campaign was different in 1982 than in 1978. As an incumbent, he tended to focus on his established record rather than on futuristic and probabilistic concerns. Furthermore, the prevailing view in the state regarding his campaign (and victory) seemed to underscore its distinct candidate orientation rather than issue orientation. In other words, the Governor--the individual candidate and his administration--comprised the key issue before Maine's voters in 1982.

On balance, Governor Brennan was portrayed during the campaign in a very positive light. Moreover, Maine residents (and perhaps more important, Maine voters) generally held "positive" feelings towards the Governor. He had established himself as a hardworking, honest, sincere, concerned, and competent chief executive. Although most persons would probably not consider him to be a charismatic leader, citizens' perceptions of competence seem to be valued heavily in this state. The Governor had not only followed through with his campaign promises of 1978, such as not raising taxes, but also had not done anything noticeably "wrong" during his first term.

LOOKING AHEAD

In the preface to a recent book on gubernatorial transition experiences and strategies, published by the National Governors' Association (NGA), Scott M. Matheson, the Governor of Utah and NGA's Chairman, observed:

> Very few leadership challenges are comparable to those presented to governors elected in the decade of the 1980s. Traditional approaches to state management and policy development will not be adequate for the difficult tasks at hand. More efficient use of resources, skillful management and creative policy choices are needed to meet these challenges. The Ameri-

can governorship has never been more open to or in need of innovation and new approaches to resolve old problems - to turn those problems into opportunities.[4]

These challenges, which confront both those who are newly-elected governors and those who are seasoned veterans, have been brought into focus even more dramatically under the present national administration. In this regard, the Reagan Administration has prescribed the elements of its "New Federalism" with the states comprising the centerpiece. Moreover, explicit (and implicit) national public policies in the domestic arena are forcing the states to take a hard look at their policy and management directions and capacities.

To an extent, of course, these external forces provide a context within which all governors must maneuver--conditioning their respective degrees of freedom as chief executives in many similar, as well as idiosyncratic, ways. In Maine, such factors have indeed left their imprints on the state, although perhaps to a lesser degree than on many other states. At least, this seems to be the case so far.[5] Although not entirely immune from the major events that occur on the national stage, the State of Maine, traditionally, has been able to retain its somewhat unique specter of Yankee self-determination, even when faced with such uncertain conditions.

Yet, while the re-election of Governor Brennan reflected, in large part, this special New England political dimension, it also could be viewed as a manifestation of Maine's link to the larger political system. The Governor had firmly established that he was cognizant of national issues, particularly as they affected the state, and had demonstrated that he could do battle with such forces, if and when necessary. Moreover, the Governor's 1982 campaign pledges not only seemed to be fewer in number than in 1978, but also appeared to be more explicitly grounded in a national context. Whereas he made a 1978 commitment against any type of tax increase during his first term, he did not offer any similar promises in 1982:

> We're not running on that commitment this time. And I say no candidate could responsibly run on that commitment in 1982, in view of the shifting sands in Washington . . . And I have a philosophy that govern-

ment's got a responsibility to meet needs, so this time I don't have any commitment in regard to not raising taxes.[6]

Compared to other states, Maine's political, economic, and social milieu was relatively calm in 1982. The state had entered the year in the black and, all things being equal, seemed to offer an ideal context for the conduct of governmental affairs. However, all was not equal or calm after the November election. The tax indexing referendum had passed, complete with a retroactive provision which threatened to cut approximately $32 million out of state coffers in the current fiscal year. This fiscal crisis delayed the planning process of the re-elected Governor pending its resolution. In early January 1983, 388 state employees actually received "pink slips," intended to terminate their employment with the state because of tax indexing retroactivity. State agencies hit hardest by this action included the Departments of Corrections (including the elimination of prison guard positions), Mental Health and Mental Retardation, and Public Safety.[7]

In his Inaugural Address on January 6, 1983, Governor Brennan referred to the dire implications of retroactive indexing and made a plea for its swift elimination early in the next legislative session. On January 14, the state legislature did agree on a compromise plan to eliminate the retroactivity provision through a one-time surcharge and change in the base year upon which it was to take effect. However, the issue did not subside gracefully. One local newspaper editorial referred to the elimination of retroactive tax indexing as the "Governor's tax increase."[8] Republican legislators attacked the new "budget surplus," the existence of which was flatly denied by the Brennan Administration. One Republican legislator tried to describe the situation in no uncertain terms: "Last week we were dancing to the only tune we thought the governor could play, a haunting, sad funeral arrangement. Over the weekend he must have taken some music lessons. There's a new melody: Spend, spend, spend."[9] Political biases aside, it was only after the retroactive tax indexing issue was put to rest that the Governor's plans for his second term could finally move ahead.

Governor Brennan, among others, views his re-election as a "ratification" of his

Administration. To the extent that popular elections do carry such an endorsement, it would not be unreasonable to expect a continuation of the activities and emphases of Brennan's first term over the next four years. The election per se can be seen as a discrete point on a governance continuum--a "linkage"--between the governor and his constituency. Indeed, one of the Governor's key advisors remarked that the Governor's "agenda" was not yet finished and that his re-election would permit continued progress among already targeted agenda items.

The nature of the Governor's 1982 campaign is instructive when speculating about his future agenda. As we have already indicated, he seemed to have made fewer campaign promises this time around. On the other hand, the Governor's campaign strategy emphasized his Administration's record of accomplishments during his first term, and stressed very heavily his leadership qualities and experience.

The governorship, it can be said, requires both leadership and management expertise. To be sure, however, the ability to "lead" does not necessarily imply the ability to "manage." Yet, given the increasing pressures on contemporary state government, governors who are strong along both dimensions are vital to public sector operations. In Maine, Governor Brennan demonstrated a basic capacity to do both during his first term. As a leader, he established credibility with the state legislature, the state bureaucracy, the press, and ultimately, the public. His vision of the role of government was translated into action in various ways, most notably when issues of social justice were at stake. His concern for reasonableness and fairness has gained him wide respect, particularly from those most concerned with social programs (and progress) in the state. He had proved to be an advocate for human services throughout his first term, but particularly when federal retrenchment in the domestic program arena became national public policy. Recent evidence suggests that the Governor will continue along this path in his second term, with perhaps more national visibility. For instance, he is already at the forefront of the child welfare issue. In this regard, he was the host for a national conference on children in the summer 1983, and conducted, through the state's Department of Human Services, a nationwide study of the status of children for the nation's governors in conjunction with the 1983 annual meeting of NGA held in Portland in August 1983.

During the campaign, the Republican candidate criticized the Governor's capacity to conduct policy planning on a comprehensive, statewide basis. Although the Brennan Administration did not produce a "Maine Plan" like the one drafted by its Republican opponent, it did provide some counter evidence to such allegations with a series of so-called "white papers" on various policy topics, such as economic development, state-local relations, human services, and others. These materials outlined the Administration's record of accomplishments, challenges still to be confronted, and future plans concerning these areas of interest.

On the management side, Governor Brennan, as a candidate for re-election, commonly described his Administration as "fiscally responsible," and cited the adoption of a "target budget" by the state as supporting evidence for his position.[10] The Governor's approach to management has also received some national attention. Recently, for instance, his use of a human resources subcabinet was highlighted as an innovative and exemplary "cabinet system" in a national magazine devoted to improving state government operations.[11] We suspect that the Governor will devote even more attention to gaining control over the reins of state government during his second term. This may turn out to be the case for several reasons. First, of course, is the influence of national trends and actions. While Maine has responded to the Reagan challenge fairly well thus far, this may be partially due to a "time lag" in the federal/state relationship. To be sure, the long-range effects of federal budget reductions, increasing state responsibilities under block grants, and national economic trends, as well as a variety of related in-state factors, are extremely difficult to forecast with any real precision. As a consequence, the state may at the moment be only experiencing the lull before the storm. The risks of ignoring such uncertain yet potentially real circumstances, one would think, far exceed the costs of preparing for them. More than likely, then, the Brennan Administration will assume a relatively proactive stance on management capacity-building in the years ahead.

The Governor also has a rare opportunity to strengthen his Administration in the second term because of his relationship with the state legislature. The Governor prides himself on his ability to work cooperatively with the legislature. Shortly after the November elections, he even served as a "faculty Governor" on this subject at NGA's New Governors' Seminar. However, because the Democrats for the first time in eighteen years obtained a majority in both houses of the Maine state legislature in 1982, the Governor's relationship is expected to be even stronger this term. Preliminary evidence on executive-legislative relations during the 1983 legislative session indicates that this will be the case. In short, Governor Brennan may gain greater control of the state government machinery because it will now be easier for him to share power with the legislature.

It is interesting to note that the governor's power of organization in Maine is perceived to be very strong in relation to other states. In fact, it has been rated third among all fifty states--only the states of Alaska and New Jersey ranking higher.[12] Yet, we expect to see greater attention given to organizational matters in the current term in order to strengthen both intra- and interorganizational systems under the Governor's authority. While the Governor, at the time of this writing, appeared somewhat satisfied with the organizational structure of state government, he conceded that organizational changes were possible this term. On a modest level, the Governor has already initiated some organizational reforms within the Executive Department in order to improve coordination of related functions. Moreover, plans to establish an office of intergovernmental affairs within the Governor's Office have been articulated, with the primary goal of improving state/local relations--clearly a major focus over the next four years. These types of activities appear to be more nonpolitical than political in nature, and reflect, in large part, the Governor's increasing emphasis on sound management practices. In many ways, these efforts are oriented towards the "fine tuning" of operating systems rather than the complete overhauling of old ones or the redesigning of new ones.

Perhaps the most significant <u>policy</u> management responsibility of the governor concerns the selection of his or her cabinet-level general executives. Clearly, these persons, while they are technically subordinates, share with the governor the policy development and implementation functions of the executive branch of state government. Accordingly, the staffing of the cabinet is often the first major symbolic step towards defining the governor's "situation," with respect to policy direction, control of the bureaucracy, and so forth.[13] In this regard, Maine's Governor has experienced a very stable beginning in 1982. With the exception of his education commissioner (the incumbent accepted a similar position in another state early in the current term), no vacancies needed to be filled nor were major changes anticipated in any of these executive posts. A related personnel issue, which has emerged recently, deserves mention. It involves one hundred or so "policy-making" executive positions which currently enjoy career civil service status. The Governor is seeking exemptions from such status for these particular positions in order to make them subject to his appointive powers. The underlying rationale for this move is that they are policy management positions and should be held directly accountable to the state's chief executive.

In summary, most observers of the state scene in Maine do not see Governor Brennan charting a much different course than that which he followed during his previous term in office. In this regard, policy emphases will again include such staples as economic development (particularly to halt an unsettling pattern of outmigration which has plagued the state for years), continued support for human services and education programs, protection of the environment, particularly its natural resources, and support for transportation programs. In addition, several areas will receive increased attention, although they are still continuations of first-term policy initiatives. The promotion of tourism and the containment of health care costs are two items that are quickly moving up the policy agenda ladder. Moreover, the state's relations with substate governments have become of primary concern because of national policy shifts, increasing public service needs at the local level, and declining financial and non-financial resources. Partially in response to recommendations that surfaced from a 1982 Governor's Conference and cabinet committee on this topic, the Governor's 1983 legislative package included a number of proposals to increase aid to municipalities under the state's general revenue sharing program, to reform county government, and to enhance intergovernmental planning. Other state efforts to provide property tax relief to local governments can be expected throughout the Governor's second term.

Continued, and perhaps expanded, attention will be given to management capacity development by the Brennan Administration over the next four years. Indeed, although retroactivity may now be a moot question, tax indexing is not. The hard realities of managing with less will only become more pronounced in the years ahead. Therefore, management expertise will certainly be a highly valued commodity in all public sector organizations, including Maine state government.

Finally, we can expect to see Governor Brennan receive, as well as seek, increased national visibility during his second term. Future political ambitions aside, there seems to be a general tendency for governors to move eventually in such a direction, particularly among those who have been re-elected to another term in office. Perhaps this phenomenon reflects an increased sensitivity to the importance of external, that is, national, interstate, and regional, factors on in-state operations. Or, it may be that over time, governors feel more effective outside of their own state environments and therefore quest after, be it conscious or not, such rewards even if only for their psychological value. Whatever the reason, the Brennan style seems to fit this national orientation rather well. Whether he uses it for purposes other than fulfilling his responsibilities as Maine's governor is a question only he can answer.

CONCLUSION

The 1982 gubernatorial election in Maine was a strong endorsement of Governor Brennan's first-term record. To be sure, the rising strength of the Democratic party contributed to the victory. The election gave the Democrats a 92 to 59 margin in the House and a 23 to 10 majority in the Senate. Brennan's position on certain issues, such as continuation of the state's commitment to human service programs, helped as well. However, the election had to be seen as primarily candidate oriented. Most voters had a positive view of Governor Brennan as an individual, especially his capacity to provide stable, competent executive leadership. He avoided making any serious errors in a political campaign, the results of which most observers regarded as a foregone conclusion.

Yet, while the electoral process proceeded smoothly in 1982, it still carried significant meaning about the path Maine will follow in the next four years. Governor Brennan placed an extensive record of policy initiatives and program management on the line, and received overwhelming electoral approval to continue in the directions he had marked out. Thus, the state will probably continue to resist, not favor, the domestic policies of the present national administration. The Governor further enjoys a new measure of confidence to proceed with the strengthening of the management capacity of state government. He will probably become even more active in national issues and in national politics. Some observers saw him as a likely candidate to run against U. S. Senator William Cohen in 1984. His style of leadership appears to be steadily assuming, in the language of James Barber's typology, an "active-positive-committed" focus.[14] In these several respects, then, the 1982 gubernatorial election in Maine was an "agenda-setting" event.

NOTES

The authors wish to express their sincere thanks to Adrianne M. Comer, research aide at the Bureau of Public Administration, University of Maine at Orono, for her assistance in the preparation of this article.

[1] New York Times, 12 February 1978, p. 20.

[2] The observations and comments in this and the next section are based on a number of personal and/or telephone interviews with a purposeful "sample" of Maine key informants, as well as content analyses of a variety of media sources.

[3] For a thorough discussion of the implications of issues, issue voting, and issue voters, see Robert Agranoff, The Management of Election Campaigns (Boston, Massachusetts: Holbrook Press, Inc., 1976), pp. 39-45, 146-151.

[4] National Governors' Association, Transition and the New Governor: A Critical Overview (Washington, D. C.: Author, 1982), p. v.

[5] For a discussion of these effects in the State of Maine, see: Kenneth T. Palmer, Alex N. Pattakos, and Stephen H. Holden, "The New Federalism Downeast: Reaganomics in Maine," in Stephen L. Schechter, ed., Publius: Annual Review of American Federalism: 1981 (Lanham, Maryland: University Press of America and Center for the Study of Federalism, 1983), pp. 83-91; and, Alex N. Pattakos and Kenneth T. Palmer, "Downeast But Not Down Under: Maine Responds to the Reagan Challenge," Publius, The Journal of Federalism, 13 (Spring 1983), pp. 39-49.

[6] Maine Municipal Association, Maine Townsman, 44 (October 1982), p. 16.

[7] Bangor Daily News, 29 December 1982, pp. 1,2.

[8] Bangor Daily News, 20 January 1983, p. 14.

[9] Bangor Daily News, 21 January 1983, p.1.

[10] Bangor Daily News, 16 and 17 October 1982, p. WE1.

[11] Lydia Bodman and Daniel B. Garry, "Innovations in State Cabinet Systems," *State Government*, 55 (1982), p. 96.

[12] Thad L. Beyle, "The Governors' Power of Organization," *State Government*, 55 (1982), pp. 79-87.

[13] Norton Long, "After the Voting is Over," *Midwest Journal of Political Science*, (1962), pp. 183-200.

[14] James D. Barber, *The Presidential Character: Predicting Performance in the White House* (Englewood Cliffs, New Jersey: Prentice-Hall, Inc., 1972).

12. THE GUBERNATORIAL RE-ELECTION OF HARRY R. HUGHES: A NON-EVENT?

PATRICIA C. FLORESTANO

THE BACKDROP FOR THE CAMPAIGN

Political Traditions in the State

Geographically, Maryland is a largely urban state that contains only one major central city, Baltimore. Historically, its southern and eastern regions display an English heritage with a distinctive southern flavor. Politically, the state demonstrates strong conservative tendencies, but it has elected to major office renowned and distinguished liberals, including both current U.S. Senators. The Democratic Party is dominant, registering 1.2 million Democrats in contrast to 480,000 registered Republican voters.

Until World War II, the state had a conservative and pragmatic political system dominated by county grass-roots parties in the rural areas and varying degrees of authoritarian urban "bosses" in the Baltimore Region. Because of the diversity of population in the state and its varying regions, ideology has never been as important to its public officials as a workable compromise. Organized labor, often the power to be contended with in such strongly Democratic states, has been an influential but not the dominating force in Maryland.

Since World War II, the major demographic factor affecting Maryland politics has been the tremendous growth in the Washington and Baltimore area suburbs. The new suburbanites, mostly migrants from out of state with no roots or ties to Maryland, have changed the cast of Maryland politics. Particularly in the District of Columbia suburbs, they show less knowledge of, and sometimes less interest in, state and local politics than they do in the activities of the federal government. While their numbers command attention, their level of participation is often disappointing.

Unfortunately, Maryland gained, in the last decade, a reputation for being a corrupt state. Since 1968, one Congressman, one U.S. Senator, two governors, two county executives, one City Council president, and one state's attorney have been convicted on various charges of tax evasion, bribery, kickbacks, and mail fraud.[1] Part of the reason for the large number of convicted public officials lies in a tradition of strong U.S. attorneys, who have forcefully prosecuted corruption at various levels of government within the state. Nevertheless, to even the most sympathetic observer, it appears that within the political climate of Maryland, payoffs and kickbacks to public officials were accepted as a way of life in the past. Peirce & Hagstrom[2] offer an interesting explanation of this phenomenon. Pointing to the tremendous influx of new residents into suburban areas, they contend that the newcomers have shown little or no interest in State or local politics or the quality of governance in their jurisdictions. At the same time, these very suburbs were the locations of massive amounts of new construction, new roads, and new facilities, activities which traditionally have been a fertile ground for corrupt practices.

The corruption "factor," coupled with the conviction and sentencing of the most recent governor, triggered the voters' desire in 1978 for a key change in politics. During a hard-fought primary battle, Acting Governor Lee, lieutenant governor under the recently convicted Mandel, was favored to win. He was strongly challenged by the Baltimore county executive, who campaigned as an "outsider," and two other challengers, the Baltimore City Council president and the former secretary of the Maryland Department of Transportation. The latter, Harry R. Hughes, running as a "reform" candidate, was given so little chance of winning that he had difficulty persuading any well-known public figure to run on his ticket as lieutenant governor. Nevertheless, in what all agree was a stunning upset, Hughes won the primary and subsequently went on to defeat the Republican candidate in the general election. In keeping with his perception that the voters desired a change from the headlines and drama of past politics, the newly elected Governor ran his administration during the first three years of his term very quietly and with little or no fanfare.

In Maryland the governor is eligible for two consecutive four-year terms and possesses those powers traditionally associated with the office. In a study of the relative powers of governors in the United States, the Maryland governorship rates as a very strong office.³

Demographic and Economic Conditions

The population of the State of Maryland totals 4,216,975, and the U.S. Census Bureau forecasts that it will grow to 4,509,501 in 1990.⁴ The Baltimore metropolitan region has grown consistently every year, with the exception of Baltimore City, which like most large old central cities has consistently lost population.

The state's economic base is roughly one-quarter wholesale and retail trade, one-quarter services, one-quarter government, one-fifth manufacturing, and the₅ remainder falls into a variety of categories.⁵ As the nation's third largest port, Baltimore is a significant part of the state's base; measured by dollar value of cargo, it is the second largest on the East Coast. The port's contributions to the Maryland economy are diverse, including vessel disbursements, crew expenditures, port-surface transportation, ship-building, steel manufacturing, tool making, and naval defense contracting.

The State of Maryland benefitted greatly from growth in the number of federal employees during the last two decades. In fact, there are more federal employees in Maryland than in any other states except New York and California. While most of the growth has been in Washington, D.C. suburbs, the Baltimore region holds the National Security Agency, the headquarters of the Social Security Administration, several smaller agencies of the Department of Health and Human Services, the Army's Aberdeen₆ Proving Ground, and the U.S. Naval Academy.⁶

The economy of the state did not fare well in the recent recession. A total of 480,000 jobs were lost between 1980-1982 throughout the state.⁷ Approximately 2,163,300 people were employed in 1983 while 169,900 individuals actively sought employment. While the state's unemployment rate of 7.9 percent was below the national average of 10.1 percent, Baltimore City's unemployment rate of 10.9 percent was consistently above the national average. The recovery of Maryland's economy after the recession was somewhat weaker than the national economy's recovery. The gross product of the state and the Baltimore region grew slowly, and incomes held steady or rose only slightly.

To finance its operations, the State of Maryland uses nineteen separate taxes, but most of its revenue comes from the individual income tax and the retail sales tax.[8] The income tax is the dominant source of income for the state, providing 41 percent of State income in 1981. In that year, sales and use taxes provided 25.8 percent of state income; motor vehichle user taxes and fees provided 14.37 percent; corporate income taxes provided 4.8 percent; and the state property tax provided 3 percent.

The state's long-term economic prospects are unclear.[9] In the past, government employment took up some of the slack caused by the decline in manufacturing jobs. Employment and revenue-raising limitations on all governments, whether legal or political, however, will not allow for the same cushion against future widespread private sector job loss. During the 1980s, the state's greatest economic problems will be the loss of manufacturing jobs and the need for the influx and development of new industry to provide employment in high technology areas.

POLITICS OF THE CAMPAIGN

Nature of the Opposition

For almost the entire three years that Harry Hughes had been Governor of Maryland, politicians, reporters, and political observers in the State Capital of Annapolis had suggested that Hughes was likely to be a one-term governor. Self-proclaimed experts tagged him as low-key, quiet, and essentially lacking in leadership qualities. His surprising strong performance during the 1982 session of the General Assembly moderated that perception sufficiently so that he was challenged in the September primary by only one fellow Democrat. Senator Harry McGuirk of Baltimore City, a sixteen-year veteran of the General Assembly and long regarded as one of the shrewdest men in the legislature, sought to unseat the incumbent Governor. Despite his attempts to picture Governor Hughes as ineffective and inept, McGuirk never generated any serious enthusiasm for his campaign. The Annapolis perception that Hughes was "politically vulnerable" to a re-election challenge from within his own Democratic party was proved to be an erroneous perception that did not exist outside of the Annapolis city limits.

Republican Robert A. Pascal, County Executive in Anne Arundel County, which has its county seat in Annapolis, had also taken that prevailing assessment to heart. He and other Republicans believed the Governor would be "politically vulnerable" in the general election. Whether or not the incumbent would have been vulnerable to a very strong challenge is difficult to say because Pascal did not mount a strong campaign. He was not totally responsible, however, for many of his problems. He was nominated by a political party that claims only 23 percent of the registered voters, and he was running against an incumbent who possessed the normal inherent advantages of staff, name recognition, and ease of fund raising. Additionally--in spite of the Annapolis experts' perceptions--the general public had no strong objections to Hughes.

Pascal was completing his second four-year term as county executive of one of the fastest growing and most affluent of Maryland's twenty-three counties. By all accounts he had been a competent, honest manager and was popular enough to have been re-elected had it not been for the county's two-term limit. His previous political experience, however, was confined to one term in the state Senate, and he had no experience at running statewide. Pascal later said that he came into the race unaware of the "enormity" of a statewide candidacy.

Longtime Maryland politicians say that because of the party's minority status, any Republican running statewide can beat an incumbent Democrat only by developing good relations with the Republican National Committee, by raising large sums of money early in the campaign for television ads to increase name recognition, and by finding a negative feature of the incumbent to exploit.[10] Pascal did none of these. For whatever reason, the Republican National Committee was quoted in the area's major newspapers early in the campaign as saying it had little hope for his election. That statement hurt Pascal's credibility and also meant that the Committee was stingy with advice and with what little money it usually gave to gubernatorial candidates. Pascal did not raise money early enough nor run television ads soon enough to increase his name recognition, which tended to hover at less than 40 percent. His first television ads did not run until mid-July when many people were away on vacation and had no interest in a political campaign. Finally, the challenger simply refused to use negative television ads to attack the incumbent. His ads portrayed him as an innovative, socially-conscious "good guy" and barely mentioned the incumbent. In the eyes of many, his campaign never got off the ground.

Campaign Organization and Strategy

Campaign Staff. Eighteen months prior to the election, a plan drawn up for Governor Hughes' re-election specified a campaign staff of six to seven persons.[11] Because of the financial limits set by the Governor, campaign staff director Joseph Coale ran the re-election campaign with the assistance of only three paid staffers.[12] The "campaign" staff, using offices in Baltimore, carefully maintained a separate existence from the staff of the Governor's Office in Annapolis as part of the Governor's intent to maintain his image as a "clean" politician with no hint of questionable practices. Officially, the Governor's Office staff did not participate in the campaign; their major role was to guide the administration whenever the Governor was campaigning.[13] Coale met with the inside staff weekly to discuss strategy and to respond to issues raised by the Republican challenger. As the campaign intensified, some spillover between the Governor's office staff and the campaign staff occurred but there is no evidence that other state employees were used in the campaign.

Campaign Strategy and Media Use. The Hughes re-election campaign strategy focused on his successful performance during the 1982 session of the Maryland General Assembly. He and his campaign staff agreed that their principal goal was to dispel any perceptions that he was in political trouble. His ability to accomplish everything on his legislative agenda during the 1982 session was highlighted in order to put to rest any doubts about his effectiveness as Governor. On the campaign themes of honesty and effective performance, he sought re-election.

Hughes and his political consultants[14] believed that television was the only medium of critical importance to his re-election campaign.

His first television spots were timed to appear in early spring at the end of the 1982 legislative session in order to capitalize on the success of the session and the Governor's bill signings. No further television spots were used until the primary. Although the Democratic challenger was never perceived to be a threat, the strategy was to maximize the Governor's showing in the primary to build momentum for the general election. Following the successful win in the primary, the campaign staff delayed extensive use of television spots until two weeks before the general election when the Republican challenger began to use them. All of the incumbent's television spots were designed to build on his accomplishments while portraying him as a warm and caring public official.

Although the Governor believed that only television was crucial in his political campaign, a small number of newspaper ads were also used during the few weeks before the general election. These were placed selectively either in community papers in Metropolitan Baltimore or in ethnic or religious newspapers such as The Afro-American, The Jewish Times, and The Catholic Review. His campaign used no radio advertisements.

Use of Polls. The Hughes campaign staff and their consultants relied heavily on polls. They conducted six, beginning in early January and ending, with declining frequency, toward the end of the campaign. According to the staff, none of the poll results were surprising, including those of the January poll, which showed the Governor as moderately vulnerable. From then on, the polls, which came roughly a month to six weeks apart, showed his public approval rating steadily improving. Rather than change the overall strategy, the poll results, which never carried any surprises, were used mainly to monitor the campaign's progress, to determine how best to use television, and to support pre-planned strategy. In addition to the polls run by the campaign consultants and the staff, newspapers in both Washington, D. C. and Baltimore conducted polls that were consistent with each other and reflected findings similar to those of the campaign.

The polls had a negative impact on the campaign of the Republican opponent because they never showed his level of public recognition rising, nor did they show the Governor's approval rating sliding. If the polls had shown some change in Pascal's standing, the psychological impact would have been helpful to his campaign.

Campaign Finances. Untypically, the incumbent Governor did not build up a sizable war chest far in advance of the campaign. His first of three fund raisers was not held until early 1982. His overall fund-raising total was $1,466,036, with individuals or organizations donating to one of three committees.[15] Hughes made large expenditures for publicity, for filming television commercials, and for buying television broadcast time. He also made contributions to many fellow Democrats running for the General Assembly.

Robert Pascal raised $843,143.[16] Pascal's financial reports reflect the difficulty he had in raising money in the final weeks of the campaign, especially after newspaper polls showed him trailing Hughes by wide margins. Not surprisingly, the reports also show that the incumbent heavily outspent the challenger on television advertisements.

THE VICTORY

Harry Hughes spent little time in his campaign making elaborate promises about his second administration. Even fewer projections were made about the future; he campaigned on his integrity and his record. Immediately following the close of the 1982 session of the legislature, the campaign strategy was shaped. The emphasis, first, would be put on the Governor as an honest, decent, hard-working incumbent, and second, on his record of solid achievements. He won because the people believed that the state had enjoyed four good years in which its resources were well managed and the integrity of the Governor's office had been restored. The Governor believes the election was also a referendum on "Reaganomics," which he attacked frequently and harshly during his campaign.

If Hughes won because of his record, why did Pascal lose? For a number of reasons, it appears. First, poor organization, or more accurately, lack of organization was a problem. At the start, he made all the decisions and relied on only one advisor, a longtime confidant who was inexperienced in statewide campaigns. In May, he hired and fired a professional campaign manager from the GOP

National Committee who knew little about Maryland. In July he chose a man to run his campaign who, like Pascal, was involved in his first statewide campaign. Second, he quite simply started too late, as evidenced in the timing of his selection of a campaign manager. It is apparent that he knew early in 1981 that he would run, yet there was little preparation for his campaign in that year.

Starting out late accentuated Pascal's third major problem, which was lack of funds. Insufficient money prevented his utilizing television to achieve more recognition in the Washington suburbs where he was almost unknown. He entered the last week of the campaign with only $65,000 to spend on media. Rather than buy television exposure in the Washington area where commercial time is more expensive than in Baltimore, he advertised in the more limited and less expensive radio market. Throughout the fall, the Pascal campaign was hamstrung because the candidate had to devote much of his time to fund raising.

Fourth, it appeared that he did not always "do his homework," raising issues for which he possessed few details. He hammered away at crime, but that never took hold as a major issue with the voters. A fifth explanation says that he did not keep as exhaustive a schedule as the incumbent, an idea which was linked to the belief of some observers that he really did not want to be governor, that he had no "hunger for the job." Finally, the factor of "Reaganomics" cannot be ignored. Pascal's discomfort with the Reagan administration showed clearly when he could not readily answer a reporter who asked him with which actions of the national administration he agreed.

In assessing the 705,910 votes cast for the Governor as compared to the 432,826 cast for his opponent (62 percent to 38 percent), how critical was incumbency to the victory? Incumbency certainly had its advantages for Hughes. He had a greater familiarity with state programs and wider recognition by voters. During the first three years of his administration, he had tended to shun some of the political techniques of his predecessors, almost to the point of seeming apolitical. During the 1982 legislative session and in this campaign, however, he proved adept at using the powerful office and its perks to win support and make friends, including the use of well-timed announcements of public works projects bringing jobs and money to areas being visited. In making appointments, one of the strongest weapons posessed by an incumbent, he showed increasing sensitivity to the needs of various special interest groups. All of this aside, probably the greatest advantage he derived from incumbency was the celebrity status of being "The Governor," an advantage clearly visible on occasions when both candidates attended the same event.

Scholars such as Tompkins, Cronin, or Turett suggest that incumbency is a "burden" and that once a candidate[17] assumes office, everything is his or her fault. This view focuses on the impact of "the accumulating weight of events and decisions," the accumulation of grievances by various groups, which over time erodes the incumbent's basis of support, and the tendency to attribute all that is undesirable to the incumbent executors.[18] Nonetheless, in the case of Harry Hughes' second campaign for Governor, incumbency was undoubtedly an advantage. Given the poorly run campaign of his opponent, Hughes would probably have won even as a first-time candidate, but the race would have been closer. As an incumbent who could point to the "restoration of integrity," Hughes gained an invaluable edge.

PREPARING FOR THE SECOND TERM

Hughes' commitment to continue "to do as he had been doing," to be honest and effective, was very important to his campaign and victory. Economic development, he said in his inaugural address, would continue to be a major priority, especially in the area of high technology. Managing the state's resources to assist local subdivisions grant property tax relief was a responsibility that he emphasized would continue. A characteristic of his first administration that would not change was the close attention it paid to the budget-making process and to the budget's use as the major instrument for shaping policy.

His blueprint for his second term is similar to that of the first. The major change promised during his campaign was the creation of a new Department of Employment and Training for the retraining of workers, especially those whose skills were in industries losing jobs. During the 1983 legislative session, he sought to expand the base for technological development in the state by establishing an engineering research center at the University of Maryland. Although an innovative idea, it was a continuation of the high priority that he had given economic development during his first administration. He also sought approval of additional correctional institutions in the state. Looking beyond the 1983 session, the Governor planned to address some broad areas during his second term, including the reduction of pollution in the Chesapeake Bay and the issue of de-institutionalization of the mentally ill and handicapped.

There was no indication at the outset of his second term that his new or continued policies required substantial changes in personnel. The only changes were necessitated by the resignation of two cabinet members and the installation of a new lieutenant governor with somewhat broader responsibilities than the first one.[19]

As provided by the Maryland Constitution, Hughes' inauguration was held one week after the General Assembly opened in mid-January. The afternoon ceremony, which includes the oath of office and the inaugural address, is the official responsibility of the state's National Guard. The evening festivities were two-part: A black tie dinner priced at $125 a person drew some 1,000 supporters of Hughes and Lieutenant Governor Curran in order to help erase their $86,000 campaign debt; after the dinner, Hughes was the host for a formal ball with moderately priced admission tickets which drew approximately 5,000 people. While the daytime governmental events were state funded, the social activities in the evening used no state money.[20] Other than his speech, none of the inaugural events were used to suggest policy directives, either new or continued, for the second term.

CONCLUSION

Following Hughes' campaign and re-election, the state government continues to run just as it had run for the previous four years: an honest and reasonably efficient executive branch driven primarily by a desire to curb expenditures. Thus, as far as changes in state policies and politics, the campaign made little difference and it would be fair to say that the campaign was a non-event.

With regard to the incumbent himself, however, the campaign may have triggered a significant change.

For three years, Hughes had presided over Maryland in a manner that self-consciously shunned politics-as-usual.[21] An intensely private and somewhat stiff man, he declined to "strong-arm" a legislature that was accustomed to previous governors doing just that. Slow to jump on burning issues, he preferred sometimes frustratingly slow analysis. Despite sixteen prior years in the General Assembly and six years leading the State Department of Transportation, he seemed unsure of his power or his role when he was elected to the statehouse for the first time. His deliberative style, reserved manner, and intentional distance from the legislature called to mind his roots in a small, conservative, rural town and led to criticism that he was indecisive and weak. In many respects, he seemed to fit into James Barber's classic typology of chief executives as the "passive-negative,"[22] an executive who does little and enjoys it less.

Whether one accepts the idea that Hughes was vulnerable at the end of his third year in office, the fact remains that he and his staff behaved as if he were. Thus, they set about changing that image. Rather than being the "laid-back," diffident official who is cautious about using his power, Hughes aggressively began demanding votes and handing out political largesse. He swept through the 1982 session of the General Assembly using all his political power and accomplishing most of his goals. Campaigning like a man who enjoyed his position and wanted to keep it, he shed any appearance of an apolitical style of leadership. Furthermore, immediately following the election, he appeared determined to surprise those politicians who expected him to slide back into his shell after re-election.

Sounding like a man who may want to run for national office, he said after the election that he would increase his interest in national affairs. His politically oriented appointments, willingness to spend more time with the legislature, and interest in a greater role in national politics seem to indicate that the activism he exhibited during the campaign will continue. Has he really switched, in the words of James Barber, from being a "passive-negative" to an "active-positive"[23] executive who is very energetic and enjoys it?

Only time will tell. If, in fact, that change has occurred, then the campaign was not completely a non-event after all.

NOTES

[1] Panos, Lou, "The Roots of Maryland Corruption," *Potomac Journal*, September 1978.

[2] Peirce, N. and Hagstrom, J., *The Book of America*, (New York: Norton and Co., 1983), pp. 130-131.

[3] Thad L. Beyle, "Governors," in Virginia Gray, Herbert Jacob and Kenneth Vines, (eds), *Politics in The American States*, 4th ed., (Boston: Little, Brown & Co., 1983), p. 458.

[4] Population data is from 1980 Census for State of Maryland.

[5] Economic data is from the State of Maryland's Department of Economic and Community Development.

[6] In Montgomery and Prince George's Counties, 32 percent and 21 percent of the work force, respectively, are employed by the Federal Government, in contrast with 6.6 percent of those in the Baltimore SMSA.

[7] All employment date is from Irene Tashlick of the State Department of Economic and Community Development. Breakdown for job loss is as follows:

```
1980 - 140,000
1981 - 157,000
1982 - 183,000
```

The figure however is not adjusted for new jobs created. The state also places retirees in this category.

[8] All state fiscal information is from the *Legislator's Guide to Maryland's Tax Structure*, Annapolis, Department of Fiscal Services, 1981, pp. 1 and 2.

[9] Center for Metropolitan Planning and Research at John Hopkins University. *Report of the Task Force on Economic Development*, March, 1978.

[10] Feistein, John. "Pascal Campaign Missing the Boat," *The Washington Post*, 14 October 1982, sec. B, pp. 1 and 4.

[11] Information on the staff and strategy draws heavily upon interviews with Joseph Coale, Ejner Johnson, and John O'Brien.

[12] John O'Brien, a former legislator, handled political contacts and coordinated Metropolitan/Baltimore; Wanda Schoeder coordinated volunteers; and Beverly Hague provided clerical support. William Boucher, the former head of the Greater Baltimore Committee was the volunteer Finance Chairman for the campaign.

[13] This was done by Ejner Johnson, the Governor's staff director, and Lou Panos, the Governor's press aide, who had worked with the Governor for several years, and John O'Brien, the Governor's legislative liaison who joined the campaign in mid-summer.

[14] Dresner and Morris; Richardson, Myers and Donofrio; and the Robert Goodman Agency.

[15] The Re-Elect Harry Hughes Committee, the Tribute to Governor Hughes, or The Montgomery County Hughes for Governor Committee. All campaign finance information is from the State Administrative Board of Election, Annapolis, 1982.

[16] The Pascal Testimonial Committee, The Pascal for Governor Committee, Democrats for Pascal (amount received, -0-); and Democrats for Pascal, Baltimore County (amount received, $1,500).

[17] Mark T. Tompkins, "The Election Fortunes of Gubernatorial Incumbents: The Quest for Successful Marginality." Paper delivered at the 1982 SPSA Meeting in Atlanta, Georgia; Thomas E. Cronin, The State of the Presidency, 2nd Ed. (Boston: Little, Brown and Company, 1980); and, J. Stephen Turett, "The Vulnerability of American Governors, 1900-1969," Midwest Journal of Political Science, 15 (1971), pp. 108-132.

[18] Ibid.

[19] Sam Bogley, Lieutenant Governor in Hughes' first term, was a very ardent supporter, together with his wife, of the Right-to-Life position on abortion, in contrast to Hughes' Pro-Life stand. On a number of occasions, the Governor was politically embarrassed by public opposition to him from his running mate. Bogley was also perceived as a weak politician who offered Hughes little in

support or ties to special interest groups. By the middle of the first term, it was evident to all observers that Hughes did not have a high regard for Bogley and that Bogley would be replaced during the second term.

[20] The cost to the state for the afternoon events was $26,000.

[21] Margaret Shapiro, "Capital Pundits Were All Wrong About Hughes," *The Washington Post*, 12 November 1982, sec. MD, pp. 1 and 4.

[22] James D. Barber, *The Presidential Character*. 2nd ed. (Englewood Cliffs, N.J: Prentice-Hall, Inc., 1977), p. 13.

[23] Ibid, pp. 12 and 13.

13. OKLAHOMA: A HISTORIC GUBERNATORIAL SUCCESSION

JEAN G. MCDONALD AND DAVID R. MORGAN

A momentous political event in Oklahoma history took place on November 2, 1982, as George Nigh became the state's first governor to succeed himself in office. The governor carried all 77 counties and garnered 61 percent of the vote as he crushed Republican candidate Tom Daxon, who ran on a Reagan-like platform supporting tax cuts and reduced state government spending. This report on the 1982 gubernatorial election in Oklahoma will set the contest in its economic and political context and provide some background on George Nigh's political career and first term as governor. Then the campaign itself will be discussed followed by a consideration of the sources of Nigh's support. The transaction from Nigh's first term to his second term in office will be covered next. Finally, an effort will be made to put the 1982 election into some broader political perspective.

THE ECONOMIC AND POLITICAL CONTEXT FOR THE 1982 ELECTION

During Governor Nigh's first term, Oklahoma enjoyed unparalleled growth and prosperity. With a growing population and low unemployment the state experienced a boom economy in the midst of a nationwide recession. The state's mineral wealth was the main contributor to prosperity; in the early 1970s oil or gas was produced in 72 of 77 counties.[1] Oklahoma ranked third in gas production and fifth in oil production. Manufacturing and agriculture were other important contributors to the state's healthy financial condition. The increase in population has not been confined to the largest metropolitan areas; rural and urban areas alike shared in the growth as Oklahoma reached a 1980 population of 3,025,290, an increase of 18 percent over 1970.[2] Still, half the state's citizens reside in either the Oklahoma City or Tulsa SMSA. Blacks and American Indians, the two major minority groups in the state, represent 7 percent and 6 percent of the population, respectively.

Oklahomans are typically conservative, yet a frontier mentality is also pervasive, reflecting the western heritage and youth of the state, not yet 100 years old. A southern heritage is manifested in some attitudes, as southerners populated the southern and eastern portions of the state; slave-holding estates existed there prior to the Civil War. Oklahoma is grouped with Arkansas, Louisiana, and Texas for census purposes, and the states are similar in important respects. For example, none has been noted for progressivism, but all have felt a touch of populism. In addition, the prevalence of fundamentalist religions and the lack of ethnic heterogeneity contribute to the conservative tenor of the state.

Historically, regional differences in the state have affected its politics and economy. Eastern Oklahoma was settled by both American Indians and southern whites, while the western half of the state, originally populated by Plains Indians, was settled by whites with northern and midwestern backgrounds. Both groups of settlers brought with them their political values and partisan attachments. Thus, southern and eastern Oklahomans have been Democratic in voting patterns, less participatory, and favored a personalized patronage form of politics. In contrast, northern and western Oklahomans have voted Republican from territorial days on, have higher rates of voting turnout, and exhibit an individualistic orientation to politics, with less emphasis on patronage.[3]

Throughout Oklahoma's history, the Democratic party has dominated the elected offices of the state. Republicans have been weak in state elections and extremely weak at the local level, despite increased support in recent years in national elections. Republicans have been able to capture the governorship only twice, in 1962 and 1966, and they have elected only a handful of state secondary officers since 1928--attorney general and commissioner of labor in 1968 and the state auditor and inspector in 1978. The mean Democratic percentage of vote for governor has been as follows: 1907-1929, 50.7 percent; 1930-1951, 57.1 percent; 1952-1980, 55.0 percent.[4] The state legislature has been heavily Democratic, with an average 75-percent Democratic vote since statehood for members of the state House of Representatives.[5] Present membership in the House is 76 Democrats and 25 Republicans; Senate membership includes 34 Democrats and 14 Republicans. Democrats virtually control county government.

Despite these statistics, the outlook for the Republican party in Oklahoma is not entirely bleak. With the exception of 1964, Oklahoma has favored the Republican presidential candidate in every election since 1952. Three Republicans have been sent to the U.S. Senate from Oklahoma since 1968, one having served two terms (Henry Bellmon). In Congress, Republicans have been weak but have held one or two seats in the six-member state delegation from either Tulsa, western Oklahoma, or currently, Oklahoma City. In fact, Republican majorities for major offices are not uncommon in Oklahoma and Tulsa counties.

THE POLITICAL CAREER OF GEORGE NIGH

George Nigh's political career spans more than thirty years of Oklahoma politics. In 1950, at age 23, he was elected to the House of Representatives from Pittsburgh County, the heart of "Little Dixie." After four terms of legislative service, Nigh decided to seek statewide office. He defeated the incumbent in a run-off election to become the youngest lieutenant governor (age 31) in state history. He served in that capacity for twenty years with two brief stints as governor when outgoing chief executives left office prematurely. During his years as lieutenant governor, Nigh's pleasant personality and promotion of industry earned him many friends and few enemies. His network of supporters was statewide, putting him in an ideal position to run for the governorship.

In his initial gubernatorial bid in 1978, Nigh faced a tough primary challenge from the incumbent attorney general and a prominent state senator. Barely missing an outright win in the primary (49.9 percent), Nigh was forced into a run-off which he easily won. His Republican opponent in the general election, Ron Shotts, was a bright, young state representative and attorney who was a former football star at the University of Oklahoma. Both campaigns were well organized and well financed. As with most gubernatorial elections since 1960, the race was highly competitive; Nigh won with only 51.7 percent of the vote.

George Nigh's first term as governor coincided with unprecedented state prosperity. Nigh was in the enviable position of presiding over an era in which the primary issue was how best to allocate vast surplus funds and which taxes to cut. His basic philosophy was conservative and cautious. In his words, "I do not believe that haste necessarily serves us well in public service. I believe in careful study and reasoned actions."[6] His personal style was to avoid controversy and work toward consensus.

Although Nigh presided over a period of record state expenditures, sixteen tax reductions were enacted during his first term, including allowing a state deduction for the federal income tax, eliminating the sales tax on drugs, expanding the homestead exemption, and reducing gift and estate taxes.

While relatively worry-free, the Nigh administration faced a few crises. The county commissioner-supplier scandal involving widespread kickbacks to commissioners, the largest of its kind in the United States, surfaced during his third year. Republican State Auditor Tom Daxon and Republican U.S. Attorney Bill Price pressed the investigation, revealing illegal practices statewide. The result was more than 200 convictions or guilty pleas on the part of commissioners and suppliers by winter 1983. The governor's response was primarily one of regret; county commissioners historically have been a very important force in Oklahoma politics. However, he did establish a task force on county government which produced several recommendations for change. He also called a special session of the legislature to consider these reforms, several of which were passed in the subsequent legislative session.

In spring 1982, a journalistic investigation revealed alleged abuses of children in state institutions administered by the Department of Human Services. The governor neither defended nor rebuked the department. When the department head resigned after thirty-one years, however, Nigh appointed former Republican Governor and U. S. Senator Henry Bellmon to head the massive agency, thus diffusing partisan opposition.

Such negative events were more than compensated for by Nigh's personal popularity. The governor loved to perform the chief of state role, obviously enjoying people. He tried to visit every county in the state yearly, at which time open meetings were held with special invitations sent to community and civic leaders. Nigh's political success had been built on his personality and need to be close to people. His style furthered that image. The governor's popularity was reflected in a 71-percent approval rating according to a statewide poll conducted in May 1982.[7]

THE 1982 GUBERNATORIAL CAMPAIGN

The Nigh re-election strategy was formulated early in 1982 after the governor announced his intention to seek re-election. While no one doubted Nigh's ability to win, the game plan was formulated anticipating opposition at the primary and general election stages. After all, Democratic candidates for governor always faced a crowded field in the primary, and since 1960, Republicans had fielded serious gubernatorial contenders. Ultimately no serious challenges emerged within his party, but State Auditor and Inspector Tom Daxon became the Governor's Republican challenger.

In contrast to the Democrats, the Republican primary was a heated battle, as two contenders fought for the opportunity to face an immensely popular incumbent. The Republican primary evolved into a bitter contest between State Representative Neal McCaleb and Daxon. While both directed their ire toward Nigh, the primary divided the usually cohesive Republican front and weakened the victor, Daxon, for the general election contest.

Needless to say, Nigh was in a considerably stronger position than his Republican adversary as the general election campaign began. Nigh's name recognition and approval ratings were high, and his campaign was well organized statewide with a sound financial base. Nigh made extensive use of television advertising, which either emphasized his strong points according to the polls--effective and honest leader--or educated the public when polls showed they were unaware of the Nigh position--the Nigh tax cuts. Throughout the campaign, his ads promoted his slogan, "Good Guy . . . Good Governor," typifying his personalistic approach to governing. Another campaign slogan stressed his experience, "Keep Nigh . . . You Know He Can Do It . . . He's Done It!" Democrats were united behind their standard bearer, and Republicans appeared to be defecting to the Nigh camp.

In contrast, Daxon was weakened by the divisive primary, shortcomings within his campaign organization, poor press relations,[8] low name recognition, and hostility from non-metropolitan areas. Rural areas tended to blame Daxon for attacking "their" county commissioners, no matter how corrupt the latter had been. One campaign participant stated, "Mr. Daxon's part in the county commissioner scandals was taken by many voters here as a move toward centralization of government in Oklahoma City."[9] Daxon also faced several financial problems, falling almost $500,000 short of his fund-raising goal.

Initial financial reports revealed Daxon collected and spent nearly $500,000, or 60 percent of his total expenditures, by the time of the primary. Daxon anticipated raising and spending $1.3 million by election day but fell far short of that goal. Governor Nigh, on the other hand, spent less than half his total expenditures by the time of the primary. In all, Daxon raised $780,779, yet spent $821,766. Nigh raised $1,233,771 in contributions and spent $1,248,778.[10]

Individuals contributed heavily to George Nigh's gubernatorial campaign, whereas PACs and political group contributions were few in number.[11] More than 4,000 individuals gave to the Nigh effort. Of that number, about 360 donated amounts of $1,000 or more, amounting to 50 percent of Nigh's receipts. Natives of Oklahoma City were far more likely than Tulsans (long a Republican stronghold) to be among the large contributors. Bankers, realtors, builders and contractors, attorneys, and doctors were prominent among the list of large contributors. While several elected state officials gave to Nigh, few offered large donations. PAC and political group money represented a negligible portion of Nigh's receipts (3.5 percent). Sixty-nine such groups, mostly within the state, donated to Nigh's coffers, but only thirteen of these contributed $1,000 or more. The three big contributors were: Oklahoma Chiropractic PAC ($4,500); Pipelines Union #798 ($5,000); and Oklahoma Medical Association ($4,800). The remainder of Nigh's funding came from thousands of contributions under $1,000.

By contrast, Daxon received far fewer contributions. One hundred ninety individuals contributed $1,000 or more. Daxon received substantial aid from the Republican Governors' Association ($20,000) and the Oklahoma Republican State Central Committee ($35,000). Nigh, on the other hand, contributed $5,000 to the state Democratic party rather than receiving funds from them; he did receive $1,000 from the Democratic National Committee.

Although Nigh's campaign was predominantly personality-oriented, a few issues did emerge during the campaign. Perhaps surprisingly, the big issue of what was beginning to happen to the Oklahoma economy in summer 1982 was never raised. Daxon, true to his conservative ideals, believed that state expenditures had been too high. He advocated further tax reductions to put the brakes on government spending. In response to this proposal, Nigh emphasized tax cuts enacted during his administration. One political observer felt it was one of the quietest gubernatorial campaigns in years.[12] Nigh's propensity to avoid controversy during his administration made it hard for opponents to criticize his administration. On many major public issues, he often let the legislature take the heat. Although he publicly stated his support for ERA, it was so passive that anti-ERA supporters could not be angry with him. A positive passive governor in the sense of James David Barber's presidential typology, Nigh's style fit perfectly with the prosperous tenor of the times.

Neither factionalism nor national events had any significant effect on the governor's race in Oklahoma. The Democratic party in the state does not have well-defined or long-standing factions. Indeed, to the extent factionalism exists it is more likely to be found in the Republican than the Democratic party. The state GOP has long been subject to moderate-to-severe tension between the rural, northwestern, wheat-growing area (from which former governor and Senator Henry Bellmon came) and the well-to-do, oil-dominated crowd centered largely in Tulsa. Contests within the Democratic party, on the other hand, are virtually always based on individual differences and are not tied to group, area, or faction.

During the 1982 campaign Nigh said little about national political figures or events. Ronald Reagan remains popular in the state, so an attack on the President certainly would not have helped the Nigh campaign. Since no other major political offices were being filled at this time, Daxon was on his own. Although some effort was made to appeal to people's fondness for Reagan, there is no indication that such efforts helped Daxon much.

No doubt, the Nigh victory was his alone; neither the Democratic party nor any faction could claim any real credit for the win. It was an individual, personal victory for a popular incumbent who had the great fortune to serve as governor during the most prosperous time in the state's history. Nigh not only carried every county, he drew support from every segment of the state's population. No one group--labor, big business, big oil, or the major metropolitan press--could properly suggest that without them he would not have won. As Gerald Pomper has noted, "Clear electoral mandates are rare in gubernatorial contests."[13] But in this case, people apparently liked the conduct of the Governor's first term and were more than willing to give him the chance to continue; this was clearly a mandate for more of the same.

PREDICTING SUPPORT FOR NIGH

Even though Nigh carried every county in the state, his support was stronger in some quarters than in others. Historically, the partisan divisions in Oklahoma tend to follow a diagonal line running from the northeast corner of the state to the southwest corner. The Democrats dominate the eastern and southern half of the state (with the exception of the Oklahoma City and Tulsa areas which increasingly vote Republican). Not only was this part of the state settled primarily by southerners, it also contains the lowest income groups and has the highest unemployment levels, largest welfare rolls, and the highest proportion of minorities in the state. Thus for a variety of reasons Nigh would be expected to run especially well in these southern and eastern counties.

What follows in Table 1 is an explicit test of this assumption using a multivariate statistical analysis. In brief, the expectation is that those counties with characteristics traditionally associated with Democratic political strength will have provided the largest vote for Nigh in the 1982 election.[14] To represent those pro-Democratic social forces, the analysis includes percentage over age 65, percentage nonwhite, percentage high school graduates, and percentage unemployed. As the first step in a hierarchical regression analysis, these four variables are used together to predict support for Nigh among the state's 77 counties. Following that, a political variable is added (percentage registered Democratic) to see if that measure can provide any additional explanation of the Nigh vote. As Table 1 shows, the four census variables can account for 72 percent of the variation in the Nigh vote. The most important of these influences (according to the standardized regression coefficients) are percentage unemployed and percentage over age 65. The higher the level of unemployment in the county and the greater the percentage of older citizens, the more support the county gave the Governor. When the political measure is added to the equation, it produces a statistically significant increment to explained variance of .10, increasing the R^2 from .72 to .82. In fact, the regression coefficient for that variable shows it to be the best single predictor for the Nigh vote.

The capacity of the four social characteristics to predict the gubernatorial vote in Oklahoma runs counter to a recent analysis of voting behavior among southern states. Using four national elections (President and Congress) between 1972 and 1976, Charles Prysby finds only a modest association between social class polarization and support for Republican candidates.[15] As Prysby suggests, part of the difficulty in establishing the importance of social class is the tendency for that measure to be confounded with geography. In the analysis above, the use of census measures makes it impossible to test whether social forces or geohistorical tendencies are really responsible for the support for Nigh. No doubt, political observers in the state would place greater weight on the effect of history and culture. Nonetheless the fact that so much of the gubernatorial vote can be explained by a limited number of social variables seems noteworthy.

Despite the rather high level of explained variance achieved when the Nigh vote is analyzed by county, support for the governor cut across all socioeconomic and demographic groups. Table 2 shows the intent to vote for the two candidates, Nigh and Daxon, according to a statewide survey done in October of 1982. As expected, Republican identifiers were not especially enthusiastic about the Nigh candidacy, but for almost every other group the differences among categories are slight. Race remains a bit of an exception, with nonwhites favoring Nigh quite substantially more than whites. But the two class measures--education and occupation--contain little variation. What differences appear are in the expected direction; those with less education and lower-status jobs tend to favor Nigh a bit more than their higher SES counterparts. In all, though, Table 2 reveals a very broad-based support for the Governor's re-election effort.

Why are the results of these two analyses--county-level and individual-level--somewhat different? Both are valid ways of examining the question of where Nigh's support originated. We need to remember, however, that when counties are analyzed, the two largest--Oklahoma and Tulsa, which together comprise over one-third of the state's population--are considered as only two of the total 77. So part of the difference results from a problem of aggregation and the nature of the unit of analysis itself. In effect, both findings are correct: counties of a certain type, which tend to be located in predominantly Democratic areas, were likely to have given Nigh strong support. Notice, for example, in Table 2 the significant difference between the Nigh vote in the two metro areas versus the balance of the state. But when the individual voter is considered, the socioeconomic and demographic determinants of support are only subtly manifest.

NIGH'S SECOND TERM

The governor and his staff were so certain of victory that no plans for a transition were ever seriously considered. Nigh's strength was solid in the spring polls and never wavered; he appeared unbeatable. Events during the course of the campaign served only to reinforce Nigh's invincibility. As for his second term, again, no planning was considered necessary. His performance as governor had been pleasing to the people of the state, so there was no reason to modify that performance. "If it ain't broke, don't fix it," was the phrase heard at staff sessions, and "don't fix it" meant do not make changes. Why depart from what had worked well during the first four years.

Once the election was over the Nigh administration prepared to resume business as usual in the low-key style evidenced before the campaign began. Such was not to be possible, however, as Oklahoma suddenly came face to face with the grim realities of recession--the boom was over! The downturn in the economy had actually begun in the summer of 1982, and by October, state revenues were down substantially. The primary reason for the decrease was diminished gross production taxes on oil and natural gas and a decline in income tax receipts. Within a week of the election, Nigh received the bad news. He was forced to turn immediate attention to finance, since the state's constitutional budget balancing amendment requires the state to spend no more than it receives. In response, Nigh ordered a hiring freeze and a 5.5 percent across-the-board cut in general fund expenditures.

Nigh continued to respond to the financial crisis as he prepared his budget for FY84. In his January 1983 budget message, the governor asserted, "For the first time in recent history we have experienced a 'failure of revenues.'"[16] As for services, the governor proposed "a lean maintenance of existing payrolls and essential services" for both FY83 and FY84, with a planned reduction of total appropriations of 3 percent for FY83. Fiscal 1984 would require a standstill budget, according to the governor's proposal. Nonetheless, Nigh hoped to avoid cutting services. In his State of the State address, he reviewed accomplishments of his first term; then he stated, "we have leveled off at a high; we have not leveled off at a rock bottom."[17] Later, he stated there would be no tax increase and no tax decrease. Funds from all possible sources would be used to "Preserve the progress . . . Continue the commitments . . . Share the sacrifices."[18]

The crisis continued throughout the winter months. By mid-March the legislature had agreed to slash $90 million from the 1983 budget in order to survive the remainder of the fiscal year.[19] The result was an overall 5-percent reduction in general revenue appropriated for current operations (excluding capital outlay), with some agencies suffering larger cuts than others. For example, higher education lost 4.1 percent, whereas the Department of Corrections, which has been under a federal court mandate to reduce crowding, actually increased its budget by 4 percent through a supplemental appropriation.

Nigh's Legislative Relations

In the midst of the financial crunch, Nigh's relations with the legislature continued much as they had in the past, although interaction was stepped up because of the crisis. Nigh's style in working with the legislature has been that of consensus; he defers to strong legislative leadership, preferring them to make the tough decisions and develop a consensus. Then he responds. In thirteen instances in his first term he responded with a veto; four times he was overridden. In all, Nigh has a relatively good working relationship with the legislature. He believes the press likes to see conflict between the two branches, but such interaction gets blown out of proportion. According to one staff member, "Sometimes it is popular to be an anti-legislature governor, but Nigh won't be among those. He likes working with the legislature. When he vetoes a measure, it is his vote on the measure, just as a legislator has an opportunity to vote."[20]

Although the governor has a partisan advantage in his legislative relations, he must still work at cultivating good legislative relations. For one thing, the Oklahoma Legislature in multi-factional, and partisan ties mean little.[21] So, Nigh holds regular meetings with the leadership; this session, the meetings were instituted earlier due to the financial situation. In fact, the Governor's staff perceives a more cooperative spirit in legislative relations this term but attributes that to the economic situation rather than to Nigh's re-election.

The Administrative Sphere

Although legislative relations were especially critical during the early part of the Governor's second term, Nigh continues to be concerned with good management. During his first term he overhauled the personnel system and continued a "mini-cabinet" arrangement created by his predecessor, David Boren, to facilitate agency coordination and joint approaches to common problems. For example, the Human Services mini-cabinet is composed of heads of the departments of health, mental health, and human services (welfare). Also as part of his official message to the legislature in January of 1980, the Governor announced he had formed the Governor's Cabinet, comprised of those agency heads who chair mini-cabinets, to provide an overall review of the management of state government.[22] More recently, he established a task force to implement a study of state financial management practices undertaken by Price Waterhouse consulting firm. Concurrently, the Governor established a task force on purchasing, procurement, and personnel. It has been estimated that the implementation of these reforms in state management information systems and financial management would save the state over $30 million.

Nigh extends his philosophy of better management to relations with the bureaucracy.

According to a Nigh staffer, the Governor is attempting to "tame the [bureaucratic] dragon rather than cutting off each of its heads."[23] Agency constituencies make it difficult to launch a frontal attack against the bureaucracy, but progress can be achieved through advocating better management, Nigh believes.

As with all Oklahoma governors, Nigh is limited in his ability to manage because few department heads are actually selected by the governor. Most major department heads are chosen by a board or commission overseeing the department.[24] The governor, of course, appoints commission members, usually on a staggered basis, but most such appointments, of which the governor has about 1,300, must be approved by the Senate. In many instances, because the governor does select the membership of these boards, he can exercise considerable control over their actions. This has been especially true with regard to the Transportation Commission, which is responsible for operating the state's highway system.[25]

Nigh will be the first Oklahoma governor to influence a majority of state appointments. Rather typically, the governor's office is not concerned solely with rewarding its friends and campaign workers; as one staffer remarked, we "reward friends, if qualified." The staffer noted the possibility that a few appointees may be asked to resign but no wholesale changes are expected.

CONCLUSION

Without doubt, the South is now far more competitive politically than in the past. Republicans can often contend almost equally with the Democrats for any major office south of the Mason-Dixon line. Yet, where the Democrats field a popular, conservative incumbent, GOP chances decline considerably. Such was the case for the gubernatorial election in Oklahoma. In 1982, the state was riding the crest of a major economic boom. Until late in the year, times were good during Governor George Nigh's four years in office. State services expanded, teacher salaries received substantial boosts, higher education received record funding increases, while taxes were reduced during each year of Nigh's first administration. Could any politician devise a better formula for success? And, Nigh's warm personality and low-key, nonconfrontational political style certainly contributed significantly to his success.

Even though the Governor carried every county in his re-election bid, some parts of the state provided much stronger support than others. This was so even though there were few large variations in the vote for Nigh on the basis of demographic groupings. While the major metropolitan papers split in their support for Nigh's re-election, he garnered the backing of a number of diverse groups including many prominent oil industry leaders and active Republicans. The message was clear: Times have been good, and we want more of the same. It was obviously an individual victory for Nigh who had campaigned vigorously on his record and his perceived image as a "good guy."

Nigh's second term undoubtedly would have begun quite uneventfully except for the sudden and sharp downturn in the state's economy. The abrupt decline in state revenue caused the Governor to become unusually involved in working with the legislature to formulate plans for cutting state spending. Nonetheless, Nigh remains committed to his basic philosophic approach to government--to remain flexible, not to express needless opinions on issues, and to let the legislature battle it out over major decisions. He continues to emphasize the long-term view; in his words, "We need to quit pressing for immediate answers."[26]

At the moment, Nigh disavows any future ambitions for public office. His actions seem to bear this out: One state legislator remarked that the only difference he could see between the first and second Nigh administrations is the Governor's apparent lack of future political ambition. Nonetheless, when 1986 draws near and an incumbent freshman Republican U.S. Senator comes up for re-election, one might assume that Nigh will feel strong pressure to run for the Senate.

In short, the historic gubernatorial succession in Oklahoma can be summarized in one work--continuity. Few changes not directly attributable to the state's financial distress can be observed in the second Nigh administration. His conservative orientation toward better management, long-term solutions, and consensus decision making remain unchanged. His superb public relations is as effective as ever. At this point, few would expect this Nigh governorship to hold any surprises.

TABLE 1

PREDICTING VOTE BY COUNTY FOR GOVERNOR NIGH
IN 1982 USING HIERARCHICAL REGRESSION

Variables by Block	r	Beta[a]	Additions to R^2 for Each Block
Block 1: Socioeconomic (1980)			
Percent over 65 years	.46	.27**	
Percent nonwhite	.32	.17*	
Percent high school	-.79	-.16	
Percent unemployed	.59	.39**	.72
Block 2: Political			
Percent registered Democrats (1983)	.82	.47**	.10**

Total $R^2 = .82$ ($\bar{R}^2 = .80$)

$F = 63.23**$

N - 77 counties

[a] Standardized regression coefficient for final equation

*p .05

**p .01

SOURCE: The socioeconomic variables are taken from the 1980 U.S. Census for Oklahoma. The political variable comes from the (Oklahoma) State Election Board, <u>Directory of Oklahoma</u> 1983.

TABLE 2

REPORTED INTENT TO VOTE FOR NIGH AND DAXON BY SOCIOECONOMIC, POLITICAL, AND GEOGRAPHIC GROUPINGS, OCTOBER 1982[a]

	Nigh	Daxon
Education		
Less than high school	66%	23%
High school graduate	65	24
Some college	54	35
College graduate	57	36
Occupation		
Professional	59	36
White collar	52	39
Blue collar	64	28
Retired	62	24
Other	63	23
Race		
White	59	32
Nonwhite	73	13
Party Identification		
Republican	36	59
Independent	47	36
Democrat	78	13
Geographic Subsample		
Oklahoma City	55	33
Tulsa	51	41
Non-metro	68	23
Total	60%	30%

SOURCE: The Oklahoma Poll, October 1982, Opinion Research Associates, Tulsa

[a] Based on the question: "Thinking now about the upcoming general election if an election were held today for the Governor's office, would you vote for GEORGE NIGH, the Democrat, or TOM DAXON, the Republican?" Undecided percentage has been omitted.

N varies from 769 to 774.

NOTES

We would like to express our appreciation to Carl Clark, Governor Nigh's Executive Assistant, and to Dean Gandy, Legislative Liaison, for their assistance in providing certain information for this study. Also our thanks go to Kenneth D. Bailey, President of Opinion Research Associates of Tulsa, for providing the data found in Table 2.

[1] Oklahoma, *Journal of the House of Representatives*, Thirty-eighth Legislature, Regular Session, 1981, p. 51.

[2] Center for Economic and Management Research, University of Oklahoma, *Statistical Abstract of Oklahoma*, 1982, p. 14.

[3] Jean G. McDonald, "Oklahoma Patronage, The Political Parties, and State Elective Officials" (East Lansing: Unpublished Ph.D. dissertation, Michigan State University, 1972).

[4] Samuel A. Kirkpatrick, David R. Morgan, and Thomas G. Kielhorn, *The Oklahoma Voter* (Norman: University of Oklahoma Press, 1977), p. 81; (Oklahoma) State Election Board, *The Directory of Oklahoma*, 1981.

[5] Jean G. McDonald, *State Legislative Competition in a Changing Party System: The Case of Oklahoma* (Norman: Bureau of Government Research, University of Oklahoma, 1982), p. 18.

[6] Oklahoma, *Journal of the House of Representatives*, Thirty-seventh Legislature, Regular Session, 1979, p. 94.

[7] Kenneth D. Bailey, *The Oklahoma Poll* (Opinion Research Associates, Tulsa), 21 March 1983, p. 2.

[8] In a panel discussion of the role of the media in state and local elections at Phillips University, October 1982, TV political reporter Terri Watkins commented that George Nigh's camp was always accessible to the press, whereas the media never heard from the Daxon organization and had trouble discovering where Daxon would be appearing during the campaign.

[9] This quote comes from a letter written to the authors by a Nigh campaign coordinator in a northwestern Oklahoma county.

[10] Daxon's expenditures were reported in an article in The Norman Transcript, 15 December 1982, p. 31. Nigh's expenditures were listed in the Daily Oklahoman, 14 December 1982.

[11] This information on campaign finances is taken from State Election Board campaign reports.

[12] The Oklahoma Observer, 25 October 1982.

[13] Gerald M. Pomper, Elections in America (New York: Dodd, Mead, 1968), p. 142.

[14] Despite the well-established decline in partisan identification and straight ticket voting, evidence persists that Democrats tend to derive somewhat more support than Republicans from groups with certain social, economic, and demographic characteristics. See Bruce A. Campbell, The American Electorate (New York: Holt, Rinehart, and Winston, 1979), pp. 215-223. Also Norman Nie, Sidney Verba, and John Petrocik, The Changing American Voter, enlarged ed. (Cambridge, Mass.: Harvard University Press, 1979), chap. 13, discuss recent changes in the appeal the parties have to various economic religious, and national-ethnic groups in the country. Specifically, they show that class cleavages along the traditional Democratic and Republican lines have begun to appear in the South as the Republican party has become stronger in that region (pp. 221-223).

[15] Charles L. Prysby, "Electoral Behavior in the U.S. South: Recent and Emerging Trends," in Robert Steed, Laurence Moreland, and Tod Baker, eds., Party Politics in the South (New York: Praeger, 1980), pp. 101-126.

[16] The following material was taken from Governor Nigh's Budget and State of the State message, January 4, 1983, Office of the Governor.

[17] State of Oklahoma Legislative Address, January 4, 1983, p. 5.

[18] Ibid., p. 6.

[19] The Daily Oklahoman, 11 January 1983, p. 1.

[20] Interview with Dean Gandy, Legislative Liaison for the Governor, March 24, 1983.

[21] Lee Bernick, "The Framework of Roll Call Voting in the Oklahoma House of Representatives: 32nd Legislature, 2nd Session (Norman: Unpublished Master's Thesis, University of Oklahoma, 1972), Chapter 4.

[22] Oklahoma, *Journal of the House of Representatives*, January 8, 1980, p. 61.

[23] Interview with Carl Clark, Executive Assistant to the Governor, February 22, 1983.

[24] According to a recent assessment of state governors' power of organization, Oklahoma ranks last. In particular the Oklahoma governor's office does poorly on span of control (over 30 departments or agencies reporting to the governor) and on the number of boards and commissions (over 100) for which the governor has varying responsibility. See Thad L. Beyle, "The Governors' Power of Organization," *State Government* 55 (1982): 79-87.

[25] For example, traditionally the State Highway Commission, legally appointed for staggering terms, resigns en masse at the beginning of a new governor's term. Consequently, the incoming governor appoints an all new highway commission, thereby indirectly controlling the appointment of the highway director.

[26] *Norman Transcript*, 6 February 1983, p. 7.

14. THE 1982 OREGON GUBERNATORIAL ELECTION: THE POLITICS OF CONTINUITY

SHELTON E. EDNER

CHARLES R. WHITE

CATHY CLARK

Events prior to the 1982 Oregon gubernatorial election appeared to portend a victory for the Democratic challenger Ted Kulongoski over the Republican incumbent Victor Atiyeh. Unemployment exceeded 12 percent; the state suffered through three gubernatorially-called special legislative sessions, each reducing spending and raising revenue in order to balance the budget, and there was a sense of political volatility with a strong property tax rebellion and move to significantly alter Oregon's land use regulations. Ted Kulongoski, had rolled to an impressive victory in the Democratic primary and was considered to have "charisma" and "leadership," in contrast to the "blandness" of the incumbent governor. However, by mid-October the polls indicated that Governor Atiyeh had moved substantially ahead of Kulongoski. On election day the Governor rolled to an impressive victory, garnering 62 percent of the vote and carrying every county in the state. Thus, even within a context which seemed to demand change, Oregon voters selected the candidate who stood for continuity, stability, and "sound management." This is our most important finding: In an extremely volatile political setting, Oregon voters overwhelmingly chose continuity over change.

THE ELECTION SETTING

The Recession and Ballot Measures

The overriding concern in the minds of the Oregon electorate in early 1982 was the recession and attendant unemployment rate of 12 percent. Oregon's economy is largely dependent on the timber and construction industries, which had been devastated by high interest rates resulting in permanent changes in the state's economic base. Layoffs and plant closures were in the headlines constantly. State revenues fell far short of projections in

1982, leading to significant cuts in state agency budgets for the biennium. Oregon is dependent on property taxes, corporate taxes, and a personal income tax. Historically, there has been strong resistance to any sales tax. Thus, the major issues the gubernatorial candidates had to face in the 1982 election were jobs and taxation.

Two major ballot measures scheduled for the November election were related to these issues. Ballot Measure Three called for a 1 1/2-percent property tax limitation, with property values based on 1977 levels, and limits on tax elections. This measure came at an inopportune time, when the state was in the middle of a fiscal crisis. More critically, such a measure, if passed, would have resulted in 20- to 30-percent reductions in revenues for local governments and school districts.

Ballot Measure Six called for ending statewide land-use planning. Oregon has had a state land-use planning law since 1973, requiring all cities and counties to have a comprehensive plan for future development. State approval of city and county land-use plans has had a tumultuous history. Some cities and counties have become embittered by state regulations and have refused to cooperate. Also, many developers have claimed that the regulations and growth limitations inhibit development. In spite of the fact that two repeal efforts had failed in 1976 and 1978, the vote was expected to be extremely close, reflecting Oregon's economic difficulties.

Both Kulongoski and Atiyeh came out strongly against Ballot Measures Six and Three. As a result, neither issue had a significant impact on the outcome of the election. Four other ballot measures, including a nuclear freeze proposal, which both candidates supported, were inconsequential to the governor's race since they lacked the political salience of the tax and land-use planning measures.

The Fiscal Crisis

Oregon's fiscal crisis began in 1979 with revenue falling far short of projections because of lower income, high unemployment, and high interest rates. Under Governor Atiyeh's leadership, state budgets were cut annually in 1979, 1980, 1981, and 1982 through reorganization, curtailed spending, and elimination of over 2400 state government jobs.

In May, 1982, Atiyeh called the second special session of the year to balance the growing budget deficit.

In early June a further deficit of $87 million developed, producing a third special session later that month. At that time the Governor proposed that $81 million be taken from the "surplus" of the State Accident Insurance Fund (SAIF), a semi-independent state agency, to avoid severe budget cuts or tax increases. Despite SAIF's attempt to block the move, the legislature approved the proposal in September, essentially solving the 1982 deficit problem. Some feel that the "SAIF solution" was merely plugging a hole in the dike, as the 1983 shortfall was projected to be $400 to $600 million. Most important, the 1983 deficit did not surface strongly in either Atiyeh's or Kulongoski's campaigns, and both were criticized for shying away from proposing solutions to the projected revenue shortfall.

Oregon Ethos

The collective Oregonian value system is a paradox of conservative and progressive values. Although the number of registered Democrats outweighs that of Republicans in Oregon, the state has a long tradition of electing moderate and even liberal Republicans to positions of leadership, such as governors and U.S. Senators, while Democrats tend to dominate the state legislature. Oregon has become a forerunner in government reform and strong environmental laws. Yet, the general citizenry seems to hold a laissez faire ethos, reflecting its history of "rugged individualism."

Party loyalty is not a strong factor and is not counted on in the state, despite a closed system of primary elections. Governor Atiyeh's campaign manager, Denny Miles, has made the observation that Oregonians merely tolerate the two-party political system as a way to select leaders and would prefer some other method. When the Governor was asked about the role of national Republican figures in the Oregon gubernatorial race, he responded that he had neither encouraged nor discouraged their participation. He also noted that Oregonians are "independent minded," and that even a visit by Vice President Bush had no real effect on the voters. This visit, however, set a state record for campaign fund raisers, producing over $100,000 in contributions for Atiyeh. In summary, Oregonians believe that they hold a set of values distinct from other states, have a distrust of outsiders, and a reputation for progressive government and non-partisan politics.

THE CAMPAIGNS

The Candidates

Definite differences were evident in the personalities of the gubernatorial candidates. State Senator Kulongoski was an outgoing, charismatic Democrat who promised leadership, direction, and action. A labor attorney, the 41-year-old Senator was chairman of the Senate Labor Committee and had also served as a state Representative in 1974 and 1976. His top priority was to create new jobs, and he clearly represented labor interests (his campaign was heavily funded by the AFL-CIO). Senator Kulongoski was in large part banking on an anti-Reaganomics sentiment to bring him to victory.

The older Governor Atiyeh, age 59, had a more restrained personality and was perceived as lacking a dynamic speaking ability. A moderate, conservative businessman, Atiyeh had been a member of the Oregon Legislature for twenty years prior to his governorship, serving in the House and Senate as Republican floor leader. Atiyeh's approach as Governor and as a candidate did not emphasize strict party lines, in spite of his background. The Governor views himself as a common man who truly stands for Oregonians. He sees his job as that of a manager whose job is to keep state spending under control and make existing programs work. Since Atiyeh took office in 1979, he has been working toward changing Oregon's anti-business image, and emphasized in his campaign that expanding existing industries and bringing new firms to Oregon were the keys to economic recovery. Atiyeh has worked to convince Oregonians that it is possible to be pro-business and pro-environment at the same time, and that he represents both interests.

The Primaries

Ted Kulongoski began his campaign vigorously, attacking Atiyeh's record on economic development as too little, too late. He also blasted Atiyeh's support for the Reagan Administration, which he intended to make a major campaign issue.

Kulongoski's major backing came from organized labor. He had the financial backing of the state AFL/CIO as well as a substantial contribution from the national AFL/CIO. Kulongoski also received the backing of the Oregon Education Association, a significant force in Oregon politics. Business associations and individual businessmen were Atiyeh's major backers. Surprisingly, given the image of conservative Republican campaign tactics, Atiyeh also had a well-organized volunteer campaign staff and many small contributors to his war chest, more than Kulongoski.

Atiyeh launched his first campaign salvo for the general election during the primaries. Anticipating the flavor of what Kulongoski's campaign tactics would be, even before Kulongoski formally announced his candidacy, Governor Atiyeh wrote a letter to President Reagan in March 1982, blaming Oregon's economic plight on the federal deficit, which was causing high interest rates and unemployment. The letter expressed "shocked surprise" over the $96.4-billion federal deficit and discussed Oregon's needs and how they could be better met by cutting the deficit. The Governor stated that although he agreed with the New Federalism concept, he did not approve of its timing. This was Atiyeh's strongest move to disassociate himself from the Reagan Administration.

State Republican leaders were upset by the letter, fearing that Reagan would not assist Republican candidates in the Oregon election. The Governor had not been expected to break his Reagan Administration ties until after the primary, and the letter's contents were released by an Atiyeh aide even though the White House had asked that they not be. This action, however, undercut Kulongoski's later claims that Atiyeh supported the Reagan Administration.

The May 1982 primary was a success for both candidates. Atiyeh won easily in the GOP primary, but not by the margin his staff had hoped for. Kulongoski won the Democratic nomination handily, with substantial leads over his opponent, Don Clark, in every part of the state.

POST PRIMARY ISSUES AND EVENTS

The Economic Recovery Issue

There was basically only one new issue in the Oregon gubernatorial campaign: economic recovery. The ballot measures relating to land-use planning and property tax limitations had been on the political agenda for some time. Since the two candidates adopted the same stance on the measures, they did not have an impact on the campaign. A major thrust of Kulongoski's campaign strategy was to make an issue out of Atiyeh's record, citing his lack of leadership and initiative. He also attempted to make energy an issue, blasting state public utilities for their high rates, lack of conservation programs, and involvement in the default of the "WPPSS" nuclear power plants for which ratepayers would ultimately have to foot the bill. Atiyeh took no interest in the energy issue for all of Kulongoski's efforts, and only near the end of his campaign did he comment on it, criticizing the Bonneville Power Administration for its California "sweetheart" power sales.

Kulongoski's attempt to make the incumbent's economic development record an issue failed for two reasons. First, Atiyeh had taken a number of steps during his governorship toward improving Oregon's economic conditions and pointed out these accomplishments in his campaign. He had introduced an economic development marketing package, a county revolving industrial loan fund, and a state computerized vacant land inventory system. Second, Atiyeh asserted his leadership role by providing a solution to the 1982 state deficit in the July special session.

In the 1982 election, Governor Atiyeh managed to convince the voters that the causes of the state's economic difficulties were national and beyond the control of the governor. Governor Atiyeh's stated philosophy was that he had faith in Oregon's economy and predicted a turnaround in the summer of 1983. He stressed his relationship with the Democrat-controlled state legislature as being a "team effort" on the subject of economic recovery.

Kulongoski's philosophy on recovery was more cynical and negative. He said that recovery would not come for a while, that the state could not depend on a federal bailout, and that it would need to initiate recovery efforts on its own. The principal source of new jobs was seen by Kulongoski as small, existing businesses that could be assisted by a tax incentive program. Atiyeh, on the other hand, focused on bringing in new, out-of-state industries, an approach with more voter appeal. In reality, Kulongoski's plan was not very different from Atiyeh's, and his only real innovation was to suggest investing Public Employees Retirement System funds to create new jobs.

The Plant Closure Bill

In 1979, several lumber mills had abruptly closed their operations with no warning at all. These closures had a devastating impact on the economic base of several Oregon communities. In response, Senator Kulongoski had co-sponsored a bill, originated by the national AFL-CIO, which would have required firms planning major layoffs to give a one-to-two-year notification to their employees. This plant closure bill was strongly opposed by business interests. Kulongoski's support for this measure became a major campaign issue, stemming from its potential impact on the ability of the state to attract new businesses. His handling of the matter also cost him substantial political credibility.

One of Governor Atiyeh's comments immediately following his 1982 primary victory was that "voters would choose him as better for the state's business image, that out-of-state businesses considering relocation would be uncomfortable with Kulongoski because of the plant closure bill." In a July 4 editorial, The Oregonian warned that business did not want to be required by law to consider labor interests when closing a plant and that Kulongoski's stance on plant closure would be interpreted as anti-business recklessness." When Atiyeh's ad campaign began in September, Kulongoski was depicted as scaring away businesses that would create Oregon jobs, a point reiterated in the ensuing gubernatorial debates.

On September 23, Kulongoski made a major blunder in an address to the National Federation of Independent Businesses, claiming that he felt the plant closure bill had been too excessive and had never testified in favor of the bill because it had never had a hearing. Three days later The Oregonian ran a front page story, following the discovery of the faux pas by local TV reporter Paul Hanson, which said that Kulongoski's denial of support for the bill was not true and that he had testified at a hearing supporting a one-year notification, expressing a concern about business obligations to employees and community tax bases. The article noted in summary that Kulongoski had flip-flopped and now opposed any legislation requiring prior notification.

One week later, Kulongoski responded, saying the error was due to his aide's use of the final legislative calendar (which was in error regarding when the bill had been tabled) to prepare his speech to the Business Association. Kulongoski explained that he had testified in broad support of the legislation but had since come to believe prior notification was harmful and would no longer support such legislation. The next week Kulongoski again responded to The Oregonian criticism by saying he would not "back away from the issue." He argued that plant closures were causing so many problems in communities that the Governor should have been seeking solutions himself instead of making a political issue of it. Four days later, the Statesman-Journal ran an article which said that Atiyeh claimed that he had knowledge of two electronics firms so frightened of the plant closure bill that they were postponing an Oregon location decision until after the elections. Atiyeh refused to reveal the names of the firms, however, when confronted by Kulongoski. Before Kulongoski's faux pas, an The Oregonian poll showed the race as being even, with Atiyeh having 42 percent of the vote and Kulongoski 41 percent. Subsequently, Atiyeh took an ever-increasing lead in the polls. Essentially, Kulongoski had hung himself on his own rope with his apparent uncertainty on the plant closure issue.

The Vulnerability List

A final event aided Atiyeh's campaign. In July, Vice President Bush visited Oregon to host several fund-raising dinners for Governor Atiyeh. In the middle of his visit, a national GOP list was published, identifying Atiyeh as one of the "vulnerable" candidates for the 1982 elections. Bush expressed shock and anger, saying the Reagan Administration was very supportive of Atiyeh. Denny Miles, Atiyeh's campaign manager, was quoted in The Oregonian as saying, regarding Bush's visit, that "the Governor's campaign would benefit more from returning Oregonians to work than from Republican vice presidential visits." Clearly this comment was meant to reinforce the idea that Atiyeh was holding the White House at a distance, yet at the same time, Miles rated Bush's visit as being "very positive."

ANALYSIS OF THE CANDIDATES' CAMPAIGN ORGANIZATION AND STRATEGIES

The campaigns run by Ted Kulongoski and Victor Atiyeh were quite different in organization structure and approach. Both campaigns adopted different decisions on the use of in-state or out-of-state campaign managers, polling firms, and ad agencies, with some important consequences. There were also differences in the impact of outside political figures and fund-raising success.

The Atiyeh campaign team was exemplified by good planning, shrewd strategy, and superior management. Kulongoski's campaign organization, on the other hand, had many problems and was rather disorganized. The Oregonian had likened the Atiyeh/Kulongoski race to a "Mercedes/VW" competition, and this analogy also held true for campaign organization.

Governor Atiyeh realized that he was in a bad position as incumbent in terms of nationwide anti-Reagan sentiment. Early in his campaign he had hired Denny Miles, then his press secretary, as his campaign manager. Miles had previously managed both Democratic and Republican campaigns in Oregon and had never managed a losing campaign. In addition, Atiyeh formed a core of executive assistants, all very competent people, to handle various aspects of the campaign. According to Miles, an overall strategy was adopted to "flesh-out the reality of the opponent" and improve the image of the governor. They needed to show Kulongoski's constituency that he did not mesh with their image of him. Several themes were to be stressed in Atiyeh's campaign:

1. "Honesty and Sincerity"
2. "Bring Jobs to Oregon"
3. "Kulongoski is dangerous to Oregon's Economic Recovery."

Miles perceived the voters as feeling that Oregon's economic woes originated outside of the state and were apathetic about whether a governor could make a difference. Reagan's policies were expected to split the electorate into thirds: one-third pro-Atiyeh, one-third anti-Atiyeh, and one-third apathetic. It was felt that Reagan would not hurt the campaign but the staff decided that they would not ask him to visit the state. Atiyeh was also advised not to spend time refuting Kulongoski's accusation of White House support.

Miles explained that one of the keys to the campaign's success was the close relationship between him, the core campaign staff, and the Governor. There was no trouble with the "palace guard," the Governor had faith in his people's decisions. When asked to reflect on how Atiyeh won, Miles identified a number of factors. The media campaign was given high priority and the radio and television commercials were very effective, placing Kulongoski in a negative light regarding the plant closure issue. The ads were prepared jointly by Miles, a local ad agency, and a political consultant. Another important move was a direct mail fund-raising letter, signed by Oregon U.S. Senator Packwood, calling Kulongoski "dangerous."

Three public debates were also favorable to Atiyeh. Consistently, his staff was stridently opposed to the idea. Atiyeh had a record as a low key, uninspiring speaker and the fear was that he would be "out-charisma'd." Yet, the Governor felt strongly that his opponent was not really in touch with Oregonians, and he did not want Kulongoski's philosophy running the state. Atiyeh wanted to challenge Kulongoski to debate, to make him stand up and reveal "who he was." He felt that Ted Kulongoski had not offered specific proposals on any issue, and wanted to pin Kulongoski down on his positions. Hence, he vetoed his staff's recommendation.

The Governor went to the debates well-prepared with rebuttals to Kulongoski's campaign arguments. During the debates, Atiyeh put the pressure on Kulongoski instead of vice versa, matching Kulongoski's challenges head-to-head. The debates were rated by various sources as being very even, an outcome favorable to the incumbent.

Kulongoski's performance in the debates reflected the overall structure of his campaign program and staff. As an accomplished public speaker, he could have done far better. Yet, his campaign staff and advisors had been pulled together late in June. His out-of-state campaign manager joined him in late June and the finance chairperson in early July. Until that point, he had relied heavily on volunteers and close friends for support and assistance in organizing his election strategies. Hence, by the time of the late summer debates he had not had enough time, election analysis, or advice to effectively debate the Governor.

In this campaign, the Governor made the major decisions such as whether or not to debate. His staff's role was in deciding where to spend the money. Atiyeh also took the initiative in insisting on a travel schedule, believing that "you should get out to build a feeling of security with the voters." Miles has remarked that "contests are on personal qualities rather than issues," and the Atiyeh campaign was aimed at the personal dimensions of what Oregonians wanted in a governor.

DIFFERENCES AND FINANCE AND SUPPORT

While Kulongoski's support came from labor, education, and public employees, Atiyeh's came from business and also a faction of the local labor movement. As a Democratic challenger seeking not only to win in Oregon but to contribute to the Democrat's national political fortunes, Kulongoski sought support from national party leaders. Consequently, he invited several national figures to campaign in his behalf. The Democratic National Committee, North Carolina Governor James Hunt, Senator Ted Kennedy, and Colorado Governor Hart were all interested in seeing an Oregon victory as a referendum on Reaganomics. Kulongoski led the polls with younger voters and with women. Atiyeh led the polls in older, male voters and independents, and received endorsements from former President Ford and Vice President Bush.

The two candidates experienced differing degrees of success with their fund raising. Even in April, Atiyeh's financing for the primary was six times that of Kulongoski's. Atiyeh had already raised $246,334, while Kulongoski had raised only $35,864. Atiyeh had many more donations of over $1,000 than did Kulongoski, with substantial backing from large and small businesses. In late July, with only three months left in the campaign,

Atiyeh had raised an additional $150,000, appointed a growing steering committee, finance directors in every county, and a long list of donors. Kulongoski had raised a negligible sum by comparison and was only beginning to form a finance organization. By mid-summer he had only begun to set up coordinators in the larger cities, with most of his effort focused on the densely populated Willamette Valley corridor. He had not yet chosen an advertising firm, and was just beginning to put a list of volunteers together.

The Atiyeh campaign was preoccupied with finance and had the assistance of two campaign finance chairmen from business and industry. Kulongoski's budget was largely based on pledges, a number of which did not come through. Although Kulongoski planned to hold fund-raisers in all the communities he visited, he did so only sporadically. While Atiyeh's advisors and supporters came from industrial and financial executives, Kulongoski's support was from liberal urban state legislators, labor, and liberal law firms. He did receive a total AFL/CIO donation of more than $100,000, more than any other state candidate in history. In advertising, Atiyeh spent a total of $347,000 with $205,000 of this total going to television ads. Kulongoski's ad budget was only $87,000. Final amounts reported for primary and general election spending were reported as:

	Raised	Spent
Atiyeh	$937,691	$963,844
Kulongoski	$550,655	$552,563

A discussion of Atiyeh's victory would be incomplete without a discussion of the role that the major state newspaper, <u>The Oregonian</u>, played throughout the campaign. <u>The Oregonian</u> consistently supported and endorsed Governor Atiyeh. It also provided substantially negative coverage of Kulongoski. Calling Kulongoski's out-of-state campaign manager a "hired gun" is one of the more blatant examples. Kulongoski's mistake regarding plant closure was given front page coverage. One editorial was entitled "Business not Hedging--the Whole Bet is on Atiyeh." This article suggested that it was unusual for Oregon business to back only one candidate, that they were scared of Kulongoski since he was pro-union and "meant more government." This relationship with the media typified the Kulongoski campaign, in large measure because he hired an out-of-state public relations director. Unfamiliar with the state's media system, this individual further hampered the campaign by not obtaining "quality" advertising space or time slots.

In October, an editorial entitled "Differences Between Still Obvious" compared the two candidates' economic development proposals and labeled Kulongoski's as "unsophisticated." When it was announced that Atiyeh had won the endorsements of all the Oregon daily papers, Atiyeh was lauded as a capable manager with a good record and as a steady leader. Kulongoski's programs were criticized for lacking detail and he was portrayed as "lacking dependability." In their own endorsement editorial, "Elect Governor Victor Atiyeh to a Second Term," The Oregonian said, "the question boils down to which candidate can be trusted to administer Oregon's shoestring budget over four lean years," and praised Atiyeh's twenty years of legislative experience.

The week before the election, it was reported that Atiyeh held a substantial lead in the polls (Atiyeh 56 percent, Kulongoski 32 percent). The Oregonian reasserted Atiyeh's major campaign thrusts, saying that the economy was the central issue, that Atiyeh held a sound management record in difficult times, and that the national economy, (not the Governor) was to blame for timber industry problems.

In conclusion, organizationally and financially, Atiyeh's campaign organization did a far better job than did Kulongoski's. Added to this advantage was the unflagging Atiyeh support of all Oregon newspapers, which certainly helped the Atiyeh campaign. As Denny Miles has stated, " . . . there are paths to victory," and apparently Miles knew the way.

The Election Results

A sunny election day, the emotionally charged land use and taxation ballot measures, and the fate of the governorship produced an eligible voter turnout of 64 percent. When the ballots were counted, Atiyeh had carried every county, including Kulongoski's home county, by a margin of two-to-one in the majority of all counties. Even the Portland urban counties had swung the great majority of their votes to Atiyeh. A summary of Portland area and total state results is:

	Washington	Multnomah	Clackamas	Oregon	Percent
Atiyeh	71,024	128,961	65,755	639,841	61.4%
Kulongoski	28,470	97,322	33,897	374,316	35.9%
Cleveland	2,631	5,468	3,013	27,344	2.7%
Other	35	185	28	458	

Atiyeh's victory margin was one of the largest in state history. It is even more remarkable, given the early perceptions of his potential vulnerability. Support from such a wide diversity of voters clearly validated his perception of empathy with Oregonians. At the same time, however, the pattern of voting was not atypical of past state elections. Despite the voters overwhelming endorsement of the Governor, they elected a Democratic majority in both houses of the state legislature. The personal appeal of Atiyeh was far more important than party politics in the election outcome.

ATIYEH'S RE-ELECTION RESPONSE

The fiscal problems of state government, the property tax issue, and land use issues had been prominent throughout most of Governor Atiyeh's first term and he was already on record regarding each issue. Thus, the major issues confronting his second term were more in the nature of unfinished business than newly identified problems. In particular, the narrow defeat of the 1-1/2-percent property tax limitation measure (50.5 percent to 49.5 percent) meant that the issue of state and local government finance would dominate the 1983 session of the state legislature. The controversy over state land-use policies faded from public view even though the ballot measure designed to abolish those policies also failed by a narrow margin (50.9 percent to 49.1 percent).

In a personal interview, Governor Atiyeh was asked whether the election results would change his style as governor. Atiyeh responded that "there has been no change," and that he felt he should continue to "do what I think is right and be who I am." In essence, he views the 62-percent voter confirmation as a mandate to continue as before. The Governor says that a pro-Atiyeh vote won the race, not an anti-Kulongoski vote. His philosophy is that "I believe that I am where Oregonians really are," and that his major political constituency is composed of "average" Oregonians. The Governor does not feel that his second term gives him the freedom to propose long-term or controversial solutions to the state's needs and problems. Further, a philosophical conflict exists between Atiyeh and the legislature. It is unlikely that he could push through any major revenue proposals because of its Democratic majority.

Some local analysts argue that Atiyeh has not taken advantage of his victory, that he is basically maintaining a do-nothing posture and not placing enough emphasis on bringing in new business. Even with an overwhelming victory and no prospect of a third term by law, there has been no extensive evidence of risk-taking leadership to meet the current needs of the state, with the exception of an ill-fated net-receipts tax.

Atiyeh continues to view his "job" as "running the company," an approach which does not call for change or innovation, but making existing programs work. This philosophy is coupled with his belief that he should do "what I think is right or in the best interest of the state." This belief has been evidenced in his support of a net receipts tax, in spite of business opposition, and his stubborn opposition to a sales tax, even though his business supporters have mounted a strong lobbying effort in its favor. Atiyeh's view of his role and his approach to it argue for carrying through with initiatives begun in the first term rather than going in new directions. Indeed, the Governor seems to be looking forward to the period after his second term as a time to assume a non-political, elder statesman role.

CONCLUSIONS

As suggested at the outset of this paper, the 1982 Oregon gubernatorial election was an affirmation of voter preference for stability and continuity in the face of substantial economic and social turbulence. This theme can also be attributed to the other elements of the election, that is, the legislative and ballot measure races. Oregon voters re-elected Democrats to the state legislature and turned back, albeit marginally, major changes to the state's land-use planning and taxation systems. These outcomes are consistent with voter behavior over the past ten years. Since the passage of the state's famous "Bottle Bill" and "Land-Use Planning Law" early in the 1970s, there has been little if any indication of voter willingness to experiment with "new" approaches or policy initiatives. A few broad social issues, such as the nuclear freeze movement, have received some voter attention and sympathy. But, for the most part, the Oregon political philosophy has tended to be status quo and state oriented. If there has been any predilection to entertain new policy or political initiatives, it has been only as a product of the intrusion of national events on state economic and social trends. Even here, however, the response has been "passive," reflecting a perceived inability to cope with what has been beyond the state's control.

This theme of continuity in the face of uncontrollable turbulence has been reflected in the actions of both Governor Atiyeh and the legislature. The Governor's second term inauguration was low key and in keeping with the tenor of the economic situation. Unlike his first inauguration, which was quite "splashy," Atiyeh chose to hold an almost "non-event" inauguration ceremony in Portland. The inauguration was held as an evening reception for state dignitaries, with no fanfare or pomp (symbolized by the serving of lemonade as the most potent beverage). Similarly, the Governor's budget was submitted to the legislature with only one major new component, a net-receipts tax to balance the budget. The remainder of the budget and related policy proposals were consistent with Atiyeh's philosophy of managing the company through tough times, that is, limited belt tightening and revenue raising coupled with greater efficiency of operations.

The legislature has followed a similar path and philosophy. While Atiyeh's tax proposals were ignored after their introduction, no other major initiatives were adopted by the legislature during the regular 1983 session. Several sales tax proposals were introduced but none passed or were referred to the voters. The legislature seemed content to balance the budget through conservative budgeting, the extension of existing "temporary" taxes enacted previously, and an increase in the state income tax. Indeed, despite the close vote on the property tax limitation measure, no new property tax relief program was adopted. The legislature adjourned without such action in the face of a promise by Atiyeh that he would call them into special session to deal with the matter. Undeterred by the Governor's threat, the legislature adjourned after its second longest session in history. There was a special session in September 1983 which produced a sales tax measure for voter action. It was declared unconstitutional by the State Supreme Court before an election could be held. Further, the actions of the legislature were almost invisible. The only substantial media coverage resulted from legislative disapproval of the Governor's net receipts tax proposal, major squabbling between the speaker of the House and the president of the Senate, and its own fumbling with other tax alternatives. The most plausible explanation of this inaction seems to be a general willingness to wait on the improvement of the economy in hopes of avoiding any actions that would irritate the voters. Also contributing were the deep divisions among Democrats on the sales tax issue, resulting in a regular session legislative stalemate.

The Relative Absence of Surprises

Only three elements of the gubernatorial race appear as surprises in the context of other state elections: 1) Atiyeh's perception of incumbency as a liability, 2) the ability of Oregon voters to separate a Republican governor from the national liability of being Republican, and 3) the relative lack of an effect of the volatile ballot measure campaigns on the race. In the first instance, Atiyeh was troubled by state constitutional provisions requiring an incumbent governor to submit biennial budget proposals within one month of the election (December 1). This provision meant that the campaign had to run parallel with an effort to continue managing the affairs of the state. While Atiyeh believes that it is necessary for a governor to maintain an image of effectiveness, the budget requirement forced him to divert substantial energy from the campaign process. Kulongoski could not capitalize on this energy drain. A more effective opponent might have turned it to his or her advantage.

On the second point, while Republicanism in the context of a national economic slump had an influence in many states, Oregon voters appeared to disassociate liability for such economic affairs from Atiyeh's abilities as a governor. Kulongoski attempted to make Reaganomics a major issue but failed, even with unemployment standing at record levels for the state. A partial explanation stems from the state's traditional maverick political behavior. Oregonians have bucked national trends before, a result consistent with an inherently parochial approach to policy issues. It is easier to sell innovative policy initiatives in Oregon based on an appeal to local values and perspectives than to argue that the state needs to keep up with the rest of the country. A related explanation may reside in the strong inclination of Oregonians to distrust political affairs. Political activities in Oregon are relatively free of graft and corruption not because of high moral behavior but because of a strong commitment to individual self-reliance. Hence, the state has a real faith in "amateur" political processes and behavior relatively uncontaminated by appeals to collective ideological movements. Consequently, "cleanliness" in politics is a form of self-protection. In the context of this strongly individualistic frame of reference, state control of its own affairs is an important value referent. While blaming others might be tolerated, Oregonians want to know what they can do for themselves.

Finally, it might be expected that hotly contested statewide ballot measures would substantially influence a gubernatorial campaign. While this has happened in Oregon in past races, this time it had little bearing on the outcome. The fact that both candidates took similar positions is a partial explanation. Just as important, the Oregon political process puts substantial weight on the initiative and referendum, that is, major policy issues will be decided by the voters. Hence, while the state has had governors such as Tom McCall, with strong policy views, such political leaders don't initiate policy arbitrarily, they facilitate its enactment and implementation. Atiyeh's philosophy of being in tune with the Oregon mind has important explanatory power. Gubernatorial candidates don't run against each other so much as they attempt to place themselves favorably in the context of public values. Candidates lose on their incompatibility with voter wishes, not because they are worse than their opponent.

Comparability with Other State Election Experiences

Several other issues are suggested by the above analysis for potential comparison with the re-election/transition experience of other states, in addition to the ballot measure and national economic/political issues discussed above:

1. The Impact of "Outside" Political Figures

2. The Role of In-State versus Out-of-State Campaign Advisors

3. Re-elections as "Non-Events"

4. The Role and Impact of State Political Culture

The impact of the first two were similar and closely related. Atiyeh chose neither to encourage nor to discourage national Republican luminaries to visit in support of his campaign. Consequently, this action appears to have had little impact on his campaign success. Kulongoski actively recruited outside supporters in his attempt to convince Oregonians that national policies were responsible for Oregon's economic woes. His actions also seem to have had little impact for similar reasons--Oregonians were blaming economic events on outside forces and were not expecting state-initiated action to solve the problems. They were, however, looking for their leaders to suggest how the state could survive the problems and not for the views and programs of national political figures.

In a parallel fashion, Kulongoski's reliance on out-of-state political advisors did not aid his campaign. These advisors were unfamiliar with state political processes and attitudes and were not able to build a campaign that would sell to Oregon voters. Moreover, since they were not based in Oregon, these advisors were unable to effectively handle local logistics, even at the level of purchasing TV time for campaign ads. Coupled with an inherently slow-to-develop campaign organization, Kulongoski was hamstrung in the critical area of campaign strategy.

Reports from some states suggest that where a re-election occurred there was relatively little impact on the governorship. This observation has led a few analysts to suggest that re-elections in these circumstances are "non-events." The Oregon experience would seem to confirm this. Yet, like "non-decisions," it is a conclusion that can be reached too quickly. While Atiyeh's second term lacked the pomp and circumstance of his first election and produced little in the way of new policy initiatives, the fact that it reflected voter preference for continuity and stability is a very important outcome. This would suggest that political observers should not too facilely attribute a lack of significant visible political events to a relatively insignificant political impact.

Finally, the Oregon experience suggests that we should re-examine the notion of political culture as a tool for explaining election outcomes in the states. This paper did not set out a model of culture for such an analysis. However, the unique attributes of the Oregon gubernatorial outcome raise some possibilities in this direction. The absence of a strong party system in Oregon forces candidates to mount strong personal campaigns. Coupled with a relatively non-ideological political environment, successful candidates are forced to wage "image" campaigns aimed at convincing the voters that they are most able to represent their views. When the election process ends, however, the personal campaign structure lacks the institutionalization of a party system for effectuating political transitions. On one hand, this gives the winning candidate a relatively free rein to pick administrative and political appointments and to manage the policy agenda. Yet, this also means that there is a significant lack of predictability in the power transference process. Successful transitions will be dependent on the incumbent's willingness to assist in the process rather than being able to rely upon a well-oiled "bureaucracy" and/or an institutionalized party structure. Success in this regard may be a "relative" phenomena. Moreover, it may reflect the level of "political development" in the state, that is, the extent to which the policy agenda is well-articulated in voter value preferences versus the politics of symbols.

15. HAVE THE TERMS CHANGED?
SOUTH CAROLINA RE-ELECTS A GOVERNOR
MARK E. TOMPKINS

"Close doesn't count," according to many, although an unhappy football coach once offered "horseshoes and hand grenades" as exceptions. Students of the political process typically argue that victory margins do count in politics. Close elections are said to encourage defeated challengers to renew their efforts in a new contest, to chasten the winner with a tangible reminder of the unpredictability of political fortune, and to limit the winner's ability to pursue political objectives by restricting available political capital. On the other hand, substantial victories evoke discussions of "mandates," political invulnerability, and political capital, which can be spent in an effort to achieve personal and policy objectives.

The 1982 gubernatorial election in South Carolina and the subsequent beginning of Governor Richard W. Riley's second term raise important doubts about whether this conception of executive resources is very useful in South Carolina. After seeking a constitutional change that would allow the governor to run for re-election, Riley sought re-election in the face of charges that "reform" was less on his mind than personal gain, established a record strong enough to preempt a challenge from former Governor James Edwards who was still quite personally popular in the state, then won re-election with the largest percentage of the popular vote in twenty years. A few short months later, the centerpiece of Riley's legislative program, a proposed "tax reform" package, had been thoroughly defeated, failing to pass either legislative house, and the remaining record of the first legislative session of his second term suggested, at best, mixed results. The clash of our expectations for the beginning of a demonstrably popular Governor's second term and Riley's personal experience must be viewed as the most interesting aspect of this period in South Carolina.

THE PRE-ELECTION PERIOD

One of the most important achievements of Riley's first term in office was his success in making it possible for South Carolina's governor to run for re-election. It required constitutional change, directly challenged the strong legislative tradition of South Carolina's political culture, faced Republican Party opposition, and suffered from

Riley's unwillingness to rule out seeking a second term for himself. Whether one approves of the current trend toward strengthening gubernatorial power or not, the formal powers of the governor of South Carolina have been among the weakest in the United States, the proposed second-term provision had been recommended by a 1969 constitutional revision study committee report, and most observers have agreed that some effort to improve the balance between legislative and executive powers has been appropriate.[1] Several previous governors openly advocated provisions for a second gubernatorial term, and Riley's 1982 Republican opponent advocated increasing gubernatorial appointment powers.[2] Still, timing may have been important; in a comparative study of states adopting these reforms, I have found that changes in gubernatorial terms of office often occur as a strong majority party's position begins to weaken perceptibly.[3] Since Riley, who is personally popular, followed the state's first Republican governor since Reconstruction, this was an auspicious time to adopt a reform that ensured that the incumbent, now a Democrat, could remain in office for eight years.

Riley's success in strengthening his office created important risks for him, however. While it is by no means clear that he was committed to running again when he proposed the change in the terms of office, he risked the public perceiving him as a "power hungry politician" once he made his decision to seek re-election. In a state with a strong tradition of legislative prerogative, this charge could be especially damaging. Accordingly, Riley and his staff exercised great care once the decision had been made, hoping to avoid providing ammunition to those who would try to portray him as overly ambitious.

The period of pre-election maneuvering was dominated by a non-event. Former Republican Governor James Edwards, Secretary of the Department of Energy during this period, appeared to be considering another race for governor. While he had indicated that he, as Energy Secretary, hoped to preside over the closing of the Department, this goal proved elusive, and by late 1981 further efforts appeared unlikely to succeed. When he left the governor's office in 1979, he was still quite popular, with one poll showing over sixty percent of those responding approving of him then. Many observers believed that he was still quite popular. Republican party officials were anxious to have him run, in part because they felt that he was their best candidate to oppose Riley, and in part because a number of other Republican candidates might be jeopardized if the campaign was dominated by an incumbent Democratic governor's easy re-election. Two of the state's six Congressional seats had changed hands in 1980, going to Republicans, while a third was open in 1982 as the result of a retirement. In addition, a strong Republican challenge was mounted in the contest to succeed the Democratic Attorney General, who retired after twenty-four years in office.

Edwards eventually decided not to run, and accepted the presidency of the Medical University of South Carolina, located in his home town of Charleston. His reasons for not running are not clear; some suggest that he simply wished to return to his dental practice in Charleston to "make some money" and bide his time until the governor's office was open and his prospects more promising. However, one poll taken in early 1982 showed Riley with a substantial margin over Edwards (55 percent to 27 percent) in a trial heat. Whether Dr. Edwards believed that he trailed by this much or not, the poll may have played a role in persuading him that the campaign would have been costly and difficult. Moreover, the economic climate was widely perceived to be unfavorable for a Republican candidate in South Carolina, with the recession weighing heavily on the state's important textile industry. These perceptions, which were reinforced by a continuing stream of news about shortfalls in state revenues, produced a series of fiscal crises that continued through the election.

Early polling data suggested another aspect of the problem: Riley presented a difficult political target, at least in some respects. His popularity appeared to be based on his personal attributes (he was regarded as "hard working and conscientious," "honest," "intelligent," a "family man," "fair," and "independent" according to responses in one early poll), but there were few important issues on which he was vulnerable. He had fought a difficult, but not entirely successful battle in the name of "reform" of the procedures for appointment of members of the state's Public Service Commission, which he had made an issue in his first campaign. Its mixed success was blamed on the legislature, which would have surrendered some of its powers if these proposals had fully succeeded. Riley also checked the growth of state government and successfully presented himself as a "fiscal conservative." At the same time, he took moderate positions on proposed spending limitations, favoring legislative action rather than constitutional change (thereby reducing its effectiveness in the eyes of conservative critics), and on the state's reserve fund requirements, favoring a reduction in the balance to be maintained. Finally, his administration sought to end South Carolina's role as a repository for the nation's nuclear waste through a continuing effort to promote the development of a national policy for nuclear waste disposal (based on regional compact arrangements) and to regulate more closely the existing site in South Carolina. While polls suggest that a majority of South Carolina residents support nuclear power, they are apparently opposed to the use of South Carolina sites to store nuclear wastes from other states. Related evidence suggests that Riley's approach to this issue was generally supported.

With former Governor Edwards unavailable, Republican Party supporters began to search for alternative candidates. One possibility involved a conservative Democratic state Senator, Ralph Ellis, who openly considered running for governor on the Republican slate. He eventually decided against the move, perhaps discouraged by evidence that he was not well-known and might not run well against the incumbent. Another candidate, Roddy Martin, a retired Army Warrant Officer, did announce his intention to run for the Republican nomination. His candidacy was not welcomed by the party leadership, in part because Martin favored legalization of gambling and opposed the state's Blue Laws. Martin's candidacy precluded the strategy of allowing Riley to run unopposed, which was unattractive to Republican party officials in any event.

Accordingly, longtime Republican stalwarts, associated with the effort to make the party competitive in the state in the nineteen fifties and nineteen sixties, asked one of their own to enter the race. They recruited William D. Workman, Jr., a onetime political correspondent for several different newspaper and subsequently editor of The State, one of the capital's two papers. Workman had run for statewide office once before, as the first serious statewide candidate offered by the modern Republican party in South Carolina, when he opposed incumbent Senator Olin D. Johnston in 1962. He fared surprisingly well in that race, holding Johnston to less than 60 percent of the vote and legitimizing the subsequent efforts to forge a Republican Party in the state. Workman saw his candidacy in 1982, at least in part, as another service to the party. At the same time, he believed that he had received assurances from party stalwarts of the necessary support to mount a credible campaign. In retrospect, it appears that he did not receive all the support he expected.

As expected, Workman had no difficulty winning the Republican Party nomination. Riley was unopposed for the Democratic nomination.

THE 1982 CAMPAIGN

The election proved to be a relatively uneventful contest. Both candidates conducted relatively quiet campaigns, which suited their personal styles. The increasingly dismal economic situation and national politics appeared to dominate much of the news.

The Governor's agenda was dominated by the state's economic situation and the legislature's inability to resolve several key issues, including Congressional and House redistricting; the status of then Senator Eugene Carmichael, who was convicted of vote-fraud but remained in the state Senate during his appeals; and the state's budget. Margaret Bethea, campaign manager both in Riley's dark-horse gubernatorial bid of 1978 and in his re-election campaign, remarked, "It's still hard work, but now we're the ones that can mess up. You are always thinking, weighing things, being more cautious."[4]

Riley's campaign was run as a separate operation, with its own staff not directly linked to the executive office. Among other consequences, this appeared to defuse any potential concern about inappropriate use of the resources of incumbency in his re-election effort. Riley reported raising $537,131 by election time. Jasper Johns, the artist, gave $5,000, while other large contributions (but none larger) came from the PACs representing banks, the textile industry, the medical and dental associations, and realtors, as well as some from several large businesses and the law firm of the mayor of the state's capital. His spending included $142,280 to Fowler Communications of Columbia (a firm headed by the former chairman of the state Democratic party); $23,542 to Peter Hart and associates for polling; $40,365 for production costs to The Big Orange, a Miami, Florida firm; and $11,232 to Campaign Systems of Washington, D.C. for telephone bank operations. Another $51,000 went to the state Democratic party, with $30,000 of that amount having been spent on direct mailings, $13,000 for telephone bank operations. Another $51,000 went to the state Democratic party, with $30,000 of that amount having been spent on direct mailings, $13,000 for telephone bank operations, and $8,000 forwarded to county parties. Some of this spending involved a calculated effort to help other Democratic candidates, particularly the candidate for attorney general (whose race was perceived as difficult) and agriculture commissioner (who ran against a Republican incumbent).

It should be noted that the candidate for lieutenant governor reported spending $540,077 in his largely separate campaign. He is widely believed to be preparing for a gubernatorial campaign in 1986; many of these contributions appeared to be in anticipation of that race and its result.[5]

Workman had substantial difficulty raising money; he eventually reported spending about $100,000, with the longtime Republican party contributor Roger Milliken giving $15,000.[6] In the week before the election, Clark Surratt, governmental affairs editor of The State, reported that Workman received no help from the national party (Workman would report receiving $5,000 from the party later) and that "a mailing sent to supposedly ripe contributors" about a month before the election produced little help. Workman's media consultant, Richard Quinn, through whom the majority of Workman's spending was funneled, argued that the lack of money was crippling and that more equal resources would have produced a very close race, a conclusion Surratt openly doubts.[7]

The most unexpected issue in the campaign emerged relatively late, following a Riley veto of state employee pay raises. After an appropriations bill, including money for raises, had passed the General Assembly, the Governor was confronted with a new report from the state's Board of Economic Advisors indicating that the proposed budget was out of balance by an additional $51 million. They had previously forced a downward revision of estimated state revenues of $38 million, while appropriations were under consideration in the House. Riley balanced the budget, as he was required to do, by vetoing state employee raises, along with some other smaller items. Workman attempted to take advantage of this veto, accusing the Governor of "attempting to balance the budget on [state employees' backs" in an open letter distributed to them. Workman argued that new hiring should have been stopped and "unnecessary expenditures" cut down instead. Although state employees were one of the few groups directly courted by either candidate, there is little evidence that the appeal succeeded, perhaps because of the puzzling picture presented by the more conservative candidate seeking state employees' votes.

The stream of bad economic news continued to dominate state government through the election and into the new term. In September, an additional shortfall of $79 million was announced by the Board of Economic Advisors; this shortfall was met by implementing a 4.6-percent across-the-board reduction in state spending. This was the third separate reduction in the state revenues estimate for the election year, each of which legally required action to bring the budget back into balance. This process may well have helped enhance the public's perception of the Governor managing the state's fiscal house. In December, the Board would announce another shortfall of $60 million, creating new difficulties which then dominated the post-election period.[8]

The other significant event in the election involved a series of "negative" advertisements that were prepared by Republican party media consultant Richard Quinn and aired in the Columbia area in September. These ads were separately funded by a group calling itself the September Committee. Quinn claimed some success with these ads, but Clark Surratt questioned their effectiveness in his pre-election column. Riley workers even suggested that they may have helped energize his campaign, since his supporters perceived the ads as unfair, personal attacks.

The ads, for example, criticized Riley for failing to respond to problems created by earlier legislation mandating statewide property tax reassessment, which did not require action until 1983. Problems arose because reassessment was postponed until the deadline year in most parts of the state and resulted in substantial tax increases for many residential property owners. Riley had proposed legislation to mitigate the impact of the resulting personal property tax increases, although it was not adopted. The ads also focused on what Republicans believed was one of their strongest issues, the so-called "leadership" question. They argued that even though Riley was obviously personally popular, he had little to show for his first term in office beyond presiding over the continuing stream of state budgetary crises (which, to be fair, had begun under the Edwards administration), observing but not influencing the legislative spectacle produced by Senator Carmichael's failure to resign following his vote fraud conviction, and preparing the way for a second term. This leadership question did not seem to take hold with the electorate.

The election results appeared to be a vindication of Riley's claim that he had done as well as could be expected, given the power of the legislature and South Carolina's economic situation. He won an overwhelming personal victory, receiving 70 percent of the vote, which was the best showing by a Democratic gubernatorial candidate since the unopposed Donald Russell candidacy of 1962. His campaign workers apparently expected to win by far less; those interviewed indicated that their expectations for Riley's share of the vote ranged from about fifty-eight percent to sixty-five percent.[9] Workman indicated that he, too, was surprised by the margin, if not the outcome of the election.

Apart from the personal victory, 1982 represented a substantial party success. Democratic candidates won races for lieutenant governor; attorney general, against a strongly mounted Republican challenge; agriculture commissioner, defeating the Republican incumbent; an open House seat in the Fifth District; and the Republican seat in the Sixth District, as well as a number of less closely contested elections. While turnout was somewhat below 1978 standards, when Thurmond's Senate seat was also involved, it was still higher than expected. Black support appeared to play an important role in some areas, as was expected in view of Riley's strong record on minority issues. Still, the election was viewed as unexceptional in many ways; an end-of-the-year survey of broadcasters and editors ranked the story of Riley's re-election below two murder trials, the national economy,[10] and the Carmichael case among the top new stories of 1982.

263

BEGINNING THE SECOND TERM

The beginning of the second term was relatively uneventful. Riley and his staff interpreted the election results as vindication of their approach to the office, as well as of Riley's own performance. As a result, few important shifts in personnel or responsibility among the immediate staff emerged.

For both candidates, the transition planning process took a predictable course. In Workman's case, limited resources required him to focus on the campaign, with little opportunity to make plans for assuming office if that occurred. As a result, the campaign staff expected to play an important role in the transition, as did those backing his candidacy, because those political resources were the basis of his effort. Workman indicated his willingness to consider holdovers from Riley's office, where partisan considerations would not interfere. It is reasonable to suggest that Workman's relatively low key campaign, coupled with the sense that the result of the election might be determined by outside events such as the economy rather than the work of the candidates and their supporters, made it easier for both camps to contemplate the consequences of a change of administrations. Riley confined planning for a second term to two key actions: He appointed a planning group consisting of his key outside political advisors. In addition, before the election, he made plans to take a trip to the Far East, following the election, which would focus on economic development. This relatively modest effort can probably be attributed to several factors, with political caution being prominent among them. Still, a key member of Riley's staff recalled one story when this issue was raised: A key advisor to one of Riley's defeated opponents in the 1978 election had reportedly claimed, "We spent too much time organizing the Governor's office and too little on winning the election." In any event, once the election was concluded, this planning group set the process in motion and Riley left the state for his trip. When Riley returned, the reports that had been produced were then employed in the process of preparing the State-of-the-State message and Riley's Inaugural Address. Another group of political supporters worked on plans for the inauguration, thus establishing three distinctive elements in planning the beginning of the second term.

Inaugural planning proceeded separately from other aspects of the process; in some respects, that seemed valuable. The most noteworthy aspect of the inauguration involved a series of maneuvers by the newly elected lieutenant governor and attorney general, widely assumed to be laying the groundwork for a gubernatorial campaign against each other in 1986, to focus public attention on their parts in the event. Matters came to a head when Attorney

General-elect Travis Medlock asked to have black U.S. District court Judge Matthew Perry administer his oath of office, rather than allow his rival, incoming Lieutenant Governor Mike Daniel, to administer it to him along with the other incoming officers. The request was ultimately denied and Medlock was reportedly forced to negotiate with Inaugural planners for enough tickets to seat those he had invited to the subsequent ball. Riley was able to remain aloof from the controversy, apart from reportedly turning down a last minute personal plea from Medlock.[11]

During Riley's absence, task forces were chartered to gather information and analyze issues, organized around eleven themes and led by key Riley aides. These reports were submitted after his return at the end of November, and figured in subsequent planning. There were few changes in personnel, with only two third-level staff positions changing hands between terms (while his legislative aide would move to a private law practice after the legislative session), and only minor changes in assignments emerged. No obvious change in Riley's concerns emerged after the election. In general terms, some interest in improving the Governor's ability to shape the state's budget was expressed, reflected in two proposals included in the State-of-the-State address. These have not yet been adopted, but there is still some interest in the issue.[12] It is not clear where this will lead, partly because the success of such proposals probably depends on whether interest in such changes is sustained by events.

Post-election stories hinted at attempts to adjust Riley's personal style. In an interview with Clark Surratt of *The State*, Riley was reported as saying he "can afford to be . . . stronger and bolder in his second term. . . ;" in a later story, Surratt also reported that "suggestions have been made . . . that Riley perhaps could improve his effectiveness if he delegated more work detail control to senior staffers in order to concentrate on broader duties of the state's chief executive."[13] Interviews with the staff confirmed this picture of Riley's attention to detail and his interest in it. However, many suggested that it was a personal trait which was unlikely to change, and one which should be appreciated as a strength in some respects, as well as a liability.

THE LEGISLATIVE SESSION

Ultimately, the beginning of Riley's second term was dominated by his proposals to the 1983 legislative session. His most important proposal was what he called a "tax equity" package. It included a proposed one-cent hike in the state's sales tax coupled with an increase in upper bracket income tax rates; provided some property tax relief; increased license fees for beer, wine, and liquor distributors; and offered a short-term bailout plan for the beleaguered state budget.

This last feature of the plan was produced as a response to yet another crisis in state revenues (recall that three revenue shortfalls had already emerged in the 1982-1983 fiscal year); this one was produced by the Board of Economic Advisors' December report of an additional $60-million shortage in projected revenues. Initially, the State Budget and Control Board, which the Governor chairs but which also includes two legislative members and two other constitutional officers, proposed dealing with the shortage through employee furloughs, school closings, and various accounting changes. In his inaugural address, Riley proposed implementing the sales tax increase on March 1, obtaining an estimated $37.5 million in 1982-1983 revenues which could be used to help meet the revenue crisis.

Several other tax proposals, along with Riley's, were placed before the legislature. A sales tax increase had tentatively been mentioned by the chairman of the Senate Finance Committee, Rembert Dennis, in 1982; he and the chairman of the House Ways and Means Committee endorsed efforts to increase the tax in 1983, with Dennis claiming that some type of increase was a "foregone conclusion."[14] The 1983 legislative agenda also included other proposals for one-cent increases in the sales tax, allocating revenues among state government, local school districts, and property tax relief in proportions differing from the Governor's version, as well as a proposal from a progressive House member for a one-and-a-half-cent sales tax increase, some of which would be used to remove the tax currently placed on food.

The resulting wealth of options and temptations may well help account for subsequent events. In 1951, when the sales tax was adopted, and in 1969, when it was increased by one cent, the General Assembly had great difficulty in choosing among the various competing approaches to raising those funds (particularly in 1969) and to allocating them. In 1951, when increased spending on education was widely perceived as vital, these controversies were subdued by then Governor Byrnes's endorsement of a proviso earmarking the revenues for educational spending.[15]

For the first few weeks of the 1983 legislative session, the House agenda was dominated by debate over the various proposals. Riley's initial proposal was defeated early, apparently, in part, because of provisions increasing income tax rates for upper income taxpayers; the progressives' proposal to end sales taxation on food purchases suffered a similar fate. Riley had evidently considered including this proposal in his package but decided not to because it did not appear politically feasible. News reports of the debate were accompanied by related discussions of contingency plans to furlough state employees for up to five days to meet the revenue shortfall in the event that the tax increase did not pass. After Riley's proposals had clearly been defeated, the House turned to various proposals to increase the sales tax by one percent, but none succeed in attracting the necessary support.

As successive deadlines for adoption of the rescue plan came and passed, it became increasingly clear that no proposal was going to succeed. Some attributed the failure of these proposals to the complexity of Riley's original package, some to anti-tax sentiment and concern over the growth in state government, and some to the lack of legislative preparation and/or leadership. One report quoted a key Senate ally as saying that the plan "could have been seasoned with more legislative input and planning," while an ally in the House argued that the legislation fell "victim to a host of competing interests . . . [which could have been anticipated by doing more] base touching and taking the temperature of the House.'"[16] In any event, the House's unwillingness to pass any measure increasing revenues in the current year left the state with a widely acknowledged budgetary crisis.

Accordingly, both houses moved to consider legislation permitting employee furloughs, believing that it was the only available approach to balancing the state's budget in the current fiscal year, since across-the-board or selective cutbacks of the magnitude required were deemed impossible. On March 9, however, the House Ways and Means Committee moved to adopt a series of measures that would erase the $60-million shortfall. Since attention had been focused on employee furloughs and other very drastic solutions, many legislators, members of the press, and, presumably, most of the public regarded the new proposal with some suspicion. Several people, including some Republicans opposed to the tax plan, charged that the "March surprise," which resolved the budget crisis, had been available for some time and hidden from public scrutiny in an effort to encourage passage of the Governor's tax plan or some other similar measure. In fact, at least one Republican called for the resignation of the Governor and the State's Auditor, who had been widely reported discussing the need for massive layoffs or the employee furlough plan, while a number of questions were raised about the role of other figures, especially the Chairman of the House Ways and Means Committee, in "finding" this money.[17]

The resulting criticism grew so severe that the Governor's aide responsible for legislative liaison prepared a memorandum explaining the process, ostensibly addressed to members of the staff but widely circulated. The various elements of the rescue plan, in fact, were already in hand--in early March they were simply assembled into a comprehensive package. The plan included $14 million in specific cuts, along with the recovery of several million dollars in Mental Health Department fees, which had been proposed the previous December; the acceleration of corporate tax collections, worth another $1.7 million; additional beer and wine taxes, worth another $4.36 million; the transfer of $1.9 million from a state authority's accounts; and, most important, the adoption of a House member's March 1 proposal to accelerate the collection of employers' income tax withholdings from a quarterly to a monthly basis, providing a one-time windfall of approximately $25 million.[18] The Governor was clearly unenthusiastic, publicly making references to "Mickey Mouse accounting techniques," while his legislative liaison said, "They've raised mediocrity to a new mediocre level."[19] However, the situation was serious enough and time was short enough that the package was quickly adopted, essentially resolving the revenue crisis.

The Governor's problems were less clearly resolved. Shortly after the fight was concluded, State Senator Ralph Ellis, who had previously considered running against Riley in 1982, and subsequently had become a Republican, announced that a poll he commissioned found that Riley was (still) more popular than Strom Thurmond, making him the state's most popular politician.[20] Nonetheless, Riley spent time meeting with members of the House, explaining the process leading to the controversies in early March, while other members of his staff made efforts to ensure that the explanation was widely disseminated. While the damage was contained, the process appeared to limit Riley's prospects for further legislative initiatives in 1983; one newspaper recapitulation was entitled, "no second honeymoon for Riley," while another headline referred to Riley's "attempt to salvage his legislative agenda."[21]

The tax equity package had not been his only proposal for this legislative session. His inaugural address included proposals for continued efforts in the area of early childhood education (a long-standing commitment), small business development, and criminal justice reforms, among other. Subsequently, he would argue for the reallocation of substantial resources going to the state's two medical schools while bolstering education in science and technology, and for the state to end the costly practice of securing the state's property insurance coverage through a third party intermediary (an insurance agency partly owned by a former member of the legislature).

Following the sales tax fight, Riley suffered several public defeats: The proposed use of an old state facility to house prisoners was rejected, the insurance arrangement continued, and a proposal to merge the state's two medical schools, which Riley endorsed, suffered one of its many defeats over the last decade. Budgetary reform measures were also essentially rejected for the 1983 session.

There were several successes at the end of the session, although Riley's role in achieving them varied. The legislature granted Riley the authority to relieve prison overcrowding through an early release program, state participation in a regional low-level nuclear waste disposal compact was approved (which was an important initiative of Riley's administration), the state's Blue Laws were eased, some changes were adopted in the drunken driving legislation, a continuing battle over the creation of an interim Court of Appeals was tentatively resolved, and a new tax was placed on "low level waste." Riley's proposals to create three new agencies were adopted. One new agency was established to coordinate planning and distribution of state health care funds, which included one gubernatorial appointee as chairman and six legislative appointees, while the other two were aimed at economic development, one to coordinate research and attract high-technology industry and the other to provide low-interest loans to small and medium-sized businesses. Still, these were not the centerpiece of Riley's program for 1983 and many represented responses to external forces, such as prison overcrowding, increased pressure on the state as a site for the disposal of hazardous and nuclear waste, and the explosive growth of public medical care costs. At the session's conclusion, Riley professed relative pleasure over its accomplishments, saying it was the best of the five that he, as chief executive, had seen, but his press spokesman refused to single out Riley's biggest accomplishment.[22] A published summary of adopted legislation suggested that fewer pieces of legislation had been adopted in the 1983 session than in any session in recent memory.[23]

This analysis, then, defines the paradox with which we started. Richard Riley won handsomely and apparently remains popular; he has changed little in his approach to government. He entered his new term committed, in Michigan Governor James Blanchard's memorable phrase, to the idea that "If you face the music early, you're better off."[24] Nonetheless, the personal mandate he secured in 1982 appears to have provided little political capital and few resources for governance. Why is that?

THE INTERACTION OF STYLE, CIRCUMSTANCE, AND SETTING

Two profoundly different explanations can be offered for this combination of political strength and legislative weakness. One centers on Riley's personal style: In this view, a political leader may be enormously popular and successful at the polls without being successful in achieving policy goals. The other explanation focuses on the constraints imposed by circumstances and settings, arguing that we often make what social psychologists call "the fundamental attribution error" in judging and ignoring the role contextual constraints play in shaping events.[25]

Examinations of personal style are often based in Barber's discussion of Presidential character.[26] In Riley's case, we find unambiguous support for viewing him as having a "positive" orientation, with no evidence of the brooding self-doubts and invocations of "duty" associated with a "negative" personal character. His conduct in office demostrates purposeful intent and focus on programmatic goals, coupled with a sense of satisfaction where progress is being made. The transition into the second term illustrates the point; the process produced general satisfaction with his approach and style, while little "agonizing reappraisal" went on. Even after the conclusion of the sales tax fight, he seemed more interested in exploring new means of accomplishing his objectives than in agonizing over the defeats.

The categorization is less clear along the active/passive dimension; in Riley's case, his energy is apparent. Several staff members evoked Jimmy Carter's appetite for detail in discussing Riley's work habits. However, in the face of substantial disappointment in pursuit of his legislative program, Riley remained personally agreeable and avoided public confrontation with those opposing him, continuing to seek mutually satisfactory resolutions of the controversies at hand, thus evoking the "receptive," "other-directed" qualities Barber associates with passivity. Several press stories underscored the point: An opportunity to address the General Assembly late in the fight over tax increase proposals was used to salute Solomon Blatt, the longtime speaker of the House; criticism of the state's Chamber of Commerce, which openly fought the proposals was limited to a few quiet comments about their failure to serve the interests of the state; and a lengthy interview with Riley in late March reported him as saying that "while the Legislature was inefficient, it was still Democratic."[27] Only one clear zero-sum struggle was reported throughout this period; once the spending bill reached Riley's desk, a privately communicated veto threat led the state's two medical schools to agree to reallocate some monies along lines preferred by Riley.[28] The entire process was played out privately in a few days. The general style of accommodation and consensus seeking, in fact, defines one of the crucial differences between Riley and Carter.

It may help to reconsider these categories: Riley is obviously purposeful in his approach to governance; a long-standing progressive agenda has been elaborated over the years and continues to guide his public behavior. He is active, seeking out problems and offering relatively innovative solutions (witness his distinctive "tax equity" package). In his decision-making style, he adopts an "inclusive" focus, however. Rather than seeking to lead a continuing coalition in a zero-sum political struggle with opponents, or to dominate all he encounters, he seeks mutual adjustment and satisfaction. Stories of political reward and retaliation are virtually absent in the local press, which instead must focus on the relative success of his efforts to achieve his goals. Friends are sometimes identified and enemies almost never are, leading to a politics of accommodation rather than controversy. As the incoming chairman of the Black Caucus put it, "He's basically been a very fair-minded person."[29]

Can we properly appreciate the Riley administration with this perspective? It suggests that Riley's successes can be understood through his positive, purposeful focus, leading the state in realistically progressive directions. His limitations come then in his failure to confront the opposition, to punish opponents, and to reward supporters. This explanation, if offered in isolation, would require us to accept the argument that important gains could be achieved through a more aggressive personal style.

Those around Riley clearly believe another explanation. In their view, setting and circumstance shape many of their constraints. This perspective cannot be dismissed lightly. Riley has been very successful in retaining his staff: Few stories of internal conflict surface in the press even though the staff's organization is best understood as "fluid" and "adaptive" with multiple points of access and only modest expressions of hierarchy. His legislative supporters publicly argue that he has been wise to stay away from the "bull in the china shop" approach and that he gets about all that he can from the legislature.[30] A key advisor suggests that Riley should be understood as an "active-positive," practicing in a political environment which would not tolerate the aggressive style Barber contemplates. Moreover, they can justly point to the style of other recent incumbents, often relatively highly regarded, who also appeared to practice the politics of accommodation.[31]

The constraints of setting are attributable to both the weakness of the governor and the power of the legislature. The Governor's weakness stems from several structural constraints. Budgetary powers are not solely vested in the governor, but rather lie with the Budget and Control Board, on which the governor serves along with two senior legislators and two other constitutional officers. Mississippi is the only other state where an arrangement of this type exists; advisors point to recent Mississippi initiatives to increase spending on education, which relied on an elaborate consensus-building process, as further evidence for the necessity for the politics of accommodation in such an environment. Agencies are governed by quasi-autonomous boards and commissions, whose appointees' terms often extend beyond a particular governor's time in office; indeed, in many cases the governor does not appoint those members. (A recent summary of the selection process for state administrative officials in <u>The Book of the States</u> indicates that South Carolina's governor appoints a smaller proportion of those officials examined than any other state's governor.[32]) A recent survey of state administrative officials found none of the South Carolina respondents ranking the governor as the "most influential" on their department's programs and objectives.[33]

Finally, save for the provision of item veto powers, the governor is also relatively weak in his ability to influence the process of legislative consideration. Dwight Drake, who had served previous governors in related capacities and who has served as Riley's legislative liaison, indicates that many previous South Carolina governors have not even had a "legislative program," so that Riley has been more active in this forum than many.[34] The continued dominance of the Democratic party in the legislature deprives the governor of another resource, based on the cohesion of a legislative majority; as Key pointed out years ago, the absence of durable factional competition undermines efforts to produce a coherent approach to public problems.

South Carolina lore understands the state to be a "legislative state," for several reasons.[35] Until the adoption of Home Rule provisions in 1975, legislative delegations were responsible for county governance; even now, they retain important formal and informal powers in their communities.[36] Seniority has played an important role in legislative leadership for decades, shaped by the powers accumulated during the years of the "Barnwell Ring" of then Speaker of the House Solomon Blatt and Senator Edgar Brown.[37] Brown's death and Blatt's aging have moderated somewhat the force of seniority. In the Senate, these changes are slight, so far, with several other senior legislative leaders assuming somewhat more diffused power. In the House, no clear, dominant leader has emerged yet, leading to a typically fragmented, and perhaps incoherent, representative assembly. In this setting, then, focused interested and fragmented consideration of proposed actions are the norms. The Governor, as we have seen, lacks many of the resources he would need to dominate such a process.[38] Indeed, Dr. John Stucker, who serves as an advisor to Riley, suggests that the

Governor's lack of budgetary and legislative leverage, coupled with his weak appointment powers, deprives him of many of the resources he would need to influence legislation more decisively. As Stucker points out, the President, who can trade support for other legislation and influence partisan rewards, relies heavily on these powers; the political power associated with a "mandate" is exercised through these more palpable tools in many cases.[39]

Circumstances similarly constrain Riley. Governor of one of the nation's poorest states, he has few resources available to solve state problems, many of which are based on the state's poverty. Much of his term in office has been dominated by national economics, which have weighed heavily on a state dependent on labor-intensive, production-oriented industries, which are vulnerable to foreign competitive pressures. Further, these events have shaped the agenda of state government, since revenue shortfalls continue and needs expand.

The agenda of an "Atari Democrat" appears irrelevant in such a setting, while Riley's emphasis on early childhood education, feasible industrial and small business development, and control of the impact of the state's long-standing role in nuclear waste disposal may have some value. Moreover, the setting constraints suggest that process reforms must precede strong leadership; Riley's success in making a two-term governor possible, and his personal role in perhaps calming the fears of personal ambition that often accompany such reforms, can be viewed as important steps in this process. Many of these setting constraints are based in once widespread traditions that are now waning in other states; as a result, South Carolinians must seek an improved climate for executive administration as a first step in the quest for state government's effort to set priorities for the use of its relatively scarce resources.

CONCLUSION

South Carolina's experience produces several cautions for students of gubernatorial politics. These include cautions about political careers, about the meaning of electoral success, and about our approach to the understanding of political executives.

Governor Riley's personal situation reminds us of the unpredictability of political fortunes. The future seemed to suggest a Senatorial race after the 1982 election, with Riley, including Fourth District Congressman and potential Senatorial opponent Carroll Campbell's name in his pre-gubernatorial election polling. Following the 1983 session, yet another poll, conducted by the Charlotte Observer, suggested that Riley was preferred by more voters than Senator Strom Thurmond in a trial heat for a 1984 Senate campaign. After a week of entertaining speculation unfolded, Riley publicly committed himself to honoring his pledge to serve out his second term.[40] Signs in mid-1983 point to Thurmond running for re-election, while one observer suggests that Riley is now more interested in seeking a judicial appointment.

Riley achieved dramatic political success in his quest for a second term in office. While this success may have made him more confident personally, it had little effect on his ability of gubernatorial capability in South Carolina, where state government is dramatically fragmented and power badly diffused.

Finally, Riley's personal qualities suggest that Barber's characterization of executive style requires reconsideration in this case. He fits Barber's conception of a "positive" orientation, but the dimension of "active-passive" does not appear useful in treating Riley's style, in this setting. Rather, we are forced to analyze Riley's decision-making style, highlighting the "inclusive" focus of his efforts to build political coalitions, coupled with his active efforts to forge them. His supporters also call our attention to the impact that the South Carolina setting has on the possibilities for executive leadership, suggesting that setting and circumstance help to frame and shape executive styles.

NOTES

I am grateful for the assistance provided to me by a number of people; both Governor Richard Riley and his staff, and his opponent, Mr. William D. Workman, Jr. and his campaign workers, have been unfailingly gracious and helpful in responding to my requests and questions. Professor Thad Beyle, Patricia Jerman, and my colleagues, Professor Blease Graham and John Stucker (who also serves the Governor), also have been very helpful and generous with their time elaborating the account I offer. I am also grateful to Clark Surratt, of The State newspaper, who helped me understand and interpret the election and its implications. While my understanding of the 1982 election and the resulting events has been substantially improved through their efforts, none of them bears any responsibility for the account that follows, nor for the interpretations I offer.

[1] Robert H. Stoudemire, "The S.C. Constitutional Revision Report," The University of South Carolina Governmental Review, XII (2), May 1970, p. 2; see also C. Blease Graham and Donald P. Aiesi, "The Role of the Governor in South Carolina," in Government in the Palmetto State, Luther F. Carter and Mann, eds., (Bureau of Governmental Research and Service, 1983).

[2] "Gubernatorial Candidates Tackle Issues," The State, 17 October 1983, sec. B, p. 1.

[3] Mark E. Tompkins, "Changing the Terms: Gubernatorial Term Reform in Modern Era," 1984 revision of paper delivered at the 1981 annual meeting of the Southern Political Science Association.

[4] Scott Johnson, "Frontrunner strategy of Riley staff far cry from 1978 excitement," The Columbia Record, 28 October 1982, sec. C, p. 1.

[5] Clark Surratt, "Daniel's Spending of $540,077 Led S.C. Races," The State, 2 December 1982, sec. C, p. 11. The most important instance of direct interests in the Governor's race involved the Riley campaign's use of former State Party Chairman Don Fowler's firm, since that firm had also worked for ChemNuclear Services, the radioactive waste disposal firm. The Riley administration was very active in nuclear waste disposal issues, of course. Clark Surratt pointed out the connection in his column, "Workman Camp Claims He's Closing on Riley," The State, 17 October 1982, sec. B, p. 4. These stories were prepared from, and supplemented by publicly available reports on file with the State Ethics Commission, filed in November of 1982.

[6] Ibid.

[7] Clark Surratt, "Campaign What-ifs Already Coming Out," The State, 31 October 1982, sec. B, p. 4.

[8] Dwight Drake, "Memorandum to Governor's Staff," dated March 15, 1983.

[9] Various pre- and post-election interviews with five individuals.

[10] "Top 10 Newsmakers," The Columbia Record, 27 December 1982, sec. C, p. 2.

[11] Jerry Adams, "Medlock Courted Favors at Inauguration," The State, 16 January 1983, sec. B, p. 4.

[12] As examples, see the following, "Proposals to Change Budget Process Debated," The Columbia Record, 24 January 1983, sec. C, p. 2; "Governor Seeks Coherent Budget," editorial in The Greenville News, 5 February 1983, sec. C, p. 2; Aubrey Bowie, "State Government Faces Management Crisis," Greenville News-Piedmont, 11 June 1983, sec. A, p. 4.

[13] Clark Surratt, "Riley Says He Can Be Bolder This Term," The State, 26 December 1982, sec. B, p. 4, and "Riley Preparing Few Changes in Next 4 Years," The State, 9 January 1983, sec. A, pp. 1 and 18. Several of those interviewed also suggested that one of the most important impacts the substantial victory margin had was to improve Riley's confidence.

[14] "Legislators Call State Sales Tax Increase Inevitable," United Press International, in The State, 10 January 1983, sec. C, p. 1.

[15] For a report of Byrnes' public endorsement of a Senate earmarking provision, "Spending Bill Shuttled to Conference Committee: School-Minded Legislators Names to Group," in The State, 3 April 1951, sec. A, p. 1 and sec. B, p. 4. Controversy over the exact form of tax measure continued through the 1969 session, although Governor McNair had publicly proposed a set of measures, including a sales tax increase, in his Inaugural.

[16] "Study: Riley State's Favorite Politician Despite Sales Tax Fight," The Columbia Record, 21 March 1983, sec. C, p. 2.

[17] As an example, see Marilyn Rauber, "Money Magic Enrages Lawmakers, "The Greenville News, 13 March 1983, sec. D, pp. 1 and 4.

[18] Drake, see note 8.

[19] Rauber, sec. D, p. 4.

[20] "Study: Riley State's Favorite Politician Despite Sales Tax Fight," On the same issue, notice that a Charlotte Observer poll in late July came to the same conclusion. See the story reported in note 40.

[21] Barbara S. Williams, "No Second Honeymoon for Riley," Charleston News & Courier, 20 March 1983, sec. A, p. 16; Chris Weston, "Riley Tries to Salvage His Legislative Agenda," The Greenville News, 10 April 1983, sec. C, p. 1 and 5.

[22] Clark Surratt, "Legislative Session Called Productive," The State, 26 June 1983, sec. B, p. 4. "Flurry of Action Ends Session, Riley Happy With Legislation," The Columbia Record, 11 June 1983, sec. A, p. 1. The reference is to the report of spokesman Russ McKinney's comments.

[23] Ibid.

[24] Jack W. Germond and Jules Witcover, "Blanchard Faced the Music Early," printed in The Columbia Record, 16 June 1983, sec. A, p. 16.

[25] Richard Nisbett and Lee Ross, Human Inference: Strategies and Shortcomings of Social Judgment, (Englewood Cliffs, N.J., 1980), pp. 120-130.

[26] James David Barber, The Presidential Character, Predicting Performance in the White House, (Englewood Cliffs, N.J., Prentice-Hall, 1972).

[27] Respectively, "Gov. Riley Drops in for a Chat," in "Palmetto Politics," The Greenville News, 20 March 1983, sec. B, pp. 1 and 9; Riley's comment that he was "disappointed with the state chamber's priority for South Carolina," appears in "Riley Criticizes Chamber Regarding Tax Relief, Budget," The Columbia Record, 28 February 1983, sec. C, p. 15; and Dean Campbell, "While Inefficient, Legislature is Democratic," The Cheraw (S.C.) Chronicle, 24 March 1983, sec. A, pp. 1 and 9.

[28] John Norton, "Medical Schools Avoid Veto Fight: Presidents, Riley Agree on Spending Package," The State, 16 June 1983, sec. A, p. 1.

[29] Clark Surratt, "Riley Preparing Few Changes in Next 4 Years," sec. A, p. 18.

[30] Chris Weston, "Riley stumbles on tax bill but recovers for final flourish," Greenville News, 19 June 1983, sec. D, p. 14.

[31] See the discussion in Jack Bass and Walter DeVries, The Transformation of Southern Politics, Social Change and Political Consequence Since 1945, (New York, Basic Books, Inc., 1976), pp. 257-264, on the adaptation of South Carolina's political leaders, including Strom Thurmond, to the changing climate of race relations in the state; also note the story about then Governor Hollings's efforts on behalf of his proposed technical education system, sought in an evening over a fifth of bourbon with state Senator Edgar Brown.

[32] The Book of the States, 1982-83 (Lexington, KY; The Council of State Governments, 1982), pp. 177-179.

[33] Glenn Abney and Thomas P. Lauth, "The Governor as Chief Administrator," Public Administration Review, 43 (1), January/February, 1983, pp. 41.

[34] Personal interview, 9 December 1982; this discussion owes much to several discussions with John Stucker about these issues--in particular, he has highlighted for me the importance of the absence of a cohesive legislative majority.

[35] See Bass and DeVries, pp. 276-281.

[36] One example of this emerged at the conclusion of the legislative session when the legislature failed to pass required legislation for the Calhoun County school budget, prompting a local funding crisis for the 1983- 1984 school year. Calhoun County is the home of the President Pro Tempore of the Senate, Marion Gressette, and had retained the old practice of establishing its taxation levels through local legislation at the State House, guided by the legislative delegation.

[37] V.O. Key discusses the emergence and role of the "Barnwell Ring" in Southern Politics, (Vintage Books, 1949), pp. 150-155; as he makes clear, the leadership was collective, but limited to a few senior members; Bass and DeVries update that account to include Edgar Brown's successors in the Senate (Marion Gressette, now President Pro Tem, and Rembert Dennis, now Chairman of the Finance Committee, posts previously held simultaneously by Brown) and the evolution of the House once Blatt gave up the post of Speaker.

[38] See the discussion in Bass and DeVries, pp. 276-278; also see Graham and Aiesi.

[39] In support of this position, consider President Reagan's victories on the budget in his first year in office; while these are widely attributed to his electoral mandate, many of the critical votes were secured through the other

resources of office. See, for example, the story about compromises struck to assure the support of Representatives from Louisiana and East Texas for "Gramm-Latta II," which lead John Breaux to report, "They're not buying my vote, only renting it," in Laurence I. Barrett, <u>Gambling With History: Reagan in the White House</u>, (Garden City, N.Y., Doubleday, Inc., 1983), pp. 160-161. The same source is useful in reminding us of the potency of the executive's symbolic and expressive powers--these, presumably, are available to a governor in South Carolina.

[40] Jim Walser, "Riley Could Unseat Thurmond in Senate, Poll Says, " <u>The Charlotte Observer</u>, 31 July 1983, sec. C, p. 1.

16. THE 1982 GUBERNATORIAL ELECTION IN SOUTH DAKOTA

DONALD C. DAHLIN

SETTING THE STAGE: A BRIEF PRIMER ON SOUTH DAKOTA

South Dakota is a geographically large, sparsely populated, and relatively poor state whose dominant industries are agriculture, primarily, and tourism, secondarily. South Dakota is also a strong Republican state although, in the present era, the two parties are more competitive than they have been in the past.

South Dakota is, as well, a politically conservative state. This characterization, however, can be overdrawn. For example, these politically conservative South Dakotans, as far back as 1916 and 1918, amended the State Constitution to allow the state to sell hail insurance, operate grain elevators, and run a cement plant, among other things. The State Cement Plant continues in operation to this day. Politically conservative South Dakotans also have elected such politically liberal U.S. Senators as George McGovern and James Abourezk. In the 1982 election, in which the voters chose among the two House incumbents (the state having been reduced to one congressional seat following the 1980 census), these voters chose the more liberal Democrat, Tom Daschle, over the more conservative Republican, Clint Roberts. What these facts suggest is that there is a strong streak of pragmatism running through South Dakota politics and tempering an otherwise clear tendency to be Republican and conservative.

As to South Dakota state government, two points seem especially relevant as general background. First, the governor's position is clearly the preeminent one in power and prestige. In part this preeminence comes from the fact that the South Dakota State Legislature is a part-time one, and in part it arises from a constitutional amendment adopted by the voters in 1972. Under the terms of that amendment the governor serves a four-year term (with a limit of two consecutive terms), appoints the heads of the major departments (currently fifteen), and has extensive powers of reorganization[1] and extensive budgetary authority over the agencies of state government.

Second, and somewhat surprisingly perhaps, the principal source of the revenue that state government spends comes from the federal government (some 43.5 percent of a $709-million budget in FY 84). The next major source of revenue is a 4-percent state sales tax. The remainder of the state's revenue comes from a variety of other charges and taxes including those on such items as gasoline, liquor, and cigarettes.

THE IMMEDIATE BACKDROP TO THE 1982 GUBERNATORIAL ELECTION

Governor William J. Janklow was elected to his first term in 1978 with 56.6 percent of the vote. The Janklow victory continued a strong resurgence of Republican strength in the state. In 1978, in addition to Governor Janklow's victory, the Republicans won four of five other contests for statewide offices, won over two-thirds control in each house of the state legislature, won one of two House of Representatives seats and one U.S. Senate seat. In 1980, the Republicans again did very well, providing strong support to the Reagan candidacy, defeating Senator George McGovern's bid for re-election and retaining their two-thirds control of the state legislature.

As the 1982 election approached, then, unless there was some major external shock to the state's political system or some major problem with the performance of the Janklow administration, continued Republican dominance in general, and re-election for Governor Janklow in particular, seemed safe predictions.

For those hoping to reverse this Republican trend, the condition of the economy in South Dakota seemed to have good potential as a political issue. The state's dominant agricultural sector was in especially bad shape as farm income, measured in 1972 dollars, had fallen from $258 million in 1978 to $172.7 million in 1982. Traditionally, rural discontent has worked to the benefit of the Democratic Party in South Dakota. Moreover, adverse economic conditions were not confined to the farm sector. Earned personal income of South Dakotans in general had fallen off since 1979 and unemployment had risen steadily, growing from 3.1 percent in 1978 to 5.5 percent in 1982. While the unemployment rate was certainly not of the magnitude of that in most states, it was becoming an increasingly nettlesome problem.

In a state heavily dependent upon federal grant-in-aid programs, the Reagan Administration budget cuts were also unsettling. For example, in 1980, the last year of the Carter Administration, federal aid to state and local governments in South Dakota totalled $443,253 million. By 1982, after two years of the Reagan administration, federal aid had fallen to $324,773 million. This loss of $118,480 million represented a 27-percent reduction in two years and, on a percentage basis, made South Dakota the biggest loser of federal aid of all the states during this time period.[2]

As a result of such economic difficulties, state revenue began to fall short of revenue projections, compelling Governor Janklow to respond in some fashion. As one response to this problem, on September 10, 1980, Governor Janklow ordered a 5-percent cut in the spending of state agencies for the remainder of the fiscal year. As a further response, in 1981 the Governor proposed a mineral severance tax designed to increase sharply the amount of taxes paid by the Homestead Gold mine. The state also passed increases in taxes on motor fuel, liquor, and cigarettes and raised a variety of user fees. At the same time, the state did not raise the sales tax rate nor impose a corporate or personal income tax.

On other matters during his first term, the Governor had more discretion in deciding what actions, if any, to take. In general, Governor Janklow brought to the task of being governor the same activist style he had used as Attorney General. In the day-to-day management of state government, for example, the Governor was successful in removing many positions from the career service which, he argued, were of a policy-making nature. Additionally, the Governor was very active in issuing executive orders to rearrange the structure of state government, eliminating the Department of Environmental Protection, for example, and abolishing and then reconstituting (in a fashion that was perceived by many to increase gubernatorial authority) many of the citizen boards and commissions.

In a similarly activist way, the Governor exercised strong leadership in a variety of public policy areas. Three examples will illustrate the point.

Example one: Rail transportation in South Dakota had been on a steady decline for several years. Governor Janklow argued that South Dakota agriculture in particular, and the state's economy in general, could not afford the loss of rail service. He therefore proposed that the state purchase and arrange for the operation of a "core" railroad system. The 1980 legislature concurred and the state purchased 780 miles of rail line. The purchase price of $21.5 million was funded by a temporary one-cent increase in the sales tax. On the issue of running trains on these rail lines, the Governor negotiated an agreement with the Burlington Northern Railroad to be the operator.

Example two: Also in 1980 at the very end of the legislative session, Governor Janklow announced that he had been in negotiation with the Citibank corporation. Citibank had decided to move its credit card operation from New York State because of New York's limits on interest rates. Citibank was looking at five states including South Dakota as possible sites for the relocation. To help insure that South Dakota was the choice, the Governor recommended that the state make several changes in its banking laws including repealing any limits on interest rates. The South Dakota legislature passed the changes in record time and Citibank did choose Sioux Falls as the place to relocate.

Example three: The development of the state's water resources, especially the Missouri River, has long been a goal in South Dakota. Because of the enormous cost involved, the state had tended to look to the federal government to take the lead in the water development area and to argue that such federal support was justified because of the loss of land involved in the construction of federal dams in the 50s and 60s. As the Janklow administration took office, the prospects for water development did not look too bright. There was considerable argument within the state over the one major federal water project that Congress had authorized--the Oahe project--which would have taken water from the Missouri and sent it to the northeastern part of the state. That internal disagreement coupled with the Carter Administration's view that most water projects were pork barrel rip offs and the Reagan administration's view that domestic federal spending had to be sharply curtailed made relying solely on federal funding for state water development less and less attractive.

At the same time in western South Dakota, the Madison aquifer, which provides the water for that part of the state, was perceived to be in some danger because of the state of Wyoming's agreement to allow the aquifer to be tapped by a consortium of large businesses operating as Energy Transportation Systems Incorporated (ETSI). ETSI wanted the water to transport coal through a pipeline from Wyoming coal fields to electrical generating plants in the South.

Negotiating secretly, Governor Janklow reached an agreement to allow ETSI to take up to 50,000 acre feet of water annually from the Missouri River for fifty years. In exchange, South Dakota would receive up to $1.4 billion over that same time period to use in developing its own water resources. Additionally ETSI agreed not to exercise its water right to the Madison aquifer. Having negotiated this agreement, in September 1981 the Governor called a special session of the legislature to approve it. Approval was quick and overwhelming. The sale of this water has occasioned a great deal of concern from states downriver from South Dakota and is currently in litigation. Governor Janklow has been very forceful in suggesting that the amount of water involved is so small and South Dakota's sacrifice of land for the construction of the federal dams in the state so large that these states really have no basis to complain.

THE 1982 GUBERNATORIAL ELECTION IN SOUTH DAKOTA

As the preceding discussion suggests, Governor Janklow's activism coupled with his incumbency insured him an unchallenged position within his own party as the 1982 election season began.

On the Democratic side, a number of possible opponents were being mentioned. They included Lars Herseth, minority leader in the state House of Representatives; Dick Kneip, former governor from 1971 to 1978; Harvey Wollman, former state legislator and lieutenant governor who also served several months as governor in 1978 after Governor Kneip resigned to become U.S. Ambassador to Singapore; Roger McKellips, state senator and the party's nominee against Janklow in 1978; Mike O'Connor, state senator from the Sioux Falls area; and Elvern Varilek, former Democratic House leader and unsuccessful candidate for Democratic congressional nominee in 1970.

As the June 1 primary date drew nearer, only O'Connor and Varilek decided to make the race. The resulting Democratic primary was both low-cost (with Varilek reporting expenditures of $20,660 compared to O'Connor's $15,894) and low-key. On June 1, 1982, with 22 percent of the state's Democrats voting, O'Connor won an easy victory, carrying 51 of the state's 66 counties and beating Varilek 24,101 (59 percent) to 16,916 (41 percent).

As of June 2, 1982, then, the major contestants for the governor's chair were set: Incumbent William J. Janklow, 43, a lawyer who had worked for legal aid on the Rosebud Indian Reservation and served one term as attorney general before being elected governor in 1978, and Mike O'Connor, 54, state senator from Minnehaha County, a Sioux Falls businessman, and the owner of a small farm near De Smet, South Dakota.

In the campaign that ensued, challenger O'Connor both attacked the performance of the Janklow Administration and offered some alternative programs of his own.

For example, on the basis of the decisions to sell water to ETSI, to allow the Burlington Northern the monopoly on the state-owned railroad system and the negotiations with Citicorp, O'Connor charged that Governor Janklow was more a friend of corporate America outside South Dakota than of the small businessperson and farmer within the state. As O'Connor saw it, if Governor Janklow had devoted his energies directly to helping South Dakota businesses and farmers, the state would have been better off.

While expressing disagreement with particular policies of the Janklow Administration, the central thrust of O'Connor's attack on the performance of the Janklow Administration was an attack on the leadership style of the Governor himself. As far as O'Connor was concerned, the Governor was too secretive in the conduct of the state's business (again the negotiations with ETSI, the Burlington Northern, and Citicorp were the main examples); the Governor also was too confrontational and intimidating in his approach to dealings with people (here the fight with downstream states over the sale of Missouri River water to ETSI was used as one example); the Governor was too much of a hip shooter in his approach to problems (here the Governor's revelation in early June that, when he was attorney general, in retaliation for California's refusal to extradite Indian activist Dennis Banks back to South Dakota, he had stopped the prosecution of ninety-three individuals on the condition that they move to California, was cited as an example); and, finally, O'Connor argued that the Governor was too personally involved in the day-to-day operations of state government with the result that there was a lack of systematic planning in dealing with the state's problems.

As for his own approach, beyond arguing that he would bring a more open, conciliatory, systematic, and businesslike approach to problem solving, O'Connor's major campaign theme stressed the importance of a healthy agricultural economy to a healthy state and national economy. To improve the health of the seriously ailing agricultural sector, O'Connor proposed creating a consortium of ten to fifteen farm states to set the price for grain in much the same way the OPEC had set oil prices. An O'Connor-sponsored measure, which would have begun the process, had passed the 1982 legislature but had been vetoed by Governor Janklow.

On the other side, Governor Janklow strongly defended both what his administration had accomplished and how those accomplishments had been achieved. He argued that the purchase of the railroad track by the state, the arrangement with Burlington Northern to operate trains on the track, the deal with ETSI, and the change in the usury laws which had brought the Citicorp credit card operations to the state, were actions in the best interests of South Dakota. Additionally, the Governor maintained that his administration had brought the growth of state government under control and hence had been able to operate in difficult economic times without the need for instituting an income tax or raising the sales tax.

As for his leadership style, the Governor argued that serious negotiations could not be conducted in the "circus atmosphere" of a public arena. The key point, in his view, was that the completed negotiations were made public and were subject to legislative debate and approval. The Governor also maintained that his heavy involvement in the day-to-day operations of state government had allowed him to bring state government growth under control. As for being a hip shooter, the Governor's response was that he didn't have time to sit around and ponder matters endlessly because the problems confronting the state required fast action. On the matter of his combative style, the Governor's argument was that he was battling for the best interests of South Dakota and doing a good job of it too.

As for his challenger, the Governor repeatedly criticized O'Connor for changing his positions on important issues (the issue of pay raises for state employees was cited as an example). On O'Connor's farm plan, the Governor argued that the plan was an unworkable political gimmick and that the O'Connor-sponsored measure that had passed the state legislature had to be vetoed because it was unconstitutional. On other proposals that candidate O'Connor made, Janklow's response generally was to raise questions about the cost of the program and/or to ask, if O'Connor really thought the idea in question was so great, why hadn't he introduced a bill on the subject as a state legislator?

This capsule discussion of the issues will mislead if it conveys the impression that the 1982 gubernatorial race in South Dakota was a hotly contested, closely fought one that dominated the fall political scene. The race was not of this sort in part because the House of Representatives race was such an important one. As earlier noted, as a result of the 1980 census, South Dakota was being reduced from two house seats to one and the 1982 race pitted the two incumbents against one another. The gubernatorial race also had trouble moving center stage because Mike O'Connor was not able to drink deeply of that mother's milk of politics, money. O'Connor had hoped to run a campaign in the $125,000 to $150,000 range. He ended up reporting expenditures of only $72,729 in the general election. By contrast Governor Janklow reported spending almost twice as much, $145,281.

Symptomatic of O'Connor's fund-raising problems was the fact that he received no money from the state Democratic Party. By contrast, Governor Janklow received $26,150 from the Republican State Central Committee plus another $6,761 in the form of a contribution of printing and postage. O'Connor also lacked the benefits of incumbency for fund-raising efforts. In comparison, the Janklow list of those who contributed more than $100 includes some twenty generally high-level state workers who gave a total of $5,125. Moreover, the Governor's list of contributors also includes sizable contributions from a number of individual lobbyists and political action committees (PACs) such as Burlington Northern and Citicorp, which had benefitted from actions the Governor had taken.

Overall, however, PACs do not seem to be a dominant force at the governor's level, as Governor Janklow received a total of only $11,950 from 20 PACs (representing mostly business and professional organizations), while Mike O'Connor was the recipient of $9,245 from 14 PACs (mostly labor organizations).

Obviously the severe shortage of money hobbled Mike O'Connor's effort to take his campaign to the people. His media campaign was almost non-existent. Instead he was forced to rely largely on personal appearances and on opportunities to debate. Governor Janklow was not at all hesitant about debating his challenger and there were six confrontations, including four televised debates, between the middle of September and election day. However, despite his best efforts, the O'Connor campaign never caught fire.

On the other side, polls done by DMI in January and September indicated that the Governor was in a very strong position. His strength and the weakness of the O'Connor campaign allowed the Governor to conduct a relatively low key bid for re-election. This meant using official appearances as much as possible to get the Governor's name and message to the voter. Only for a couple of weeks in mid-October did the Governor use a motor home to barnstorm the state.

Governor Janklow's campaign mounted a more substantial media effort than Mike O'Connor's but did not use as much media advertising as they were prepared to if the race had been closer. Radio was the principal medium for the advertising involved because the Governor believes radio is the best way to reach voters in South Dakota. The focus of the ads was on individual South Dakotans stating why they believed Governor Janklow should be re-elected.

In conducting his campaign, the Governor was clearly in charge. His chief of staff, Ron Williamson, assisted in determining who was responsible for such activities as canvassing and getting out the vote. Ron Williamson also had the job of following up to be sure that people did what they were supposed to do. The Governor's campaign headquarters was located in his home town of Flandreau and was headed by his sister. The routine work of the campaign, such as mass mailings, was done out of this office. The Governor also had an operations headquarters in Pierre.

As this discussion suggests, the Republican party organization did not play a big part in the Janklow campaign. Beyond the substantial financial contribution there were some joint mailings and some joint telephone canvassing work.

In a campaign where, for different reasons, neither side is aggressively reaching for the voters' attention, the role of the media is especially critical. In the 1982 gubernatorial election, three comments about the media's role need to be made. First, in terms of overall coverage, as already noted, the governor's race played second fiddle to the race for the House of Representatives seat. Second, on two or three issues, the media reported that Mike O'Connor had taken inconsistent positions on issues, a point of view that Governor Janklow was pushing as well. For example, on a pay increase for state employees, O'Connor indicated to the State Employees Convention that he had favored an increase for state workers. However, the media reported that a video tape of the legislative debate had been reviewed showing O'Connor against any raises for state employees that year. "I was wrong and the Associated Press was right," the story quoted O'Connor as saying.[3] Third, on the editorial pages, all of the state's major daily newspapers endorsed Governor Janklow for re-election. Overall, then, media coverage hurt the O'Connor campaign.

Given this discussion, the news that Governor Janklow easily won re-election will come as no surprise. If there was any surprise in the results, it was in the size of the Governor's victory margin. At 70.9 percent of the vote, Governor Janklow's vote percentage set a new record in gubernatorial elections in South Dakota.

In attempting to explain the size of the Governor's re-election victory, a good place to start is with Governor Janklow's activism on some of the traditional major political issues in South Dakota--water, transportation, economic development, and the cost of government. Clearly the voters were impressed with the actions the Governor had taken in these areas. Moreover, these actions allowed the Governor to distance himself from the national perception that adverse economic conditions were the fault of the Republicans in general and Reaganomics in particular.

On the other side, in emphasizing agriculture so strongly in his campaign, Mike O'Connor was following a trail that previously had taken Democrats to power in South Dakota. It was unfortunate for O'Connor that he was not able to convince the agricultural community that his grain consortium plan would work.

As another part of the explanation, in tough economic times a challenger may find it more difficult to argue for new programs because of their costs. Thus, for example, O'Connor proposed that the state pay all the costs of elementary and secondary education but the cost of such a move meant the proposal was never taken seriously. In this view, then, in difficult economic times, more so than in more prosperous times, the election becomes a referendum on the incumbent's performance in managing the fiscal affairs of the state. Governor Janklow's action in curtailing state spending by 5 percent when the state revenues seemed to be faltering, coupled with the facts that the state had not raised the sales tax or instituted an income tax and that South Dakota seemed to have its financial affairs in order when compared to Minnesota, which was having terrible budgetary problems, all worked to the advantage of Governor Janklow.

On the issue of the Governor's leadership style, obviously the voters came down on the side that the Governor's aggressive style was a real advantage for the state. In this regard, Governor Janklow was helped by the miscues of his challenger. The fact that O'Connor was shown to have changed his stands on issues, for example, served to blur the leadership choice.

The size of the Governor's victory margin is no doubt also attributable in part to the O'Connor campaign's financial difficulties. Mike O'Connor simply lacked the funds to run a vigorous, highly publicized campaign.

Overall, then, the results of the 1982 gubernatorial election in South Dakota should be seen as a referendum on the performance of the Janklow Administration during its first term[4] and, more specifically, as a personal triumph for the Governor.

THE SUCCESSION FROM THE FIRST TO THE SECOND

JANKLOW ADMINISTRATION

The succession process in a state where the governor has won re-election is likely to be much less formal and much simpler than in a state where one governor is replacing another. Certainly the gubernatorial succession process in South Dakota was a simple, informal one. No succession coordinator was appointed. Instead, the Governor's chief of staff, Ron Williamson, provided the coordination that was needed. Nor was there any need to establish new machinery to assist in such responsibilities as the appointment process or the budget development process.

At the same time, the incumbent governor who has won re-election does need to be concerned about the dangers of complacency and stagnation both on his own part and on the part of the rest of his administration. To counter this danger, Governor Janklow set up an internal review process. The process started toward the end of November and involved each cabinet-level appointee conducting a self analysis of that person's agency answering such questions as "Where have we been?" and "Where are we as an agency going?" The results of the review were then presented by each of these cabinet-level officials at a meeting in Sioux Falls in December. Listening to the reports and advising the Governor at this meeting were the Governor's personal staff as well as external advisors whom the Governor has used over the years. According to Clyde Saukerson, the Governor's legal counsel and a participant at this meeting, these sessions allowed the Governor to evaluate his top management people and get a sense of policy and program priorities that might be pursued during the second term.[5]

In Saukerson's view, at least three concrete results flowed from this meeting. First, the Governor came away with a renewed sense of the need for exercising leadership in the field of education at all levels. Reflecting this emphasis, in his State-of-the-State address the Governor called for a high level study to define more precisely what role each of the state's seven publicly funded institutions of higher education should be playing. Additionally, as a part of his 1983 legislative package, the Governor proposed several measures including bonding authority to make loans available to the children of middle income families whose income was too high to qualify for federal loans, and for a waiver of tuition for students intending to become science and math teachers. Finally, the Governor made a key personnel change in the education area. The Governor appointed Judith Meierhenry as secretary of Education and Cultural Affairs. Ms. Meierhenry, 39, is a lawyer, and a former high school teacher with extensive prior experience in the Janklow Administration, having served previously as director of the state Economic Opportunity Office and as secretary of the Department of Labor. Indeed, in what is probably a unique situation in the United States, Ms. Meierhenry continues to serve as secretary of Labor in addition to holding her new post as secretary of Education and Cultural Affairs.

A second result of the December meeting was again in the form of a reaffirmation of a first-term initiative: diversification of the South Dakota economy. Reflecting this emphasis, through an executive order, the Governor created a new Department of State Development to get more concentration and coordination in this area. The Janklow Administration's 1983 legislative package also reflected this emphasis. In a proposal that stirred considerable debate outside South Dakota, the Governor recommended and the legislature approved a plan to allow national bank holding companies to buy state chartered banks. In turn, state chartered banks are now allowed to own insurance companies. The effect of this legislation is to permit national bank holding companies to circumvent the federal law that prevents them from owning insurance companies.

A third result, which Saukerson feels will flow from the December reassessment, will be an increased emphasis on personnel management. According to Saukerson, the Governor spent more time in his first term on program management than on personnel administration. The second term will see increased emphasis on recruiting able people to management positions, on identifying current employees with management potential, on providing opportunities for those employees to develop that potential, and on better evaluation of management personnel. Both Citicorp and Burlington Northern have offered to loan some of their executives to assist the state in this area.

In addition to mentioning these three areas as important ones to watch during the second Janklow term, there are three other areas that early signs suggest also will receive emphasis.

First, transportation will continue to be a priority but the emphasis will shift from railroads to highways. Symbolic of this shift in emphasis was the elevation of Jim Myers to secretary of Transportation. During the first term, when railroads were a major priority of the Janklow administration, Mr. Myers had provided strong leadership as director of the Division of Railroads in the Transportation Department. In promoting Myers to the position of department head, the Governor seemed to be signaling his desire to emphasize improving the state's highway system in his second term.

Second, the Governor has indicated a desire to improve relations between Indians and non-Indians in the state. This topic emerged as a major theme in his inaugural address. While no specific proposals to accomplish this objective have emerged as of yet, presumably this area also will receive emphasis.

Third, the second Janklow Administration will continue to use creative financing to allow the state to embark on new programs without the need to raise the sales tax or institute an income tax. The use of the state's bonding authority to provide student loans has already been mentioned. Additionally, in 1982 the Governor called for additional bonding by the State Housing Authority and for the creation of an Agri-Business Bonding Authority. The Governor also proposed and the legislature approved a bill which takes advantage of federal tax laws by allowing the state to provide tax write-offs to wealthy investors through the sale of state facilities such as the State Cement Plant. As the plan is designed, the state will get enough revenue from the interest on the invested purchase money to pay for new projects as well as for leasing back the facility. At the end of the lease period, the state buys the facility back with the original money which has been invested all these years.

Finally, in analyzing the succession from the first to the second Janklow Administrations, the extent of high level personnel changes should be mentioned. In addition to the already cited changes in the position of secretary of Education and Cultural Affairs, and in Transportation, changes have also taken place at the top in the Departments of Agriculture, Military and Veterans Affairs, and Health, in the Bureau of Administration, in the Bureau of Intergovernmental Affairs, and in the position of the Governor's chief of staff. As the earlier discussion has indicated, the changes in Education and Cultural Affairs, and in Transportation, represent a commitment to give priority to these areas. The final significance of the rest of these changes is less clear at this time. At the least, they would seem to represent a desire to avoid complacency during the second term. In most instances they also represent the desire to reward people who had performed ably during the Governor's first term.

CONCLUDING COMMENTS

Given the fact that Governor Janklow's re-election percentage was the largest of any governor elected in South Dakota's history, and given the further fact that the state's Constitution has a two-consecutive-term limitation on gubernatorial service, some brief comment on Governor Janklow's future political plans would seem appropriate. At this time, the best guessing in the state suggests that in 1986 the Governor will seek the Senate seat presently held by fellow Republican Senator James Abdnor.

Whether out of interest in a different office or out of increased confidence in his subordinates, in talking with key officials in the Janklow Administration, the impression emerges that the Governor will be more willing to delegate authority to subordinates during his second term than he was during his first. If correct, this point raises the general question: Do governors delegate more authority in their second and subsequent terms than in their first?

Finally, in her book <u>Managing the State</u>, which is based on an analysis of the Francis Sargent administration, Martha Weinberg argues that "The most important characteristic of elected chief executives, if the Massachusetts case is representative, is their reliance on crisis management."[6] Crisis management is used in the sense that a governor and the governor's staff spend most of their time dealing with what they perceive to be critical incidents, many of them unpredictable and uncontrollable.

The experience during the first term of the Janklow Administration would seem to be supportive of Weinberg's analysis. Much of the success of the Governor can be attributed to his ability to respond to critical but often unplanned incidents in a way that was perceived as effective by the voters. As two quick examples, which have been previously discussed, the danger to the Madison aquifer from Wyoming's sale of water rights spurred the Governor's negotiations with ETSI, and Citicorp's desire to move their credit card operations out of New York created an unplanned but critical incident to which the Janklow Administration responded.

Weinberg's analysis leads her to caution against the uncritical transference of private sector concepts about what it means to be a chief executive. In the context of considering gubernatorial successions, her analysis and the South Dakota experience also suggest that no matter how carefully planned the succession, much of the ultimate success of any incoming governor will depend upon that governor's ability to spot critical problems and respond appropriately to them.

NOTES

[1] In a comparison of all fifty states, South Dakota along with six other states is ranked in the "very strong" category in terms of the governor's power of organization. See Thad L. Beyle, "The Governors' Power of Organization," State Government 55 (Number 3, 1982): 79-88.

[2] "South Dakota is No. 1 Loser of Federal Aid," Sioux Falls Argus Leader, 13 April 1983, sec. A, p. 1.

[3] "O'Connor Says His Statements Were Conflicting," Sioux Falls Argus Leader, 5 August 1982, sec. C, p. 1.

[4] For an analysis that makes the same point see Alan L. Clem, "The 1982 Election in South Dakota," Public Affairs (Vermillion, SD: Governmental Research Bureau, February, 1983).

[5] Interview with Clyde Saukerson, Pierre, SD, April 4, 1983.

[6] Martha Wagner Weinberg, Managing the State (Cambridge, Mass: The MIT Press, 1977), pp. 208-209.

[7] Ibid., pp. 20-26.

17. THE 1982 GUBERNATORIAL ELECTION IN TENNESSEE

MICHAEL R. FITZGERALD
FLOYDETTE C. CORY
STEPHEN J. RECHICHAR
ABIGAIL S. HUDGENS

HISTORICAL BACKGROUND

To properly understand the nature of the 1982 gubernatorial campaign and its effect on state government in Tennessee, it is first necessary to place this election in appropriate historical context. Since its 1796 admission to the Union, Tennessee's political panorama has been defined by two forces: sectionalism and factionalism. These factors constitute the political past upon which the state's political present is drawn. As such, sectionalism and factionalism have significantly influenced gubernatorial elections and have had a concomitant effect upon state government--largely by inhibiting the capacity of newly elected governors to affect the operation and direction of major state agencies.

Sectionalism and Factionalism

Tennessee politics has traditionally been a matter of factional conflict within the dominant party. Thus in the early nineteenth century, the cliques within the old Republican party were predicated upon the personal rivalry between William Blount, whose strength was greatest in West Tennessee, and John Sevier, whose power base was East Tennessee. From the Blount faction emerged Andrew Jackson, who forged the new Democratic party, and based in great measure upon anti-Jackson sentiment, the Whig party in turn built a formidable political organization in Middle and West Tennessee. For twenty years the Democrats and Whigs engaged in genuine two-party competition in the state, and during this period the Whigs won six of nine gubernatorial elections. Until recently this brief era was the only time of effective two-party competition in Tennessee history. The cultural, socioeconomic, and geographic differences between East, Middle, and West Tennessee were exacerbated by the bitter divisions engendered during the Civil War and Reconstruction. East Tennessee was staunchly unionist and after the war became rock-ribbed Republican. Middle and West Tennessee, the former Whig strongholds, were secessionist and became Democratic bastions. Thus, although the state's electorate following Reconstruction became preponderantly Democratic, the Republican party was able to dominate elections in East Tennessee.

In the twentieth century, Democratic dominance of the state electorate in all but East Tennessee meant bifactional state politics. Until the mid-sixties the strongest faction coalesced around E. H. Crump and his awesome Memphis-Shelby County political machine. Crump's control of Shelby County's votes was enhanced by his ability to win support from East Tennessee Democrats, who comprised a minority in that region. For them, supporting victorious gubernatorial candidates, as part of a Crumpled coalition, was an opportunity to obtain patronage in state government denied them by the Republican majority. Conversely, Middle Tennessee was a center of the anti-Crump Democratic faction, which regularly fought Crump's machine in statewide primaries. Despite an occasional victory, Crump's patronage-based alliance with East Tennessee Democrats kept the power of the anti-Crump Democrats constricted for many years.

Thus, at mid-century Tennessee was actually two one-party systems. The Democrats controlled local government in West and Middle Tennessee as well as the majority of the statewide electorate while the Republicans ruled East Tennessee. Statewide elections went to the Democrats virtually by default as regionally based factions within the party engaged in lively, even ferocious, intraparty competition. This intraparty friction hampered effective administration of state government because a newly elected governor faced a state legislature that included hostile elements of his own party's rival faction and a cohesive Republican contingent from East Tennessee.

Insurgent Republicanism

After 1948, Republicans were able to break the Democratic monopoly on statewide votes involving presidential elections. Between 1952 and the present, Republican presidential candidates won more votes statewide than their Democratic rivals in six of eight elections. Not until 1966, however, did this growth in Republican strength manifest itself beyond presidential elections, for in that year Howard H. Baker, Jr., became the state's first popularly elected Republican U.S.

senator. Republican William Brock's victory over the incumbent Democrat, U.S. Senator Albert Gore, in 1970, coupled with Howard Baker's successful re-election in 1972 and 1978, reenforced the emergence of two-party competition in Tennessee in presidential and senatorial elections. In 1970, just four years after the Republicans failed to field a nominee to challenge incumbent Governor Buford Ellington, Winfield Dunn became the state's first Republican governor in fifty years. Dunn's victory was largely the product of insurgent Republican strength outside of East Tennessee, most especially in the increasingly populous suburbs of Memphis in the West and Nashville in Middle Tennessee. It was also partly attributable to what one astute observer called gubernatorial politics that had settled into "a generation of factional fighting within the Democratic fold."[1] Thus, by the early seventies, party politics in Tennessee had "trickled down" from presidential to gubernatorial elections. The failure of the "trickle" to continue downward, however, meant that the new Republican governor faced Democratic majorities in both houses of the state legislature.

The Blanton Debacle

In 1974, with Governor Dunn constitutionally prohibited from succeeding himself, the Democrats struggled through their usual acerbic, multifactional primary fight with former congressman Ray Blanton winning the nomination. Since Tennessee does not conduct run-off elections, Blanton consequently won the nomination with a mere plurality of 22 percent. Determined to recapture the governor's mansion, the Democrats emphasized party loyalty in the general election. This effort was aided by Watergate and a national economy in the throes of recession. The Democratic strategy proved successful, and Republican nominee Lamar Alexander was soundly defeated in the general election.

Yet, the Blanton victory eventually proved Pyrrhic for the Democrats as his administration became the most unpopular and scandal-ridden one since Reconstruction. Throughout his term, Blanton engaged in a running battle with the media. Much adverse publicity was generated by Blanton's open use (many called it abuse) of the prerogatives of the governor's office. Allegations of political favoritism and outright corruption proliferated as the governor, close aides, political allies, relatives, and business associates became targets of state and federal investigations. These inquiries revealed extensive sales of clemency by members of the Blanton administration; also allegations of liquor license sales involving the Governor himself were rampant. Although a 1978 amendment to the state constitution now allowed the governor to succeed himself, the brewing scandals associated with the administration, and his low standing in the straw polls, led to Blanton's decision not to seek re-election. Nevertheless, Ray Blanton and his besieged administration became the focus of the 1978 gubernatorial race.

With Blanton out of contention, the Democrats engaged in their traditional factional primary fight. The two strongest segments were those led by Bob Clement (son of a popular former governor, the late Frank Clement and heir to his father's wing of the party), and Jake Butcher, a prominent Knoxville banker. After a hotly contested battle, Butcher won a narrow primary victory to become the nominee of a split party. Lamar Alexander won a token Republican primary with approximately 86 percent of the vote. Unlike 1974, the Democrats were unable to reunite after the primary. Alexander won several eminent defectors from the Clement faction of the Democratic party, and he continuously belabored the unpopular scandal-burdened Democratic governor. Fear of offending Blanton and other powerful Democratic stalwarts prevented Butcher from effectively answering Republican charges. In addition to the onus of an unpopular incumbent administration, Democrat Butcher had his own image problems. The Republicans cast the wealthy Butcher in the role of a rich "wheeler-dealer" banker and a high roller intent on purchasing the governor's chair. At the same time, Alexander projected the image of a down-to-earth East Tennessean, who was close to the people--an image highlighted by a walk across the state in an open-collared, plaid, flannel shirt that became a campaign symbol.

The result was a smashing Republican victory in 1978. Alexander not only carried East Tennessee, he was the first Republican gubernatorial candidate to win majorities in the western and middle divisions of the state. Just four years after being thoroughly defeated by Blanton, Alexander carried the four major metropolitan areas in Tennessee--despite the fact that his Democratic opponent had outspent him by better than two-to-one. The unpopularity of Ray Blanton and his administration, Jake Butcher's big-money image, Republican insurgency in Middle and West Tennessee, Democratic defections unable to tolerate the Butcher faction, and Lamar Alexander's attractive image (carefully developed by Doug Bailey of Bailey-Deardourff Consultants)--all contributed to the stunning triumph.

The Democratic debacle precipitated by Ray Blanton's scandal-plagued administration was completed when Lamar Alexander, at the behest of the U.S. Attorney's office, was sworn in three days before the scheduled inauguration. Thus, the new governor assumed the helm of state government in the midst of an explosive situation in which public opinion was incensed by the performance of his predecessor. Blanton created a situation in which his successor, simply by operating in a low-key fashion emphasizing dignity and probity in executive operations, earned the approbation of a state electorate traumatized by four long years of unrelenting controversy and scandal. Nonetheless, the Tennessee General Assembly remained firmly in the hands of a Democratic majority.

The First Alexander Administration

Following his startling electoral victory, Lamar Alexander brought a forthright approach to the governorship. Alexander promised honest, non-partisan administration and indicated that he would attempt few innovations through legislation. Toward that end, and to the chagrin of some Republicans, Democrats and Independents were appointed to the cabinet. The new governor also eschewed the use of county-patronage committees in making other appointments.

In lucid contrast to his fiercely partisan and combative predecessor, Governor Alexander declared that nonpartisanship and cooperation would be the hallmark of executive relations with the state legislature. Unlike Blanton, Alexander took great pains to cultivate members of the press--among some of his closest aides were several former journalists. He also made clear that clemency would be exercised strictly on the basis of merit and never upon political considerations. Essentially from the opening day of his term, Lamar Alexander assumed the role of caretaker and declared his intention to restore confidence and trust in state government.

The new governor proved as good as his word; his first legislative package included just twenty-nine bills, the smallest proposed by a Tennessee governor in recent years. Also, the first Alexander budget was a status quo document involving no new programs or proposals for new taxes. In the words of one observer, it was a budget "providing everyone a little something or a little more to cover inflation, meet basic needs, maintain harmony, and avoid controversy."[3] Subsequent Alexander budgets were similar in design if not detail.

In his first term of office, Governor Alexander engaged in several skirmishes with the Democratic-controlled legislature over issues such as interest rate ceilings, fuel tax increases, and funding levels for education, but he avoided major battles. The Governor eventually earned the enmity of only one major statewide interest group, the large and powerful Tennessee Education Association (TEA). This group was highly displeased by the Governor's refusal to allocate a greater proportion of his proposed budgets to education. Members of the TEA were especially upset when, in January 1982, the Governor announced that controlling state expenditures and increasing family income took precedence, in his budget plans, over enlarging state spending for education. Mounting TEA displeasure with Alexander's budgetary priorities, accompanied by Democratic charges that the governor had done little for education in his first three years, prompted Alexander to open his fourth year with a resounding defense of his commitment to education.

At the Tennessee Press Association's annual meeting, Alexander, using a statewide television hookup, unveiled a five-year statewide "Basic Skills Program" to upgrade the reading and math skills of children and adults. Further, in defense of his commitment to education, Alexander noted that his 1983 budget would allocate 27 percent more for education than his first budget. The TEA was not satisfied and proved an active critic of the Republican governor, but Alexander eventually won modest legislative support for his basic skills initiative. The legislative session was, however, frequently punctuated by Democratic charges that the Governor simply was not exerting enough leadership in state government. Election year political posturing greatly strained executive-legislative relations, and before the dust finally settled the legislature overrode six Alexander vetoes. It did approve a budget and program that accommodated Alexander's "steady course" approach to state government.

Although Lamar Alexander's caretaker perspective generated some claims that the Governor was not a forceful leader, the unpopular Blanton administration remained the principal standard against which the Republican chief executive was measured. Throughout Alexander's first term, the public was reminded of the scandal associated with the previous administration; the state's print and broadcast media regularly reported stories that redounded to the discredit of the former governor and his years in power. Amidst a blare of publicity Blanton was indicted, tried, and convicted of bribery; at the same time, nineteen of his relatives, friends, and associates were indicted (most of whom eventually pleaded guilty or were convicted), on charges of bribery, extortion, bid-rigging, and perjury. The trials, convictions, and subsequent appeals of Blanton and others spread as a dark shadow over Alexander's first four years in office, constantly reminding the public of what had gone before in Tennessee government; it made a "caretaker" administration exceedingly attractive and gave the Governor's partisans effective ammunition against his critics. Thus, in 1981, as an approaching gubernatorial election year warmed the political air, the state Democratic chairman took the Republican Governor to task for a long list of problems, among them a rising state crime rate. In reply, a Republican state Senator noted that: "Crime in the governor's office has decreased 100% since Alexander became governor."[4]

Alexander's administration was fundamentally free of scandal charges. The contrast between the bad publicity associated with the former governor and the favorable press generated by the present was not lost upon most Tennesseans. In this Lamar Alexander won much gratitude for his restoration of previously damaged state pride.[5]

THE 1982 GUBERNATORIAL ELECTION

The 1982 gubernatorial campaign officially opened in May when Lamar Alexander announced his candidacy for re-election. In so doing, the Governor ended widespread speculation that he might challenge incumbent Democrat James Sasser for his

U.S. Senate seat. No rival for the Republican nomination came forward, and Alexander was able to concentrate fully upon the Democratic challenge. Although nine candidates declared for the Democratic nomination, the real contest was between only two, state Senator Anna Belle Clement O'Brien and Randy Tyree, mayor of Knoxville. While the 1982 Democratic primary did not produce the equivalent acrimony as that of 1978, Lamar Alexander was nonetheless to benefit from residual divisiveness stemming from the unhealed Democratic split between Clement/O'Brien and Butcher/Tyree factions.

Senator Anna Belle Clement O'Brien was prominent in the Tennessee Democratic party as a member of one of the state's first political families--the Clements. Her brother, the late Frank Clement, served three terms as governor and was one of the most powerful political figures in Tennessee history. During her brother's administration, O'Brien served as a staff assistant concerned chiefly with patronage affairs. Subsequently she served in the state Senate, generally representing rural interests. In 1978, O'Brien was a central figure in the unsuccessful bid of her nephew Bob Clement (son of the late governor) for the Democratic gubernatorial nomination. Senator O'Brien enjoyed extensive name recognition as a member of the Clement clan; she had also won considerable recognition and respect for her work both in the legislature and on behalf of her party. Despite vacillating on her decision to seek the nomination, O'Brien was an early favorite among the majority of party leaders and was considered the front-runner by most political observers. Still, the late start proved a serious handicap for Senator O'Brien as she scrambled in the late spring of 1982 to raise campaign funds and assemble an organization.

In contrast, Mayor Randy Tyree was known to have his eye upon the governor's race for at least a year before his official April 1982 announcement. Twice elected mayor of the state's third largest city, Tyree hoped to capitalize upon publicity attending the opening of the 1982 World's Fair in Knoxville. Despite the Fair, however, Tyree remained relatively unknown outside East Tennessee. As he mounted his first statewide election bid, the mayor enjoyed the backing of the Butcher faction of the Democratic party with its considerable financial resources. Thus, in many ways the

O'Brien-Tyree battle in 1982 represented a rematch of the truculent Clement-Butcher contest four years earlier.

To overcome his relative anonymity, Mayor Tyree mounted a campaign that relied primarily upon the electronic media. Availing himself of the services of prominent political consultant Matt Reese (who had earlier handled successful campaigns for John Y. Brown in Kentucky and John Glenn in Ohio), Tyree shunned traditional courthouse campaigning with its reliance upon established political organizations. The centerpiece of this media effort was a mid-summer television blitz, in which Tyree effectively appeared in polished and extremely expensive commercials. Conversely, Senator O'Brien relied upon the time-honored Tennessee style of campaigning with emphasis upon meeting the electorate one-on-one or in small groups, and of stressing party loyalty. Yet, O'Brien ran into difficulty with this campaign style because of poor staff management and organization, schedule mishaps, and money problems. Eventually Tyree's campaign took hold. As O'Brien's original name-recognition advantage gave way, her early lead in straw polls vanished, and she was unable to establish any momentum of her own.

As for Governor Alexander, he was far from idle. The incumbent spent $1.3 million in the uncontested pursuit of the Republican nomination, again availing himself of the services of the prestigious consulting firm of Bailey-Deardourff and Associates. Doug Bailey, image maker for such Republican luminaries as Gerald Ford, Jim Thompson (governor of Illinois), and James Rhodes (former governor of Ohio), handled Alexander's 1978 campaign and had been on retainer ever since. During the primary, Alexander conducted another campaign in which the modest image of a hardworking executive with close ties to the people was cultivated. He studiously avoided references to the Democrats, leaving their contenders to fight among themselves.

The Democratic primary in August produced Randy Tyree as Lamar Alexander's opponent in the general election. The mayor's 42,500 vote victory margin over Senator O'Brien was largely the product of votes won in West Tennessee, where the political machine of Congressman Harold Ford delivered the black vote in Tyree's behalf. O'Brien outpolled

Tyree in his home county in East Tennessee, an embarrassing result that was capitalized upon immediately by Alexander. The Governor wryly observed: "The most interesting thing . . . is that the people who know her best voted for Miss Anna Belle and the people who know Randy Tyree best voted for Miss Anna Belle."[6]

Without question the key to Tyree's victory involved his superior financial resources and his sophisticated use of the electronic media. The mayor raised nearly $976,000 in contributions and loans and spent approximately $1 million; close to $550,000 in expenditures were given over to media and polling services. In contrast, Senator O'Brien raised only $295,000 while spending about $430,000.[7] Even though 55 percent of O'Brien's expenditures were devoted to advertising, the monies were ill-spent. As one veteran analyst explained: "You can't run a 1950s campaign in this modern media age, [Miss Anna Belle was] a poor media candidate."[8]

The General Election

In the general election the initial odds were even more unfavorable for Tyree. Although 1982 was a difficult year for Republicans--Alexander had been targeted for defeat by the Committee to Elect Democratic Governors--the incumbent was heavily favored to win in November.[9] Alexander's strategy was to capitalize on his image of integrity as a stark contrast to that of the discredited Blanton administration. The primary goal was to personalize the campaign in such a fashion as to make the fundamental issue <u>Alexander the man</u>. As for other issues, Alexander presented the image of a man who was doing his best under very difficult economic circumstances. Avoiding overt attacks on the Democratic party, Alexander aimed his appeal to the whole electorate. The Governor hoped for a large crossover vote to insure a victory of major proportions. Alexander ardently desired such a grand triumph, and this feeling permeated his entire campaign. In retrospect, one of his closest aides commented: "[We] always thought that we could win and win <u>big</u>."[10]

Throughout the campaign, Alexander was extremely successful in using the concept of "Community Days." Developed by political consultant Doug Bailey, this theme promoted the Governor's image as a man close to the people. A

Community Day was ostensibly a public service event focusing on the "volunteer spirit in Tennessee." In classic "media opportunities," Alexander joined the citizens of a community, and together with sleeves rolled up, they attacked some community problem. During the forty-five Community Days held in 1982, over $860,000 was raised and donated to the host communities.[11] The power of incumbency provided Alexander with an extraordinary advantage, and he maximized it through the "Community Days" program. As one state Democratic official later caustically remarked: "He got all the boy scouts and girl scouts walking down the road with him, and that's heady wine for the public."[12]

Through his Community Days activities, Alexander tried to focus attention on the good things occurring in Tennessee and to establish a positive tone to his campaign. In so doing Alexander sought to disengage himself from any association with the sour national economy--his hope was to persuade Tennesseans that the recession was not his fault. In distinct contrast, Randy Tyree sought to tie the Republican Governor to the Republican administration in Washington and the recession. Tyree relentlessly criticized the economic issue and Reaganomics and tried to bind Alexander to Reagan at every turn. The Mayor and his professional political consultant, Matt Reese, were convinced that the chances of being elected would improve substantially if the Tennessee election could be turned into a referendum on Reagan's economic policy. Thus, Tyree portrayed Alexander as a do-nothing administrator who evaded the tough decisions needed to help the economy and reduce the unemployment rate in Tennessee. In turn, Tyree characterized himself as an able, energetic administrator who as governor would initiate bold economic projects, similar to the World's Fair, as a means of stimulating the state economy.[13]

Alexander's leadership and the economy were the main topics of three debates (one in each grand division of the state), held in early September. Tyree hammered away at the economy as a Republican problem that was severely debilitating the state. Alexander, refusing to concede his responsibility for a national recession, emphasized the probity of his administration in sharp juxtaposition to the corruption of his Democratic predecessor. Furthermore he tried to deflate Tyree's proffered image as a competent administrator of Knoxville.[14]

Lamar Alexander successfully negated his challenger's efforts to transform the state's gubernatorial election into a referendum on Reaganomics. Though Randy Tyree was unable to convince Tennessee voters of the Alexander-Reagan connection, it was not for want of effort. Nor to many was it for want of justification. A Knoxville Democrat reflected: "Shortly after the 1980 presidential election, Alexander was often on television coming out of the rose garden hand-in-hand with Ronald Reagan. But Alexander eventually disassociated himself from Reagan, and Tyree let him do it."[15]

As the campaign entered its final weeks, the pace and intensity increased. Claiming that "we have no place in this party for mugwumps," Randy Tyree pushed a loyalty resolution through the Democratic Executive Committee. This unanimous resolution, passed in the aftermath of endorsements for Alexander by two Democratic county executives, banned from party office anyone who publicly supported a GOP candidate.[16] Immediately dubbed "Randy's Rule," this gambit placed Tyree on the defensive. Alexander was quick to seize "Randy's Rule" to remind audiences about the blatant partisanship of the Blanton administration and once again offered his less partisan administration for comparison.

Despite "Randy's Rule," Tyree actually enjoyed less than wholehearted support, and the traditional Democratic vote never coalesced for him. He did receive formal endorsements from such leading Democrats as House Speaker Ned McWherter and Lieutenant Governor John Wilder, but not until just three weeks before the election. Additionally, defeated primary opponent Anna Belle Clement O'Brien canvassed the state on Tyree's behalf. There were, however, many Democratic power brokers throughout the state who simply sat out the race, and their absence seriously hurt Tyree.

Without solid party support, Tyree relied upon modern campaign methods to support his candidacy. He invested over a half million dollars and a great deal of faith in the pet technique of political consultant Matt Reese, the Prism System. Described by Tyree's staff as a phone bank, the system was based on identification of forty different socioeconomic clusters around the state that were indexed into message groups such as "shotguns and pickups," "furs and stationwagons," and "sharecroppers." This system was then targeted with advertising to elicit favorable responses from the particular groups.[17] Tyree's organization hoped Prism would overcome Alexander's name recognition advantage, and by October talk flourished of a big upset in November.[18] A month before the election Tyree's pollster, Pat Caddell, released figures showing the mayor trailing Alexander by only ten points with fourteen percent of those polled undecided. Caddell's release also showed Tyree ahead by seven points in Shelby County, the state's most populous county.[19]

Yet the big upset did not materialize. Alexander's campaign in the closing weeks became increasingly aggressive. In late October Alexander ran a series of Knoxville-based, man-on-the-street interviews which devastated Tyree's chances of victory. For example the last person to speak in the ad responded by expressing personal distrust of Tyree. Coinciding with these commercials were the Alexander attacks on Tyree's campaign financing. Alexander intimated that $1 million of Tyree's financing had come from prominent East Tennessee banker and former Democratic nominee for governor, Jake Butcher. Try as he might to refute the charges, Tyree was mired in the controversy and spent the last weeks of the campaign defending both himself and Butcher. Several months afterwards, the defeated challenger conceded that "[the Republicans] timed their negative ads to come in at a key point and put our whole campaign on the defensive for the last two weeks."[20]

While personal contributions from Butcher were approximately $15,000, Tyree's campaign was in debt to Butcher-controlled banks for $615,000. Despite no actual proof of wrongdoing, the campaign-funding issue raised spectres of past political ghosts, and Tennessee voters could not countenance another potential scandal. In the words of a senior Tyree campaigner: "Visions of Ray Blanton were always over the shoulder."[21] Thus, on election day Alexander won by a landslide receiving 736,589 votes to Tyree's 499,059 and became the first Tennessee governor to win consecutive four-year terms. Tyree lost every congressional district except the ninth, which was heavily influenced by Tyree supporter, Congressman Harold Ford. While Tyree carried 39 of 95 counties (all of which were rural), Alexander won every metropolitan area.

In retrospect, Alexander's victory was clearly for the man and not for the party. Democrats won twenty-seven of the thirty-six governorships contested nationally in 1982. Furthermore, Tennessee Democratic nominee James Sasser scored an equally impressive win over his Republican opponent Robin Beard. Thus, Alexander's personal popularity carried him through what was a very strong Democratic year.

The 1982 gubernatorial election proved to be a statewide referendum on the personality and style of incumbent Lamar Alexander. During his first four years in office there was no definitive Alexander program--except for cautious, honest management of the affairs of the state with "steady course" budgets. Alexander's opponent endeavored to raise questions about the Governor's leadership ability and offered to provide leadership that would seek to control economic conditions rather than give way to them--only to fall victim to accusations of partisanship and shady financial connections because of his relationship with the Butcher faction of the Democratic party. Tennessee voters refused to blame their incumbent governor for the recession and were unimpressed by Tyree's promises of new initiatives for state government. If Lamar Alexander was a caretaker during his first term, the November election returns proved that he was an extremely popular one.

Postmortem

For both the victorious Lamar Alexander and the vanquished Randy Tyree, the 1982 election was one of accomplishment. Alexander had the traditional incumbent goal of retaining office through an impressive victory. After the landslide triumph, the Governor's aides were candid about such aspirations. As one of Alexander's campaign directors noted: "The only goal is to win because if you don't then there's nothing."[22] Alexander's 60-40 margin reflected a statewide vote of confidence in his leadership, and flowing from this confidence the Governor has embarked on a more aggressive course of action. In turn, it may be stated that Randy Tyree accomplished two things. Even in defeat, Tyree brought attention to the need for more assertive leadership on various statewide policy issues, most significantly economic development. Also, Tyree radically enhanced his name recognition should he decide to run again for a statewide office. As the Mayor himself observed:

"I was like the Chinese philosopher sending the message whether it gets received or not. Plus my name recognition is now 76%."[23]

EFFECT OF THE ELECTION ON STATE GOVERNMENT

During 1982 the gubernatorial election had the general effect of slowing the pace and diverting the attention of many administrators in state government. Department commissioners served in the well-organized "Surrogate Program" in which the governor's top level political appointees travelled around the state appearing on Alexander's behalf and defending his record. Moreover, lower level state employees experienced the typical anxiety that accompanies a possible post-election change in state administration. As the head of one of the state's largest agencies later observed:

> I think it's a very painful thing to go through a gubernatorial election if you're you're in state government. I had a new appreciation [after going through this this election] of what state employees must suffer through every four years. The uncertainty of knowing whether projects will be completed before the end of the administration creates an immense amount of anxiety.[24]

There is no evidence that the effect of the Surrogate Program or of the traditional anxiety over administrative succession had any significant deleterious effect upon state operations in 1982. In fact, maintenance of efficient program administration was of paramount importance to Alexander. One of his closest advisers attested: "We told the administrators we could run an A+ campaign, but we had a big problem if they ran a C+ state government."[25]

Executive Organization, Style, and Program

From the beginning of his second term, Lamar Alexander shifted his executive organization and style from that of "caretaker" to that of "program promoter." First, through executive order and proposed legislation, the Governor took steps to reorganize the executive branch. Citing the need to streamline state government, this sweeping effort involved about 1,600 state employees from 14 executive departments, 9 independent agencies, and the governor's office itself. Four independent agencies were abolished and 150 positions eliminated, at an estimated savings of $2 million.[26] Second, Alexander's desire to inject new energy into the administration was apparent in eight cabinet-level personnel changes. These appointments drew heavily upon the private sector and illustrated Alexander's desire to utilize professional managerial expertise for state operations.[27] Third, the Governor's original Policy Group, which in the first term had served a liaison function between the governor, the legislature, and executive departments, was reduced in size and converted into a special projects advisory group. With this change Alexander tried to "cut out the intermediary between himself and the cabinet members and wanted to give the departments greater responsibility."[28] Fourth, Cabinet Councils were formed and charged with the responsibility of coordinating Alexander's program initiatives and assuring that, insofar as possible, all departments were prepared to support and implement new policy.

In this fashion Governor Alexander set the organizational framework for moving beyond a caretaker role, and he thus assumed a more aggressive posture. During a series of meetings with administration and legislative leaders, the Governor emphasized that bold policy initiatives were forthcoming. Alexander personally promised to work diligently for passage and implementation of his programs. Furthermore, he expected others in state government to do the same.

The Governor's televised budget message in January showed the entire state a polished, dynamic performance. Alexander thereby served public notice that he would fight for his new programs. Subsequent months found the Governor continuing in this style as he sought to build, within the legislature and throughout the state, a coalition for his budget and program. The budget document itself symbolized Alexander's change in philosophy because it was an innovative four-year proposal indicative of the Governor's desire "to leave his mark in education and economic development."[29]

The multi-year financial prospectus was accompanied by striking programmatic recommendations. Corrections reform was a major issue in Tennessee, and since 1978 the state had been under federal court order to improve prison conditions.

Consequently under the rubric, "A Correction Plan introduced a major overhaul of the corrections system. The components of the plan included a more integrated prison system, management innovations, and establishment of inmate work programs designed to defray partially the costs of incarceration. Additionally, the second term opened in the middle of a fiscal year in which severe revenue shortfalls led to the impoundment of funds for most state operations--especially higher education. Thus, the Governor also found himself under pressure from educational interests and concerned citizens to promote dramatic increases in educational funding, even if this meant imposition of a state income tax.

Coupled with burgeoning state and national concern over the quality of education, this pressure for increased educational funding provided Alexander with an opportunity to exercise leadership, and he seized it dramatically. The "Better Schools Program" unveiled in January 1983 was explicitly designed to promote education as an instrument of economic development. While promoting the program, Alexander told one group: "Better schools are the key to better jobs and we have a chance to lead the nation."[30] The education program's cynosure was a "Master Teacher Plan" in which outstanding elementary and secondary teachers would receive pay raises commensurate with their excellence. According to Alexander, by designating the best educators as "Master Teachers" and providing them with proper recognition and higher salaries, Tennessee would keep its best teachers and provide incentives for improvement of the educational system. Funding for the Better Schools Program and raises for other state employees required additional revenue which Alexander proposed to raise with a two-percent increase in the state sales tax.

The Governor's deliberate shift in executive style is exemplified in Alexander's Better Schools Program proposal: The leadership of the Democratic majority in the state legislature was already on record against any tax increase, and there was little evidence that the electorate favored any tax increase. Clearly, program innovation and higher revenues promised a major battle not easily won. Alexander, however, pushed forward a plan calling for greater educational spending, as well as a tax hike to cover it. The Governor's assertiveness was also illustrated by the announcement that he would

<u>only</u> support increases in educational funding which were tied to educational improvement; Alexander further noted that he was prepared to take the political heat involved in financing the change--<u>if</u> his "Better School Program" was approved. Otherwise, he vowed to veto any tax increase. Alexander aggressively promoted his "Better Schools Program" by personally lobbying key individual legislators, appearing before a variety of foremost groups around the state, and even writing guest editorials that were published in newspapers. Eventually the Governor won a significant level of bipartisan support in the legislature, as well as endorsements from such prominent interest groups as the Tennessee Manufacturing Association, the Tennessee Taxpayers Association, and the Tennessee Association of Teacher Education.[31]

But the Governor was unable to cultivate the largest and most powerful state educational interest group, the Tennessee Education Association (TEA). TEA particularly objected to what it considered the "merit pay" element of the Master Teacher Plan, and eventually TEA killed the Governor's plan in the Senate Education Committee. The Governor immediately vowed to renew his fight for the Master Teacher Plan in the next legislative session. Toward that end he has promoted the plan with widespread national publicity and acclaim during an appearance on the MacNeil-Lehrer Report, a feature article in U.S. News and World Report, and a speech before the American Federation of Teachers National Convention.[32] In June 1983, Alexander appeared in Knoxville with President Reagan and won a presidential endorsement for the plan.

Thus, midway into the first year of the second term, the re-election of Lamar Alexander had certain tangible effects upon the organization and style of this Governor. Casting aside the caretaker role played during the first four years, Alexander reorganized his administration and assumed a bolder style. Early indications show that his administrative consolidations and aggressive leadership have met with a positive response from Tennesseans. For example, an April 1983 poll conducted by Peter Hart gave Lamar Alexander's job performance a 63-percent rating.[33] Still, in the first major legislative battle over his pioneer education program, the Governor was fought to a frustrating draw by the powerful TEA and its legislative allies; a landslide personal victory at the polls did not produce the coalition necessary to match a program-promoting organization and style with legislative success.

SUMMARY AND CONCLUSION

The 1982 gubernatorial election once more illustrated the influences of sectionalism and factionalism on Tennessee politics, for East Tennessee's bedrock Republicanism and internecine Democratic rivalries provided a solid anchor for Lamar Alexander's re-election. The personal nature of Alexander's triumph also underscored another fact of Tennessee political life: As Greene has stated, "Tennessee political life is intensely factional and personal. Party organization is loose, intermittent, and weak."[34] This dearth of party strength continues to plague efforts at effective governance. Past compromises due to factional squabbles have given way to current compromises caused by the emphasis on individual candidates. In both cases, the results are ironically similar; a new governor faces a resistant and ambitious legislature which owes little or nothing to his leadership and goals. So in spite of Lamar Alexander's devastating margin of victory, he has not yet generated a successful governing coalition.

Consequently, the 1982 Tennessee gubernatorial election carries fundamental implications for contemporary American political life. First, as this election makes clear, the traditional role and effect of political parties on statewide elections has drastically diminished. Candidate image and personality, not party image and loyalty, now tend to define gubernatorial elections. The withering of party strength and prestige, in turn, can tarnish the most conclusive electoral triumph, for as Greene has observed, a governor's "preeminence is strengthened by the conditions and activities of political parties."[35] In Tennessee, as elsewhere in the Union, we now see the unmistakable "presidentializing" of gubernatorial elections with all of the attendant implications.[36]

Second, professional campaign consultants working largely through the electronic media, not the party professionals and organizations, dominate gubernatorial campaigns. The Alexander experience since 1978 indicates that the "new politics" is extremely effective in promoting the career of a given politician by building the requisite electoral alliance necessary to win high public office; the Tennessee experience indicates that this politics can create the partnerships to support a caretaker administration. But, recent months suggest that the new politics is much less effective at constructing a governing coalition capable of sustaining a program-promoting administration. Though it is early in the second Alexander administration, the present situation in Tennessee shows every sign of confirming Sabato's observation that:

> Political consultants and the new campaign technology may well be producing a whole generation of officeholders far more skilled in the art of running for office than in the art of governing.[37]

NOTES

[1] J. Leiper Freeman, *Political Change in Tennessee, 1948-1978: Party Politics Trickles Down* (Knoxville: University of Tennessee, Bureau of Public Administration, 1980), p. 26.

[2] *Tennessee Journal* 5 (February 26, 1979), p. 1.

[3] M. Lee Smith, *Tennessee Journal* 5 (March 5, 1979), p. 1.

[4] State Senator Victor Ashe as quoted in the *Tennessee Journal* 7 (June 29, 1981), p. 6.

[5] This gratitude was reflected in Alexander's immense personal popularity among the Tennessee citizenry. According to Thomas J. Ingram, deputy to the governor, Alexander's pollster Robert Teeter reported that the approval rating for the governor in the last year of the first term was "higher into the term than [the rating for] any other governor Teeter had polled into a similar term." (Interview, Nashville, Tennessee, February 7, 1983)

[6] As quoted in the *Tennessee Journal* 8 (August 9, 1982), p. 1.

[7] These and all figures relating to campaign finance in this chapter were derived from the campaign disclosure reports filed by the candidates with the state librarian and held in the State Archives in Nashville.

[8] M. Lee Smith, *Tennessee Journal* 8 (August 9, 1982), p. 1.

[9] "Demo Governors Put Alexander on 'Hit' List," *Knoxville News-Sentinel*, 11 August 1982, sec. C, p. 1.

[10] Interview with Thomas J. Ingram, deputy to the governor, Nashville, February 7, 1983.

[11] David Lyons, "Tyree May Try It Again," *Knoxville News-Sentinel*, 3 November 1982, sec. A, p. 3.

[12] Interview with J. D. Wallace, State Democratic Party Treasurer, Knoxville, January 26, 1983.

[13] Interview with Mayor Randy Tyree, Knoxville, January 26, 1983.

[14] Joel Kaplan, "Alexander, Tyree Score Each Other," *Nashville Tennessean*, 8 September 1982, p. 1. Alexander reminded the Nashville voters that "four years ago . . . we were embarrassed all over the country . . . we heard stories of whisky licenses being sold and money passing through the governor's office."

[15] Interview with Randy Nichols, Knoxville, November 19, 1982.

[16] As quoted by Robert Sherborne, "Full Party Loyalty A Must for Office Seekers," *Nashville Tennessean*, 29 August 1982, p. 1.

[17] Bill Fletcher, "Tyree's Phone Blitz to Target Social Groups," *Nashville Banner*, 13 October 1982, p. 1.

[18] Roger Harris, "Recession Issue Tyree Aides Say," *Knoxville News-Sentinel*, 17 October 1982, sec. B, p. 12.

[19] Ibid.

[20] Interview with Mayor Randy Tyree, Knoxville, January 26, 1983.

[21] Interview with Thomas Mattingly, Tyree campaign staff assistant, Knoxville, November 23, 1982.

[22] Interview with Stephanie Chivers, campaign director, Nashville, February 7, 1983.

[23] Interview with Mayor Randy Tyree, January 26, 1983.

[24] Interview with Commissioner Sammie Lynn Puett, Department of Human Services, Knoxville, February 2, 1983.

[25] Interview with Thomas J. Ingram, deputy to the governor, February 7, 1983.

[26] Joel Kaplan, "Plan to Streamline Government Told," *Nashville Tennessean*, 8 January 1983, p. 1. The agencies abolished were the Tennessee Energy Authority, created in 1977 to manage energy conservation and fuel allocation programs; the

Health Planning and Resource Development Agency; the Statewide Health Coordinating Council; and the Tennessee Corrections Institute, which served as a training facility for state and local corrections officers.

[27]M. Lee Smith, Tennessee Journal 9 (January 3, 1983), p. 1. Smith, a longtime observer of Tennessee politics, noted," . . . Alexander has sought department heads who are managers as opposed to professionals in the field. Alexander's philosophy is that large state agencies are best run by generalist managers . . . Eight of the 19 commissioners [appointed for the second term] had prior management experience as chief executive officer of a large business."

[28]Thomas J. Ingram, deputy to the governor, in a letter to Michael R. Fitzgerald, February 16, 1983.

[29]Interview with Commissioner Sammie Lynn Puett, Department of Human Services, Nashville, March 16, 1983.

[30]Ed Cromer and Jim O'Hara, "Alexander Says Sales Tax Hike is 'Best Choice,'" as quoted in the Nashville Tennessean, 23 March 1983, p. 10.

[31]Steven D. Williams, "Alexander's Master Teacher Program Fails in Tennessee," Comparative State Politics Newsletter 4 (May 1983), p. 11.

[32]Tennessee Journal 9 (June 13, 1983), p. 4 and Tennessee Journal 9 (July 11, 1983), p. 4.

[33]Tennessee Journal 9 (May 2, 1983), p. 1.

[34]Lee S. Greene, David H. Grubbs, and Victor C. Hobday, Government in Tennessee, 4th ed. (Knoxville: University of Tennessee Press, 1983), p. 103.

[35]Ibid., p. 99.

[36]See Robert Agranoff, "The New Style of Campaigning: The Decline of Party and the Rise of Candidate-Centered Technology," in The New Style in Election Campaigns, 2nd ed., ed. Robert Agranoff (Boston: Holbrook Press, 1976), pp. 7 and 10.

[37] Larry J. Sabato, *The Rise of Political Consultants: New Ways of Winning Elections* (New York: Basic Books, 1981), p. 337.

18. WYOMING RE-ELECTION: FROM AFFLUENCE TO RECESSION WITH STABILITY

JANET CLARK

Although he vowed[1] to wage the "hardest campaign" of his career,[1] from the minute that he declared his intention to seek an unprecedented third term, Governor Ed Herschler's re-election was never in doubt. Despite the fact that he was only the second Wyoming Governor to serve two terms,[2] Herschler scored an easy victory over his Republican opponent, winning by the largest margin of his three gubernatorial races. Several factors contributed to his landslide. First, this Democratic Governor is personally very popular in a state where the people are generally conservative and Republican. Second, the Governor had served during a period of growth and prosperity for the state. The energy boom had brought new population and income to a relatively poor state about the time that Herschler had first come to office. He was able to capitalize upon Wyoming's individualism, populism, and concern for preserving its environment and upon the general satisfaction of a complacent electorate. Finally, he was assisted by problems regarding the Republican nominee.

THE ENVIRONMENTAL SETTING

The national recession was rather slow in hitting Wyoming. The economic crunch had not begun to squeeze the voters much before the 1982 election. As late as June 1982, Wyoming ranked fifth among the states in per capita income,[3] and the unemployment rate was well below the national average. Even in those energy-impacted areas that were economically depressed, the people had little reason to blame a Democratic governor for the international oil glut or for the Republican President's domestic and economic programs. Yet, even the Republican incumbents in Congress fared well in the 1982 election, for Wyomingites were still basking in the economic development of the 1970s when the state's population grew by nearly 41.6 percent to 470,816 and per capita income went from twenty-sixth in the nation to second by 1980.[4] With few exceptions, incumbents from both parties were re-elected by wide margins. The public seemed generally satisfied with their lot in life and with the performance of their government officials.

THE CAMPAIGN

The main suspense of the gubernatorial race occurred early in the year, long before the contest began. The real question was whether Governor Herschler would break with Wyoming tradition and seek a third term as governor or whether he would follow in the footsteps of Wyoming's former great leaders and use the governorship as a stepping stone to the U. S. Senate.[5] Senator Malcolm Wallop was facing re-election in 1982, and many observers felt that he was in a relatively vulnerable position. Governor Herschler appeared to be a major contender for the Democratic nomination. By March, however, he indicated that he was no longer considering the senatorial race, and it was assumed that he would stay in the Governor's Mansion. He faced only minor opposition in the September 14 primary. His opponent, an Albany County rancher named Pat McGuire, was best known for his reports[6] of "flying saucers" landing on his ranch. Herschler sailed through the primary, winning 85 percent of the vote.[7]

Governor Herschler has always been fortunate regarding his Republican opponents. In 1974 when he first sought the office, the Republican candidate, Dick Jones, had battled three others to narrowly win the nomination with 26.5 percent of the vote. One of his opponents, Malcolm Wallop, had painted Jones as an extreme conservative who was anti-environmentalist and pro-mining industry. Herschler adopted this issue and used it effectively against all of his Republican opponents.[8] Herschler won the 1974 election with 56 percent of the vote because of the environmental issue, fallout from the Watergate scandal and Nixon pardon, and voter perceptions of his honesty, friendliness, and concern for the common man.[9]

In 1978, Herschler faced a difficult race. Evidence of organized crime in Wyoming was revealed on a national television program, and his appointed attorney general was under indictment. Following the primary, he was 12 to 15 percentage points behind his opponent, and 80 percent of the public believed that organized crime was a serious problem in Wyoming and that the Governor was not doing enough about it. Nevertheless, Herschler managed to close the gap and win the race with a little help from other Republicans. Again the Republican candidate, John Ostland, had faced a difficult primary battle and had used up much of his campaign treasury. As a result, he lost precious time at the start of the campaign, and the initiative shifted to Governor Herschler. He attacked Ostland as an anti-environmentalist and a friend of the mining interests. His biggest gains, however, came from his proposal to cut property taxes in the state and to increase mineral severance taxes. As a result of the popularity of this plan, he managed to eke out a 50.9 percent victory.[10]

Leaders of the Republican Party in 1982 tried to avoid the circumstances which they felt had robbed them of the governorship in the previous two races. They believed that the primary battles had been fatal to the party which had a 50 percent to 37 percent advantage over the Democrats among the registered voters.[11] Therefore, they decided to avoid a contested primary by meeting in May to select a party-backed candidate and give him full party support throughout the summer. Unfortunately, Unfortunately, the campaign of the annointed candidate, Nels Smith, former Speaker of the Wyoming House, got off to a slow start. Perhaps seeing the handwriting on the wall, Smith withdrew from the race only a week before the filing deadline.[12] On July 10, Republican leaders met again to find a new candidate who was to be relatively "well organized, well heeled and well known."[13] They tried to draft U. S. Representative Dick Cheney, but when he refused, selected Warren Morton, another former Wyoming House Speaker from Casper.[14] Morton, a petroleum engineer and manager of the MKM Oil Company, proved to be the perfect opponent from Herschler's point of view because he was highly susceptible to anti-environmentalist charges. Morton easily defeated two opponents in the primary, winning with 74 percent of the vote.

Facing an extremely popular incumbent, Morton fought an uphill battle all of the way. He outspent the Governor by three to one. His expenses totaled $596,860.77 while he received $567,215.59 in contributions including significant grants from the Wyoming and National Republican Party and loans from himself. On the other hand, Governor Herschler spent only $192,068.48 and received $226,872.68.[15] Both candidates used professional polling organizations to help isolate issues for the campaign. Governor Herschler used the Peter D. Hart Research Association of Washington, D.C. Warren Morton used V. Lance Torrance of Houston, Texas. Neither candidate published the results of his polls, but occasionally Morton's organization would release figures showing him closing the gap or raising questions about the public's support for a third-term governor. Herschler's campaign manager was quick to rebut these findings without releasing the Hart data.[16]

The major difference in the costs of the two campaigns resulted from Morton's heavy reliance on professional campaign consultants to produce and coordinate his media advertising despite the fact that Congressman Dick Cheney was nominally his campaign manager. Governor Herschler, by contrast, relied upon his regular campaign staffs of volunteers operating out of two offices, one in Cheyenne and one in Casper, under the direction of two campaign coordinators. For the Governor, the major expense was television advertising, which absorbed nearly one-third of his total expenses. Both candidates saturated the broadcast media using both radio and television extensively. Morton also purchased ads in the local newspapers across the state in an effort to overcome his relative disadvantage.

Both candidates received many large contributions from individuals and from PACs. While both had many out-of-state donors, Morton received a much larger proportion of his $1,000 contributions from persons living outside Wyoming, over one-third as compared to one-tenth for the Governor. This difference was important as it allowed Herschler to charge Morton with being the tool of the oil companies. Particular emphasis was placed upon the fund-raising activities of Denver oilman J. W. Vander Beek of Amoco on behalf of Morton.[17] However, Herschler received nearly $10,000 more in PAC money. The majority of his PAC receipts came from labor organizations while Morton's were mainly from business groups. Similarly, Herschler received endorsements from Wyoming's labor organizations (the AFL-CIO, NEA, Teamsters) and the environmentally-concerned Outdoor Council while Morton was endorsed by the Wyoming Truckers and the Life Underwriters Associations.

During the campaign the candidates engaged in three debates in different locales in the state.

Morton scored the Governor on four issues. He attempted unsuccessfully to develop anti-third-term sentiment among the public. This issue was hard to press because Republicans had previously urged their own Governor Hathaway to seek a third term in 1974. Furthermore, the Republican incumbent in another statewide office, the secretary of state, had held office since 1962. Morton attacked the Governor's budget and the growth of state government spending. He alleged that government spending had increased 250 percent in Herschler's two terms, even when adjusted for inflation and population growth.[18] The major issue was an attack on Herschler's popular water development program. Morton called it a "rehash" of projects proposed much earlier after years of delay.[19] Finally, he described the Governor's administration as one of inaction and inertia. He accused him of standing by as hundreds of miners lost their jobs.[20]

Governor Herschler defended his record, indicating that conservatives in the state legislature, like Morton, had blocked the earlier development of the water projects by failure to increase the severance taxes to make the necessary funds available. He challenged Morton to specify what he would do as governor and where he would cut spending and he painted him as an anti-environmentalist tool of outside interests.[21] In the absence of any popular overriding issue to galvanize the electorate, the campaign tended to degenerate into foolishness. At one point the organizations of the two candidates were feuding over the actors used in campaign commercials. Apparently, voters were supposed to be concerned over whether these actors were registered Wyoming voters.[22]

THE VICTORY

In the end, Morton was unable to impress Wyoming voters with any of his issues. Governor Herschler won the most complete victory of his career. He garnered 63 percent of the gubernatorial vote and won in twenty-one of the twenty-three counties. His previous margins were much smaller, 56 percent in 1974 and 50.9 percent in 1978, and in both of the earlier races he had carried only ten counties. The extent of his victory becomes clear when compared to the normal Democratic vote of Wyoming which is 43 percent.[23] His 1982 percentage of votes was lower than that of 1974 in only three counties (Campbell, Sweetwater, and Uinta), and the two counties (Campbell and Park) that he lost were both strongly Republican. Voter registration in Campbell County is 74 percent Republican to 19 percent Democratic, and in Park County it is 73 percent to 19 percent.[24] Nevertheless, neither county is among the most Republican counties of the state. Big Horn, Johnson, Niobrara, Sublette, and Weston all have higher percentages of registered Republican voters. Table 1 shows the Governor's margin of victory in the five most Democratic counties in the southern part of the state versus the remaining eighteen Republican counties for all three elections. The vast changes in popularity over the three elections resulted from defections in the Democratic region in 1978 and from a large percentage of crossovers in the Republican region in 1982.

Public opinion data also show that Herschler's much larger margin of victory in 1982 primarily resulted from converting previous opponents.

Table 1

PERCENTAGE OF HERSCHLER VOTES BY REGION

	1974	1978	1982
Southern, Democratic counties	68.2%	58.4%	71.6%
Republican counties	49.6%	47.3%	58.4%
Total	56%	50.9%	63%

Source: 1975 and 1979 Wyoming Official Directory and Election Returns and "Summary--General Election Official Vote, November 2, 1982" compiled by Secretary of State Thyra Thomson.

Table 2 shows the correlations between vote for Herschler and several political and socio-economic factors based on surveys conducted by the Government Research Bureau of the University of Wyoming. Sex and age had little impact upon these gubernatorial votes. Income and education have a fairly similar pattern. Both were unrelated to Herschler's support in 1974, while in 1978 there was a moderately strong tendency for the less educated and poorer to be more supportive of Herschler, as is true for many Democratic candidates. (Both gammas were about -.30). These differences were moderated in 1982, primarily because of increased support for Herschler among the wealthier and more educated. See Table 3 for the percentage of voters supporting Herschler in the various groupings. The relationship between union membership and Herschler's vote also dropped from .30 to .18 between 1978 and 1982, principally because of increased non-unionist support for Herschler. Union support for Herschler dropped between 1974 and 1978 following the political scandal in Rock Springs, which is one of the strongest union centers in Wyoming.

As would be expected, partisan factors are strongly related to voting in Wyoming as party identification, party registration, and vote in the

Table 2

CORRELATIONS OF SOCIO-ECONOMIC AND POLITICAL FACTORS WITH VOTE FOR HERSCHLER
(Gammas)

	1974	1978	1982
Socio-Economic			
Age	-.07	-.05	.08
Sex	-.08	-.15	.02
Education	-.09	-.29	-.22
Income	-.07	-.31	-.08
Union membership	.53	.30	.18
Political			
Ideology	--	.35	.38
Party ID	.79	.76	.67
Party Registration	--	.75	.62
Previous Presidential Vote	--	.72	.66*

*Carter and Anderson voters in 1980 Presidential election combined.

previous presidential elections have gammas of about .75 with gubernatorial vote in 1978. These correlations dropped to about .65 in 1982 because of Herschler's increased success in attracting Republican support, because he received 48 percent of the votes of registered Republicans, 43 percent of the Republican identifiers, and 50 percent of the 1980 Reagan voters. Finally, liberalism had a moderate correlation of about .35 with support for Herschler in both 1978 and 1982 as both liberals and conservatives, but not middle-of-the-roaders, increased their electoral support of the Governor quite significantly.

Herschler's personal popularity seems to be the major reason for his re-election. The pre-election survey results indicate that the campaign issues played a very small role in determining votes. Most persons who planned to vote for Herschler felt that the state was in good shape and that he had done a good job. On the other hand, the main support for Morton was based on shared party ties. He had little personal appeal and many voters opposed him because of his ties to big oil companies. Table 4 presents the reasons given for favoring or opposing both candidates. Among the few who planned to vote against Herschler, the most common reason given was opposition to the third term.

The general prosperity and well-being of the state played the main role in determining the outcome of most statewide races. Clearly, incumbency was far more important than party in winning. While Herschler won a spectacular victory, his was not the largest landslide in the 1982 election. The incumbent State Auditor, Jim Griffith, captured 74 percent of the vote, and U.S. Representative Dick Cheney won 71 percent. Both of these Republicans carried every one of the twenty-three counties. The other Democratic incumbent, Superintendent of Public Instruction Lynn Simons, won with 57 percent of the vote and carried thirteen counties. The voters were apparently satisfied to retain people with whom they felt familiar and comfortable. The only incumbent eligible for re-election who won by less than 55 percent of the vote was the Republican Secretary of State. She garnered less than her usual share of the vote, as she faced a well-known opponent. Also she may have been hurt by her party's campaign efforts to hold Herschler to two terms. She was running for her sixth term of office.

Table 3

VOTER SUPPORT FOR HERSCHLER BY POLITICAL AND SOCIO-ECONOMIC GROUPINGS

	1974	1978	1982
Education			
Grade School	66%	83%	84%
High School	57%	60%	67%
College	58%	48%	59%
Family Income			
Under $12,000	63%	68%	66%
Over $12,000	60%	52%	63%
Union Membership			
Nonmember	57%	52%	61%
Member	82%	67%	69%
Ideology			
Conservative	--	43%	54%
Middle-of-the-Road	--	64%	66%
Liberal	--	66%	83%
Party ID			
Republican	33%	29%	43%
Independent	59%	74%	66%
Democrat	88%	82%	87%

Table 4

REASONS FOR VOTER ATTITUDES REGARDING CANDIDATES

Pro Herschler
Percentage of total sample = 53%
Percentage of those making response

Has done a good job	68%
Know him personally	5%
Democrat	5%
Environment policy	4%
Water policy	4%
Severance tax	3%
Against big business	3%
For working man	3%

Anti Herschler
Percentage of total sample = 19%
Percentage of those making response

Time for a change	68%
Water policy	11%
Has done a poor job	5%
Corrupt	3%

Pro Morton
Percentage of total sample = 15%
Percentage of those making response

Republican	34%
Oil and Gas position	15%
Conservative	9%
Water policy	6%
Know him personally	6%
Will provide jobs	5%

Anti Morton
Percentage of total sample = 13%
Percentage of those making response

Pro big oil	55%
Dishonest	14%
Campaign tactics	12%
Pro big business	2%
Against state employee	2%
Against teachers	2%
Water policies	2%

STARTING THE THIRD TERM

In the next four years, Governor Herschler faces a different economic condition for the state from that of his first two terms. Following the election, he was quick to perceive the need to change his policy approach from his previous terms when the state enjoyed prosperity punctuated with treasury surpluses. The Governor felt that he could no longer do all that he would have liked to do because of the lack of available financing. Wyoming operates under a biennial budget adopted in February of even-numbered years. By the end of 1982, it was clear that revenues were falling short of projections and that new programs would be difficult to undertake. The prosperity of the 1970s which had enabled the massive growth of expenditures to catch up from years of neglect resulting from Wyoming's economic hardtimes in the 1950s and 1960s was now apparently over.[25]

The changeover in attitudes and expectations went smoothly. The Governor retained his entire office staff and many heads of the state agencies. One major new appointment was the attorney general. Governor Herschler has had a new attorney general for each term of office, while changes among his office staff have been few. He has had the same three secretaries and administrative assistant since he first took office. Structural changes in his staff operation have developed slowly, with the main change occurring around the start of this decade when emphasis shifted from support for public relations operations to administration and intergovernmental affairs. The Governor appears to be moving slowly in the direction of long-range planning and priority setting as necessitated by declining revenues.[26]

The first public statement of Herschler's changed approach to state government was the State-of-the-State Address given to the 47th Wyoming Legislature in January 1983. He "painted a largely pessimistic picture of the state's economy, urged legislators to restrain spending and outlined his support for new programs. . . ."[27] Herschler has always supported environmental protection and conservation in the state. He requested the creation of a wildlife and conservation trust account and proposed the establishment of a youth conservation corps to assist economically disadvantaged youths. He urged continuation of the water development program adopted in the 1982 session but attempted to balance his requests for new funds with recommendations for reductions in the appropriations for state agencies.[28]

For the most part, the austerity program was well received by the conservative, Republican-dominated legislature. The House leadership, in particular, seemed to want to "out save" the Governor. Most of the legislation proposing new programs was killed in House committees. The Republican leadership rescinded a 9-percent raise for state employees adopted in the biennial budget and replaced it with a 2-percent raise after attempting to pass zero-percent raises. Perhaps the only significant legislation to survive the session was a law to equalize school financing throughout the state, brought on by a Wyoming Supreme Court decision ordering the legislature to act.[29]

EVALUATION

The governorship of the state of Wyoming is neither a uniquely strong nor overall weak institution. For the most part, the governor's success depends upon his personal leadership skills and party support.[30] Governor Herschler likes being governor and enjoys very much the powers and perquisites of the job.[31] Yet, he does not seem to be among the most active or influential of the state's governors. His approach to the office appears to be incremental and reactive rather than innovative and creative.[32]

Wyoming's legislature meets for very limited sessions--forty days in odd-numbered years and twenty days in even-numbered ones. For this reason, governors have traditionally played the major role in developing policy. The legislature has merely reacted to gubernatorial initiatives. Until the creation of the Legislative Service Office in 1971, the legislators were without the technical support to draft bills or research their implications. Since then, the balance of power between the legislative and executive branches has begun to shift. Legislators now take a greater initiative in drafting their own programs and are no longer content to merely react to the governor's policies. At times, they appear to try to encroach upon the governor's administrative turf. Governor Herschler has complained specifically about legislative incursions into his power.[33] While

Governor Herschler likes to use his party members in the legislature to influence legislative outcomes, he does not use the full strength of his office or personal prestige to guide his programs through the session. Rather, he avoids issues that might hurt his image and reacts to the legislature by vetoing bills he does not like.[34] During the eight years of his gubernatorial career, he has vetoed more bills than were vetoed by all twenty-six preceding governors combined.[35]

Nevertheless, Governor Herschler's relative weakness in policymaking may not reflect a difference in personality or style from previous governors. Rather, it may well be a function of the fact that Herschler is a Democrat who has been faced regularly with significant Republican majorities in both legislative houses. It would be difficult for an opposition governor under any circumstances to control the actions of the legislature, and now that the Republican-dominated legislature has the technical support of the Legislative Service Office, it can be relatively free of gubernatorial dominance. At any rate, Governor Herschler's lack of dominance has not hurt him in the eyes of Wyomingites. He won an unprecedented third term in a landslide in the 1982 election, capturing the support of almost every group of voters, and he remains popular as "Gov Ed" today. Some observers expect that he will live out the rest of his life in the Governor's Mansion.

NOTES

[1] *Laramie Boomerang*, 16 September 1982, p. 18.

[2] B. Oliver Walter, "Wyoming: Conservative and Republican But Not Always So," *The Social Science Journal*, 18 October 1981, p. 134.

[3] *Laramie Boomerang*, 27 June 1982, p. 20.

[4] Walter, p. 131.

[5] Tim R. Miller, *State Government: Politics in Wyoming*, (Dubuque, Iowa: Kendall/Hunt Publishing Company, 1980), p. 143.

[6] *Northern Wyoming Daily News*, 7 July 1982, p. 9.

[7] *Laramie Boomerang*, 16 September 1982, p. 10.

[8] Walter, p. 134.

[9] *Wyoming State Tribune*, 2 April 1975, p. 1.

[10] B. Oliver Walter, "Wyoming" in B. Oliver Walter, ed. *Politics in the West: the 1978 Elections*, (Laramie: Institute for Political Research, Department of Political Science, University of Wyoming, 1979), pp. 194-196.

[11] "Summary of Voter Registration in Wyoming, January 20, 1982," prepared by Thyra Thomson, Secretary of State of Wyoming.

[12] *Gillette News Record*, 9 July 1982, p. 1.

[13] *Northern Wyoming Daily News*, 10 July 1982, p. 1.

[14] *Northern Wyoming Daily News*, 10 August 1982, p. 5.

[15] Candidate Campaign Reports filed with the Secretary of State's Office, Cheyenne, Wyoming.

[16] *Laramie Boomerang*, 2 October 1982, p. 5.

[17] *Powell Tribune*, 16 September 1982, p. 5 and *Laramie Boomerang*, 26 September 1982, p. 11.

[18] *Northern Wyoming Daily News*, 15 July 1982, p. 1.

[19] *Gillette News Record*, 10 September 1982, p. 1.

[20] *Northern Wyoming Daily News*, 17 August 1982, p. 1.

[21] *Powell Tribune*, 16 September 1982, p. 5; and *Laramie Boomerang*, 3 October 1982, p. 17; 7 October 1982, p. 3; and 13 October 1982, p. 23.

[22] *Laramie Boomerang*, 22 October 1982, p. 11.

[23] *Wyoming State Tribune*, 4 November 1982, p. 1.

[24] "Summary of Voter Registration in Wyoming, January 13, 1983," prepared by Thyra Thomson, Secretary of State of Wyoming.

[25] Personal interview with Governor Ed Herschler, Cheyenne, Wyoming, 27 January 1983.

[26] *1975-1983 Wyoming Official Directory*, compiled by Thyra Thomson, Secretary of State of Wyoming.

[27] *Laramie Boomerang*, 13 January 1983, p. 1.

[28] Ibid.

[29] Janet Clark and B. Oliver Walter, "Wyoming Reapportionment: Does It Make A Difference?" paper delivered at the 1983 Annual Convention of the Western Political Science Association, Seattle, Washington, 24-26 March 1983.

[30] Miller, p. 150.

[31] Miller, p. 136.

[32] Personal interview with Wyoming Representative Jacques Sidi (R.-Natrona County), Speaker Pro Tem, Cheyenne, Wyoming, 16 February 1983.

[33] Miller, p. 146.

[34] Personal interview with Wyoming Representative Jacques Sidi (R-Natrona County), Speaker Pro Tem, Cheyenne, Wyoming, 16 February 1983.

[35] *Laramie Boomerang*, 17 March 1983, p. 18.